UNDERSTANDING DATA

Bonnie H. Erickson
Department of Sociology
University of Toronto

T. A. Nosanchuk
Department of Sociology
Carleton University

McGRAW-HILL RYERSON LIMITED

Toronto   Montreal   New York   St. Louis
San Francisco   Auckland   Bogotá   Düsseldorf
Johannesburg   London   Madrid   Mexico   New Delhi
Panama   Paris   São Paulo   Singapore   Sydney   Tokyo

UNDERSTANDING DATA

ISBN 0-07-082452-5

1 2 3 4 5 6 7 8 9 10 BP 6 5 4 3 2 1 0 9 8 7

Printed and bound in Canada

Care has been taken to trace ownership of copyright material
contained in this text. The publishers will gladly take any
information that will enable them to rectify any reference
or credit in subsequent editions.

Canadian Cataloguing in Publication Data

Erickson, Bonnie H., 1944-
  Understanding data

Bibliography: p.
Includes index.
ISBN 0-07-082452-5

1. Statistics. I. Nosanchuk, Terry A., 1935-
II. Title.

HA29.E75   519   C77-001233-7

TABLE OF CONTENTS

PREFACE FOR TEACHERS

Probably everyone who has written a statistics textbook, or indeed any book, believes that book to be importantly different from all others. Certainly we believe this of *Understanding Data*, and think that after reading it you'll agree. The clearest and most important difference is in the heavy utilization of exploratory data analysis, developed by John Tukey.* Traditionally, most of the effort in social science statistics textbooks has been directed toward the testing of hypotheses, with little attention being given to the complementary problem of finding hypotheses. Tukey's exploratory material makes it possible to address this latter problem through a set of fast, resistant, straightforward, and mainly intuitive techniques for pulling ideas and hypotheses out of a body of data.

Exploratory data analysis is well worth knowing for its own sake, as experienced data analysts will see at once. Further, the exploratory techniques provide a solid intuitive base for learning traditional hypothesis testing material; the exploratory tools are intuitive and data centred and hence easy to learn, while being sufficiently parallel to traditional tools to illuminate them. Finally, an emphasis on exploratory materials produces a statistics course which is fun to learn and fun to teach.

It never used to be much fun to teach or learn statistics. In traditional courses (which we both have taken and given) the students frequently fear and dislike the material, learn it poorly, and forget it quickly. This was all the more frustrating because we knew the material was important to the students and quite exciting under the right circumstances. After all, a student who loathed the statistics course one year might turn up a few years later saying, "*Now* I see what all that was about; it's good stuff after all." The change usually came about after the student got involved in a research project which was important for him, so that the value of dealing with data became apparent. We wished that sort of thing could happen more often: how?

Clearly a different kind of textbook was needed. The traditional text suffered from many of the following ailments: artificial problems, examples and illustrations arousing no-one's interest and drawing on a no-one's social scientific insight, for which there were unique right answers and little or no room for judgement; an emphasis on mathematical proofs and probability material that turned the students off rather than helping them to understand what was happening; and, in general, dull technical prose and a strong technical orientation. Mediocre students with some math background often did better than very good students with genuine social science insight and training; the strengths of the latter kind of student were not drawn on.

We're not the first to see these problems. Several of the newer texts have been responsive to the same issues; one can now find well-written texts using

---

*John W. Tukey, *Exploratory Data Analysis*, Addison-Wesley, New York 1977 (expected).

realistic illustrations, often drawn from the literature. But even these texts have not gone far enough, in our opinion; they do not sufficiently involve the student in data and data analysis, they do not break down the student's frequent fear of numbers, they don't teach the student how to develop ideas of his own. To go far enough, we believe, one must go beyond conventional statistics.

This is where Tukey's exploratory techniques come in. These provide efficient ways of searching for patterns and exceptions to patterns, for the data features that spark ideas. All good data analysts do this sort of thing, but because there has never been a well-documented, explicit set of procedures, they have tended to do it less efficiently than necessary, and each person has had to "discover the wheel" for himself. Perhaps the best short way to describe these tools is to repeat the comment made, over and over, by working researchers who have been introduced to the Tukey material: "But a lot of this is just what I've been doing, in a rough-and-ready way, all the time!" There are also new estimation procedures being developed by Tukey and his students; we won't go into those here although the teachers using this text may well want to know of such procedures for their own use.

The consequences of emphasizing exploration are quickly apparent. Proofs are irrelevant, a background in mathematics beyond high school algebra is quite unnecessary; instead, good exploration calls for quite different things: patience, curiosity, background knowledge of the subject matter, orderliness, playfulness of mind. Exploratory work draws on the strengths of the typical social science student, not on his weaknesses. Hence he can learn the material easily, gaining confidence in his ability to work with data effectively and enjoyably.

But exploration by itself would not be enough; ideas must be tested as well as developed, the encounter with hypothesis-testing must be faced at some point, if only to enable the student to read the literature. As we have mentioned, however, it is faced far more easily with exploratory training in hand. The confirmatory material can be understood as a more formal analogue of the exploratory material already mastered. This brings us to a major point of organization in the book: for each broad problem type, we first work through a set of exploratory tools and then move to the parallel confirmatory materials. We have tried to underline the links between exploratory and confirmatory tools in several ways: in the writing of the chapters, in the explicit bridging sections headed "Exploratory and Confirmatory" found at the end of most chapters, and in the use of illustrations and assignments in which the same data are analyzed from both an exploratory and a confirmatory perspective.

Let us consider the organization of the book, and suggested course organization, in a little more detail. The text is designed for a two-term course of approximately twenty-six weeks. Most of the chapters fit comfortably into a week, except that chapter 1 can be assigned along with chapter 2 and two weeks might be allowed for 15 and 20, and perhaps for 11 also if time permits. Dropping chapters is less easy, since the book was written as an integrated introduction to a way of thinking rather than the more usual combination of text and reference book; but if time pressure is serious, one could talk around chapters 6, 12, 16 and 20 more easily than the others (especially if working with graduate students, who can do the book in one term quite readily).

The chapters are organized into five major sections, from batch analysis to multiple regression and some of its exploratory analogues; each section is followed by one or more data sets suitable for use as a review exam. We recommend using these five reviews rather than the more usual Christmas and final exams. The former structure gives the students a review period when one is needed and each section goes over more smoothly once the previous section has been well digested. Also, five exams are usefully out of phase with panic periods in the student's other courses most of the time. We have found it useful to assign little if any other work while a review exam is in progress and to allow two weeks for the exam, including a review lecture. You should be aware that the review exercises are much more time-consuming than they appear. This has the side effect of creating a strong incentive for the student to use the computer. We have had good results with the SNAP-IEDA package, one of the few presently offering both exploratory and confirmatory options, and one of the easier to use.

The review examinations and virtually all the homework problems are real data sets which the student may analyze as he sees fit. Problems with "right answers" do not teach a student how to analyze data; only analyzing data can do that. The student must learn to ask his own questions, to use his own judgement in applying tools to a problem, to make sense of the results and discuss his insights in reasonably clear ways. This means a lot of work and thought for the student, but it also means he has a lot more fun and learns a lot more. He learns not only technique, but that poorly defined though very real property "judgement." He gets a feel for data, a nose for problems, a confident independence in reading about other people's research or planning his own.

Assigning data sets rather than problems also means more work for the teacher, but he too gets a lot more for his trouble. Be prepared to see assignments that are really essays reporting the sometimes tortuous path of an investigation. As essays, these will often be rather poorly organized since data investigations routinely include dead ends, blind spots, delayed insights and so on. Try to read them as narratives. Such assignments are harder to grade than problems; what about the paper with inhumanly tidy technical work but few ideas versus the chaotic but analytically acute paper? What about sheer volume, when an average student hands in four hundred pages or more over the year? But the assignments are also interesting to grade. You don't just make ticks or crosses; you can see the students learn, each one a bit differently, and you can learn from them—for they will come up with ideas that you would never have thought of.

We encourage our students to form working groups for both assignments and review exams. The benefits from this are numerous; bull sessions can be powerful learning settings, students enjoy working on things together, and the working group is a close approximation of the real world work setting many of the students will enter subsequently. On the other hand, it is subject to abuse; we try to keep this at a minimum by asking each student to prepare his own assignments, that is, to restrict group work to sharing and checking computations and bull sessions. We also try to make clear to students how to avoid being ripped off by others.

By now it is probably evident that this is a new kind of textbook that will require a rather new kind of teaching; in order to help in the transition, we have written a teacher's manual discussing the issues above in more detail as well as some of the problems that are likely to arise. We would be most interested in getting comments and suggestions from those who use the text. In particular, we are always eager for fresh data sets that go over well with students. We have tried to provide sets with a great deal of variety in the topics, the units of analysis, the level of difficulty, and the data quality. But we take it for granted that teachers will want to bring in other data sets, to suit their own interests or to orient the course more closely to the interests of their students. Often the students will have data that they want to work on, especially graduate students. In trying new data sets, remember that they tend to be far more work than you would ordinarily expect.

There are two books which we have found to mesh well with this approach. The first is Tanur, *et al.*, *Statistics: A Guide to the Unknown*, a collection of short, well written articles on a wide variety of applications of statistics, such as smoking and lung cancer, under-representation of women on juries and the early prediction of election results. The other is Huff, *How To Lie With Statistics*, a witty and intelligent book on misuses of statistics from which nearly anyone can profit.

Thus far, we've discussed *Understanding Data* as a textbook for an organic statistics course. It is possible for the text to be used in other ways as well. For example, it could be used as a primer in exploratory techniques in conjunction with an instructor's favourite conventional text; for such a use, Tukey's text should also be considered. *Understanding Data* could also be used as part of data oriented methods courses.

This book could not have been written without the co-operation, tolerance and support of several hundred students at both the University of Toronto and Carleton University. We acknowledge a special debt to John Tukey whose immensely creative work has, among other things, helped put the fun back into teaching statistics. Numerous typists have suffered through the various editions of this book, two in particular being Nazira Conroy and Nancy Allingham. Dean Wendt of Carleton University provided a grant for typing expenses. Thanks also to Jane Abramowitz, Tom Archibald, and others at McGraw-Hill Ryerson for their advice and support. We are grateful to the Literary Executor of the late Sir Ronald A. Fisher, F.R.S., to Dr. Frank Yates, F.R.S. and to Longman Group Ltd., London, for permission to reprint Tables III and IV from their book *Statistical Tables for Biological, Agricultural and Medical Research.* (6th edition, 1974.)

EDITOR'S INTRODUCTION

Several decades ago C. Wright Mills warned sociologists of the twin pitfalls of "abstracted empiricism" and "grand theory." In this respect, he was agreeing with Robert Merton's now widely accepted dictum that sociological theorizing must be at the "middle range," moving readily and frequently between high-level abstractions and observable reality, exploration and confirmation. Yet if most sociologists have come over to this point of view, the statistical tools at their disposal have not eased its adoption. Classical statistics were developed to meet the requirements of the natural sciences; as such, they reflect the more deductive nature of hypothesis development in these sciences. By contrast classical statistics have offered the sociologist little in the way of techniques for exploring messy data in the context of incomplete theories.

The present book by Professors Erickson and Nosanchuk follows in the path of Professor John Tukey, in an attempt to fill these gaps and remedy these weaknesses. This is a book of statistics for middle-range theorizing, and it emphasizes exploratory data techniques, not found in other books, which sociologists will find useful in their day-to-day research. The primary characteristics of exploratory techniques discussed by the authors are simplicity, resistance and elucidation. For statistics to be used by sociologists, and especially by students of sociology, they must first be easy to understand and use. Accordingly this book is aimed at that legion of professional sociologists and students who have always feared numbers; it employs much visual display, for example, as an easy way into the data. Also, the book is written in a relaxed and enthusiastic way that encourages the intimidated student without watering down what he must be taught.

But second, exploratory statistics must be resistant, able to deal with the kinds of data most sociologists find themselves handling. The contradiction we must always explain to our students, and perhaps not very satisfactorily, is that most of our data-handling techniques depend upon assumptions (e.g. normality, independence of errors, homoscedasticity) which our data almost never meet. True, there are data transformations which remedy some of these problems; and Erickson and Nosanchuk provide the student with a variety of transformations to be used especially at the exploratory stage. Yet the dominant spirit of this book is that if you don't have the techniques you need, you will have to find new ones or use combinations of existing techniques in their place. There is never a single, perfect technique; and maybe, no optimal technique yet exists for a given problem. If this kind of viewpoint and the creativeness it engenders is familiar to statisticians, it is still new and much needed among sociologists.

Finally, this book aims to teach techniques of data exploration which elucidate — cast the maximum light upon — the interwoven relations within a body of data. The sociologist of the 1950s went into his data with one or two hypotheses and a desire to test for "significance." The so-called significance test controversy raged and abated and we found ourselves, in the 1960s, being more concerned with "explaining variance" and, latterly, with decomposing correlations. Behind such powerful techniques as regression and path analysis lay the assumption that doing sociology consisted in manipulating a well-defined, easily quantified model comprising a few variables. In the 1970s, however, sociology has moved in a number of directions which reject these assumptions. As we rethink what sociology ought to be, many even reject the proposition that sociology can be quantitative at all; this is almost a natural consequence of the desire to return to a kind of sociology more like that of Weber, Durkheim, Marx and the other founding fathers. Yet it is more profitable if we retain quantitative analysis, while rejecting abstracted empiricism. Like the founding fathers we should ransack our data and become thoroughly familiar with the social and cultural dynamics which produce them.

This introduction may seem overly general because I feel sufficiently confident that Professors Erickson and Nosanchuk will make the particulars evident in short order. The many readers of this book in manuscript, not least the undergraduate students who have been taught out of it for several years, are happy to see the book finally come into print, for it will change the way we do sociology. It is therefore an exciting addition to the McGraw-Hill Ryerson Series in Canadian Sociology.

LORNE TEPPERMAN

1

Understanding Data

Many of the readers of this book, we suspect, are approaching it with a sense of dread. Students, especially in the behavioural sciences, often believe that while other courses may be enjoyed, statistics courses must be endured. We believe that statistics is not only useful and important, but also enjoyable. Students believe this too, *after* they have overcome some initial stumbling blocks. The first problem to be faced is the problem of numerical illiteracy: unnecessary difficulty in reading numbers.

Look at it this way: students are expected, and expect themselves, to be able to read at very high levels. They read complex ideas as presented by difficult writers, and deal with the ideas intelligently and critically. It may take time and even be painful but the reader, being confident, is spurred by his confidence and usually is successful.

But suppose he or she is beginning to read a table of numbers, not a chapter of words. That's quite another story! Many students who are bright with anything but numbers freeze up when numbers come along. They don't even try to cope; instead they immediately succumb to "data-phobia." The symptoms of data-phobia are easy to spot when reading an article with tables in it. The poor victim of the phobia reads the text confidently, absorbing the argument and possibly taking issue with it. Then comes a table: and the data-phobe may avert his eyes, stare at the table helplessly without knowing what to make of it, or skim the table very quickly to see if he can find what the author says is there. He never really gets into the table for himself, but relies on asking, "What does the author say the table says?" Unless there are really gross departures from this in the table, our data-phobe is likely to find the author's explanation acceptable, even when the reader agrees with nothing else in the paper. It may surprise some readers to learn that authors' interpretations of tables are sometimes incorrect. More commonly, authors will fail to remark on important aspects of their own data, aspects that the reader may be interested in. The author may overlook these features because they do not seem important to him; he may misjudge their importance or they may not matter as much in his theoretical or evaluative framework as in the reader's. The author may even ignore these features because he did not notice them; he may have run out of time, he may be a data-phobe himself, or he may not be a very good analyst (that's possible!). For all sorts of reasons the reader simply cannot rely on a paper's author to get everything out of the paper's data, and one certainly can't expect that he will always interpret the data the way the reader would like to do.

It is, therefore, up to the reader to read the numbers as carefully as the words; he has a lot to gain by doing so. Well, why doesn't he? Why don't you? Numbers, after all, are a far more simple and unambiguous form of information than words. If you can read and understand books expressing difficult ideas and using complex language, why can't you read numbers critically? Certainly, there are reasons: for one thing, we've been carefully trained to be literate in the usual sense of being able to use and understand the written word; but very few of us have been trained to be numerically literate. If anything, our training tends to make us fearful rather than inquiring when faced with numerical data. We usually start with a deeply rooted conviction that it is just going to be too hard for us. As a result, we don't try very hard, and don't get very far. When we end up doing poorly our initial expectation is confirmed — a good example of the self-fulfilling prophecy.

One of the major goals of this book is to break up this self-defeating pattern, to demonstrate that data analysis is not difficult. The bulk of data analysis is comparatively simple; the bread-and-butter work that keeps most of social science research going is no more difficult than reading ordinary textual material. Indeed, routine data analysis uses tools much like those used in routine reading: some thought, some common sense, some orderly reasoning, some imagination, some background knowledge of the area. If you have read this far, you can read the rest of the book; if you are verbally literate, you can develop numerical literacy.

At this point you may be thinking, "It's all very well to talk about common sense and so forth, but statistics is full of mathematics — and that's not like reading words and I definitely will not understand it!" However, it isn't necessary for data analysis to involve complex mathematics. At this level, in an introductory course, we rarely need any math beyond counting and arithmetic. Our big mathematical weapon turns out to be subtraction! We also make use of a few familiar techniques like drawing graphs. But what you really need is judgement, persistence, paper, a pencil, and a willingness to use your eyes and your head. Basic data analysis is easy and you *can* do it.

There is another misconception about statistics that we would like to demolish. Analyzing numbers is not painful and boring: it can be engrossing and a lot of fun. We can't convince you of that just by saying so, but you can and will convince yourself by doing some data analyses and experiencing the pleasures of discovery and understanding at first hand. There is nothing more exciting than learning something about social reality through data, learning it through your own efforts: once you get started, it is hard to stop — like eating peanuts!

We hope to turn you into data-philes rather than data-phobes, into people who can deal with numbers sensibly and critically and who can enjoy the process. We have promised you some simple tools to help you do this. Now it is time to describe the two kinds of data analysis dealt with in this book and give some idea of the book's overall strategy.

We will discuss two general approaches to understanding data: exploratory and confirmatory. Exploratory techniques make it easy to see into the data, to poke around some information in search of ideas about how things work. These procedures can generate the hypotheses which are sometimes taken to be the starting point of the scientific enterprise. Confirmatory techniques are directed to testing these hypotheses, once we have them, provided that we also have good data that are relevant to the hypotheses. Looking for ideas and trying to test them are two different things, so the two sets of techniques are different also.

We will try to approach problems first through exploration and then through confirmation. There are several reasons for this order. A lot of research is done in this way: the researcher explores an area and then tests the resulting hypotheses that look most promising and sensible. Besides, the exploratory methods are particularly easy to understand, and once familiar with the exploratory methods, the parallel confirmatory statistics are far easier to follow.

Exploring Data

The spirit of exploratory data analysis is a lot like the spirit of classic detective work. If you enjoy mysteries you could get into the right frame of mind by reading some Sherlock Holmes stories. Both detection and exploration require tools, some understanding of the material examined, and relentless following up of clues. The detective needs to know the tools of his trade, whether fingerprinting or classification of tobacco ash, in case he needs them. Similarly, the data analyst should know at least one way of tackling each of the major kinds of data he may run into. For this reason you will learn a range of useful basic tools even though this book cannot cover all the available techniques. The detective needs to have background knowledge, from timetables to laws of inheritance, to make sense of the clues he gets. Similarly, the data analyst should be able to call on his basic knowledge to interpret clues in numerical form. This does not mean that you must have an advanced degree before reading this book, only that you should use knowledge you have already or can find quickly. For example, if you find that English and French Canadians are different in some way you should be able to think of many reasons for the difference. Or if you find that cities differ in migration patterns, say, you can easily look up some possible reasons, such as size or growth rate, by spending a few minutes with a yearbook. Finally, the good detective finds his way to a solution to the case at hand by following through on clues, by pursuing and checking the possibilities which clues suggest to him. Similarly the data analyst checks and pursues insights by trying them out against available information. Sometimes the insight does not work out; that is fine, you have learned something and can test another idea. Sometimes the insight works but not perfectly; that is fine too, as you can look for additional insights to improve your explanation. Sometimes an insight really takes care of a problem by explaining almost all the data you have; and that is terrific, but it doesn't happen very often!

One of the nice things about detective stories is that the detective usually takes time at some point to explain just how he interpreted clues and followed them up (few published research articles do this, which is a pity). For example, consider how Sherlock Holmes works in "Silver Blaze." First we quote a narrative passage showing Holmes at work, and then give his explanations of what he was doing and why.[1]

> As we stepped into the carriage one of the stable-lads held the door open for us. A sudden idea seemed to occur to Holmes, for he leaned forward and touched the lad upon the sleeve.
>
> "You have a few sheep in the paddock," he said. "Who attends to them?"
>
> "I do, sir."
>
> "Have you noticed anything amiss with them of late?"
>
> "Well, sir, not of much account, but three of them have gone lame, sir."
>
> I could see that Holmes was extremely pleased, for he chuckled and rubbed his hands together.
>
> "A long shot, Watson, a very long shot," said he, pinching my arm. "Gregory, let me recommend to your attention this singular epidemic among the sheep. Drive on, coachman!"
>
> Colonel Ross still wore an expression which showed the poor opinion which he had formed of my companion's ability, but I saw by the inspector's face that his attention had been keenly aroused.
>
> "You consider that to be important?" he asked.
>
> "Exceedingly so."
>
> "Is there any point to which you would wish to draw my attention?"
>
> "To the curious incident of the dog in the night-time."
>
> "The dog did nothing in the night-time."
>
> "That was the curious incident," remarked Sherlock Holmes.

Now, what was all that about? "The incident of the dog in the night-time," which is quite a famous one, is an example of interpreting a clue using background knowledge. As Holmes explains,

> "I had grasped the significance of the silence of the dog, for one true inference invariably suggests others. The Simpson incident had shown me that a dog was kept in the stables, and yet, though someone had been in

---

1. The three passages are from *The Complete Sherlock Holmes* by Sir Arthur Conan Doyle, with preface by Christopher Morley, Doubleday and Company, Garden City, New York, 1930.

and had fetched out a horse, he had not barked enough to arouse the two lads in the loft. Obviously the midnight visitor was someone whom the dog knew well."

When Holmes asks after the health of the sheep, he is checking an earlier conclusion by looking for further related evidence:

"My final shot was, I confess, a very long one. It struck me that so astute a man as Straker would not undertake to lame the horse without a little practice. What could he practice on? My eyes fell upon the sheep, and I asked the question which, rather to my surprise, showed that my surmise was correct."

We want to be able to find clues, get ideas about them, and follow up on the ideas in search of hypotheses as we explore our data for insights about some problem. We cannot be sure of where our search is going to lead us; if we could, why would we be searching? We may have to make several stabs at the data before we work out a possible interpretation that looks good. Now, just how good does it have to look? Here is a point where our analogy to detection breaks down. In mystery stories the solution the detective works out has to be not only good but perfect; there is only one true version of how the crime was done and that is the version which the detective must find and prove. That's fine for fiction, where the author can invent a crime designed just so that it can be solved, but it will not do for real-life data analysis. There is no use looking for perfect interpretations of data: it would be terribly hard to find perfection if it were available, and it isn't. You never look for *the* interpretation of a complex data set, or *the* way of analyzing it, because there are always lots of interpretations and lots of approaches depending on what you are interested in. There are many good answers to different questions, not one right answer as in the detective story.

In principle, the one perfect analysis does not and cannot exist. In practice, if you stick to looking for "the right answer" you are in for a terrible time, constantly bedevilled by loose ends that won't quite fit. You may get so frustrated that you give up because you can't get the right, the perfect, result; consequently you may end up with nothing when you could easily have found half a dozen different ideas that were good even if not perfect. This is one situation in which Voltaire's aphorism, "the best is the enemy of the good," applies. Don't worry too much about "the best": look for things that appeal to you, that make sense to you and seem worth following up. Look for good ideas and plan to work with them.

Now just about every data set with anything to it can generate several good leads, but that does not mean that you will find one at the first shot. Your first few hunches may not lead anywhere; or you may have several hunches and want to work a little on all of them to see which is the most promising. One way or another you often have to make several tries on your data.

It follows that your tools have to let you be flexible, which means that they have to be quick and easy to use. The exploratory techniques take very little time to learn or to use. This means that you can (and should) use them often, to investigate a set of numbers from different points of view. If the techniques were time-consuming and difficult they would be less useful for exploration because we just would not use them. We might admire them greatly, but life would be too short for exploring with them. So the first requirement for an exploratory tool is *simplicity*.

What other features should a useful exploratory technique have? Well, let's think about what we are exploring when we use the techniques. If the data on a problem are in beautiful shape it is usually because the exploration stage is long past; we usually explore before going to the expense of collecting good clean data. The explorer, therefore, must use whatever is on hand, and often only "dirty" data, filled with errors and gaps, will be available. Still, even poor data can generate useful insights if we are unlikely to be seriously misled by occasional wild or erroneous observations. Hence we want our tools to have *resistance*. By this we mean resistance to things which are probably misleading: to extreme cases that may be flukes, measurement errors, or highly special instances that need special attention. For example, suppose we were looking at salaries for junior and senior members of a firm and found that the "average" (arithmetic mean) income was the same for both groups. Using our background knowledge we decide this is very strange since income usually increases with age or years of service. Perhaps we look more closely and find that the average for juniors has been pulled up by one person with a very large income. We may have misplaced a decimal (giving him $50,000 instead of $5,000 a year) or made some other mistake; or perhaps there is something special about him — he may be the world's leading authority on computers, or the boss's son. In any case it seems reasonable to put him aside for special attention and conclude that, excepting a few cases, the average senior makes more money than the average junior. This "setting aside" of extreme cases is one way of making an analysis resistant. There are of course others.

You may be wondering why we spend so much time learning how to cope with bad data. Why not get good data and use the confirmatory tools, which are not very resistant but are popular? Why have two sets of statistics? First of all, exploratory tools are useful for exploring even good data; remember, they are very fast and easy to use. Secondly, there are many situations in which you have to use very imperfect data because of pressures of time, money, etc. You may not be able to wait five years for the results of the next census, for example, or may simply want to follow up a new and rather wild idea at little cost in time, effort and money. Any information when used with proper caution is better than none.

One final feature of exploratory methods is a little harder to pin down here, although it will be obvious after you have worked with exploration for a while. This feature could be called insight. After all, the purpose of exploration is finding good ideas about how the world works, so the tools should help us to get insights. They do, and for the most part they do so by quite literally letting us see into the data. A crucial component of every exploratory analysis involves finding ways of looking at the data. Of course you have to do this yourself; a method cannot see or think for you. But the method will help by displaying the data in highly visual ways and by clearing away the parts you think you understand so that you can look harder at what you are still puzzled about.

Confirming Hypotheses

Confirmatory techniques are designed to test hypotheses, not find them. If you have a clearly formed idea and some high-quality data that bear on the idea, then you turn to confirmatory statistics to find out whether or not your idea is acceptable in light of the evidence. Where exploratory work is like detection, confirmatory work is more like the courtroom trial that follows. In confirmation, a possible hypothesis has been found and its truth must be tested; in the court, a possibly guilty person has been found and he must be tried. As we follow this new analogy we will see that confirmation has a different role in data analysis than exploration has, and this different role is carried out in a different way; both, however, remain important.

Confirmatory procedures, like courtroom trials, are supposed to gather unbiased evidence, to examine it rigorously in accordance with the standard rules, and to demand very convincing evidence before deciding that something is so. In the courts the relevant data are supposed to accumulate without bias through the efforts of the judge, the prosecution and the defence, the last two working as adversaries; while the scientist is expected to get good unbiased data on his own. Actually, science does have something like the adversary system of the courts in that an assertion made by one scientist will be disputed by another if the assertion seems unwarranted. Good unbiased data are essential because we are hoping to draw conclusions about the issue in question: to decide that a person is or is not guilty or that a hypotheses is or is not true. Naturally, our conclusions can't be worth much if our data are not good. The nature of "good" data, from a confirmatory viewpoint, will be clarified in chapters 7 and 8.

The conclusions will also be worthless if we take the data and handle them improperly. We want to make inferences from the evidence systematically, as exactly as we can, and in ways that are comparable to other tests or other trials; all this will help us to be accurate and objective in our conclusions. The best way of doing this, in courts and in confirmation, is to use agreed procedures which have been very carefully worked out and have well-understood strengths and weaknesses. That is one reason (not the only one) why confirmatory statistics are so much more rigid and formalized than exploratory ones. In exploration, you feel free to modify or invent techniques to suit your particular problems and your own style of thought; but in confirmation you have a decision to make, one which other people will expect you to be able to defend carefully.

Finally, courtrooms and data analysts try to avoid positive decisions (that a person is guilty or that a hypothesis is correct) unless the evidence is very strong indeed. A mere hint of proof is not enough; if that is all you have, you declare that no one's guilt can be shown or no hypotheses can be proven. This is stringent, and in fact both the court and the scientist enhance this stringency by assuming the *opposite* of what the prosecution or scientist would like to prove, i.e., they assume the defendant is innocent or the cherished hypothesis is false. The assumption is rejected only if it is distinctly unreasonable in the light of the evidence. In courtrooms this means that an accused is "presumed innocent until proven guilty beyond a reasonable doubt"; indeed one rule of thumb declares it is better that a hundred guilty men go free than a single innocent man be convicted. In science one begins by assuming a "null hypothesis" — if seeking a link between income level and level of education, for example, the null hypothesis would state that income is not related to education. The opposing hypothesis, that a link exists, is acceptable only if the evidence is overwhelmingly in favour of it as against the null. We will go into all this in more detail, expanding on the courtroom analogy somewhat, when we begin to discuss the logic of confirmatory statistics.

For now, the main thing is to note the importance of making a well-supported decision about how the world works, and to see what making such a decision demands. We must have good data for a basis; in exploration no one objects to having good data, of course, but good data are not essential. We must also have clearcut rules for reaching decisions, and clearcut hypotheses to test; in exploration, on the other hand, we may have no hypotheses to start with and we look around for them in ways designed to be free and easy rather than rigorous. Overall, confirmation is much less flexible and much more precise than exploration; they have to be different in these ways to do their different jobs.

As we have seen, the job of exploration is creating ideas, and the beauty of it is its openness and playfulness. The job of confirmation is making careful decisions, and the beauty of it is its power. If a few important assumptions (like random sampling) are met, then one can make very strong statements from modest amounts of data. For example, quite elaborate and informative studies using national samples of fewer than a thousand respondents have been carried out; many important studies use under a hundred. This is quite impressive when you think of how complex social reality is and how hard it would be to study it without statistics. This power has a price tag: you have to follow the rules, you have to spend some time on the calculations (or, better, get a computer to do it), and you have to spend a lot of time and money getting good data. But presumably the price tag is a reasonable one because you are getting a solid test of hypotheses which look important and plausible in the light of previous exploratory or theoretical work.

Now, how do you learn to follow the rules, do the calculations, and so on? In this book we assume that the essential thing is to understand the logic of what goes on when a test is made. This logic is easy to see once you have learned the exploratory approach to a problem; the confirmatory approach is usually just a tighter version of the same thing plus the making of a decision. If you see what is going on, you do not have to settle for "cookbook" approaches to your data — approaches that you stumble through by rote, not really understanding or learning anything. Nor do you have to steel yourself for massive doses of mathematics to "help you see how it works." Few students see anything that way so we have left most of the mathematical derivations out of the main text. We're interested in having you develop a feeling for and understanding of the tools. And how do you understand? By seeing what the tools actually do to the data, which again is something we learn through exploration.

We will make no attempt in this book to survey all of the confirmatory statistics; there are far too many for any single course, for one thing. Instead we will concentrate on a relatively small number of the more basic and popular techniques, discussing their logic and some of their properties as well as presenting relatively simple computing forms. Most of the more complicated ways to test hypotheses use the simple approaches we will deal with as starting points, so you can work up to the more dazzling techniques as the need arises. In short, we stress confirmatory statistics that are easy to do, easy to understand, generally used, and basic to more advanced methods.

Confirmation and Exploration Together

So far we have stressed the differences between the two kinds of statistics, hoping to clarify each of them. But it is important to realize that they are complementary as well as different: you can't do without either one, and the good analyst is the one who can work with both together. The easiest way to work with them together is to use them in alternation. We have already said that people often start on a problem with exploration, get some ideas, and then move to confirmation to test the ideas. And what comes after testing the hypothesis? More exploratory work, of course! There is almost always something unexpected and interesting, or something that doesn't fit, and a good researcher can't resist asking why: "if you know all the answers, you haven't asked all the questions." A lot of important new ideas are found in exactly that way, by following up the odds and ends (or "deviant cases"). So exploratory work is naturally followed by confirmation because you want to test good-looking ideas once you see them, and confirmatory is naturally followed by exploratory because you will want to push an explanation a little further if you can. The process doesn't terminate until the researcher runs out of time, energy, information or interest. Both ways of looking at data are essential parts of doing science; neither is better nor more important than the other.

The alternation between exploration and confirmation can take place from minute to minute in the researcher's mind, or from decade to decade as the status of a problem changes, or over longer periods of time as a whole discipline changes gears. In the case of long-term change we get something like the alternation Kuhn (1960) sees between "normal" and "revolutionary" science. In normal science, paradigms provide our hypotheses so confirmatory statistics are generally more important, though exploration still plays a role. However, in revolutionary science what is primary is the discovery and interpretation of the unexpected, a very important payoff from the exploratory approach.

Even though both approaches are essential, they do not both get the same amount of publicity. Confirmation gets more attention and recognition because it is more formalized, which means that it looks more rigorous and impressive. Besides, it shows up in the most polished phase of research, the testing of clear hypotheses with clean data, which is the phase that usually gets published. The formality and familiarity of confirmatory statistics make them very useful for public communication of findings. By contrast, exploratory analyses are fluid and require more explanation to an outsider so they tend to be done privately to help the researcher clarify his ideas in his own mind. Exploratory tools are not only less standard and more private, they are also just plain unknown to most researchers. But don't let that fool you: exploratory tools belong in your tool kit.

There are many fine standard sources for confirmatory statistics; two that we have used are Hays, *Statistics for Psychologists* and Brownlee, *Statistical Theory and Methodology in Science and Engineering*. All of the exploratory material in this book is drawn from the innovative work of John Tukey. Most of the material, plus additional refinements and more advanced exploratory tools, can be found in his book *Exploratory Data Analysis*. On some minor points we have followed an earlier version, *Exploratory Data Analysis: Preliminary Edition*. Sometimes our language is a little different from his, largely because we have tried to use standard terms whenever possible. Information on his terms and usages can be found in the "Exploratory and Confirmatory" sections following most chapters, as well as in the glossary. We plan to cover rather less of both approaches than can be found elsewhere, but hope to clarify both by showing how they can fit together.

In this introduction we have often talked about analyzing data, getting ideas from data, seeing things happen in or with data, and so on. None of this is going to occur without data! So data there will be, believe us, and lots of it! All the remaining chapters contain examples which are based on real data, and the homework is based on real data too. Nothing else would be suitable; after all, you are taking the course to learn how to analyze data and you don't learn that from anything else but analyzing data.

You may wonder why we bother to say such obvious things. The reason is that it seems they are not so obvious: have a look at the problems in most standard statistics textbooks and see how many of them are based on simplified problems of questionable relevance, such as picking coloured balls out of urns or estimating how long you will have to wait until the next bus arrives. Artificial examples and assignments like these can be fast to compute, and they can be set up so that there are "right answers" but they are not very helpful in learning how to use statistics in social science research. Data analysis is something that has to be done, and done for actual situations, to be understood. We think that it also has to be done for real situations to be enjoyed. Genuine data about social life are often messy, complicated, time-consuming — and fascinating.

One final word about doing data analyses: you do them to learn how to use tools and, more importantly, to learn about data and how to understand them. To acomplish this aim, make sure your work is never just a bunch of calculations. It's what the calculations, displays, and so on, tell you that counts, so you should always *discuss* your results in words at some length. We have found a good rule of thumb to be that every assignment or examination should have at least as many pages of verbal discussion as of calculations or graphs or other nonverbal analyses. The discussion can be quite simple — you can't expect to get earthshaking ideas every time — but it has to be there.

Section One:
Exploratory Batch Analysis

Chapters 2 to 6 introduce the idea of "batches" and show some basic ways to explore batch data. Three aspects of batches are stressed: levels, spreads, and shapes (or central tendency, dispersion, and distribution in more common language). Section Two will turn to the confirmatory analogues to some of the ideas in Section One.

At the end of this first section, right after chapter 6, there are several sets of batch data. Your instructor may assign one of these sets as homework or as exam material.

2
Organizing Numbers

Perhaps the single most important thing in data analysis, both exploratory and confirmatory, is learning to look hard at data. It may sound embarrassingly simple-minded, but it isn't. We must learn to look not only at a data set but also into it. We have probably all had the experience of looking at a large complex table without really knowing how to begin to extract the juice from it. We stare sightlessly long enough to placate our consciences and then turn gratefully to the text where we are told what the table says. And if it is hard to see very far into a table where the numbers are already organized in some useful way, how much harder it is to see anything in a set of numbers which have not been analyzed at all! We have to find ways of putting numbers into arrangements of some sort which let us look at them, and then we must learn to see them effectively. In this chapter we start right at the first stage of inquiry with some simple ways of organizing numerical information.

Picking Your Numbers

Consider the rich array of numbers in Table 2.1, which gives some suicide rates for various countries by sex and age. There is a lot there; enough, in fact, to serve as example material for this chapter and the next few chapters as well. We could just stare hard and think hard, and we would dig some interesting things out that way. Try it now for a few minutes before reading on.

No doubt you have seen several important things; for example, you have probably noticed that the male rates are higher than the female ones. Country and age seem to be important too. But if we want to get further than very general impressions like these, we must look harder at some of the numbers; we can't see everything about all of them at once.

We first decide to look only at male rates (leaving the female rates as a possible homework assignment). The male and female rates are clearly different, with male rates always higher than the corresponding female rates, so it will probably be useful to look at the sexes separately. This leaves us with male rates for various age groups and various countries; it might seem

13

natural, then, to ask what effect age has on suicide rates among males. This is still too big a question to start with; five age groups for fifteen countries is a lot of numbers. Starting may be easier if we look hard at just two age groups, develop some ideas, and see how the ideas work for all the age groups later. What two groups? Such choices depend on the tastes and judgments of the analyst. Here, we decide to do the oldest group (65–74) and the youngest (25–34) on the grounds that a big age difference would be likely to highlight any effects age might have. Other choices would also have been plausible; for example, if you were looking at retirement as a major crisis point in life, you might contrast the 55–64 group to the 65–74 group because the first is probably mostly men at the end (and often the apex)

Table 2.1

Mortality from Suicide, 1971: rates per 100 000

Country	Sex	Age				
		25–34	35–44	45–54	55–64	65–74
Canada	M	21.6	27.3	31.1	33.5	23.5
	F	7.8	11.5	14.8	12.3	9.2
Israel	M	9.4	9.8	10.2	14.0	27.3
	F	7.6	4.2	6.7	22.9	19.1
Japan	M	21.5	18.7	21.1	31.1	48.7
	F	14.0	10.3	13.2	21.0	40.1
Austria	M	28.8	40.3	52.3	52.8	68.5
	F	8.4	16.4	22.4	21.5	29.4
France	M	16.4	25.2	36.1	47.3	56.0
	F	6.6	8.9	13.0	16.7	18.5
Germany	M	28.3	34.6	41.3	49.1	51.8
	F	11.3	15.6	24.2	25.6	27.3
Hungary	M	48.2	65.0	84.1	81.3	107.4
	F	12.7	18.4	26.9	34.7	47.9
Italy	M	7.1	8.3	10.8	17.9	26.6
	F	3.5	3.7	5.5	6.7	7.7
Netherlands	M	7.8	10.6	17.9	20.2	28.2
	F	4.7	8.2	10.5	15.8	17.3
Poland	M	26.2	29.1	35.9	32.3	27.5
	F	4.4	4.7	6.6	7.3	7.0
Spain	M	4.1	7.0	9.6	15.7	21.9
	F	1.4	1.6	3.8	5.4	5.7
Sweden	M	27.6	40.5	45.7	51.2	35.1
	F	13.0	17.5	19.6	22.4	17.1
Switzerland	M	21.7	33.6	41.1	50.3	50.8
	F	10.4	15.9	18.2	20.1	20.6
UK	M	9.6	12.7	14.6	17.0	21.7
(England and Wales)	F	5.1	6.5	10.7	13.0	14.1
United States	M	19.6	22.2	27.8	32.8	36.5
	F	8.6	12.1	12.5	11.4	9.3

Source: *World Health Statistics Annual 1971*, vol. 1; Geneva, World Health Organization, 1974.

of their careers while the second group is mostly retired men; if retirement is traumatic, the second group should have markedly higher rates of suicide. The general point here is: pick out the sets of numbers that suit your interests. Don't try to see everything straight away; feel free to concentrate on whatever interests you.

Batches and Units of Analysis

Now that we have started by picking some numbers to concentrate on at first, what do we have? We chose the youngest and oldest males' rates as a starting point. These numbers have been copied out in Table 2.2A so we can see them more clearly, uncluttered by all the other numbers in Table 2.1. Each of these sets of rates is a *batch*: a set of related numbers. The rates for males 25–34 can be considered a batch because they are all of a kind. The rates for males 65–74 are also all related numbers. If we had suicide rates for Canada, divorce rates for Israel, mean income for Japan, etc., we would have, not a batch, but a bunch of unrelated numbers. Numbers go together in a batch because they appear to belong together. Each of the numbers stands for the same kind of thing: here, for the number of suicides per 100 000 males of a given age group for various countries. As we will discuss later, the meaning of these figures may vary slightly from country to country; nonetheless, they are enough alike to be called a batch. Since the numbers in the two batches, each corresponding to an age group, are alike, we may

Table 2.2A

Mortality from Suicide, 1971, for Males 25–34 and 65–74

	Males 25–34		Males 65–74	
	Unrounded	Rounded	Unrounded	Rounded
Canada	21.6	22	23.5	24
Israel	9.4	9	27.3	27
Japan	21.5	22	48.7	49
Austria	28.8	29	68.5	69
France	16.4	16	56.0	56
Germany	28.3	28	51.8	52
Hungary	48.2	48	107.4	107
Italy	7.1	7	26.6	27
Netherlands	7.8	8	28.2	28
Poland	26.2	26	27.5	28
Spain	4.1	4	21.9	22
Sweden	27.6	28	35.1	35
Switzerland	21.7	22	50.8	51
UK (England and Wales)	9.6	10	21.7	22
United States	19.6	20	36.5	37

Rounding rule: 0–4 down, 5–9 up

compare the batches. Otherwise, we would have no basis for comparison.

Numbers have to belong to things — here, the suicide rates have to be attached to various countries. The countries are the *units of analysis* or *units of observations*, the things that were observed to get the numbers. In this particular case the countries themselves recorded the suicide statistics and passed them on.

More will be said about batching just following chapter 6, after you have become at home with batches.

Simplifying Numbers

Before starting to organize numbers it often pays to simplify them, especially if an electronic calculator isn't easily available. You can usually gain in ease of calculation without losing anything; you keep all the accuracy you really need, or believe in. In any case, figures often appear more accurate than they really are, and can often be simplified without any loss in accuracy at all.

Consider the suicide rates. There is a strong tendency to regard these data as virtually perfect, because they come from authoritative-sounding sources like national governments and a United Nations agency. However, at least two major problems are associated with these data. First, different nations have different procedures for determining cause of death; for example, if a person deliberately shoots himself but does not die for a week, his death may or may not be classified as a suicide. Secondly, while the rates are calculated on a base of 100 000, which sounds like a lot, the groups involved may actually be smaller, thus reflecting only a very few actual suicides. As a result, the rates may fluctuate wildly from one year to the next. For example, Israel had a population of about three million in 1970, and probably less than half were aged between 25 and 74, the ages for which we present figures. How many of these are males between 65 and 74? Probably far fewer than 100 000, with perhaps fewer than 25 actual suicides (remember, the rate is 27.3); a few errors in classification or even random fluctuations could markedly alter this figure.

As a result, small differences between rates should probably be ignored in cases like this. Thus, when we wish to simplify our figures, we shouldn't feel badly if some of the apparent accuracy is lost. In fact, even if the figures are very accurate, we may simplify for ease of calculation as long as we do not obscure the general trends.

Rounding is the most familiar simplifying procedure and can be done in several ways. Table 2.2A illustrates one fairly common way: decimals from .0 to .4 are rounded to the whole number below them, while .5 to .9 are rounded to the next higher whole number. Note that we jotted our rounding choice down at the bottom of the table so we would not forget what we had

Table 2.2B

Rounded Suicide Rates, Males 25–34

Original Rates; per 100 000	Rounded; per 10 000
21.6	2
9.4	1
21.5	2
28.8	3
16.4	2
28.3	3
48.2	5
7.1	1
etc.	etc.

Rounding Rule: 0–4 down, 5–9 up

done to the numbers. A look at the rounded numbers shows that they are not really any less informative than the original figures: the differences from one country to another are still clear. This is because the changes due to rounding are small in relation to the overall range of the numbers: for the younger batch, the rates vary from 4.1 to 48.2, so a change of 0.5 (the largest possible when using this method) is not likely to make an important difference.

Other methods of simplification are available. If you want to be very quick, you can simplify by truncating, or chopping off the ends. In our example, we could have just cut off the decimals so that 21.6 would become 21 and 9.4 would become 9.

Rounding does not have to be restricted to decimal places. For example, we could round off the units as well as the decimal place. Then 21.6 would become 2, 9.4 would become 1, and so on; in short we would be left with rounded rates per ten thousand. This would be meaningful — rates can be per 100 000, per million or whatever — and is sometimes helpful. Here, it is less helpful because the numbers become uninformative. In Table 2.2B we see what happens to our younger batch: when rounding goes too far, too many numbers end up looking the same when they are actually different in ways that may well turn out to be interesting (e.g. both 21.6 and 16.4 become 2). So how far should you round in a particular case? This is a matter of judgement, like a lot of data analysis; it will depend on the accuracy of the original figures, the range of the figures in the batch, and the use you intend to make of the rounded figures. Common sense and a little experience make this decision an easier one.

Still, even a lot of experience doesn't always guarantee that you'll make the right rounding decision every time. On reading Tennyson's "The Vision of Sin" Babbage, the famous mathematician and puzzle solver, is said to have written to the poet,

"In your otherwise beautiful poem there is a verse which reads:
'Every moment dies a man,
Every moment one is born.'
It must be manifest that, were this true, the population of the world would be at a standstill. In truth, the rate of birth is slightly in excess of that of death. I would suggest that in the next issue of your poem you have it read:
'Every moment dies a man,
Every moment one and one-sixteenth is born.'
Strictly speaking, this is not correct. The actual figure is a decimal so long that I cannot get it on the line, but I believe one and one-sixteenth will be sufficiently accurate for poetry."[1]

Well, we've started; we have chosen the batches we want to begin with and we've simplified the data by rounding. But it is still hard to see much because the data aren't organized. Surely it would be convenient to *order* the rates by size so we can look for patterns, for regularities and for departures from these patterns and regularities.

Ordering Batches

There are many ways of organizing the data in Table 2.2A. A familiar way is to gather the numbers into categories as in Table 2.3, a tally. Just to remind you of how this works, in Table 2.3 for males 25–34 we see that one country had a rate between 40 and 49; eight countries had rates between 20 and 29; two between 10 and 19, and four between 0 and 9. We get these tallies by going through the raw numbers and marking each one off in the appropriate category. This is quite easy to do (as long as you don't have too many numbers) and it is quite useful too. For example, we can see that the rates for the older batch are higher and also more spread out than the rates for the younger group.

Why do older men have higher rates of suicide? Many possibilities come to mind. The end of one's working life may indeed, as suggested earlier, be a blow for some people, diminishing the sense of self-worth and increasing financial problems. Older people generally have poorer health and fewer social contacts. In general, the problems of life grow and the resources for meeting them shrink. Why are the rates for older men more diverse? Perhaps the experiences of old age are more different, country to country, than those of youth — for example some countries may have better social services for older people, which in turn might result in lower suicide rates for this group. Older people may also be more diverse in their values and beliefs (including values related to suicide) because they grew up in earlier periods when countries were less "homogenized" by industrialization and higher

1. From the Mathematical Gazette, cited by J. R. Newman (1956).

Table 2.3

Tally of Table 2.2A, Rounded Figures

Males 25–34		Males 65–74	
100–109		100–109	1
90– 99		90– 99	
80– 89		80– 89	
70– 79		70– 79	
60– 69		60– 69	1
50– 59		50– 59	111
40– 49	1	40– 49	1
30– 39		30– 39	11
20– 29	H̶H̶ 111	20– 29	H̶H̶ 11
10– 19	11	10– 19	
0– 9	1111	0– 9	

levels of international communication. You may have some other suggestions.

In general this approach is good for finding gross similarities or differences between batches. On the other hand, it is poor at giving details. Looking at Table 2.3, how can we know just where a case fits in an interval? We can't. The only way we can get this sort of detail is to go from the tally back to the original numbers, which can be a nuisance — especially if these original numbers are somewhere else (perhaps in a reference book we used) or no longer available (perhaps we were counting things as they happened and the behaviour we looked at is now past and gone). Fortunately there is a way to jot down numbers that takes no more time than tallying and does not throw away information; we can get something for nothing, if we spend a few minutes learning more efficient techniques.

Suppose, instead of a range to the left of the "bar" we have only the leading digit(s), and to the right of the bar, we have our next digit. In this way, we retain the quick visual impact of the tally, and moreover, retain the richness of the original table! Tukey refers to this as a *stem-and-leaf* display. Table 2.4 gives stems-and-leaves of the batches from Table 2.2A. Let us look at the first few lines of the stem-and-leaf for the younger batch to see how this works. The first several lines with stems 5 to 10 have no leaves; this means no countries had rates in the fifties, sixties, etc., for males 25 to 34. The line with a stem of 4 has a leaf of 8, which means one country had a rate of 48. The stem 3 has no leaves, so there were no rates in the thirties. The stem 2 is very popular, with eight leaves. So there were eight countries with rates in the twenties. We could see that much from the tally, but here we have the graphic quality of the tally and we have not had to sacrifice information. You can read off the original numbers just by tacking the leaves onto their stems.

A stem-and-leaf is easy to read; it is also easy to make. First put down the stems in order; in Table 2.4 we put down 10, 9, 8 and so on. This is much like listing the intervals for a tally except simpler: instead of 100–109 we write 10, instead of 90–99 we write 9, etc. When the stems are ready, go through the numbers in the data source and record leaves next to their stems as you come to them.

Table 2.4

Stems-and-leaves for Table 2.2A,
Rounded Figures

Males 25–34		Males 65–74	
10		10	7
9		9	
8		8	
7		7	
6		6	9
5		5	621
4	8	4	9
3		3	57
2	22986820	2	4778822
1	60	1	
0	9784	0	

	stem:	*leaf*:		*stem*:	*leaf*:
	tens	units		tens	units

Let's go through an example in detail. We want to make a stem-and-leaf of the older males' suicide rates. Working down the column of figures in Table 2.2A, we meet the numbers in this order: 24, 27, 49, 69, 56, and so on. The first number has a 2 in the tens' place, so its stem is 2; and it has a 4 in the units' place, so the leaf on that stem is 4. Similarly, 27 has a stem of 2 and a leaf of 7. Table 2.5A shows the stem 2 and leaves 4 and 7 placed on a stem-and-leaf. Table 2.5B shows how the first five rates are added to a stem-and-leaf.

Table 2.5A

Different Leaves on the Same Stem

24
27
stem   leaf
2 | 47

Actually, it's one of those things that takes longer to describe than to do. Writing numbers down in stems-and-leaves takes no longer than just copying them. You don't even need a table like Table 2.2A, which we use here just to clarify what is happening by taking it one step at a time. You

Table 2.5B

Making a Stem-and-Leaf

Number	Stem	Leaf	Stem-and-Leaf	
24	2	4	6	9
27	2	7	5	6
49	4	9	4	9
69	6	9	3	
56	5	6	2	47
			1	
			0	

stem: tens *leaf*: units

can copy straight from a source (like Table 2.1) to a stem-and-leaf (like Table 2.4).

The first few times you try this it may seem a bit awkward, but a little practice pays big dividends. With minimal expenditure of energy, we have a data representation which is graphic and complete. We can see all that can be seen from a tally, plus some things which are difficult or impossible to see there. For example, if we look hard at Table 2.4 we begin to see that the numbers in both batches cluster a lot. In the younger batch, there seem to be several clusters of numbers. The numbers in the high twenties (Austria, Germany and Sweden, and perhaps also Poland) form one cluster, the numbers in the low twenties (Japan, Switzerland, the U.S.A., Canada, and perhaps France) form another, and the countries with rates of ten or less also seem to cluster. In the tally we could see that there were a lot of rates under ten and a lot in the twenties, but we could not see whether the "teens" rates went with either of the clusters. We will return to the clusters later.

The stem-and-leaf is very little work (actually a little less than straight copying when you have learned to do it) and gives lots of information in an organized form. It is one of the basic tools of exploratory analysis, especially batch analysis. Here is a list of steps to follow when doing stems-and-leaves:

1. Choose your stems. Run your eyes over the numbers you plan to work with. Find the biggest and the smallest and make sure your stems cover that range. In Table 2.2A it was easy to see that the rates went from 4 to 107, so stems from 0 to 10 would handle all the numbers. You don't have to worry about anything but coverage to start with, because as we will see in a moment, it's easy to change your stems if you decide you want to.

2. Order your stems. We like to put the biggest one at the top as in Table 2.4, so that numbers "higher" on the page are "higher" in size as well. This saves a lot of verbal and visual confusion. However, you can order in the other direction if you like.

3. Always make a note of the stem and leaf units. In Table 2.4 we noted:

"stems are in tens, leaves are in units." Otherwise you can't tell how large the numbers are.

4. Check quickly. To be sure you haven't skipped a number, count the number of leaves. In Table 2.4, each stem-and-leaf should (and does) have 15 leaves because there were 15 countries.

Different Kinds of Stem-and-Leaf

Changing Stems

The stem-and-leaf gives us a lot for a little bit of work. It also turns out to be a flexible tool. To illustrate this, we carry on with the suicide data using different variations on the basic stem-and-leaf, each of which shows us something a bit different. For example, if we look hard at Table 2.4 we see that we do not really need two sets of stems here because the stems for the two batches are identical. We can use just one set of stems and put one batch (say the younger) to the left and the other to the right. This gives us Table 2.6, which contains the same information as Table 2.4 in a form which makes comparison a little easier. This is called a "back-to-back" stem-and-leaf and is very handy when you want to compare two rather similar batches for detailed differences.

Table 2.6

Back-to-back Stem-and-Leaf

Males 25–34		Males 65–74
	10	7
	9	
	8	
	7	
	6	9
	5	621
8	4	9
	3	57
22986820	2	4778822
60	1	
9784	0	

stem: tens   *leaf*: units

In our example it is hard to see much that is new in Table 2.6 because we have already looked rather hard at these batches. Table 2.6 stresses the size difference; the older men's rates look much higher than the younger men's, with the former starting almost where the latter ends.

The most important variations are variations in the kinds of stems and/or leaves used. By varying the kind of stem, we can change "magnifi-

Table 2.7

Compact View: Double Stems

Males 25–34		Males 65–74	
10, 11	:	10, 11	7:
8, 9	:	8, 9	:
6, 7	:	6, 7	9:
4, 5	8:	4, 5	9:621
2, 3	22986820:	2, 3	4778822:75
0, 1	9784:60	0, 1	:

stems: tens
leaves: units

cation" from a very compact view to a very detailed one. Compactness comes from putting more than one stem on a line. We can make Table 2.4 more compact by, say, cutting the number of lines in half as in Table 2.7 where each line has double stems. To keep track of which leaf goes with which stem, we can use colons to divide the leaves; the leaves on the right of the colon go with the stem on the right. Consider this line from Table 2.7 for the younger batch:

$$0,1 \mid 9784{:}60$$

The leaves to the right of the colon go with the stem to the right; the rates are 16 and 10. The leaves to the left of the colon go with the stem to the left; the rates are 9,7,8, and 4. Compared to Table 2.4, this more compact form makes overall features (like the younger group's less diverse rates) easier to see.

By using more lines, "opening up" the stem-and-leaf, we can get a picture that emphasizes details more. In Table 2.8 we double the number of lines compared to Table 2.4 (our original stem-and-leaf): each line is now half of a stem. That is, there are two lines for the stem "6"; the upper one gets the upper sixties, 65–69, and the lower one gets the lower sixties, 60–64. In the younger group we can easily see the two clusters in the twenties and also the one around ten; in the older group we see a cluster in the high twenties and, perhaps, another more spread-out cluster around the fifties and high forties.

You may ask, which form is best? Which should I use? There is no one answer: what you use depends on what you want. Sometimes the little details of figures are what count, sometimes not. Sometimes you want a compact stem-and-leaf and sometimes you want the data spread out well. Since each kind of display shows something a little bit different, you should often find yourself doing several different stems-and-leaves rather than worrying about what the "right" one is. You might well want to use Tables 2.4, 2.7, and 2.8: 2.7 for a quick overview, 2.4 for moderate detail, and 2.8 for intensive detail. If you have any one of these, others are easily made from it; you don't have to go back to the original data source.

One final caution: for our example, the most detailed stem-and-leaf happened to be one with half stems. For a different problem the most detailed version may have single or double stems. The nature of the data and your requirements should be the criteria governing your choice of a kind of stem.

Table 2.8

Detailed View: Half Stems

Males 25–34		Males 65–74	
10		10	7
10		10	
9		9	
9		9	
8		8	
8		8	
7		7	
7		7	
6		6	9
6		6	
5		5	6
5		5	21
4	8	4	9
4		4	
3		3	57
3		3	
2	9868	2	7788
2	2220	2	422
1	6	1	
1	0	1	
0	978	0	
0	4	0	

stems: tens
leaves: units

Changing Leaves

So far we have only considered the simplest kind of stem-and-leaf where each leaf is a single digit. This organization is a good general one that you will use often, but it is not the only kind. For example you may want to keep more numerical information than Table 2.4 (and its relatives, Tables 2.6–2.8) provide. You may want to copy out the decimal places from a source like Table 2.1, which is a pretty good idea if the source is one which you'd find it a nuisance to consult again and you think the details may turn out to be interesting. The extra information can be worked into a stem-and-leaf by using double-digit leaves, as in Table 2.9. This is the same as 2.4 but with more detail. The top line for the older group is

$$10 \mid 74$$

which does not mean two rates of 107 and 104 here, but one rate of 107.4.

Table 2.9

Table 2.4 with double digit leaves

Males 25–34			Males 65–74
10		10	74
9		9	
8		8	
7		7	
6		6	85
5		5	60, 18, 08
4	82	4	87
3		3	51, 65
2	16, 15, 88, 83, 62, 76, 17	2	35, 73, 66, 82, 75, 19, 17
1	64, 96	1	
0	94, 71, 78, 41, 96	0	

stems: tens
leaves: units and tenths

We do not bother to put the decimal points in the leaves because it is un-necessary, as long as a footnote that explains what you've done is included. If you prefer, you could think of these numbers as rates per million instead of per 100 000 so that the decimal points go away. Then the stems would be hundreds, and the leaves tens and units.

We have lost one piece of information that we had in the original table, the association of a rate with a country. With a little ingenuity, we can man-age to keep this too. We need only to give up the "units" information in the leaves and put in their place country identifications, nominal leaves. In Table 2.10 we do this for both the batches "back to back." In this form, we

Table 2.10

Using Names as Leaves

Males 25–34		Males 65–74
	10	HUN
	9	
	8	
	7	
	6	AUS
	5	FRA, GER, SWI
HUN	4	JAP
	3	SWE, US
CAN, SWI, SWE, POL, GER, AUS, JAP, US	2	CAN, ISR, ITA, NET, POL, SPA, UK
UK, FRA	1	
SPA, NET, ITA, ISR	0	

stems: tens
leaves: first three letters of country names

can most easily think about the clusters which we have noted so often. We can immediately see which countries cluster together, and think about what they may have in common that produces similar suicide rates.

Spain, Netherlands, Italy and Israel come on the same line for both batches. Their rates are somewhat higher in the older batch, but are still low for that batch. This suggests that these four countries may be similar in some way that keeps suicide rates relatively low. There are a lot of similarities, and different people will find different similarities thought-provoking. One possibility: all four have relatively mild climates. Does warmer weather mean a less stressful life, perhaps because expenses are lower and the climate less depressing? One could follow up on this possibility in various ways. On the one hand, some information about the climates would be useful. How severe are the winters in the 15 countries? On the other hand, we could look beyond the four countries whose similarity caught our eyes: what are rates like in other warm countries?

We could use the nominal leaves to ask other kinds of seminal questions. For example, why is Hungary so much higher in both batches, the highest by far? Why is it that age does not seem to make much difference for Poland and Canada although it does for other countries?

Overview

Where has all this gotten us? Well, having our batches organized in even these rudimentary ways has made it possible to look at these numbers painlessly, to start thinking and speculating about them. Many interesting questions have emerged: why are Hungarian rates so high and Spanish rates so low? Why do France and Austria increase so much from one batch to the other? What do Israel, Italy, Spain and the Netherlands have in common? Furthermore, some possible hypotheses have emerged: suicide may be a function of stress points that are related to age and/or may be a function of climate. Other hypotheses could be made, and some simple lines for further research have been suggested: for example, looking up data on climate would help us to check some of our hunches. You can get a lot out of a little data just by looking hard.

We have just gone through the first stage of analysis of a very simple set of data and it has been relatively painless; using the stem and leaf, all we've done is transcribe our data (we must do this in any event) and look at it (no formulae, no complications). Questions and patterns have emerged almost effortlessly. After all, before we can hope to find useful answers to a problem, we must ask questions of our data; the better our data presentation is, the more easily productive questions will emerge. You have also been introduced to the simplest form of data in a body, the batch. Besides the suicide rates seen here, other examples of batch data are: batting averages for various baseball teams, ages of members of your class, the ages of a set of survey respondents, etc. Remember that the numbers in a batch should belong together: the numbers should emerge from the same process. Sometimes this is obvious: who would try to mix suicide rates with the heights of volcanoes? The two sets of numbers obviously do not belong in the same group. Sometimes deciding what can go into a common batch is less obvious. For example, does Japan belong in our suicide batches? You might argue that it does not, because its culture is so different; among other things, suicide is traditionally regarded as honourable in certain circumstances, and this tradition remains influential. Or you might argue (as we did) that Japan does belong with the rest because it is a highly industrialized and Westernized nation.

To describe these ideas in another way, a batch consists of numbers generated by the same process: by factors underlying suicide (suicide rates), by demographic processes (ages), by skill and training (batting averages) and so on. If we suspect that the process does not always work the same way, we might break up our batch into several subbatches. For example, the male suicide batching by age lets us see if suicide rates seem to be at all different for men at differing points in their lives. We could subbatch further to check out factors which we suspect are related to suicide. We could divide the countries into warm or cold, Catholic or Protestant, politically repressive or politically open, and so on. This would give us some idea whether climate, religion, or politics really does make some difference to suicide rates. If we are unable to decide in advance, a couple of approaches can be tried to see what makes the most sense.

In this section we have taken the first steps in a data analysis: looking hard at data, asking questions, some of which we can perhaps answer later. We have also begun to see what is meant by "doing better," getting more information or clues without proportionally more effort. Minimum effort is an important criterion since we will want to do a great many things, and will only do them if they are not too difficult or time-consuming. People, after all, are not computers: we can weary of a task, or simply become bored. The more we can get done before this point is reached, the more likely we will be to master the problem.

Large Batches

Even the stem-and-leaf is a bit slow when you have a very large collection of numbers. What if you have hundreds of numbers in a batch? There are two major ways to cope. First, if you are exploring you don't need hundreds of numbers; fewer numbers would actually be better, easier to work with and see and think about. So don't use them all: select a manageable quantity randomly and save the rest for later use, perhaps to test ideas developed in exploration. A second major way of coping is the computer, which can organize lots of numbers in various ways very speedily. But a computer can overwhelm a researcher with numbers: too much, too fast, with too much precision (often specious). In addition, sometimes we expect the computer to tell us everything, or assume that anything the computer doesn't tell us isn't worth knowing. When we plug in the computer, we often "unplug" our brains.

Peculiarities of Our Example

Our example had some special features; any example would. Just remember that stem-and-leafing is not confined to the kind of batches we happened to use here. We compared batches that had equal numbers of entries (15 per batch), which won't often happen. We might have batched by region, say, and compared rates for European and Asian countries, and we would not likely get exactly the same number of each. Further, our batches happened to have the same cases (countries) appearing in each batch. This is interesting for discussion but not at all necessary for batch analysis in general.

We also chose to work with national statistics. We've listed examples of other kinds of batch data above, but national statistics happen to be very handy; you can easily get answers to questions you think up, you can look up urbanization, climate, or whatever you require in almanacs by spending a few minutes in any library.

Exploratory and Confirmatory

This is the first of several "translation" sections which will appear at the ends of many chapters. The idea is to provide standard, or confirmatory, equivalents of the relatively novel exploratory language (due mainly to Tukey) so that you can describe your work to others in the language they are most likely to understand. Sometimes it really is just a translation; we use some term which is simpler than the standard one, or more evocative, but means the same thing. Sometimes it is a little trickier because we are talking about exploratory tools that have no exact equivalent in the tool kit of standard approaches. The stem-and-leaf is one of those tools.

There are a couple of standard techniques which are closely related to the stem-and-leaf and can be very quickly found from stems-and-leaves. They are not nearly as good as stems-and-leaves for exploratory work, but they are often more useful for communication; after all, many people have not heard of the stem-and-leaf technique, and it's a nuisance to be explaining it all the time. One thing you can get from a stem-and-leaf is a frequency distribution: the number of cases per interval or category of cases. You can

Table 2.11

Males 65-74: Alternate Presentations

Stem-and-Leaf		Frequency Distribution		Histogram	
10	7	100–109	1	100–109	▢
9		90– 99		90– 99	
8		80– 89		80– 89	
7		70– 79		70– 79	
6	9	60– 69	1	60– 69	▢
5	621	50– 59	3	50– 59	▭
4	9	40– 49	1	40– 49	▢
3	57	30– 39	2	30– 39	▭
2	4778822	20– 29	7	20– 29	▭
1		10– 19		10– 19	
0		0– 9		0– 9	

stems: tens
leaves: units

see how to get this by comparing the stem-and-leaf in Table 2.4 to the corresponding tally in Table 2.3. In the stem-and-leaf for the younger batch, the stem 0 has four leaves; this means there are four cases from 0 to 9; so the frequency of the interval 0–9 is four. Each line is converted to an interval (just jot down the range of numbers that would be stored on that line); and the number of cases on each line is recorded. Table 2.11 gives a stem-and-leaf, and corresponding frequency distribution for rates for males aged 65–74.

Frequency distributions are useful summaries when you have a lot of cases; in this case stems-and-leaves become cumbersome. If we had hundreds of cases per line, the stem-and-leaf would be quite something! The exploratory tools are designed for fast work with a modest number of cases, remember. If we had hundreds of cases we just would not look at them all when we explored, we would select a manageable subsample: at most a hundred, often less.

Another popular tool is the *histogram*. Again you start with intervals and represent the number of cases per interval, but you do it graphically rather than numerically by putting bars opposite each category; the length of the bars is proportional to the number of cases in the intervals. The width of the bars is (usually) the same for all of the bars. Table 2.11 presents the suicide data for older men in bar graph form as well as stem-and-leaf and frequency distribution. Note how easy it is to get from the stem-and-leaf to the other two. The histogram may look a little difficult at first glance because you have to draw little bars of the right length; for example, in our histogram we have used an eighth of an inch per case so we have to make a bar one eighth of an inch long for the interval 100–109 which has one case, three eighths of an inch long for the interval 50–59 which has three cases and so on. But look at the histogram and look at the stem-and-leaf: the histogram is just the outline of the stem-and-leaf's leaves! If you write down your leaves so that they are fairly evenly spaced, the stem-and-leaf is a histogram: the longer the lines the more cases there are.

So it is clear that the stem-and-leaf tells you everything the other two displays tell you, and it can be converted to either form quickly to make communication easier. It should also be clear that the stem-and-leaf is much superior for two reasons: it is quicker to do and it contains far more information. It tells you not only how many cases there are per interval, but also what they are. Thus we intend to use the stem-and-leaf as our basic tool for preliminary data organization.

Homework

1. *Do-it-yourself Data*
It is a little extra work but a lot of fun to collect your *own* data. Count some things, get at least one batch of numbers, stem-and-leaf in a good variety of ways and discuss. Why did you decide to count what you did? What does it mean? What do the stems-and-leaves tell you? What would you like to do next to follow up on your ideas from the analysis?

In the past students have gathered numbers about all sorts of things. One student, for example, was interested in whether male students or female students had better concentration when they were studying. So he went to the library, spread out some work so he could fit into the background, and discreetly observed male and female students working at the library tables. He watched each person for two minutes, counting the number of times the person looked up from whatever he or she was doing (the idea being that the people who looked up more were concentrating less, probably). So he ended up with two batches: a set of counts for female students and a set of counts for male students. Each count was a number, the number of times that a person looked up. Curious about how it came out? Try it in your own library.

Another student was interested in how traffic patterns around her home changed during the day, so she counted the number of vehicles passing by during five-minute intervals in the morning, the afternoon, and the evening. After several days she had several counts of traffic flow for each period: a morning batch, an afternoon batch, and an evening batch. One could introduce many variations on this, depending on the amount of time one had and what was most interesting.

Still another student wanted to figure out what television programmers were up to, so she counted several kinds of things like the number of commercials for programmes of various types. For example, she would watch several documentaries, count the number of commercials in each one, and note several counts; or she would watch police dramas and get several counts of the number of commercials on each of them. Thus she got a documentary batch, a police story batch, etc. (and if anyone complained about all this TV, she was doing her statistics homework!).

Another thing which might be useful is to find out "where all the money goes"; carry around a little notebook and jot down the amount of every purchase and the sort of thing it is for (food, stationery, etc.).

Implicit Comparisons

These possible mini-studies bring up a point not obvious for the suicide data: interpreting batch data often includes comparisons to background knowledge, whether or not the comparison is explicit. Suppose the student recording television commercials found three in a half hour; is that many or few? Few if our comparison is with North American commercial TV; many if it's educational TV. We all have a surprisingly large range of knowledge about how big things tend to be, so that we can recognize unusually sized things easily: a four-pound baby is tiny, while a four-pound diamond is too large to be credible. For some kinds of data like suicide rates, few of us have much feeling for size at first. Is a rate of 10 per 100 000 a lot or a little? Who knows? But looking at batch data quickly changes this. We have already seen that Hungary's rates are high and Spain's low, because we have seen these rates in comparison with others. So if you have background comparison knowledge, use it. If you are starting fresh, you will soon learn from the data.

2. *Female Suicide Rates*
We will not be working with the female rates in the text, so you can work on them for the next several chapters. Pick a couple, put these batches into all the various kinds of stems-and-leaves, and discuss what you see. For next week's homework you will need all five batches in comparable stem-and-leaf format.

General Comments on Homework

All homework assignments have two parts: technical work and discussion. They are equally important and they both must be done. This week, for example, you must get used to the basic batch technique: assorted stems-and-leaves. But you don't just stem-and-leaf the numbers and stop! Look at the displays, think about them, write down the things you see (main features of the data) and the things you think of (questions, hypotheses). The discussion in the chapter gives you some idea of the sort of thing we mean, although your discussion will naturally stress the data more and the technique less than ours has to.

Numerical work alone is boring for you, indigestible for the reader, and ambiguous for the grader (do you really understand what you've done?). For everyone's sake, always discuss.

3

Using Numerical Summaries

We have now seen how the stem-and-leaf can help us get a quick feel for one or two batches of data. Unfortunately, when we have more batches, the amount you can see is limited in some ways. Two stem-and-leaf arrays can be seen if arrayed back-to-back, as in Table 2.6. However, it is difficult to see beyond a mere jumble of numbers if three or more data sets have to be compared, and the interesting problems often involve many batches. For example, Table 3.1 gives suicide rates for all five age groups for males rather than just the oldest and youngest. Five batches altogether now; that's a lot of numbers and we may have difficulty coping with them. Table 3.2 does about as well as we can do with the tools of the last chapter alone: we have used a single common stem followed by the five columns of leaves side by side. It is possible to see a few things in this maze of numbers if you work at it, but it is hard work and it's difficult to be sure of what you are doing.

Table 3.1

1971 Mortality Rates from Suicide for Males
(rates per 100,000)
(Rounded to nearest unit)

	1971				
	25–34	35–44	45–54	55–64	65–74
Canada	22	27	31	34	24
Israel	9	10	10	14	27
Japan	22	19	21	31	49
Austria	29	40	52	53	69
France	16	25	36	47	56
Germany	28	35	41	49	52
Hungary	48	65	84	81	107
Italy	7	8	11	18	27
Netherlands	8	11	18	20	28
Poland	26	29	36	32	28
Spain	4	7	10	16	22
Sweden	28	41	46	51	35
Switzerland	22	34	41	50	51
UK (E & W)	10	13	15	17	22
USA	20	22	28	33	37

Table 3.2

Stems and Leaves for Data in Table 3.1

	25–34	35–44	45–54	55–64	65–74
10					7
9					
8			4	1	
7					
6		5			9
5			2	310	621
4	8	01	161	79	9
3		54	166	4123	57
2	22986802	9275	18	0	4778822
1	60	0913	01805	4867	
0	9784	87			

stem: tens
leaf: units

We want to have some simple ways of comparing a lot of batches easily. In this chapter we will learn how to compare some important features of batches very easily using numerical summaries. A series of summary numbers can be seen easily while a series of data sets can't. Of course, we can only summarize after deciding what we want summarized, that is, after deciding what features of the batches are important enough to put in a summary and what can be left aside as mere detail. Now, what are some of the major features of batches? Our explorations of the suicide data in the previous chapter suggested several things that are likely to be of interest for many different kinds of data:

1. Level, or how big the numbers are "on the average." For example, it looked like suicide rates for older males were higher than those for younger males.
2. Spread, or how compact the batches are. For example, the rates for older males appear to be more spread out, more different from one another, than are the rates for younger males.
3. Clumping, or how the batch is clustered into groups of numbers. For example, for the rates of the 25–34 age group in Table 2.4, twelve of the fifteen rates are on only two stems.
4. Shape, or how the numbers are distributed. Do they trail off nearly evenly above and below the middle or do they trail off primarily in one direction? For example, the older batch tended to trail upward.
5. Unusual numbers, or numbers that seem rather high or rather low compared to the rest (like Hungary).

If we could satisfactorily summarize these features of batches, broad comparisons of batches would be greatly simplified. We would still be interested in some details, and would expect to return to them from time to time, but a good summary would do for a first look and would also, by implication, tell us which details need special attention because the summary describes them poorly.

As it will turn out, the numerical summaries we will use can do a very good job of summarizing level, spread, shape, and unusual values. They won't tell us much about clumping; fortunately that is one thing we can see pretty easily from stems-and-leaves.

In this chapter we will deal with ways to summarize level and spread. The next chapter will show how these summaries can be made more effective using graphic techniques, and the last two chapters of this section will describe techniques and strategies for working with shape.

Level: The "Centre" of the Data

Perhaps the single most important feature of data description is the batch *level*: where the batch is centred. Among other things, this provides a quick best guess about the magnitude of values a given process might generate. Thus, in baseball for example, a pitcher's "earned run average" (E.R.A.) gives a best guess as to the number of earned runs he will allow in the next game he pitches. Level is also a familiar idea which people use, in a rough-and-ready way, all the time. Comments like "doctors make more money than teachers" are typical. This doesn't mean that every doctor in the world makes more than every teacher; it does mean that the overall level of incomes is higher for doctors than for teachers; that doctors earn more "on the average." The general idea of level or centre is familiar, but many people don't realize that this general notion includes many different kinds of levels. For any batch, there are different centres for different purposes. Here we describe only four especially useful kinds of level, starting with two familiar ones and then discussing two that are less familiar but very handy.

The Mean and the Median

The most familiar, most frequently used level is the *mean*. To find the mean of a batch, add up the values of all the observations and divide by the number of observations (the *count* of the batches, whose symbol is N). For example, the mean of the 25–34 batch in Table 3.1 is:

$$\frac{\text{Total}}{\text{Count}} = \frac{22 + 9 + 22 + 29 + \ldots + 22 + 10 + 20}{15}$$

$$= \frac{299}{15} = 19.933\ldots$$

By the way, how precisely should we report figures like these? For example, should we make this mean 20, 19.9, 19.93, 19.933, or what? As a general rule of thumb, we suggest: keep as many significant digits as there are in the data, or perhaps one more. Here we used numbers with at most two significant digits (units and tens) so the mean would be calculated as 20 or as 19.9. More precision (e.g. 19.93) is really fake precision, since the data themselves were not this precise. Less precision might be too crude here, although it might be acceptable for another data set. Well, what about 19.9 versus 20? This is not too important as a rule; we will sometimes do one thing and sometimes another. When you get to Table 3.3, you will find various levels reported with different degrees of precision: some with no decimal places, some with quarters, some with one decimal place. This is of no consequence, since the table has all the information we need for our exploratory work. If you want a guideline (your common sense is really enough) you might try starting analysis with one more significant digit than the data and drop this extra digit if and when you can see you don't need it. If you are already familiar with significant digits and scientific notation, read on. If not, this is a good time to learn, so turn to the section on significant digits in the technical appendix.

There is another technical detail worth noting since things like it often crop up for rates. We just found the mean of the rates of countries, not the mean rate of suicide of men in the youngest age group in all countries. To find the overall rate per 100 000 men we would have to allow for the fact that some of these countries have more people than others. Israel with a fairly low rate has many fewer people than Hungary with a high rate but when we average the rates we treat them as if they had the same population base.

The mean is just one kind of level, good for some purposes and not so good for others. For confirmatory work the mean is very useful indeed. It uses all the data; it is easily understood, although sometimes tedious to compute by hand; and it has mathematical properties which are very convenient for confirmatory statistical problems. However, we don't like the mean for exploratory purposes because it is more laborious than other levels and, more important, it is not resistant. "Not resistant" means that a few wild observations or errors can affect its magnitude dramatically. To illustrate, consider the kingdom of Frammistan in which the 999 peasants earn $1 per year while the king collects $1 000 000 000 per year. The mean income of our mythical Frammistanis is about one million dollars per year, a figure which misleads because it is not even approximately true of anyone in the society.

We might do better here by asking not, "how much do people earn on the average?", but rather, "how much does the *average* man earn?" We would then rank the 1 000 inhabitants of Frammistan and take the middle observation; here this is the mean of the 500th and 501st, or $1, which gives us a better indication of the income level. This measure is called the *median*, symbolized Md. (By the way, this example is really not so far-fetched as all that; there are many nations in which the top 10% have a share of the total income many times as large as that of the bottom 90%.)

The median is the number such that half the batch is greater and half is smaller than it; if we have an odd number of cases, there is a middle one and that's the median, while if there is an even number of cases, there are two middle ones, and the median is half way between them. Finding the median can be a nuisance if the batch isn't ordered, but it's very easy from stems-and-leaves like those in Table 3.2. For the youngest group, for example, the number N of figures in the batch is 15, so we want the eighth largest or eighth smallest number (the same thing); we just start at the top (or bottom) of the stem-and-leaf and count toward the centre in order of magnitude (not in the order the numbers are written) until we get to the 8th largest or smallest, here, 22. On checking, we see that seven of the batch values are bigger than this and seven are smaller.

Of course, you want to know how to remember how far to count in! That's the only problem in computing a median. It's easy enough if you use a mnemonic device of Tukey's, *grows to*. A number that is not an integer grows to the next higher integer; e.g., 8.0001, 8.25, 8.875 all grow to 9. On the other hand, any integer grows to itself plus one-half; e.g., 8 grows to 8.5, 13 grows to 13.5, etc. Now the median observation (Md) is the observation that $N/2$ grows to. We just did an example for odd numbers: for the suicide batches $N = 15$ so

$$\frac{N}{2} = \frac{15}{2} = 7.5 \rightarrow 8$$

(the little arrow means "grows to"). What about even numbers? Take, for example, the batch

$$3 \qquad 7 \qquad 16 \qquad 19$$

Here N is 4. So

$$\frac{4}{2} = 2 \rightarrow 2\tfrac{1}{2} \quad .$$

We count in $2\tfrac{1}{2}$ from top or bottom and find ourselves halfway between the 2nd and 3rd values, or 7 and 16; their mean,

$$\frac{7 + 16}{2} = \frac{23}{2} = 11.5 \quad ,$$

is the median of the batch. Again the rule works: half the values are above 11.5, half below.

The median is a very familiar level, probably the commonest after the mean. How do the two compare? The mean uses all the information but at the cost of occasionally being "victimized" by stray observations. To guard against strays, the median sets aside both the upper and lower halves of the data taking only the middle one or two. This makes it very resistant. For example, the means and medians of the five suicide batches are listed in Table 3.3, which also sums up other things we'll get to shortly. Note that the mean is higher than the median for four of the five batches; and it is especially higher for the oldest batch. If you look back at Table 3.2 you soon see that the mean is overreacting to the rates for Hungary; the rates for Hungary are so extreme, so large compared to the rest, that the mean is being pulled up a lot by this single value. Of course, the median is not affected; it reflects what happens in the middle of the batches, ignoring what happens at the extremes. This resistance to extreme cases is desirable in exploration, where you often use data of erratic quality. The median uses very little of the data and yet loses less information than you might think; if the data are free of strays then the median gives results much like the mean, while if the data do have erratic values then the median often fits our intuitive impression of overall level better than the mean does. Nevertheless, the median does force us to rely on one or two observations, a somewhat uncomfortable situation.

We would like a measure that uses more of the data without relying much on the extreme observations. In the next part of the chapter we present two measures of the level that give us this sort of compromise.

Middle Means

The basic strategy for using more data than the median while avoiding extremes is to take levels from the usually more reliable middle half of the data. This strategy is one aspect of the more general approach of trimming off some part of the less reliable extremes. You may well be familiar with one sort of trimmed level in common use, especially in sports like gymnastics or diving. For example, a gymnast's performance is judged by several experts; the highest and the lowest judgements are thrown out, and the score is the mean of the remaining judgements. Often this keeps a gymnast from being unduly penalized because one judge loathes the performance for idiosyncratic reasons; equally, the procedure sometimes keeps a competitor from being unduly rewarded because one judge has an exceptionally high score for him.

For our trimming, we want a procedure that will be generally useful for various kinds of data and sizes of batches; trimming off the highest and lowest quarters usually works out well. So we need to know how to find the *quartiles*, those values that quarter a batch. (Sometimes you see two analogous terms: deciles, which divide a batch in tenths, and percentiles, which divide a batch in hundredths.) You already know one quartile, the median, or second quartile, which divides the top two quarters from the bottom two. To find the other two quartiles we break the top and bottom halves of the batch in half again, and it is easy to do this by using the concept *grows to* again. We find what $N/4$ grows to; counting in that amount from the top gives the upper quartile, counting in that amount from the bottom gives the lower quartile. Here is how it works for the youngest suicide batch.

$$N = 15, \text{ so } \frac{N}{4} = \frac{15}{4} = 3\tfrac{3}{4} \to 4 \quad ;$$

we want the fourth largest and fourth smallest values. From the stem-and-leaf we quickly find these numbers: 28 and 9. See how they divide up the batch:

Counting in:

1	48	
2	29	
3	28	
4	28	Upper Quartile $= q_U$
	26	
	22	
	22	
	22	Middle Quartile $=$ Median $=$ Md
	20	
	16	
	10	
4	9	Lower Quartile $= q_L$
3	8	
2	7	
1	4	

If N happens to be a multiple of 4 then q_U and q_L may not be values in the batch. For example if we have

$$2 \quad 5 \quad \underset{\underset{q_L}{\uparrow}}{} 7 \quad 10 \quad 13 \quad 17 \quad \underset{\underset{q_U}{\uparrow}}{} 18 \quad 20$$

then

$$\frac{N}{4} = \frac{8}{4} = 2 \to 2\tfrac{1}{2} \quad ;$$

the quartiles are halfway between the 2nd and 3rd values counting in from each end; here

$$q_L = \frac{5+7}{2} = 6 \quad \text{and} \quad q_U = \frac{17+18}{2} = 17.5 \; .$$

The summary Table 3.3 gives q_U and q_L for all five suicide batches.

Now that we know how to find batch middles we can discuss the middle means. The easiest middle mean to compute is the *trimean*, which just uses what we've already found:

$$\text{Trimean} = \text{TRI} = \frac{q_U + q_L + 2\,Md}{4}$$

For the 25 to 34 age group we know q_U, q_L and Md so the trimean is

$$\text{TRI} = \frac{28 + 9 + 2(22)}{4}$$

$$= \frac{81}{4} = 20\tfrac{1}{4}$$

The trimean uses more data than the median by including the upper and lower quartiles, which give extra information about the location of the centre, while still avoiding extremes. The trimean weights the median doubly because the median is, after all, close to the centre and the centre is what we're after. Obviously this weight is slightly arbitrary: for example, we could easily have decided to weight the median triply and divide by five. However, this formula will turn out to have some desirable properties, is quick and easy to compute, and gives a measure that combines many of the nice properties of the mean and median.

There are other middle levels, the best known being the *interquartile mean*, or the mean of the numbers between the upper and lower quartiles. It is the mean of the middle half of the data, excluding the quartile values themselves. Using the 25 to 34 batch again,

$$\text{Interquartile mean} = \frac{26 + 22 + 22 + 22 + 20 + 16 + 10}{7}$$

$$= \frac{138}{7} = 19.7$$

Since the interquartile mean is just the mean of the middle, Tukey suggests the less cumbersome title *midmean*, or MID for short. There is just one little thing to be careful about when using this straightforward measure: repeated values. Some or none of the repeated values may be included in the calculation, depending on how many are needed to get half the data (the middle half) into the midmean. For the suicide batches, each of the extreme quarters has 4 observations, leaving 7 for the middle half. In the 25 to 34 batch, q_U is 28 and 28 occurs twice; neither 28 is used in the midmean because the middle has seven values without the 28s. By contrast, in the 45 to 54 batch q_U is 41, 41 occurs twice, and one of the 41s must be included in the midmean to get a full 7 cases in the middle. With a little practice, you can easily set aside top and bottom quarters from the stem-and-leaf.

The midmean is somewhat more work than the trimean while giving very similar results (as you can see in Table 3.3), so in general we prefer the trimean. On the other hand, the midmean is fairly well known under its ponderous name "interquartile mean"; it is thus a good level if you want to explore levels using a resistant measure and then easily communicate your results to a wide audience.

Both midmean and trimean resist the effects of wild values, use the usually more stable central values, are easy to compute, and give about the same results as the more comprehensive arithmetic mean when the data are well-behaved, that is, when the data are smooth and there are no wild outliers, like the Hungary rates here.

All four levels can be compared for the suicide batches by looking at Table 3.3. All three resistant measures (Md, TRI, MID) give similar results, with the trimean and midmean perhaps closest together (they usually are). The mean is clearly different from the resistant trio: again, the mean is much affected by Hungary's unusually high rates. These differences are important because the numbers give us different first impressions of what is happening in the data, once we get past the obvious common message that suicide rates increase with age. The mean seems to be saying that suicide rates increase at about the same rate as we pass from one age group to another except between the 45–54 group and the 55–64 group where the increase is slightly lower. The more resistant measures appear to show a relatively large increase from 35–44 to 45–54, and a relatively small increase from 55–64 to 65–74. The rates are high and similar for both older groups. This could lead us to speculate that retirement at age 65 is not as important a factor in suicide as we had suggested earlier. On the other hand, the greater difference from 35–44 to 45–54 might reflect the fact that the older group is exposed to certain difficulties that the younger group does not face; the older men are more likely to lose their jobs with little chance of re-employment, more likely to get ill, less likely to have children at home. The resistant levels give a sensible picture and one that is true to more of the data, while the mean seems to be reflecting the extreme nature of a single piece of the data (Hungary) too much.

Table 3.3

Comparison of the Levels of Five Suicide Batches

	25–34	35–44	45–54	55–64	65–74
Mean	19.9	25.7	32.0	36.4	42.3
Md	22	25	31	33	35
Tri	$20\frac{1}{4}$	24	29.5	33.5	$37\frac{1}{4}$
Mid	19.7	24.1	30.1	35.1	36.4
q_U	28	35	41	50	52
q_L	9	11	15	18	27

All types of levels have their advantages; which to use is a matter of judgement. If you have trouble deciding, try two or three and see what happens. All the levels have problems with some sorts of data; even the resistant measures are not always best. If you do meet some batches to which the exploratory levels do not do justice, remember that many of the rules for the exploratory levels (for example, the weighting of the median when calculating the trimean) are a bit arbitrary and can be adjusted to suit particular needs. You should feel free to make such adjustments but if you do, make them consistently for any batches that you want to compare. And, of course, tell your reader (and yourself: you might forget) what you are doing.

Get to know all four levels, so you can use the best one for each job; no single measure can be best for all purposes.

Hiatus: Some Necessary Symbols

Since the mean is easy, we use it as a vehicle to introduce some important and recurring symbols. We symbolize our batch values with x, their mean with $\bar{x}$ (read "x bar"), and the rule for finding the mean with

$$\bar{x} = \frac{\sum\limits_{i=1}^{N} x_i}{N}$$

which is just

$$\text{mean} = \frac{\text{total of all the } x \text{ values}}{\text{count}}$$

as above. Here is a glossary of these symbols.

x represents the elements of a set of numbers, here the batch (definitely *not* "the unknown").

$\bar{x}$ is the mean of x.

i the subscript "i" is an *index number*; if there are ten observations in a batch, "i" stands for the numbers 1, 2, ..., 10. These index numbers have nothing to do with the value of the x referred to (any more than a house number tells you anything about the residents' age), but rather specify which of the x's is being referred to.

Σ is the Greek capital letter sigma which stands for "sum" (a handy sign since we add a lot of things).

$\sum\limits_{i=1}^{N} x_i$ means "add up all the x_i's, where i goes from 1 to N". In other words

$$\sum\limits_{i=1}^{N} x_i \text{ means } x_1 + x_2 + \ldots + x_N .$$

N stands for the number of x values that we have, the count.

Most of the time we will just want to add up a bunch of numbers called x so we simplify by leaving out the i's which distinguish one x value from another, thus:

$$\text{mean of } x = \bar{x} = \frac{\sum x}{N}$$

The Spread of the Data

As we have seen, knowing the approximate centre of a batch of data is extremely useful. Clearly, this by itself is not enough. We would also like to know something about the amount the batch can be expected to vary about this centre, the *spread* of the data. When spread is low, the level can provide a very good guess; where spread is high, knowing level won't help a lot in predicting any particular outcome. You may have heard the old saw about the man who drowned in a river where the average depth was one foot. Returning to our baseball example, a team whose pitcher has allowed an average of two earned runs per game can lose to a team whose pitcher has allowed an average of four runs per game (and often does; otherwise there would be little mystery in predicting the outcomes of such encounters). Managers may prefer the consistent (low spread) player to the erratic or "streaky" (high spread) player. For the suicide example, we argued in the previous chapter that the oldest group's rates were more spread out than the youngest and this suggested some interesting possibilities, such as the "homogenizing" effect of industrialization.

Once again, there is a variety of measures available. One extremely simple and well-known measure is the *range* of a batch: the smallest number subtracted from the largest. For the 25–34 batch, a glance at the stem-and-leaf shows

$$\text{range} = 48 - 4 = 44$$

We label the smallest number X_L (lower extreme) and the largest number X_U (upper extreme) so another definition of range is:

$$\text{range} = X_U - X_L$$

The range is very easy to find; unfortunately it is not very resistant because it is based on precisely those values that are most likely to be erratic: the extremes.

A good combination of resistance, ease of calculation and use of a reasonable amount of the data is again probably to be found in the middle of the distribution. We define the *midspread*, or spread of the middle, to be the difference between the upper and lower quartiles (dq for short).

$$\text{midspread} = dq = q_U - q_L$$

For the 25–34 batch, $dq = 28 - 9 = 19$. In more standard language this measure labours under the title "interquartile range," which is descriptive but cumbersome. The midspread or, alternatively, difference of quartiles, dq, is the principal exploratory measure of spread that we'll use.

When we turn to confirmatory statistics, we will find another spread measure to be important, the *variance*. Very roughly speaking, the variance measures spread by looking at how much the batch values differ from their mean. We can see exactly what happens by following through the example in

Table 3.4

*Work Sheet for Variance Computation, 25-34 Batch:
Long Method*

x_i	$x_i - \bar{x}$	$(x_i - \bar{x})^2$
48	28.1	789.61
29	9.1	82.81
28	8.1	65.61
28	8.1	65.61
26	6.1	37.21
22	2.1	4.41
22	2.1	4.41
22	2.1	4.41
20	0.1	0.01
16	−3.9	15.21
10	−9.9	98.01
9	−10.9	118.81
8	−11.9	141.61
7	−12.9	166.41
4	−15.9	252.81
$\bar{x} = 19.9$	$\sum(x_i - \bar{x}) = 0.5*$	$\sum(x_i - \bar{x})^2 = 1846.95$

$$\text{Variance} = \frac{\sum(x_i - \bar{x})^2}{N - 1} = \frac{1846.95}{14} = 131.93$$

* Theoretically, this sum should be zero. We can use this to check our calculations. Here the sum is 0.5, which is within rounding error of zero; so our calculations are probably correct.

Table 3.4. The first column gives x, the batch values, again for the 25–34 batch. From this we obtain the mean $\bar{x}$, which we earlier found to be 19.9. Next we want to know how much the batch values differ from $\bar{x}$; that is the next column, $x_i - \bar{x}$ or each of the x values minus the mean. (These are often called "deviations" from the mean). So far so good; the more spread out the batch is, the bigger these deviations will be, so we can measure spread by some summary of the deviations' sizes. Would the mean of the deviations be suitable? No: it's easy to demonstrate that the deviations must add up to zero. Well, we could get rid of the minus signs. One way is to drop them and then take the mean of the results, which gives us the "mean of the absolute deviations" (MAD). The MAD is a measure of spread, but one hardly ever seen outside of statistics books. The preferred method for handling minus signs is to square the deviations, getting the third column of the work sheet Table 3.4. Our final step is to find the overall level of these squared deviations:

$$\text{VAR} = \frac{\sum(x_i - \bar{x})^2}{N - 1}$$

This is just the mean of the squared deviations (except for the $N-1$ instead of N in the denominator; we use $N-1$ because, for technical reasons, it is better than N in just about all applications of the variance).

The variance is a very important measure with some good points and some bad points. First the good news. The variance uses all the values in a batch whereas the range and dq use only two; the variance is broadly based. From a mathematician's point of view, the variance uses all the observations in a very simple way; only MAD (the mean absolute deviation) could be simpler, and MAD has unappealing mathematical properties. The variance has more appealing properties that make the construction of confirmatory statistics easier. The variance therefore plays a major role in the most popular confirmatory statistics and we will have to get to know the variance well.

And now for the bad news: from an exploratory point of view, the variance is terrible. It is not resistant; it is tedious to compute; and it is not very intuitive. The variance is even less resistant than the mean because it is even more affected by extremes. Look at Table 3.4 again. The extreme cases like 48 and 4 are farthest from the mean, so their deviations are the largest ones; when these values are squared they become extremely big. The value 48 alone contributes 789.61 to the total of 1846.9 for $\sum(x_i - \overline{x})^2$: over a third from just one case! Any unusually high or low values really blow up the variance.

The variance is more work than the range and dq, each of which requires only a subtraction once the batch is ordered. Well, at least we can minimize the computational work by using a fast form of the variance formula:

$$\text{VAR} = \frac{\sum x^2 - (\sum x)^2/N}{N - 1}$$

This is not as forbidding as it may look if you have been away from basic algebra for a while. The numerator of the expression has two parts, each easy to compute:

$\sum x^2$ says: first square each of the x values, then add all the squares up.

$(\sum x)^2/N$ says: first add up all the x values, then square the total, and finally divide the squared total by N.

Table 3.5 contains a worked example of this faster form of the calculation for variance. Note the difference between squaring x, then adding it and adding it, then squaring it! Always make sure you do the arithmetic in the right order. Naturally, the answer we get with the fast method of Table 3.5 is exactly the same as the slower method of Table 3.4.

Finally, we remarked that the variance is low on intuitive appeal as well as on resistance and computational speed. Somehow you can't *see* a variance. With the dq or the range, one can see the spread right in the batch; thus the spread has a direct and obvious meaning. But the variance puts a number of things together (all the N deviations from the mean) in a number

Table 3.5

Work Sheet for Quick Variance Computation,
25-34 Batch

x_i	$x_i{}^2$
48	2304
29	841
28	784
28	784
26	676
22	484
22	484
22	484
20	400
16	256
10	100
9	81
8	64
7	49
4	16
$\sum x_i = 299$	$\sum x_i{}^2 = 7807$

$(\sum x_i)^2 = 89401$

$$\text{Variance} = \frac{\sum x_i{}^2 - (\sum x_i)^2/N}{N-1} = \frac{7807 - (89401)/15}{14} = 131.92$$

$$\text{SD} = \sqrt{\text{VAR}} = \sqrt{131.92} = 11.5$$

of steps (the deviations are squared, then their level is taken) which goes beyond what visual imagination can handle. Most people never visualize the variance, they just get used to it.

Part of the problem is that the variance can't be readily compared to the numbers it is based on, because the variance is in different units: the data units squared. We can overcome that hurdle easily enough by taking the square root of the variance, thus getting us back to the data units. This slightly more intuitive measure of spread is the *standard deviation*:

$$sd = \sqrt{\text{VAR}}$$

often further abbreviated:

$$s = \sqrt{s^2}$$

For the 25–34 batch we know that VAR = 131.92, so *sd* is the square root of this or 11.5. We can use the standard deviation to talk about the relationship of a value to the rest of a batch.

For now, we will give you a few examples illustrating important aspects of how the standard deviation works. Then we will discuss *sd*, *dq*, and range for the suicide batches. First consider Table 3.6. In part A we see four batches that are just the same except for one value, the X_U, which increases

Table 3.6

Some Properties of the Standard Deviation

A: *Lack of Resistance*

Batch 1	Batch 2	Batch 3	Batch 4	Batch 5
9				2
8			2	
7		2		
6	2			
5 2				
4 37	37	37	37	37
3 926	926	926	926	926
2 428	428	428	428	428
1 39	39	39	39	39
0 5	5	5	5	5

stem: tens   *leaves*: units

sd = 14.2	15.8	17.7	19.9	22.2
$\bar{x}$ = 30.0	30.8	31.7	32.5	33.3

Increases

sd	1.6	1.9	2.2	2.3
$\bar{x}$	0.8	0.9	0.8	0.8

Md is 30 and *dq* is 20.5 for all 5 batches

B: *Independence from Mean*

Batch 1 Plus 100

15	2
14	37
13	926
12	428
11	39
10	5

sd = 14.2
$\bar{x}$ = 130.0

C: *Why "Standard" Deviation*

Batch 1

Batch 1—All Doubled

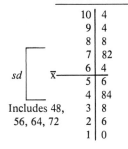

5	2
4	37
3	926
2	428
1	39
0	5

$\bar{x}$ sd

↑ Includes 24, 28, 32, 36

Includes 48, 56, 64, 72

10	4
9	4
8	8
7	82
6	4
5	6
4	84
3	8
2	6
1	0

sd = 14.2
$\bar{x}$ = 30.0

stems: tens
leaves: units

sd = 28.4
$\bar{x}$ = 60.0

by equal amounts from batch to batch. The mean increases too, of course; we have seen that the mean is not resistant. But the standard deviation increases faster and faster; it is even more sensitive than the mean. By the way, we have not invented a bizarre example with no practical importance: look at the oldest suicide batch. It is not at all uncommon to find batches with values that look far more unusual than the X_U in batch 4 of Table 3.6 part A. (Note that the exploratory tools like Md and dq are not affected at all by X_U's behaviour here.)

Let's get a litle more feeling for the standard deviation's behaviour by looking at part B of Table 3.6. Here we have just changed the level of batch 1 from part A by adding 100 to everything. The mean increases by 100, but the standard deviation does not change at all. This makes sense; the numbers are no more or less spread out than before, they are merely higher up. Level and spread are separate issues. Finally, Part C of 3.6 gives some idea of why the sd is called the *standard* deviation. Part C shows batch 1 again and batch 1 with all values doubled. The sd and $\bar{x}$ also double. But the sd continues to do the same job. We have marked the amount of the standard deviation (one sd) around the mean for both batches (e.g. for the original batch 1 the square bracket covers the mean (30), plus and minus half the sd, a range of one sd altogether). The four values in the middle of the batch are those within half a standard deviation of the mean; and this is true whether we use the original figures or the doubled ones. We can think of "one standard deviation" as a unit of spread that will mean the same thing for any batch. We will develop this idea further in the next chapter when we talk about standardization.

Now let us turn to a comparison of different spread measures in action by looking at the midspread, range, and standard deviation for our suicide rate batches. We could try to compare these spread measures' values for one batch, like the 25–34 batch:

$$\text{standard deviation} = 11.5$$
$$\text{range} = 44$$
$$\text{midspread} = 19$$

but a moment's thought shows that we can't compare these numbers the way we compared the levels. All the levels were trying to locate the same thing, the centre of the data, and were easily comparable, but the spreads are doing rather different things; for example, the range can't possibly be smaller than the midspread: it covers more ground. But we can compare the spread measures in action by computing each of them for all five suicide batches and considering the messages each of them sends.

Table 3.7 gives the standard deviations, ranges, and midspreads of all five batches of suicide rates.

Let's look first at the broad relationships among the spread measures. The range is always the largest. By comparison, the dq and sd are in roughly

Table 3.7

*A Comparison of the Range, dq and sd for
Male Suicide Rates*

	25–34	35–44	45–54	55–64	65–74
10					7
9					
8			4	1	
7					
6		5			9
5			2	013	126
4	8	01	116	79	9
3		45	166	4123	57
2	20226889	7259	18	0	4227788
1	06	0139	00158	4678	
0	9784	78			
sd	11.5	15.8	19.9	18.7	23.0
Range	44	58	74	67	85
dq	19	24	26	32	25

the same ballpark, with the *dq* a bit larger. The *sd* can be larger than the *dq*; this usually means there are some very atypical values in the batch as in batch 5 of Table 3.6A, where the *sd* is larger than the *dq* and there is one quite unusual-looking upper value.

Now let's see what the three measures tell us about the five suicide batches' behaviour. As we go from the youngest batch to the oldest batch, the *range* increases at every step except from 45–54 to 55–64, increasing faster and faster; the *standard deviation* increases at every step but one, increasing about the same amount each time except for the step from 45–54 to 55–64 where it declines; the *midspread* increases pretty steadily except for the last step, from 55–64 to 65–74, where the *dq* drops sharply, and the move into the middle group where the increase is slight. In a very broad way, the messages are the same: spread increases as we go from younger to older batches. But the messages are different in details that may be important. First, why are they different? Because of the different characteristics of the different measures, characteristics we pointed out above. The range was said to be unreliable, being based on just two points and those the most extreme. Sure enough, a hard look at the stems-and-leaves of Table 3.2 shows that Hungary, the highest value in all the batches, fluctuates rather briskly and pretty much on its own; Hungary does not look like a good guide to the spread of the batches as a whole. For example, when the range suggests that spread declined in the 55–64 batch, it is only that the rate for Hungary declined in that batch. The standard deviation was said to be nonresistant. Again we see this in the suicide batches: the standard deviation reflects the behaviour of Hungary in rather the same way as the range, although not as strongly because the standard deviation is based on all the observations rather than just the extremes.

Finally, what about the midspread, dq? It reflects the main body of the data quite well; for example, the middle mass of the oldest batch is a little more compact than that of the second oldest batch, largely because the countries with lower rates for 55–64 have similar but higher rates for 65–74, while those already high for 55–64 increase only slightly by 65–74. Perhaps the transition from 55–64 to 65–74 is not an important one for the higher rate countries; for example, perhaps retirement ages are spread out over those 20 years.

The range is easy but not resistant; the variance and standard deviation are a lot of work and not resistant; the midspread is easy and resistant. We think that the dq is giving us the most accurate and resistant picture of batch behaviour, and this together with its ease of computation make it our preferred measure for exploratory work. You should get to know the variance and standard deviation, though, since you will need them soon for confirmatory work.

Numerical Summaries

Now we are in position to give the quick summaries of important batch features which we promised at the start of the chapter. The discussion so far makes it clear that we need to know how many things there are in a batch (N), what the batch level is, what its spread is, and what the extreme values are like; all of these have played a role in our computations and discussions. The most economical way of doing these things is to list N, the quartiles, the median (or another level if you prefer), and the extremes. The dq does not have to be written in because you can read it off from the quartiles. It makes sense to list these summary numbers in the same order in which they occur in the batches, that is:

N the count
X_U upper extreme value
q_U upper quartile
Md median (or substitute other levels)
q_L lower quartile
X_L lower extreme value

Table 3.8 gives numerical summaries for all five batches of suicide data. We can see the flow of the batch levels from the medians, we can see the extremes, and we can read off spreads quickly. We also get the ingredients of trimeans. Comparisons of the major features of the batches are much easier in the condensed form of Table 3.8 than in the densely detailed form of Table 3.2.

Table 3.8

Numerical Summaries for All Suicide Batches

	Batch				
	25–34	35–44	45–54	55–64	65–74
N	15	15	15	15	15
X_U	48	65	84	81	107
q_U	28	35	41	50	52
Md	22	25	31	33	35
q_L	9	11	15	18	27
X_L	4	7	10	14	22

Exploratory and Confirmatory

The following terms are more or less standard:

mean	interquartile range
median	range
quartile	variance
interquartile mean	standard deviation

We prefer to use midmean for interquartile mean and midspread for interquartile range because these terms are less cumbersome. The only unusual measure we have introduced is the trimean,

$$\text{TRI} = \frac{q_U + q_L + 2\,\text{Md}}{4}$$

What we call level is usually called central tendency, and spread is often called dispersion.

Tukey uses some different terms, such as *hinge* for upper or lower quartile; thus upper hinge for upper quartile, lower hinge for lower quartile, and H-spread for midspread.

Tukey also uses a different way to display the numerical summary; in his most recent work he prefers a box display like this:

$$N \quad \begin{array}{|cc|} \hline & \text{Md} \\ q_L & q_U \\ X_L & X_U \\ \hline \end{array}$$

We find this somewhat less easy to read than the display in this chapter, which is similar to Tukey's earlier (1970) suggestion. Finally, Tukey has some additional terms and display methods which we do not cover here.

Homework

1. Since the main point of this chapter is to learn about two really funda-
mental features of batches, level and spread, a good idea for homework is
trying out the various level and spread measures on several batches to see
them at work. We suggest that you find all the level measures and range and
midspread for the female suicide rates in Table 2.1. Find variance and
standard deviation for one or two of these batches.

It is fastest to go about this in some orderly way. We suggest working in
stages like this:

    a. Stem-and-leaf your batches.
    b. Find your numerical summaries and jot them down under the stems-
       and-leaves they go with. (Step 3 is easy after step 2.)
    c. Find the various levels (mean, median, midmean, trimean) for each
       batch, note them down in some neat array, and discuss.
    d. Find the ranges and midspreads of each batch and discuss (again,
       very easy from step 2). Also find variance and standard deviation
       for two batches — these are time-consuming so do not do too many.
       Discuss.
    e. Discuss any remaining aspects of the data which have caught your
       eye: behaviour of extremes, batch differences or similarities, or
       whatever.

2. We have often mentioned the importance of resistance as a characteristic
of numerical summaries. To see how different levels are affected by extreme
values, calculate mean, median, trimean and midmean for the male suicide
data, *without* Hungary. How do these compare to the values calculated
including Hungary? Describe the changes in the various levels and discuss
why these changes happen.

4

Graphs: Seeing and Setting Aside

In the last chapter we saw how quick numerical summaries could help us when we had to compare many batches of data, something for which the stem-and-leaf is poor. Numerical summaries seemed quite good for this, and we will see in the next few chapters that they can be enormously helpful. However, they lack the visual impact of the stem-and-leaf. In this kind of situation, we will find that graphical displays can help.

All of the things we have done so far with numerical analyses of batches of data can be done with graphs, usually with less effort. We have seen from stems-and-leaves how quickly and easily a visual presentation can be digested. In the end, we will see that there are things that can be done better with graphs and things that can be done better with numbers. Often we will find that we can do still better with both; there are no hard and fast rules here. Being a good data analyst involves judgement, but personal preferences are not irrelevant: we will usually want to use those tools that we feel most comfortable with. On the other hand, we should want to be comfortable with as many tools as possible.

First of all we will discuss some general points related to the presentation of any kind of graph: the magnification of the graph (like the magnification of a stem-and-leaf) and the use of a zero point on a graph's scale. Both these procedural points make differences to the ways that graphs are seen. Then we will show you a special kind of visual presentation, the schematic plot, which we will find very useful. Finally, we show how to remove level and spread from batches once they have been sufficiently examined through numerical summaries and/or schematic plots.

The Magnification of a Graph

Graphs often make it possible to communicate complex ideas easily but there are many types of graphs and one must be careful to select the right sort for each job. Often there will be several types that will be useful, each telling a different important thing about your data. One feature of graphs is magnification: the more we blow our graphs up, the more easily we can see details and the less easily we can see overall features. This point was illustrated for stems-and-leaves in chapter 3 where we showed the same batches in three kinds of magnification (Tables 2.4, 2.7, and 2.8). The same point holds for graphs: use the magnification that best shows what you want to see, and use several different magnifications if you want to see different things.

Using the Zero Point

When preparing graphs for public viewing, one should always show the zero point as part of the graph because this gives an immediate feeling for where the data are centred (their level). Otherwise one has to look carefully at the numbers on the scale and a careless reader may get the impression that the bottom line is the zero level.

In Table 4.1 the medians of the five suicide rate batches are plotted without including the zero point. A quick glance (which is all that most readers give to a graph) gives the impression that the elderly are just lined up on bridges and tall buildings waiting to jump off! But in Table 4.2, which does include the zero point, the rate of increase with age seems more moderate. For publication purposes it is more honest and informative to use the Table 4.2 format rather than that of Table 4.1 (Huff, *How to Lie With Statistics*, has an excellent and very entertaining discussion of many kinds of misleading graphs).

But the format in Table 4.1 does have advantages over that in 4.2: it shows details more clearly, since it is a kind of close-up, high-magnification graph. Thus it is a bit easier to see that the increases from 45–54 to 55–64 and from 55–64 to 65–74 are the smallest ones while the 35–44 to 45–54 increase is much bigger. With a more complex graph, say one with more points plotted, a close-up would be essential for seeing detail. Often it makes sense to plot both with zero point included (so you can see the overall level of the data and their overall pattern, as in Table 4.2) and also without to get a detailed view as in Table 4.1. Tukey argues that if we are interested in a detail of a graph, we ought to make a new graph in which this is no longer a detail, but rather is a central feature.

Remember that we are talking here about exploration which is mainly intended for private use. You won't be misled by the detailed graph because you will know how it was constructed and you will already have seen and absorbed the graph with zero point. For public presentation, however, statistics designed to convey information honestly and accurately to a general audience that may be very short of time or expertise are to be preferred. Such an audience may be misled by graphs that focus on particular aspects of data while taking other aspects (like general level) for granted. Exploratory statistics are definitely not intended for these unwary readers but for the

Table 4.1

Suicide Batch Medians, No Zero Point

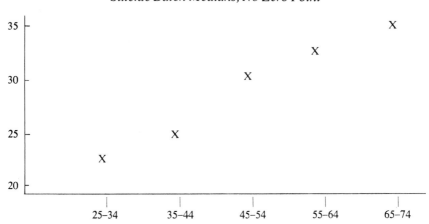

Table 4.2

Suicide Batch Medians, Zero Point Included

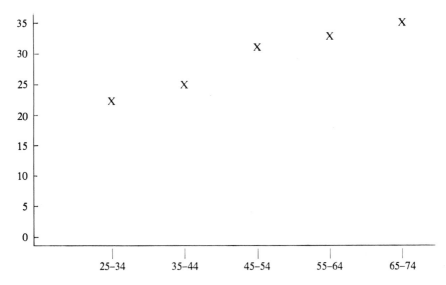

analyst committed to deeply probing some set of data. Setting some aspects of the data aside while going deeply into others is the sort of thing an analyst can and must do. When he reaches conclusions that should be made public, he switches back to the public mode of presentation. That is not to say that what we are learning here is irrelevant to the public aspect of analysis. Our exploratory skills (like knowing how to find a good magnification and type of display quickly) can be helpful in this public mode too.

The Box-and-Dot Plot

To compare batches quickly, we want graphs that retain important features but leave out unnecessary detail, and we want graphs that can be quickly plotted. The numerical summaries from the previous chapter gave important features of batches in just five numbers, so why not simply plot them? This is the basic idea behind the box-and-dot plot.

Table 4.3 shows the batch of suicide rates for males 65–74 in a stem-and-leaf and in a box-and-dot. As you see, the main trick is putting the important summary numbers (the ends, quartiles, and median of the batch) as far apart on the paper as they are in numerical size, which allows us to literally see how far apart they are. To do this we need a scale, off to the left in this case, which is roughly similar to the stem part of the stem-and-leaf. Now, when we plot the graph, we can use various kinds of marks for different essential features of the batch to display them clearly.

As we have remarked several times, the middle half of the batch is very important: it holds a lot of the data, and the data there are more reliable on the whole. We use a box for this part, called the *midbox*, with lines across the ends of the box marking the upper and lower quartiles and a line in the

Table 4.3
Plotting the Males 65-74 Batch

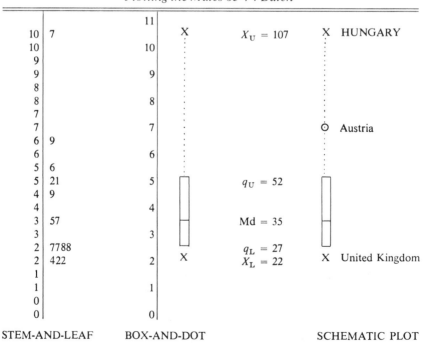

| STEM-AND-LEAF | BOX-AND-DOT | SCHEMATIC PLOT |

middle part for the median. Usually it is easiest to draw lines for the median and quartiles and then draw the vertical lines to make the box. One advantage of the box is that it makes the size of the midspread very clear; just the length of the box. This takes care of everything but the extremes, which are marked with X's; the range, of course, is just the distance between the X's. Thus we can see level and spread at a glance. We can also easily spot upward or downward trends and many sorts of asymmetry. For example, in the box-and-dot of Table 4.3 the median is not quite in the centre of the midbox; it is closer to the lower quartile than to the upper. This suggests that the data might be trailing off upward, as they are. Of course, all these insights *can* be obtained from the numerical summaries, but they must be looked for, whereas these features in plots *demand* to be seen. In addition, with only slightly more than a glance, you can see the trimean. Find the point halfway between the ends of the box: halfway between this point and the line for the median is the trimean. It can be done by eye, quickly, which is one reason for defining the trimean the way we do.

All of the required values can be obtained directly from our stem-and-leaf, needing little computation even with large batches of data. The actual plotting is no trouble, especially if you use tracing paper. You can put some tracing paper over some graph paper, mark off a scale, and then mark off the crucial values. You then remove the graph paper so no guide lines remain to mar the simplicity of the plot. Another trick is to simply lay the tracing paper over the stem-and-leaf and, using the stem as a Y axis, indicate the median, quartiles and extremes directly from the stem-and-leaf. If we are comparing several batches, we can only use this method if we are using identical stems for each batch. This method also requires stems-and-leaves with the same stems from top to bottom, evenly spaced. Often we change stems in the middle of a stem-and-leaf to fit in batch values conveniently; but we almost never do this in a plot. The strength of a plot is its quick visual impact, and the visual impression can be quite misleading if the scale is not consistent throughout the plot.

Can we do better still? Well, we have marked off extreme values, but it would probably also be useful to note those observations straying from the main body of the data, whether or not they are extremes. These strays should be unusual enough to be worth special attention: they should be not only outside the middle half of the data, but well outside it. How far outside? Some rule based on the midspread should be useful, since the midspread tells us how spread out the main body of the data is. Tukey suggests some rules of thumb using the *step*, or one and a half midspreads:

$$step = 1.5 \, dq$$

Observations a step or more from the middle of the data are quite different from most of the batch, while observations two or more steps from the middle are very different indeed. Hence two new terms and some rules of thumb connected with them:

> *outside observations* are at least one step above the upper quartile, or at least one step below the lower quartile; we usually call them *outliers* for short.

> *far outside observations* are at least two steps above the upper quartile or at least two steps below the lower quartile; *far outliers* for short.

Let's work through an example for the 65–74 suicide batch, using the numerical summary and the stem-and-leaf in Table 4.3A. The dq is 25, so one step is 1.5(25) or 37.5. An upper outlier must be at least q_U plus a step, or $52 + 37.5 = 89.5$. From the stem-and-leaf we see there is only one such case, 107 (the rate for Hungary), so there is one upper outlier. Is it "far out"? Clearly not, but let's check the arithmetic just to be sure; q_U plus two steps is $52 + 2(37.5) = 52 + 75 = 127$, and none of the values in the batch is that big. Thus there is just one upper outlier, which is not "far out." How about lower outliers? They would be q_L minus a step or smaller, or at most $27 - 37.5 = -10.5$. Nothing can be that small, since negative suicide rates are impossible, so the batch has no lower outliers and thus no low "far out" values either.

In practice, this goes very quickly. Table 4.3A shows the kind of work sheet you will probably find handy. The stem-and-leaf, and the numerical summary along with it, you get routinely. Then comes the essential arith-

Table 4.3A

Checking Outliers for Oldest Batch

Males 65–74			
10	7	N	15
9		X_U	107
8		q_U	52
7		Md	35
6	9	q_L	27
5	126	X_L	22
4	9		
3	57		
2	4227788		
1			
0			

$dq = 25$ step = 37.5

outliers: upper threshold $= 52 + 37.5 = 89.5$; one upper outlier, 107.
　　　　　lower threshold $= 27 - 37.5 = -10.5$; no lower outliers.
far outliers: upper threshold $= 52 + 75 = 127$; no upper far outliers.
　　　　　lower threshold $= 27 - 75 = -48$; no lower far outliers.

metic for finding outliers: *dq*, step, q_U + step, and so on. When you have become used to this process you may want to put down even less here, perhaps just which values are outliers or far outliers. Table 4.3B gives a more pictorial version of finding outliers.

There is only one other outlier, again upper, for the 45–54 batch (check this). Since outliers should get special attention, we want them to be unusual cases, so it is possible to have a set of several batches with no outliers at all. On the other hand, some batches have several outliers, so don't automatically stop checking as soon as you find one; scan the stem-and-leaf carefully and make sure you find them all.

Since outliers are uncommon, it pays to look hard at a few more values as well. Tukey suggests noting the highest and lowest values in the batch that are not outliers. Tukey calls these values *adjacent*: they are the values next to being outliers. In the 65–74 batch we just looked at, the upper adjacent value is 69 (the highest non-outlier) and the lower adjacent value is 22 (the lowest non-outlier). In a batch without outliers, like three of the remaining suicide batches, the adjacent values are just the extremes.

Table 4.3B

Checking for Outliers: Picture

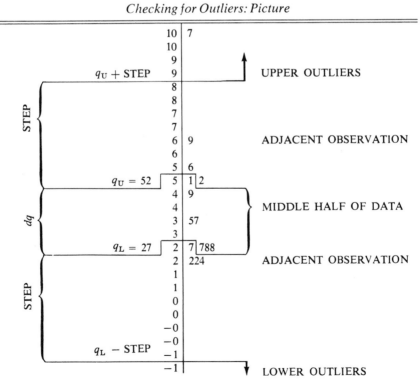

Both outliers and adjacent values should be clearly identified to make it easier to think about them. This brings us to the *schematic plot*: a box-and-dot plot with all outlying or adjacent values marked in, the outlying values labelled in capital letters and the adjacent values in small letters. For example, look at the third part of Table 4.3, a schematic plot for the batch of rates for males 65–74. It is immediately clear that Hungary is an upper outlier: HUNGARY is in capitals. (Besides, we can see that this value is more than one and a half box-lengths above the upper end of the box, or more than one step above the upper quartile.) We can see that the lower extreme, United Kingdom, is *not* an outlier since its label is in small letters. When we have a far outlier we give it a really eye-catching label, upper case letters with underlining (and maybe a different colour of ink as well, something we cannot show in this text). You will see examples in Table 5.12. The labelling system provides an immediate visual summary of the arithmetic we did to find outliers. Moreover, it tells us what the unusual cases *are*, often helpful when trying to figure out what makes the cases unusual.

Table 4.4 gives the schematic plots of all five suicide batches. For an

Table 4.4

Five Age Batches Compared With
Schematic Plots

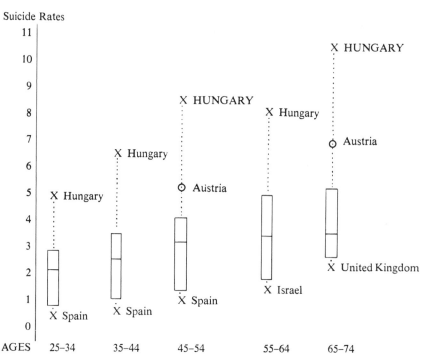

overall visual comparison of the five batches, the schematic plot form of Table 4.4 is clearly a good one. It shows summary values, thus avoiding the too-rich detail of the stem-and-leaf; and it shows them in directly visual form, thus avoiding even the little time it takes to interpret a numerical summary.

The schematic plots show the relationship between age and suicide rate level and spread at a glance. They also show the behaviour of the extreme cases, both in raw value and in relation to the rest of the data in their batches. The lower extreme is Spain in the three youngest groups, then Israel and last, the U.K., though Spain's rates stay quite low for the latter two groups as well. The lower extreme is never far from the rest of the batch, never an outlier. The upper extreme is always Hungary, whose rates tend to increase with age and to become more unusual (compared to other batch values), the only break in the pattern being the 55–64 age group. Clearly special research on Hungary and perhaps Spain will be needed. Finally, the schematic plots show us shape more easily than other displays. All batches trail up in the extremes, the two oldest batches being the only ones to trail up in the middle with the other midboxes all trailing down. Perhaps the extremes all trail upwards because the numbers can't go very far down. (there's no such thing as a negative suicide rate). A lower limit on a batch's possible values is called a *floor*, and an upper limit a *ceiling*. The presence of floors or ceilings often affects shape.

Schematic plots show off most important batch features very well. But remember that they do not show everything. To be simple enough to show some major features really well, the plot must suppress other features. Probably the most important suppressed feature is clumping. For example, consider Table 4.3 again. The stem-and-leaf version of the 65–74 batch suggests there may be two clumps, one in the twenties and one higher. The plot only shows that higher rates are, on the whole, more spread out.

Setting Aside Levels

By now we are well equipped with ways to find, look at and interpret two of the main features of batches: level and spread. But there are other features of batches as well, such as shape. These features are usually less striking than level and spread and will not show up too clearly while level and spread differences dominate our batch comparisons. It would be nice to be able to get level and spread differences out of the picture (once we have looked at them thoroughly) in order to see the subtler features more clearly. This order of battle is one which will become very familiar to us:

1. Summarize, display, and interpret a big noticeable feature of the data.
2. Get the feature out of the way once you understand it.
3. Look for the next most noticeable feature, which will now be easier to see.

In our case the big features so far are levels and spreads. Now, how can we set them aside?

We will illustrate the setting-aside techniques with the suicide batches (but cheer up, we are almost finished with them). First of all, let's think about getting level differences out of the suicide batches. We are not losing the level differences; we have thought about them, and we will keep a note of them. We just don't want to be distracted by them. We can set them aside by literally taking them away: by subtracting them! In more detail, go to the first batch, look up whatever level you want to work with, and subtract that level from every case in the batch. Then go to the second batch, find the same kind of level for it, and subtract it from all the cases. Continue until every batch has had its level taken away.

Now, after subtracting each batch's own level you are left with several new batches of numbers derived from the old ones. What levels do the batches have? All zero! If you start with a batch which has (say) a mean of six, and you subtract six from everything in the batch, you get a new set of numbers whose mean is zero (of course, the median or other levels may not be zero). We now have a set of batches all having the same level. Therefore, contrasting the levels to make inferences about the batches is impossible. Level has been set aside, and we are now free to examine other features of the data.

Remember, if you are going to compare batches you should subtract the same kind of level from all of them. Most often it will be the batch's own level, but sometimes it will be the level of all the batches and sometimes some theoretical level. This last sort of level removal should be familiar to golf fans in particular. Scores in a tournament are often given relative to par, making it possible to easily compare scores of players who have completed play with others still on the course. Also, this system allows us to see at a glance whether a given score on a hole is good. Four will be a good score, for example, where the par is five, meaning a score of minus 1; it will be a bad score where par is three, meaning a score of +1. Level removal makes such comparisons possible and easy.

Table 4.5 gives an example using the 45–54 suicide rates. The level subtracted is the median, which is 31. There is a stem-and-leaf of the original batch, and a stem-and-leaf of the new batch to show what has changed and what has not. The level has changed: the new median is zero. Has anything else changed? No; nothing else has changed at all. We have put the two stems-and-leaves side by side to make this really clear. The "before" and "after" pictures have the same spread, same shape, and in fact are alike in every way except for level. This means that we can take levels out of the picture by subtraction without fearing that we may be taking out something else as well without realizing it. Note a couple of procedural points. The new stem-and-leaf has been clearly labelled with the level we subtracted: again, we have not lost this level, or thrown it away, just put it aside. Also

Table 4.5

Removing a Level from Male Suicide Rates, 45-54

Rates	Rates–Md (ie 31)					
84	53	8	4		5	3
52	21	7			4	
41	10	6			3	
41	10	5	2		2	1
46	15	4	161		1	005
36	5	3	166		0	550
36	5	2	18		−0	3
31	0	1	01805		−1	036
21	−10	0			−2	110
28	−3					
10	−21	Original Data		Md = 31 Subtracted		
10	−21					
11	−20					
18	−13					
15	−16					
Md = 31	Md = 0					

note that the new stem-and-leaf has two stems called zero, one positive and one negative. That is because we want stems to cover the same amount throughout a basic stem-and-leaf. In this case the stems cover ten units. Now 0 to 9 is ten units and so is 0 to −9 so we need two zero stems. (Zero itself is a moot case: people usually put it with the plus-zero stem.)

This removal of differences in level by subtraction is easy enough, but since we enjoy being lazy we are pleased to be able to tell you that there is a still easier way to get levels out! Look hard at what we just did with the 45–54 rates and you will see that we simply moved the scale of the stem-and-leaf until the midpoint was opposite the zero part of the scale. Moving a scale up and down is just like adding and subtracting. This technique works beautifully with schematic plots and tracing paper: draw a scale on a sheet of tracing paper and draw a faint guideline through the zero level. Lay this paper over a schematic plot so that the guideline is just over the median line in the schematic plot. Trace the plot, and there you are: you have the plot for the batch with its median removed. All the other points (upper extreme and so on) are just where they should be. Try it and convince yourself. This approach can be a time-saver when you want to compare several batches after removing levels. You do the same thing for all the batches, remembering to line up each batch's median with the zero-level guide line before tracing.

By the way, the schematic plot, unlike the stem-and-leaf, doesn't require two zero entries on the scale. The entry −3 in Table 4.5 would simply be located between 0 and −10 as in any standard plot.

Table 4.6 shows the results of this subtraction-by-tracing with the five suicide plots of Table 4.4. The effect is as though we had passed a string through each median and then pulled it taut so that lower batches came up and higher ones went down till all the levels were on a line. Note that the original median of each batch is recorded underneath it. This plot does not make as much difference to the suicide batches as it does to most since the medians were quite close to start with, but even so it is now easier to see some things, especially the play of the extremes relative to the median. The pattern of the extremes is not entirely neat, so it could be summarized in various ways. We see a mirror-image pattern: both X_U and X_L first pull away from the batch centre and then come in again. There is one exception, Hungary in the oldest batch. This pattern suggests that intermediate age groups are most spread out. Earlier we saw that the dqs increase with age except for the oldest batch. Why?

We can often get interesting results by reordering the plots according to their original levels. Here, the plots are ordered by level already but often they are not. Ordering by level may show that spread increases with level (as it does for the suicide data up to a point); and sometimes shape is

Table 4.6

Suicide Batches with Level Removed

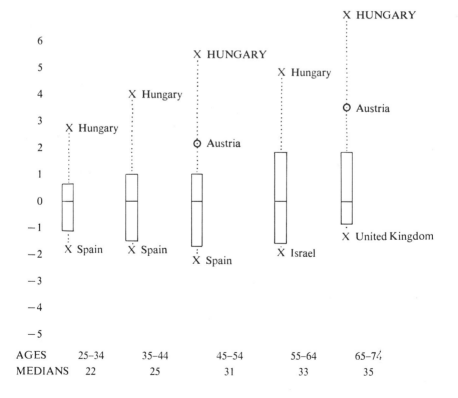

AGES	25–34	35–44	45–54	55–64	65–74
MEDIANS	22	25	31	33	35

related to level. Sometimes ordering by level shows nothing at all, but it's so easy to do that it is always worth a try.

Standardizing

Spread is another major data feature which, like level, tends to obscure subtler aspects of the data. We have seen that the suicide batches have spreads that increase with age, except for the oldest batch; this pattern is especially clear in Table 4.6 where the removal of level has lined the boxes up so that they can be very easily compared. Perhaps we were right earlier in suggesting that older men were socialized in periods when the nations were more different. If so, why does the 65–74 batch not fit? Why isn't its dq the largest one instead of being smaller than the dqs for the two next oldest batches? Well, this could be a chance fluctuation; after all, the range fits the pattern of increasing spread with age. Or it could have something to do with retirement; perhaps the difficulties of being old and out of work are so severe, and so similar from place to place, that they swamp the cultural differences between older men. In that case it's the extremes that don't quite fit for this batch. We could explore these ideas further, perhaps by seeing whether other rates become more diverse with age and by comparing the services for older people in our 15 countries.

Having obtained some ideas about what the spread might mean, we would like to remove differences in spread, as we did with level, so that we can look more deeply. We can't do this with subtraction, for we have already seen that increasing or decreasing the numbers in a batch does nothing to the spread. We can equalize spread by simple arithmetic, however; we use division. Specifically, we divide each batch by its own spread (this is parallel to subtracting its own level). We have done this for the 25–34 batch in Table 4.7, removing the midspread ($dq = 19$). The new batch of numbers has a dq of 1.0. This is exactly what will happen with any spread measure using the original data units (midspread, range, or standard deviation, but *not* variance): whatever the spread of the original batch, the new spread will be 1.0 after we divide the data by the old spread. Thus we can equalize the spreads of a number of batches by dividing each by its own value of some chosen spread, getting new batches which all have the same spread: one. This could get a little tedious in practice so we usually do not divide every number in every batch, only the summary points and unusual points needed for our schematic plots. Before leaving Table 4.7 note what does change and what does not. The level is affected; the spread, of course, becomes one; but nothing else is altered. The relative positions of the extreme values, the general shape of the batch and so on are the same. However, unless we've removed differences in level the effects on level can be confusing. For example, in the original data the median for the youngest group (22) is

Table 4.7

Removing a Spread

25–34 Batch	Divided by $dq = 19$
48	2.5
29	1.5
28	1.5
28	1.5
26	1.4
22	1.2
22	1.2
22	1.2
20	1.1
16	0.8
10	0.5
9	0.5
8	0.4
7	0.4
4	0.2
$dq = 28 - 9 = 19$	$dq = 1.5 - 0.5 = 1$
$Md = 22$	$Md = 1.2$

lower than that for the next oldest (25). If we remove the midspread, the median for the youngest group becomes

$$\frac{22}{19} = 1.2 \text{ and the median for the next oldest becomes } \frac{25}{24} = 1 ,$$

a reversal. We don't want such confusing changes in the order of something as important as level, so we routinely remove differences in spread after level has been set to zero, never differences in spread alone. This treatment of the data is known as *standardization*. Thus, if we want to remove both level and spread, we just find

$$\text{Standard Score} = \frac{\text{observation} - \text{level}}{\text{spread}}$$

Looking at this simple equation it is easy to show why the standardized data must have zero level and unit spread. Suppose that our level is the mean. If we subtract the mean from everything in the batch we get, in symbols, $x_i - \overline{x}$ and the mean of this is

$$\frac{\sum(x_i - \overline{x})}{N} = \frac{\sum x_i - \sum \overline{x}}{N} = \frac{\sum x_i}{N} - \frac{N\overline{x}}{N}$$

$$= \overline{x} - \overline{x}$$

$$= 0 .$$

Or suppose that our spread is the midspread. Then after we divide the elements of the batch through by the midspread we get x/dq and the spread of these new values is

$$\text{New } q_U - \text{New } q_L = \frac{\text{old } q_U - \text{old } q_L}{\text{old } dq}$$

$$= \frac{\text{old } dq}{\text{old } dq} = 1$$

The same sort of thing can be done with any type of level and any type of spread. It should be clear, though, that if you standardize using mean and standard deviation you may well get a transformed batch with a median and midspread that are not zero and one and conversely. Just in passing: it is possible to get a dq of 0. Should that happen use some other spread measure for standardization, as division by zero is meaningless.

Suppose we use an exploratory kind of standardization on our suicide data. Table 4.8 shows the arithmetic. For example, for X_U in the youngest batch the standard score is

$$\frac{48 - 22}{19} = \frac{26}{19} = 1.4 \ .$$

Since the arithmetic does take a little time we have standardized only summary numbers plus any additional outliers or adjacent values. The new values do have zero level and unit spread (you may get 1.1 or .9 as a spread, but this should just be rounding error).

The standardized summary numbers are plotted in Table 4.9. Note that the outliers and adjacent values are the same as before. Remember, we have changed level and spread but nothing else, so things other than level and spread are still to be seen and can be seen more easily. This is the best view

Table 4.8

Standardizing the Suicide Batches

Numerical Summary Values					
	25–34	35–44	45–54	55–64	65–74
X_U	48	65	84	81	107
q_U	28	35	41	50	52
Md	22	25	31	33	35
q_L	9	11	15	18	27
X_L	4	7	10	14	22
dq	19	24	26	32	25
adjacent			52		69
Numerical Summary Values, Standardized					
X_U	1.4	1.7	2.0	1.5	2.9
q_U	0.3	0.4	0.4	0.5	0.7
Md	0.0	0.0	0.0	0.0	0.0
q_L	−0.7	−0.6	−0.6	−0.5	−0.3
X_L	−0.9	−0.8	−0.8	−0.6	−0.5
adjacent values			0.8		1.4

Table 4.9

Plots of Standardized Suicide Batches

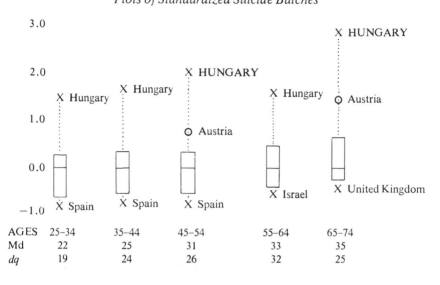

AGES	25–34	35–44	45–54	55–64	65–74
Md	22	25	31	33	35
dq	19	24	26	32	25

of shape we have had. We can see that shape fluctuates upward as age increases; the rates for the youngest group trail down in the midbox, the rates for the oldest group trail up. The behaviour of extremes is clarified since we see how extreme they are allowing for batch spread. In this example standardization (in 4.9) reinforces our impressions from the raw data (in 4.4): Hungary becomes more and more unusual as we go from younger to older batches with one exception. The lower extremes are in about the same relative position in all batches.

One often standardizes data sets that were measured by different rulers: heights measured in feet and metres, incomes measured in dollars and pounds, IQ measured by Stanford-Binet or Wexler-Bellevue, etc. This is a way of getting rid of arbitrary features of measurement; for example, choosing a yardstick instead of a metric rule. In our case, though, the level and spread differences of the two batches are not simply accidental byproducts of a measurement scale. The difference between suicide rates of 20 or 35 per 100 000 is a very real one. We do not want to get rid of level and spread here, but rather to note it carefully and then to set it aside so other things can be seen. What we can see most vividly, of course, is shape; with more basic things like level and spread out of the picture, shape shows up very clearly.

At first, students often have difficulty seeing how standardization might be useful. This illustration might clarify matters.

Often, the absolute level of a variable is less important than the comparative level; relative deprivation is such a case. In the same way, how well-educated a person is considered to be may depend on more than the simple number of years of schooling accomplished. Thus a man born in the backwoods in 1900 with a high school diploma might be seen to have relatively more education than a man born in New York City in 1950 with two years of university. Standardization provides a way of comparing the educational achievents of these two men controlling for their different backgrounds. Part of this background is the different levels in 1900 and 1950, in the backwoods and in New York City. Another important part is the spread in educational achievement in the two settings. Once we've controlled for these two effects by computing "standard education scores," comparison is more direct and meaningful.

Fits and Residuals

In passing we have had a very brief and rather trivial introduction to a technique which will be used throughout in exploration and often in confirmation; the separation of an observation into a *fit* part and a *residual* part. At each stage in the analysis, we think carefully about those aspects of the data that are easiest to see; and when we think we understand these, we remove them, and set them aside (not throw them away). We do this because obvious features of a body of data may partially obscure subtler things, so removing what is now obvious makes those more subtle components stand out more clearly. This is rather like the steps in a dissection; first study the surface layer, understand it and then cut it away, leaving the next layer as the new surface. That is, one can't clearly see the musculature until the skin is removed, and similarly, the skeleton is obscure until the musculature is removed (after it is "understood," of course).

Since we go through this process so often it is useful to have basic terms for its steps. In the first step, we find and explain a feature of the data; for example, we found batch levels and tried to come to terms with them by thinking about why suicide levels should increase with age. The data feature is summed up in appropriate numbers (here, the batch medians) which we call a *fit*. In the second step we remove the feature just explained by setting aside the fitted values; for example, we set aside the level fit by subtracting each batch's median from the batch values. When the first layer of fit is found, explained, and set aside we get *residuals* from the first fit, or leftover aspects of the data which still need attention. Here, we saw that spread was a notable feature of the residuals from level in Table 4.6; we tried to explain it too; and in Table 4.9 we went on to another wave of residuals with two layers of fit (level and spread) removed. There are still other features of the data to see, notably shape, which we'll soon learn how to deal with as well. The process continues through fitting, finding residuals, finding new fits for the residuals, and so on until you run out of time or out of ideas for new fits. Each layer of fit is removed in an appropriate way: level fits by subtraction, spread fits by division, and shape fits by transformation (the subject of the next two chapters).

Exploratory and Confirmatory

The magnification of graphs and the use of zero points are things you have to think about whether you are doing exploration or confirmation. When doing exploration, suit yourself; try this and that till something pays off. When doing confirmation you are often also planning to do publication (if only of a limited sort like handing in a paper), so you ought to present the data in whatever way gives the most honest initial picture.

Standardization is a common term and the technique is often used. In most published sources it is taken for granted that standardization is confirmatory standardization: subtracting the mean, dividing by the standard deviation. But, as we have seen, you can and should use sturdier and faster exploratory versions as well.

The major business of this chapter, the schematic plots, have no standard equivalents. But these tools are so useful that it is sometimes worthwhile to use them for public presentation, explaining as necessary, and it is always worthwhile to work with them routinely in exploratory analyses.

The terms "fit" and "residual" are used in both exploratory and confirmatory work; the kinds of fits made tend to be different, with exploratory work relying more on fast, resistant, approximate fits.

As before, the reader familiar with Tukey (1977) will note some discrepancies. Most of these are merely terminological; where more or less standard terms exist, we've tended to use them as a way of providing a bridge to the less familiar material.

One thing you might watch for; we denote adjacents and outliers with names in lower and upper case, respectively, the treatment Tukey gives to outliers and far outliers, respectively. Generally, readers familiar with this material from one source should have little difficulty following it in the other.

Homework

1. Using the numerical summaries and stems-and-leaves you have made for the female suicide rates,

a. find any outliers and detached values;

b. make schematic plots and discuss;

c. make plots with levels removed and discuss.

If you have time left over, pick two batches you would like to compare; standardize, plot, discuss.

Improving Your Homework

By this time, your discussion of the numeric results in your homework should be getting much more analytic; you should be finding it easier and easier to see patterns in the data, to develop possible explanations for them, and to think up ways to explore or check out these explanations. There is nothing especially difficult about this set of activities (except, possibly, getting started; and you should be well started by now). The very brief discussion of suicide spreads on page 65 is a modest example. We noted a pattern of spread increasing from younger to older batches, except for the oldest batch. We suggested an explanation for the overall pattern. Then we looked a bit harder at the oldest batch, which didn't fit the pattern, and tried to explain that too (milking as much as possible from the data at hand). Then we suggested ways to follow up on the possibilities emerging from a hard look at the spreads. We don't mean to imply that you will always do exactly these things in this order, by the way. Sometimes the availability of one kind of easily obtained background data (easy follow-up) leads you to try for explanations to which those data are relevant. Or you may play with some additional information because you have a hunch it might be helpful. Or you may note a pattern and take a while to come up with a satisfying explanation or two for it. As always, feel free to do what you enjoy and want to do. But try, always, to push yourself towards more detailed and clear explanations that are more data-centred. This is the goal, however you get to it.

5

Transforming Data

So far we have learned how to deal with two of the major feaures of batches, level and spread. We learned how to summarize these fits and how to remove them so that we could look more deeply at the residuals for further features. The most notable "further feature" so far has been shape, which turns out to be a very important batch feature indeed. So we would like to be able to summarize and remove shape as well as level or spread. For levels, we subtracted; for spreads, we divided; for shape, we turn to *transformation.*

In this chapter we will give you some feeling for how transformations deal with shape by discussing and illustrating the most important transformation, the logarithm. The logarithm is worth special attention because it is the most frequently used transformation and because it needs a little more explanation than other common transforms (even so, it is very easy, at least the way we do it here). In the next chapter we will discuss some other simple transformations, suggest how to decide which transform fits the shape best, and begin to discuss how to interpret shapes. But for this chapter we stick with one transformation for one kind of shape in order to simplify your introduction to shape summary and removal.

A Simple Application

Let's begin with an unusually simple example in which logging works well for easily understandable reasons. Later we will move on to an example that is a little less clearcut but a lot more typical. Consider Table 5.1, which gives population sizes for the United States and for Canada for twelve consecutive censuses. Clearly population grew dramatically in both nations. We can get a more detailed picture of how population grew by looking at the columns headed "growth," which give the differences between each census and the one before. For example, between 1851 and 1861 the Canadian population count grew by .79 million. Clearly the amount of growth is larger for later years than for earlier ones in both countries. To see some further important features of the data, let's look at the schematic plots in Table 5.2. We immediately see that the U.S.A. batch has far greater level and also far greater spread. By looking slightly harder, we can also see that both batches tend to trail upwards: the upper extreme is farther from the midbox than the

Table 5.1

Population, 1850-1961

Canadian Population (in millions)			U.S. Population (in millions)		
		Growth, since previous census*			Growth
1851	2.44		1850	23.2	
1861	3.23	.79	1860	31.4	8.2
1871	3.69	.46	1870	39.8	8.4
1881	4.32	.63	1880	50.2	10.4
1891	4.83	.51	1890	62.9	12.7
1901	5.37	.54	1900	76.0	13.1
1911	7.21	1.84	1910	92.0	16.0
1921	8.79	1.58	1920	105.7	13.7
1931	10.38	1.59	1930	122.8	17.1
1941	11.51	1.13	1940	131.7	8.9
1951	14.01	2.50	1950	150.7	19.0
1961	18.24	4.23	1960	178.5	27.8

Source: Statistics Canada and *Statistical Abstract of the United States; 1971* (92nd Edition). US Bureau of the Census, Washington, D.C. 1971.

*"Growth" between adjacent censuses is defined as the difference between the populations they show.

lower extreme is, and the upper quartile is farther from the median than the lower quartile is. That is, within the batches we find that higher values are more spread out than lower ones. We have also seen that this is true between batches: the batch with higher level (U.S.A.) has higher spread too. Level and spread *covary* (i.e. vary together), a data feature that is frequently encountered.

At first glance this may seem like quite a bundle of data features, but one simple idea will explain most of them. Populations gain by births and immigration, and lose by deaths and emigration. If these four factors operate at roughly constant rates, or their net effect simply remains about the same, then population changes by a roughly constant *rate*. Does that seem to be happening here? Let's look at Table 5.3, which gives the ratio of each population figure to that from the preceding census. Table 5.3 shows us a kind of growth rate, while Table 5.1 showed us growth amounts. The ratios look rather similar from census to census, which suggests that both countries have indeed generally had steady rates of growth. Since the 1850s death rates have declined a lot but so have birth rates, so it is reasonable that population growth has been roughly steady. The ratios also look similar between the batches (both have a median ratio of about 1.2), which suggests that both countries have been steadily growing at about the same rate. This makes sense: Canada and the U.S.A. are neighbouring countries with many historical similarities and closely related economies and cultures, so it is reasonable that their populations grow in roughly the same way.

Table 5.2

Plot of Raw Population Data

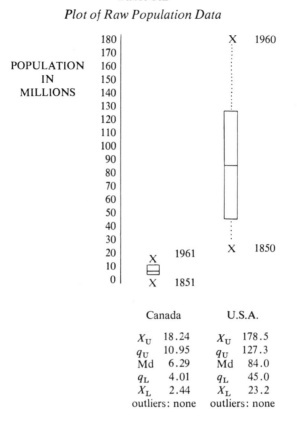

	Canada	U.S.A.
X_U	18.24	X_U 178.5
q_U	10.95	q_U 127.3
Md	6.29	Md 84.0
q_L	4.01	q_L 45.0
X_L	2.44	X_L 23.2
outliers: none		outliers: none

A constant rate of growth explains a lot about the data. First, we can now see why the amounts of growth in Table 5.1 are larger for later years: later years have larger populations, so the same growth rate means bigger growth amounts. This is precisely like getting compound interest on a fixed amount of savings. To illustrate with a very simple and probably familiar example, imagine $100 in an account earning 10% interest compounded annually. At the end of the first year, the account contains $110, a gain of $10, while at the end of the second year, the account is at $121, a gain of $11. But the *rate* of increase is unchanged; the two ratios,

$$\frac{110}{100} \text{ and } \frac{121}{110}, \text{ are equal } \left(\frac{11}{10}\right),$$

as they should be. Second, we can see why the two batches trail off upward. If the larger figures (populations in later years) are growing by larger amounts, then they are more different from each other and more spread out. Finally, we can see why the U.S.A. batch is more spread out than the Canadian batch. The U.S.A. figures are much larger to start with, so again they differ from

Table 5.3

*Ratios of Adjacent Censal Years For
Canada and U.S.*

Canada		U.S.	
1861/1851	1.32	1860/1850	1.35
1871/1861	1.14	1870/1860	1.26
1881/1871	1.17	1880/1870	1.26
1891/1881	1.11	1890/1880	1.25
1901/1891	1.11	1900/1890	1.20
1911/1901	1.34	1910/1900	1.21
1921/1911	1.21	1920/1910	1.14
1931/1921	1.18	1930/1920	1.16
1941/1931	1.10	1940/1930	1.07
1951/1941	1.21	1950/1940	1.14
1961/1951	1.30	1960/1950	1.18

1.3	240		1.3	5
1.2	11		1.2	66501
1.1	471180		1.1	4648
1.0			1.0	7

Md 1.18   Md 1.20

each other by larger amounts. We would have to look elsewhere for an explanation of the differences in batch level (history and climate seem like obvious places to start) but the other major features of the data all seem to stem from a roughly constant rate of growth.

Now we know what we're dealing with; but we're not dealing with it very effectively. Using ratios is good in some ways — it's easy, familiar, and clearly brings out the rate of growth idea — but it has two annoying problems. First, taking ratios involves simple but somewhat time-consuming arithmetic. Second, once you find ratios you can't get back to your original numbers. Consider a ratio of 1.21. What pair of population sizes does that ratio go with? There are infinitely many possibilities. In our example we have two: the 1951/1941 values for Canada, or the 1910/1900 values for the United States. We can't tell which from the ratio. And in general, it is hard to analyze the ratios much further.

Thus, what we are seeking is a transformation that controls for the compound interest effect, that is painless to compute, and still leaves the original numbers recoverable. Taking logarithms is such a transformation. Results for our example are shown in Table 5.4, *Logarithms of Population Sizes*, and the corresponding plot on Table 5.5. For the moment, let's not worry about where these logs came from or how they were calculated; let's see whether the logs are coping with the data as we would like them to.

First, we'd like to see that the compound interest effect is removed: that differences from census to census are no longer greater for later periods

Table 5.4

Logarithms of Populations Sizes

	Canada	Growth		U.S.A.	Growth
1851	6.39		1850	7.37	
1861	6.51	.12	1860	7.50	.13
1871	6.57	.06	1870	7.60	.10
1881	6.64	.07	1880	7.70	.10
1891	6.68	.04	1890	7.80	.10
1901	6.73	.05	1900	7.88	.08
1911	6.86	.13	1910	7.96	.08
1921	6.94	.08	1920	8.02	.06
1931	7.02	.08	1930	8.09	.07
1941	7.06	.04	1940	8.12	.03
1951	7.15	.09	1950	8.18	.06
1961	7.26	.11	1960	8.25	.07

Logged Population		Logged Population	
7.2	6	8.2	5
7.1	5	8.1	28
7.0	26	8.0	29
6.9	4	7.9	6
6.8	6	7.8	08
6.7	3	7.7	0
6.6	48	7.6	0
6.5	17	7.5	0
6.4		7.4	
6.3	9	7.3	7

stem: units and tenths
leaves: hundredths

with larger populations. To check this, we found growth figures for logged data in Table 5.4 as we found growth for raw figures in Table 5.1. Growth in logs does seem pretty even for Canada, not noticeably higher for earlier or later years. For the United States, growth in later years appears slightly smaller than that in earlier years, very different from the picture given by the raw data. This is a suggestive feature and we will return to it. Second, if logging captures the constant rate of growth idea then the batches should not trail upward after logging. If we look at the stems-and-leaves for logged population in Table 5.4, or the schematic plots in Table 5.5, it is clear that the upward trailing we found in the raw data is indeed gone. The Canadian batch is especially neat, with both the extremes and the quartiles well balanced around the median. In the U.S.A. batch the median is nearly between the quartiles but the extremes now seem to straggle downward a bit. But overall, the higher values and lower values are now equally spread out in both batches. Finally, the two batches now have virtually equal spreads (both in terms of *dq* and in terms of range). The covariation of level and

Table 5.5

Logged Population Figures,
U.S. and Canada

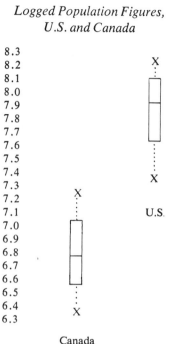

spread, a feature we attributed to the roughly constant rate of growth, has been fully removed.

Logging sets aside most of the data features that caught our eyes at first; does it also help us to understand them? Certainly. Table 5.4 showed us that the logged population figures grow by a roughly constant amount from one census to the next. In the next section we will see that addition in logs is like multiplication in raw numbers, and subtraction in logs is like division in raw numbers. So the roughly constant differences from census to census in logs are the same thing as the roughly constant ratios from census to census in the raw data. The logs, like the ratios, indicate a roughly constant rate of population growth. Logs can do all that ratios do, and more; for it is easy to see further with logs, to set the constant growth pattern aside thus illuminating detailed deviations.

But before going on to details, let's go over what logs are and how they can be found quickly. You may be finding it hard to believe that logs can be easy. Fear not; the massively detailed fine-print pages and esoteric rules you may be thinking of are not really needed in exploratory work. In fact, we prefer logs to other similar transforms because they are actually much easier.

Table 5.7

Break table for two-decimal logs

A) MAIN BREAK TABLE

Break	log	Break	log	Break	log	Break	log	Break	log
9886		1567		2483		3936		6237	
	.00		.20		.40		.60		.80
1012		1603		2541		4027		6383	
	.01		.21		.41		.61		.81
1035		1641		2600		4121		6531	
	.02		.22		.42		.62		.82
1059		1679		2661		4217		6683	
	.03		.23		.43		.63		.83
1084		1718		2723		4315		6839	
	.04		.24		.44		.64		.84
1109		1758		2786		4416		6998	
	.05		.25		.45		.65		.85
1135		1799		2851		4519		7161	
	.06		.26		.46		.66		.86
1161		1841		2917		4624		7328	
	.07		.27		.47		.67		.87
1189		1884		2985		4732		7499	
	.08		.28		.48		.68		.88
1216		1928		3055		4842		7674	
	.09		.29		.49		.69		.89
1245		1972		3126		4955		7852	
	.10		.30		.50		.70		.90
1274		2018		3199		5070		8035	
	.11		.31		.51		.71		.91
1303		2065		3273		5188		8222	
	.12		.32		.52		.72		.92
1334		2113		3350		5309		8414	
	.13		.33		.53		.73		.93
1365		2163		3428		5433		8610	
	.14		.34		.54		.74		.94
1396		2213		3508		5559		8810	
	.15		.35		.55		.75		.95
1429		2265		3589		5689		9016	
	.16		.36		.56		.76		.96
1462		2317		3673		5821		9226	
	.17		.37		.57		.77		.97
1496		2371		3758		5957		9441	
	.18		.38		.58		.78		.98
1531		2427		3846		6095		9661	
	.19		.39		.59		.79		.99
1567		2483		3936		6237		9886	

When in doubt use an even answer, thus 1462 gives .16 and 1496 gives .18.

Table 5.7 (cont'd)

B) SETTING DECIMAL POINTS

1			1
	+0	−1	
10			0.1
	+1	−2	
100			0.01
	+2	−3	
1,000			0.001
	+3	−4	
10,000			0.0001
	+4	−5	
100,000			0.00001
	+5	−6	
1,000,000			0.000001

C) EXAMPLES

Number	B	A	log Number
log 137.2	2 + .14 =		2.14
log 0.03694	−2 + .57 =		−1.43
log 0.896	−1 + .95 =		−0.05
log 174,321	+5 + .24 =		5.25

Source: Tukey, *Exploratory Data Analysis*, 1977, Addison-Wesley, Reading, Mass.

Easy Logs

We will always use logs to the base ten because computation is easier with them, making them better than Napierian logs for our purposes. But how are logs found? Well, perhaps you remember that the log of x is the power to which you raise ten in order to get x:

$$x = 10^{\log x}$$

So finding the log of any power of ten is pretty easy. Here are a few examples:

$$\log 1\,000 = 3 \quad (1\,000 = 10^3)$$
$$\log .001 = -3 \quad \left(.001 = \frac{1}{1000}\right)$$
$$\log 10 = 1$$
$$\log .01 = -2$$

and so on. Now whenever we get a number that is not quite this easy we can break it up into two parts, one that is a power of ten (and easy) and one that is a number with one non-zero figure in front of the decimal place (a standard form that we can look up in the "Break Table" of Table 5.7). Say our number is 1 735. First we get it in the standard form:

$$1\,735 = 1.735 \times 10^3$$

The log of the 10^3 part is easy; it's just 3, the power of 10. The log of the other part we get from Table 5.7. The break columns give values of numbers in standard form with the decimals left out to save space and visual confusion. So to find the log of 1.735 we look for the pair of break values that it fits between and we find

   1718
   1758

in the second break column. 1735 falls between these two so we look between these two to the right where the logs column is, and find .24 in line with the gap between 1718 and 1758.

   $\log (1.735) = .24$

Now all we have to do is combine the logs of the two parts of our original number, 1 735. To do this remember that logs were used by lazy people in the old days when no one had an electronic calculator. Logs were designed to make life easier when doing arithmetic by substituting easier arithmetic operations for harder ones:

   addition for multiplication
   subtraction for division

Now our original number was the *product*

   1.735×10^3

so the log of that number is the *sum* of the logs of the parts of the product:

   $$\log (1\ 735) = \log (1.735) + \log (10^3)$$
   $$= .24 + 3$$
   $$= 3.24$$

The same rules go for numbers less than one (decimal something). Say we want log (.0893). First into standard form:

   $$.0893 = 8.93 \times \frac{1}{100}$$
   $$= 8.93 \times 10^{-2}$$

We find that 893 falls between 8810 and 9016 in the breaks so the log is .95. Thus

   $$\log (.0893) = -2 + .95$$
   $$= -1.05$$

(Note that the log is *not*, definitely not, -2.95!) There are a few more examples in part C of Table 5.7.

   Try various ways of finding the whole part of the log, the power of ten involved. Some people like the way above. Some find the little diagram in part B of Table 5.7 easier. To use part B, fit your number between the powers of ten that it falls between in size. For example, 1 735 falls between 1 000 and 10 000 and .0893 falls between .1 and .01. Then follow along the gap between those figures in part D till you find the whole part of the log — in our examples we get the same answers as before (3 for 1 735 and -2 for .0893), as we should. Still others would rather count than anything, so they count the number of places the decimal in the original number has to be shifted to get the number into standard form:

$$1.\underbrace{785}_{\text{3 places left}} \qquad\qquad \underbrace{08.}93_{\text{2 places right}}$$

Again, for our examples we get 3 and −2. All these procedures give the same result, so suit yourself.

Earlier we noted that taking ratios made the original data unrecoverable. This is definitely not true for logging, because we can always get back to the original data by finding the *antilogs* of the logs. To take antilogs, find the number that the number to be transformed would be the log of, i.e. do logs in reverse. For example, what is the antilog of 3.52? The 3 tells us that we want 10^3 times something in standard form. The break table tells us that .52 is the log of something between 3.273 and 3.350 — let's take the mean of these, 3.312. So the antilog of 3.52 is $10^3 \times 3.312$ or 3 312. The antilogs of negative numbers are just a shade trickier because you need a positive fraction to look up in the break table. For example, the antilog of −1.43 is found by this route:

$$-1.43 = -2 + .57$$
$$\text{antilog } (-2) = 10^{-2}$$
$$\text{antilog } (.57) = 3.716$$
$$\text{thus antilog } (-1.43) = .03716$$

You must add one to the decimal part to get something positive for the break table, so you have to subtract one from the integer part to even up. Going from raw data to logs and back to unlogged data may introduce some rounding error because we don't bother with tedious many-place tables; if that is important for some reason, accurate log tables are readily available.

A break table like 5.7 is easy to use for logs or antilogs; it is also highly portable. A break table can be put on a wallet size card and used even when civilized niceties like calculators and computers are distant: on picnics, planes, wherever. It is no small advantage to be able to do some preliminary analysis when an idea hits you and ideas don't always hit in the presence of a sophisticated calculator.

Finding logs good enough for exploratory work is just as fast and easy as exploratory tools are supposed to be. When you've got the logs, they are easy to work with: mere addition and subtraction do what it takes multiplication or division to do in raw data. And the original data are never lost; we can always recover them.

Returning to Our Example

Now that you have learned (or remembered) how logs work and how to find them, it is time to go back to our example and examine the log transformation in more detail. Earlier we saw that logging removed the "compound interest" effect of roughly steady growth rate and the effects of such a growth rate: larger increases for larger populations, plus larger spread for larger numbers both within and between batches. Logging is therefore a fit for the process of growth at a constant rate: when we log, the effects of that process are removed from the data. Like any fit, logging leaves *residuals* or details that do not fit the overall pattern and hence call for special attention. In our example, residuals are given in Table 5.6. First we found the median growth amount in logs: in both countries, one census figure tends to be .08 greater than the previous one. (Remember, this corresponds to the

Table 5.6

Growth of Logged Population
Figures

Canada		U.S.
X	.13	X
X	.12	
X	.11	
	.10	XXX
X	.09	
XX	.08	XX
X	.07	XX
X	.06	XX
X	.05	
XX	.04	
	.03	X

Md = 0.08 Md = 0.08

Growth of Logged Population
With Level (0.08) Removed

Canada		U.S.A.	
To:		To:	
1861	.04	1860	.05
1871	−.02	1870	.02
1881	−.01	1880	.02
1891	−.04	1890	.02
1901	−.03	1900	.00
1911	.05	1910	.00
1921	.00	1920	−.02
1931	.00	1930	−.01
1941	−.04	1940	−.05
1951	.01	1950	−.02
1961	.03	1960	−.01
Md = 0.08		Md = 0.08	

roughly constant ratio of 1.2 between adjacent census figures in the raw data. In fact, .08 is the log of 1.2, as it should be.) Then we subtracted .08 from each of the intercensal differences in logs (found in Table 5.4 under "Growth.") If population really did grow quite constantly, we would have only zero residuals but in fact we have many that are non-zero because the population sometimes grew by more than .08 (positive residuals) and sometimes grew by less (negative residuals).

Getting these residuals is one of the main benefits of transformation; for now we can see beyond the overall pattern of roughly constant growth rate to less obvious details, the interesting discrepancies that prevent growth rates from being perfectly constant. We could have looked at these details in the raw data, but only with a lot of trouble; and in practice it is so much trouble that we are not likely to get around to it. So back to the residuals in Table 5.6.

The picture for the U.S.A. data seems simplest: relatively rapid growth before 1890 in the heyday of expansion and immigration, followed by slower growth after immigration was restricted and particularly slow growth in the depression decade. In Canada there were similar influences though in a less neat pattern of years: immigration booms for Confederation, whole provinces added in later years, the settlement of the wheatlands, slower growth in economically slow decades.

The growth picture may also have been affected by changes in birth and death rates. Death rates have declined fairly steadily over this period, but birth rates have declined more erratically (they went down during the depression, producing lower than usual figures in 1940 or 1941, and rose again after the second World War, producing the "baby boom" which shows up in higher figures for later years). You could pursue any of these points further, or ask yourself why the Canadian figures have more extremes of large or small increases than the U.S.A. figures do.

Some Uses of Logging

Hopefully this example has convinced you that logging is easy, often makes clear sense, and is very much worthwhile. We saw that logging was a good *fit* for a *process* of steady growth rates. It was good numerically, in that it neatly removed the compound interest effect. It was good analytically, in that we could easily understand why logging worked numerically: addition in logs is like subtraction in raw numbers. Best of all, logging helped us to sort out what belonged to the overall constant growth pattern and what did not. After logging, it is easy to examine the residuals from a constant growth process and see the things that don't fit such a process and hence have to be explained with other factors (like changing patterns of immigration). We have stressed the intercensal growth figures, but logging sheds light on other facets of the data as well. For example, in the raw data the upper extremes look a bit unusual in both batches, though they are not outliers. After logging, we see that these population figures are not especially high (see Table 5.5); in fact, the U.S.A. figure (for its 1960 population) looks a bit low, if anything. That means these values are in line with what we expect given a constant rate of growth; they are pretty big in raw numbers, but only because the growth rate has been applied to a big base figure (the population in the previous census).

It's Seldom So Simple

Our first example, though simple, illustrated several important points very well. Hopefully these points are now clear enough, so that we can move on to a kind of analysis that is both more common and more complex. Analogous issues will come up, although we will not always be able to resolve them in as straightforward a way.

The main uses of transformation are fitting shape, and removing shape to allow us to see more. Let's begin, then, with a discussion of what we mean by shape. Next we will turn to another example using population data but of a different kind. The differences won't make logging any less useful, but they will change the nature of our interpretation.

What We Mean by Shape

Table 5.8 offers some simple examples of what we mean by shape. In the first example the batch "straggles upward": the small values are clumped relatively close together, while the larger values trail off. Conversely, the data in the third example "straggle down": here it is the high values which are bunched and the lower ones which are more spread out. In the second example, the batch is symmetric: most of the observations are in the middle, with the higher and lower values both trailing off at the same rate. Scores of all North American eight-year-olds on a standard I.Q. test would look like this. All the first three batches are basically single-peaked, unlike the fourth which has two peaks.

All our procedures for summarizing and removing shape are designed for single-peaked data. Transformations that can cope with data having many peaks do exist but we ignore them here. They are not useful all that often, they are less easy, and you can usually avoid them. If you do get a batch with many peaks, like the fourth one in Table 5.8, it is often because two or more different batches with different levels (and/or spreads and shapes) have been mixed together. You can remove the many-peakedness and avoid fancy transforms by breaking the batch down into sub-batches, which is

Table 5.8

Different Shapes

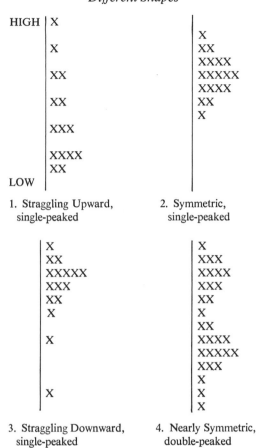

1. Straggling Upward,
   single-peaked

2. Symmetric,
   single-peaked

3. Straggling Downward,
   single-peaked

4. Nearly Symmetric,
   double-peaked

probably the better, as well as the more convenient thing to do. For example, consider Table 5.9. Part A gives a stem-and-leaf for 24 districts in Vancouver; on the right is the rate of turnout in the 1970 municipal election and on the left either W (if the district is part of the generally wealthier West End) or E (for East End). The plot may look roughly single-peaked and symmetric over-all but a close look shows some clumping at both the top and bottom, with Ws at the top and Es at the bottom. So we go to Part B, separate plots for West and East rates. Clearly this is a difference worth knowing about; for example, the East End rates are lower and less spread out. Some further sub-batching might be useful here since the two new batches (especially the West End batch) still show clumping.

Finally, note that the importance of peaking as part of shape underlines the importance of the stem-and-leaf in judging shape. Schematic plots show

Table 5.9

Municipal Election Turnout: Vancouver 1970

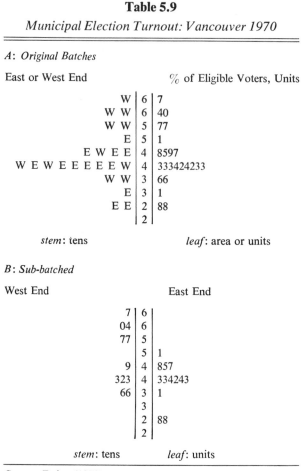

A: *Original Batches*

East or West End   % of Eligible Voters, Units

```
              W │ 6 │ 7
           W  W │ 6 │ 40
           W  W │ 5 │ 77
              E │ 5 │ 1
        E W E E │ 4 │ 8597
W E W E E E E W │ 4 │ 333424233
           W  W │ 3 │ 66
              E │ 3 │ 1
            E E │ 2 │ 88
                │ 2 │
```

            stem: tens   *leaf*: area or units

B: *Sub-batched*

West End   East End

```
   7 │ 6 │
  04 │ 6 │
  77 │ 5 │
     │ 5 │ 1
   9 │ 4 │ 857
 323 │ 4 │ 334243
  66 │ 3 │ 1
     │ 3 │
     │ 2 │ 88
     │ 2 │
```

            stem: tens   *leaf*: units

Source: Ewing (1972).

symmetry or asymmetry very well but do not clearly reveal whether the data are single-peaked. Remember, in chapter 4 we pointed out that plots do not show everything: they do not show clumping. It's best to use both plots and stems-and-leaves in working with shape.

The Standard Shape: Symmetric and Single-Peaked

What do we do about single-peaked shapes? Before, for levels and spreads, we set aside batch features by making them standard, getting levels to be zero and/or getting spreads to be one. In a similar spirit we remove shape by trying to get a batch into a standard shape: symmetric. Why a standard shape? To make batch comparisons easier and to avoid arbitrary fiddling with shape. Batch comparison is easier if all or nearly all the batches are in the same standard form, because differences in shape can get in the way of seeing and interpreting finer aspects of the data. A standard shape also gives a clearcut goal for transformations which saves time and cuts down on arbitrary transformation. If a standard shape, why the symmetric? Well, it's the most "neutral" shape. Batches usually straggle up or down for a reason and we try to figure out what the reason is; but a symmetric batch doesn't call out for shape explanation in the same way. Further, symmetry is the standard goal for compelling practical reasons: the confirmatory statistics we will soon be turning to assume *normally distributed* data. A single-peaked symmetric batch may not be quite normal but is usually close enough so confirmatory tools that assume normality can be used safely. We will have more to say about this issue from chapter 7 on.

Most of the batches we will meet begin with some straggle (most frequently upward straggle) and become roughly symmetric after a suitable transformation. The suitable transformation is very often logging, which is one reason why we spend so much time here on this transformation. Some batches are so "ugly" that no transform can make them roughly standard. Even the U.S. and Canadian census data don't end up perfectly standard. The figures are quite symmetric, but they are not single-peaked; instead they tend to be nearly evenly spread over their stems, close to what is sometimes called a "uniform" distribution in which all the stems have the same number of cases. This is one unusual feature of our first example and we will now see another, which will become clearer by contrast with our next example.

A More Typical Example

Table 5.10 presents the 1970 populations of some African, American, and European nations according to estimates published by the United Nations. First let's describe the data a bit. We chose to use 1970 estimates rather than census counts because the dates of the most recent available censuses varied so greatly: as recent as 1975, and as old as 1950. Many countries simply cannot afford routine accurate census taking, so the data are often rough (especially for underdeveloped countries), but at least we have rough estimates for the same time period for all cases. After some hesitation we decided to use only independent nations as cases. We could have used all territories (including some, like Angola, which became independent after 1970) but most of these are too small to be viable political units. Finally, we used all reported cases for the Americas, with the United States and Canada included in the Europe batch because they are more similar to this region than to the rest of the Americas in demographic patterns. Since Africa and Europe included a somewhat unwieldy number of cases, we selected representative subsets (by a procedure to be described in chapter 7).

Table 5.10

National Populations, 1970 (Estimated) in Thousands

Africa		Americas (excluding USA, Canada)		Europe Plus USA and Canada	
Algeria	14,330	Argentina	23,748	Albania	2,136
Burundi	3,544	Barbados	238	Austria	7,391
Congo	1,191	Bolivia	4,931	Belgium	9,656
Equatorial Guinea	285	Brazil	93,319	Bulgaria	8,490
Guinea	3,921	Chile	9,369	Canada	21,324
Kenya	11,225	Columbia	21,118	Finland	4,606
Lesotho	931	Costa Rica	1,727	France	50,768
Liberia	1,523	Cuba	8,472	German Democratic	
Madagascar	6,750	Dominican Rep.	4,062	Republic	17,058
Mali	5,047	Ecuador	6,093	Greece	8,793
Niger	4,024	El Salvador	3,534	Hungary	10,338
Nigeria	55,073	Guatemala	5,097	Iceland	204
Rwanda	3,679	Guyana	709	Italy	53,661
Somalia	2,789	Haiti	4,235	Liechtenstein	21
South Africa	22,469	Honduras	2,509	Monaco	23
Swaziland	422	Jamaica	1,869	Netherlands	13,032
Togó	1,960	Mexico	50,695	Norway	3,877
Uganda	9,806	Nicaragua	1,833	Portugal	8,663
Tanzania	13,273	Panama	1,434	Romania	20,253
Upper Volta	5,380	Paraguay	2,386	Spain	33,779
		Peru	13,586	Sweden	8,043
		Trinidad–Tobago	1,027	Switzerland	6,187
		Uruguay	2,886	United States	204,875
		Venezuela	10,275		

Source: *United Nations Statistical Yearbook 1975*, United Nations Statistical Office, New York, 1976; Table 18. Copyright, United Nations (1976). Reproduced by permission.

In some ways this example is awfully familiar! We see the U.S.A. and Canadian populations again, this time for 1970 (by the way: are these values what we would predict from our earlier analysis?). But though we have the same subject matter, we do not have the same kind of problem. For example, we cannot explain features of this data set using the idea that worked so well for the previous one: a roughly constant rate of growth. Such an idea makes no obvious sense here, since we do not have an over-time picture of the same units going through a growth process. Instead, we have population figures for each unit at just one point in time — at just one moment in whatever processes underly the population sizes. However, we can and will still use the data to think about what the underlying processes may be, and to generate ways of checking up on our speculations. Our current example is far more typical of data batches, since most data are collected for just one point in time.

The raw data are stemmed-and-leaved in Table 5.11. Clearly there is an upward straggle. The stems-and-leaves trail off upward strongly in all three

Table 5.11

Populations, Stems-and-Leaves

Africa		Americas (excluding U.S.A. and Canada)		Europe (including U.S.A. and Canada)	
5	5	9	3	20	5
5					
4					
4		5	1	5	14
3		4		4	
3		4		4	
2		3		3	
2	2	3		3	4
1		2		2	
1	4103	2	41	2	10
0	575	1		1	7
0	41041344022	1	40	1	003
		0	59865	0	7859986
		0	0244143221213	0	00042

For all: *stems*: ten millions
leaves: millions

	Africa	Americas	Europe
N	20	24	22
X_U	55,073,000	93,319,000	204,875,000
q_U	10,516,000	9,822,000	20,253,000
Md	3,973,000	5,014,000	8,728,000
q_L	1,742,000	1,851,000	4,606,000
X_L	285,000	238,000	21,000

batches. For easier comparison we turn, as usual, to schematic plots, in Table 5.12. Looking first at the middle of the data, we see that there is upward straggle in each midbox: the upper quartile is farther from the median than the lower one is, showing that the third quarter of the data is more spread out than the second. Turning to the top and bottom quarters, we see first that the upper extreme is much farther from the box than the lower extreme, and second that there are seven upper outliers and nothing even close to a lower outlier; again the higher values are much more spread out. Data with strong straggle are often hard to plot; in this case we could not fit in the U.S.A. value without making the rest of the data very cramped, so we broke the scale as indicated by the two zigzags. Note that we put a zigzag right in the Europe plot, as well as in the scale on the left, so that the reader cannot miss the really unusual size of the U.S.A.

The shape is clear: upward straggle in all three batches. We have also noted the outliers. How about level and spread? The level is highest for Europe, and similar for the other two with the median for the Americas a shade higher. The spread is also highest for Europe, with the other two batches relatively alike but the African batch a shade larger in midspread and a bit smaller in range.

Table 5.12

1970 Populations, Schematic Plots

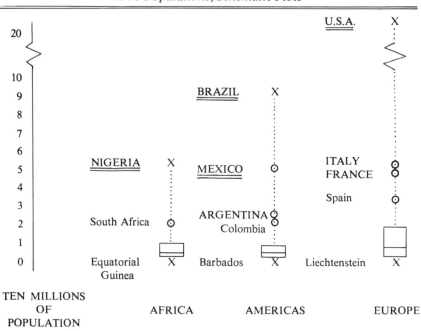

TEN MILLIONS
OF   AFRICA   AMERICAS   EUROPE
POPULATION

All of these data features should be explained. But before we do so, might it not be a good idea to transform the data? Some of the outliers may not look so unusual after we transform, thus removing the effects of the upward straggle pattern. Similarly, the batch differences in spread may look different afterwards. Spread and level appear to roughly covary here, with the highest level going with the highest spread; a transformation that removes upward straggle may remove inequalities of spread too. If transforming removes features then they are probably part of an upward straggle pattern and so may not need a separate explanation. Let's try logging these data and see.

The logged data are recorded in Table 5.13, stemmed-and-leaved in Table 5.14, and plotted in 5.15. The stems-and-leaves are now much closer to standard shape than they were before logging. All three batches have just one major peak, with a small lower cluster in the Europe batch. All three are roughly symmetric in the middle. None have perfect standard shapes (you will not see many real data batches that do!). To examine the shape more closely, let's turn again to schematic plots as in Table 5.15. Here we can easily see that the numerical summary values are very symmetric: the median is in the middle of each box and also about half-way between the extremes. The one exception to a very prettily balanced picture is the lowest

Table 5.13
Logged 1970 Populations

Africa		Americas		Europe	
Algeria	7.16	Argentina	7.38	Albania	6.33
Burundi	6.55	Barbados	5.38	Austria	6.87
Congo	6.08	Bolivia	6.69	Belgium	6.98
Equatorial Guinea	5.45	Brazil	7.97	Bulgaria	6.93
Guinea	6.59	Chile	6.97	Canada	7.33
Kenya	7.05	Colombia	7.32	Finland	6.66
Lesotho	5.97	Costa Rica	6.24	France	7.71
Liberia	6.18	Cuba	6.93	German Democratic	
Madagascar	6.83	Dominican Rep.	6.61	Republic	7.23
Mali	6.70	Ecuador	6.78	Greece	6.94
Niger	6.60	El Salvador	6.55	Hungary	7.01
Nigeria	7.74	Guatemala	6.71	Iceland	5.31
Rwanda	6.57	Guyana	5.85	Italy	7.73
Somalia	6.45	Haiti	6.63	Liechtenstein	4.32
South Africa	7.35	Honduras	6.40	Monaco	4.36
Swaziland	5.63	Jamaica	6.27	Netherlands	7.12
Togo	6.29	Mexico	7.70	Norway	6.59
Uganda	6.99	Nicaragua	6.26	Portugal	6.94
Tanzania	7.12	Panama	6.16	Romania	7.31
Upper Volta	6.73	Paraguay	6.38	Spain	7.53
		Peru	7.13	Sweden	6.91
		Trinidad–Tobago	6.01	Switzerland	6.79
		Uruguay	6.46	United States	8.31
		Venezuela	7.01		

Table 5.14
Logged 1970 Populations, Stems-and-Leaves

	Africa	Americas (excluding U.S.A. and Canada)	Europe (including U.S.A. and Canada)
7	7	8 | 0	8 | 3
7	21401	7 | 7	7 | 775
6	66876657	7 | 40310	7 | 032013
6	1203	6 | 79686765	6 | 99796998
5	56	6 | 2433240	6 | 3
5		5 | 9	5 |
4		5 | 4	5 | 3
4		4 |	4 |
		4 |	4 | 34

stems: units
leaves: tenths

	Africa	Americas	Europe
N	20	24	22
X_U	7.74	7.97	8.31
q_U	7.02	6.99	7.31
Md	6.60	6.62	6.94
q_L	6.24	6.27	6.66
X_L	5.45	5.38	4.32

Table 5.15

Logged 1970 Populations, Schematic Plots

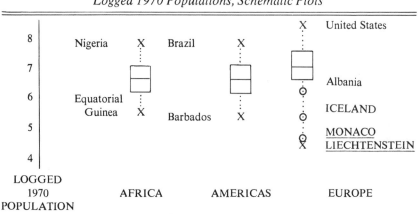

quarter of the Europe batch, which has three lower outliers (two of them far outliers). Logging has done an excellent job of removing upward straggle. What else does it remove? First, it leaves us with no upper outliers; even the United States value looks quite ordinary now. The seven upper outliers in the raw data were not as unusual as they appeared; they were just part of an overall pattern of upward straggle. Second, it has virtually removed differences in spread. The midspreads of the three batches are nearly equal now; the African and American ranges are nearly equal, and the Europe range would probably be similar if it weren't for the lower outliers we have already noted.

Therefore transformation has simplified our list of things that have to be explained, because some things — covariation of level and spread and seven upper outliers — are part of upward straggle, as we can tell when we find that they are removed by the same fit (logging) that removes the upward straggle itself. Now that we have that sorted out, we have to get on with the explanation! First, since we've been looking so hard at shape, why do the raw data straggle up? Why are the larger nations comparatively few and far between? Looking at the plots, it is hard not to be struck by the possible role of area: Brazil is huge and Barbados is tiny, the United States is far larger than Liechtenstein, and so on. Sheer size is not everything — Canada has greater area than the United States, but a lot of it is rather hard to live in. Perhaps the important thing is a combination of resources needed to support population: area, arable land, and resources generally. A few of the countries have a lot of such resources (and large populations) while relatively more nations have less of such resources (and smaller populations). How did such resources come to be unequally distributed? Well, resources usually are unequally distributed. For example, in every country with recorded income distributions the incomes straggle up: a few people get a lot and a lot get less. A common explanation is that these unequal distributions result in part from competition. A few people (or families, or nations) begin with some competitive advantages and get more resources, which in turn increase their advantage so they get still more resources, and so on; as a result, the higher values keep getting more and more spread out generating the observed upward straggle. Note what we have done here: we've tried to trace the shape of our data, population sizes, to the shape of an underlying variable, resources; then we try to explain the shape of resources. We could check on this further by looking at area and so on to see if resources do straggle up, and by looking at history to see if countries that start off with more resources tend to get more, for example by absorbing new territories (as Canada, like many other countries, did several times).

Let's try another kind of explanation of shape. We have seen that populations grow by larger and larger amounts as time goes by; perhaps some of these countries are larger because they have been growing at high rates for longer. Many of the larger nations have been developed for relatively long periods of time; this means they may have had more adequate health care for longer, leading to lower death rates and higher population growth rates. However, development usually brings lower birth rates too, so that population growth slows down after a while; but the population base can get pretty big before the birth rates start to fall. We could pursue this possibility by, for example, looking at indicators of health care like number of doctors per capita. Have the more populous states had better care for longer?

Probably both the suggested processes play some part in population sizes, and so do other processes we have not considered. The overall upward-straggling shape is not a simple phenomenon, as it's certainly a result of many underlying processes working in combination. This is a more complicated kind of problem than in our first example, also a more typical one; but one that we can still handle, by making sensible speculations and following them up.

We have some ideas about shape, so let's go on to the other main features of the data. Why is the level higher for the Europe batch? Perhaps because resources which support population (including advanced technology) are well developed there, health care reached a high level there at a relatively early period, and nation-states have been established there for longer so that countries have had a longer time in which to grow larger by absorbing their neighbours. Even as recently as the twentieth century, Yugoslavia was formed from several smaller countries. Note that Europe had the highest level before and after transformation, while Africa and the Americas had roughly equal levels both before and after transformation. The transformations that we use always leave the order of the levels the same (though they may change the relative sizes of the levels).

Turning to spread, we saw earlier that most of the original spread differences were just part of upward straggle and do not need special attention. For example, in the raw data Europe was more spread out, but that was primarily because the European nations were larger on the whole and the larger values tend to be more spread out. Explanation of spread is simplified, but we still have something to do. After all, the three midspreads are not exactly the same after logging. Instead, the Europe midspread is a bit smaller than the other two. Why? First, perhaps, we should clarify what has happened here. It may seem a bit odd: in raw data Europe has the largest midspread, now in logged data it has the smallest! But this is not so odd if we remember what logs do: subtraction in logs is like division in raw numbers. So the small difference of quartiles in logged data means that the Europe batch had a small ratio of q_U to q_L in the raw data. (Check this out with the summary values from Table 5.11.) Thus the European sizes are more spread out in the raw data but they are less disproportionate. After logging we find that the Europe values are not quite as spread out as we would expect them to be given their level. Again, why? Perhaps the long history of merging states, referred to earlier in two different contexts, has some relevance here too: perhaps many of the smaller states have not been able to survive. Or perhaps the European nations are relatively alike in population sizes because they are so alike in their economies and cultures. The poorer nations of Africa and the Americas have more varied levels of development and more varied societies.

Having considered the three major overall features of the data (level, spread, and shape), we now turn to the outliers. The seven upper outliers in the raw data are no longer outliers in logged data, while three cases that did not look especially unusual in the raw data become outliers in the logged data. Again we can see how this happens if we consider ratios. Take the most extreme cases, the U.S.A. (quite an outlier in raw data) and Liechtenstein (quite an outlier in logged data). In the raw version, the U.S.A. looks vastly more unusual; it is $204\,875\,000 - 20\,253\,000 = 184\,622\,000$ from the q_U, while Liechtenstein is $4\,606\,000 - 21\,000 = 4\,585\,000$ away from the q_L. But the U.S.A. value is only about ten times the q_U while the q_L is over 200 times the size of Liechtenstein. In relative terms, the Liechtenstein value is much more unusual, though this is hard to see in the raw data because the lower values are so crowded compared to the higher ones.

The seven nations which are outliers in the raw data but not in logged data have large populations, but no larger than we expect given that there is an overall upward straggle. We often refer to such cases as *false outliers*: they seem unusual at first because they are outliers in raw data, but they stop being outliers once the data have been balanced by a suitable transformation. Since our seven false outliers are now revealed as not especially unusual, we do not need to discuss them further. This data set also offers us some examples of *hidden outliers*, or cases that are not outliers in the raw data but become so after a suitable transformation; that is, cases that are more unusual than they look in raw data. Here, Iceland becomes an outlier while Monaco and Liechtenstein become far outliers after logging. They are far smaller than we would expect given the overall pattern, so we do need to think about them. How did a few unusually tiny states manage to survive in a region that has seen much merging of states? It is easy to see how Iceland remained independent in spite of its size: it is far away from the European continent on a small island without great natural wealth. Liechtenstein is not in fact all that independent, having very close ties to Switzerland: for example, Switzerland supplies the border guards for Liechtenstein. Similarly, Monaco has long been under the dominance of France. Thus these two tiny areas have a limited independence, which they maintain in part by staying neutral in wartime and in part by offering specialized conveniences (tourism and tax shelters) in peacetime.

This example did not lead to the same clearcut picture that the first one offered, even though both examples use population sizes. But logging was productive in both examples; even in the more complex second example, logging clarified the analysis greatly by clearing away the effects of upward straggle so that more could be seen. Perhaps the most dramatic benefit was in the analysis of outliers, where seven false ones were identified and three hidden ones were made visible. We still do not know for sure why the data straggle up in the second example, but we do have several ideas that might profitably be pursued. Another benefit is one that is often overlooked: by reducing spread and level differences between batches, transformation makes the data easier to plot and to see. This is no small advantage, since looking hard at data is one of the most important aspects of exploration.

Some General Remarks about Transformation

Transformation lets us work with shape as we work with level and spread. We define a standard shape (symmetric and single-peaked) as we defined standard level (0) and standard spread (1). We can fit almost any single-peaked batch shape by finding the transformation which puts the batch most nearly into standard form; this transform is a fit for the shape which summarizes and removes it. We try to explain the fit (for example, we argued that population batches become standard after logging because the resources which support population tend to be unequally distributed) and then go beyond it by looking hard at the transformed data.

It is important to note that our transformations are made on the raw data, and not, for example, on standardized data. It often happens that transformation does most or all of your standardization for you; usually level differences are reduced and spread differences are much reduced or eliminated. Besides, it is easier to understand and interpret transformations if they are as simple as possible, and transformation of raw data is simpler and more easily communicated. Furthermore, standardizing makes some transformations effectively impossible; we can't take logs of negative numbers, for example. So if you want to get some level or spread differences out of some batches after transformation, go ahead and do it in the usual way on the transformed batches. Batches with transformed numbers in them are still batches and can be batch analyzed like any other numbers.

In particular, they can be examined for outliers. After transformation many things can happen to outliers: outliers in the raw data may stop being outliers, they may persist, or new outliers may be revealed. Take the transformed version of what is or isn't an outlier more seriously; when a batch is symmetrized, upper and lower ends of the batch are treated more even-handedly in defining outliers, and the overall pattern of the batch is allowed for.

Of course, a foolish or unscrupulous person could use transformations to create or destroy outliers to suit himself; for example, logging often gives new lower outliers and eliminates upper outliers and never the opposite (why?) while the reverse may occur for some other kinds of transformation. This is one reason why we argued that having a standard form is useful in part to avoid arbitrary transformation: if the goal of the transform is clear then the choice of transform is restricted.

We'll be meeting batches of various shapes, so we need to have several transforms in our toolkit and we need to know when to use them. That's in the next chapter.

Exploratory and Confirmatory

As we remarked at the start of this chapter, transformation is also very useful in confirmatory work since the most widely used confirmatory tools are meant for data with a special kind of standard shape. If your data do not have this shape, they can often be transformed so that they do have it.

We have spoken here of "single-peaked" and "multi-peaked" data. In standard language it is more usual to speak of unimodal and multimodal data. The *mode* of a batch is the most frequent value, the value which occurs most often. If two values occur equally often and more often than any others, the batch is bimodal; if several values are tied for first place, the batch is multimodal. In Table 5.8, where several kinds of shape are illustrated, the first three batches are all unimodal. The fourth batch is double-peaked, but not (as it may at first seem) bimodal: one stem has five cases and no other stem has as many, so this batch is unimodal too. This example should be enough to show why we have not used the "mode" language very much: batch 4 in Table 5.8 very clearly has two clusters, but the mode language does not capture this. Like all confirmatory measures, the mode is very exactly defined and can sometimes be misleading.

Homework

Do ONE of **1, 2,** or **3.**
1. Return to the suicide data in chapter 2. For either the male rates or the female rates,
   a. log the rates
   b. stem-and-leaf and plot the transformed batches
   c. discuss what's happened. Which batches are more symmetric or less than before? Why? Do logs seem to work? Why might they work?

2. Consider Table 5.16 which gives the 1970 populations of the 22 largest metropolitan areas in the U.S.A. and the 1971 populations of the 22 largest metropolitan areas in Canada. Metropolitan areas include governmental units like core cities *plus* surounding suburbs; the census takers try to define these areas so that they are meaningful population units. Plot the raw data; then log the data and plot again. What did the logging do? How close to standard shape do the batches come, before and after logging? Why do the data straggle up? Shape is the main topic here but discuss any other data features that seem important.

Table 5.16

22 Largest Metropolitan Areas

	CANADA
Metropolitan Area	1971 Population, thousands
Calgary	403
Chicoutimi-Jonquière	134
Edmonton	496
Halifax	223
Hamilton	499
Kitchener	227
London	286
Montreal	2,743
Ottawa–Hull	603
Quebec	481
Regina	141
St. Catharines–Niagara	303
St. John's, Nfld.	132
Saint John, N.B.	107
Saskatoon	126
Sudbury	155
Thunder Bay	112
Toronto	2,628
Vancouver	1,082
Victoria	196
Windsor	259
Winnipeg	540

Source: Statistics Canada, 1971, Table 8.

Table 5.16 Continued

Metropolitan Area	U.S.A. 1971 Population, thousands
Anaheim–Santa Ana–Garden Grove	1,420
Atlanta	1,390
Baltimore	2,071
Boston	2,754
Chicago	6,979
Cincinnati	1,385
Cleveland	2,064
Dallas	1,556
Detroit	4,200
Houston	1,985
Los Angeles–Long Beach	7,032
Milwaukee	1,404
Minneapolis–St. Paul	1,814
New York	11,529
Newark	1,857
Paterson–Clifton–Passaic	1,359
Philadelphia	4,818
Pittsburgh	2,401
St. Louis	2,363
San Francisco–Oakland	3,110
Seattle–Everett	1,422
Washington	2,861

Source: Statistical Abstract of the United States; 1971 (92nd ed),
U.S. Bureau of the Census. Table 18. pp. 19–20.

Table 5.17

Per Capita Gross Domestic Product, Selected
western hemisphere countries (1971, in U.S. $)*

Argentina	1260	Jamaica	740
Bolivia	219	Mexico	712
Brazil	452	Nicaragua	471
Canada	4317	Panama	782
Costa Rica	586	Peru	356
Ecuador	306	Uruguay	836
Guatemala	371	U.S.A.	5121
Haiti	110	Venezuela	1151

Source: Yearbook of National Accounts Statistics 1973,
Vol. III, International Tables, United Nations,
New York 1975. Copyright, United Nations,
1975. Reproduced by permission.
*Gross Domestic Product is a measure of wealth very
similar to the more familiar GNP.

3. Plot the 1971 per capita GDP figures in Table 5.17; then log and plot again; discuss. The numerical work is less here, which means you could spend more time on pursuing ideas by doing extra analysis or by looking up useful information to test your ideas. One handy source of data is the *World Handbook of Political and Social Indicators*, volumes I and II. Your library almost certainly has some other sources as well.

6

Finding the Best Transformation

In the last chapter one very important transformation, the log, was described, not only for its own sake but also to help illustrate how transformation works in general and what some of the reasons for transformation are. This chapter is necessary because batches can have many different shapes. So we need to know several kinds of transformations, each a fit for a different shape; and we need to know how to choose among them. We explain the use of several transforms; we offer two procedures that may help you to find an appropriate transformation quickly; and we give some guidelines for deciding when a transformation is appropriate.

Other Useful Transformations

Relax: we are not about to dazzle you with a mass of weird and unfamiliar functions. Almost all the shapes you'll run into can be handled quite adequately with logs or one of a very few familiar alternatives. First, consider batches that straggle up, similar to those in the last chapter.

Sometimes when we try logs on such data, we find that we have overshot the mark: the new batch now straggles down because we've overcorrected. So we turn to a more moderate correction than the log transform, the square roots of the data. This is easy to handle, as many statistics books and books of statistical tables have square root tables more than adequate for exploration, and many inexpensive electronic calculators will give square roots. Suppose instead that logs undercorrect the data, that is, the batch still straggles up after logging. Then we want something stronger and might turn to the negative reciprocal (or $-1/x$), a somewhat stronger transform. You use negative reciprocals because that keeps the order of the numbers the same. For example, 2 is bigger than 1 but when you take reciprocals $1/2$ is smaller than $1/1$; using $-.5$ and -1 is fine because $-.5$ is bigger (less negative) than -1.

Let's try these three transformations on the same batch to see how they work. Table 6.1 gives data on the number of housing starts in the

Table 6.1

Private Nonfarm Housing Starts,
U.S.A., 1966-1968

Month	Number of Units Started		
	1966	1967	1968
January	78,500	57,700	79,800
February	74,800	60,200	82,800
March	115,900	89,200	123,900
April	138,600	112,000	159,100
May	126,700	129,700	139,000
June	118,200	123,400	136,000
July	97,600	124,000	137,300
August	99,600	123,600	134,500
September	86,900	119,500	132,400
October	74,400	133,100	138,100
November	71,400	116,800	125,100
December	58,900	79,100	95,500
Entire Year	1,141,500	1,268,400	1,483,600

Source: Bureau of the Census.
NOTE: Components may not add to totals due to rounding.

United States, 1966–68. The data have been stemmed-and-leaved and plotted in Table 6.2 so we can get a better look at them. Some things are clear at once; in Table 6.1 we can easily see that the time of year makes a big difference to housing starts, which is simple enough to explain: it's much harder to pour foundations in January than in July in most of the United States. In Table 6.2 we see that the level of housing starts went up quickly, and that none of the months in any of the years seemed different enough from the others to be outliers. Looking a bit more closely we see that the shapes of the batches are interesting. The 1966 batch straggles upward just a bit and 1967 and 1968 straggle down rather substantially. The fact that the shapes are different from year to year is intriguing and suggestive, and we will discuss that more later.

Take 1966. It straggles up; and in fact most of the social science data you will ever see will straggle up. This is in part because we often deal with variables which have clear floors but where ceilings are vague or absent: income, age, population, gross national product and so on. So the transformations that make upwardly straggling data symmetric are particularly useful. Square roots, logs, and negative reciprocals are given for the 1966 batch in Table 6.3. With this batch of numbers, square roots are not a strong enough transformation; the batch still straggles up. The logged data look good, essentially no straggle still remains. Taking negative reciprocals is fine for the middle mass of the data, but makes the data beyond the quartiles very asymmetric. Overall, the logged data are probably the best compromise, though as usual, there is some judgement involved. More generally, you can

Table 6.2

Private Nonfarm Housing Starts, U.S.A.

1966		1967		1968	
13	9	13	30	15	9
12	7	12	3440	14	
11	68	11	27	13	967528
10	0	10		12	45
9	8	9		11	
8	7	8	9	10	
7	9541	7	9	9	5
6		6	0	8	30
5	9	5	8	7	
				6	

stems: ten thousands
leaves: rounded to nearest thousand

	1966		1967		1968
q_U	117	q_U	124	q_U	138
Md	93	Md	119	Md	134
q_L	75	q_L	84	q_L	109

see that these transformations have different effects and so will be appropriate for different data sets.

What do you do if a batch straggles down? You want to spread out the higher values and pull the lower ones together to make the batch symmetric. This is easy to do by trying powers of the batch numbers: x^2, x^3, x^4, or whatever it takes. This is pretty simple so we have not bothered to work out examples for you. The antilog transformation corrects for downward straggle too (being the opposite of logs) but is awkward if the data are large numbers; the antilogs can really get enormous. Consequently this transform will rarely be used as a way of handling shape, though it is used in getting results from log transforms back to the original data units. For most data which straggle down, finding squares or cubes is likely to be adequate. You should feel free to try powers or roots or negative reciprocals or any other function of the data that will make them amenable, so become familiar with enough options to be flexible.

Table 6.3

1966 Housing Starts, Transformed

Square Roots	Logs	$-1/x$
3 | 70, 60	5.1 | 40	-7 | 29
3 | 40, 40, 20, 10	5.0 | 670	-8 | 56
2 | 94, 82, 76, 70, 64	4.9 | 940	-9 |
2 | 46	4.8 | 875	-10 | 02
	4.7 | 7	-11 | 5
		-12 | 7
stem: hundreds	*stems*: units and tenths	-13 | 35
		-14 | 1
q_U 340	q_U 5.07	-15 |
Md 302	Md 4.97	-16 | 9
q_L 276	q_L 4.88	*stem*: ten millionths
		q_U -86
		Md -109
		q_L -134

(all observations $\times 10^{-7}$)

Choosing an Appropriate Transformation

By now you have seen, and can easily work with, several kinds of transformation. Different transformations have different effects on data; some
spread the data out where values are high and condense them where values
are low, some do the opposite. In addition some change spread a lot more
than others. How do you decide which to use? Let us first consider choosing
a transformation for one batch, and then for several related batches.

When working with a single batch you want to get it as close as possible
to standard form: single-peaked, symmetric, and falling off smoothly on both
sides. The middle part of the data is particularly important and, other things
being equal, we choose that transform which symmetrizes the middle. Thus,
we chose a log transform for the Canadian population data (Table 5.5).
But if we have two transforms that are pretty good for the middle we can
choose between them by looking at how they handle the observations beyond

the quartiles. Consequently, we rejected the negative reciprocal in favour of logs for our housing start data (Table 6.3).

Now we want to show how you can quickly choose symmetrizing transformations for whatever batches come your way. We want a better choice procedure than hit-or-miss, trial and error, because that takes time and work. The first step is to get an orderly idea of what transformations do what kinds of things. In Table 6.3 we saw that square roots, logs, and negative reciprocals all correct for upward straggle to varying extents; the square root transform is weaker in its effect than logging, which is in turn weaker than negative reciprocals. We can also see with a little thought that powers of x correct for downward straggle and do so to varying extents. Consider a little example: the numbers 5,6,7. If we transform these by squaring we get 25, 36, and 49. The smaller pair are one unit apart in the original form and are 11 apart in the squared form. The larger pair are again one unit apart in the original form, but are further apart than the smaller pair after squaring: 13 vs. 11. And these are numbers that are not very different in the first place. Now suppose we try x^3, getting 125, 216, and 343. Now the smaller pair are 91 units apart and the larger pair are 127 apart. Again the larger numbers have been spread out relatively more, with a higher power of x exaggerating the effect. In general, the higher the power of x the more the larger numbers are stretched compared to the smaller ones (or the more the smaller ones are squeezed together compared to the larger ones).

We can sum up this useful information by what Tukey calls the *ladder of transformations*:

$-\dfrac{1}{x^2}$	$-\dfrac{1}{x}$	$\log x$	$\sqrt{x}$	x	x^2	x^3	antilog x
STRONGER		MILD	NO SHAPE CHANGE		MILD		STRONGER

← CORRECT UPWARD STRAGGLE ————— CORRECT DOWNWARD STRAGGLE →

Moving to the right spreads out larger x values and clumps the smaller ones; moving to the left spreads out smaller values and clumps the larger ones. Suppose you start with original data that straggle down. You might try x^3 and, alas, this straggles up. Try x^2 then, of course. One or two stabs are usually enough to identify a good transformation. But even this sounds like work! With bad luck we could end up doing several transformations on a batch, taking up time that we would rather spend on thinking about what the data mean. There is an easier way to handle this problem. Think back to the numerical summary. We can get the extremes, quartiles, and the median of a batch quickly by now and we will have gotten them anyway when we first looked at the raw data, so that is no problem. Transforming five numbers (and perhaps a few others for added reliability if there is time)

Table 6.4

Finding a Good Transform Using Numerical Summaries

Canadian Population = X

	X	$\sqrt{X}$	Log X	$-1/\sqrt{X}$
X_U	18.24	4.27	1.26	−.23
q_U	10.95	3.31	1.04	−.30
Md	6.29	2.51	.80	−.40
q_L	4.01	2.00	.60	−.50
X_L	2.44	1.56	.39	−.64

| X | $\sqrt{X}$ | log X | $-1/\sqrt{X}$ |

is not hard or time-consuming. And the summary numbers are good guides to the batches they summarize: if the transformed quartiles and extremes look symmetrical around the median then we probably have a transformation that will work on the whole batch. To get a quick feeling for how symmetric the summary numbers are after transformation we again can use a fast and familiar tool: box-and-dot plots. Consider Table 6.4, in which we look at trial transformations on the Canadian population data (because we already know what the "right" answer is). We can see very easily that the raw population figures straggle up; the square root figures are a bit more symmetrical but still straggle up; and the negative reciprocals of the square roots straggle down slightly. Clearly the square root transform undercorrects and the negative reciprocal overcorrects, while the log transform is "just right." As we have already seen, the message from the summary numbers is accurate in this case since a full-scale log transform of all the population figures was very effective.

Using summary numbers and the ladder of transformations is easy and fast and works most of the time, which is just as well, since it wouldn't be worth much otherwise. Once in a while you will run into intermediate cases.

For example, you might find that x^2 undercorrects your batch and x^3 overcorrects it. What then? If you are extremely precise you may want to find the transformation that symmetrizes the data exactly — but that will be something in between x^2 and x^3, say $x^{2.314}$. Now you can do this if you insist (you do it with the help of logs) but it is a lot of work and only rarely worth the trouble, even in confirmatory work. For most exploratory work we suggest not taking the trouble. Decide which simple transform looks better and go ahead with it.

If the decision between the two transformations is really close, you might pick the one that is easier to do (that's quite reasonable) or the one that makes more sense. For example, we saw that the U.S.A. population figures were slightly overcorrected by a log transformation, and one could argue for taking the square root of the batch or possibly even leaving it alone. But the log transform makes a lot of sense for populations so we used it anyway, and then we got some discussion out of the slightly imperfect nature of the transformation — the transformed data straggled down a little and that led us to think about declining immigration rates and other things interfering with the theoretically normal pattern of constant increase. Like a lot of data analysis, the choice of a good transformation is often a matter of judgement and taste. Besides, we can do more than one analysis.

Choosing a Transformation for Several Related Batches

Balancing Batches

For one batch we try to even up within-batch spread, so that the upper and lower halves of the batch straggle about the same amount. For several related batches we try to even up spread within each batch and between batches as well. The ideal multi-batch transformation will result in all the batches having medians well centred between both the quartiles; the extremes equally far from the quartiles; and each of the batches having similar spreads even if their levels differ. How often do you get a set of batches which can be transformed so neatly? Well, let's get back to the real world.

It can be tricky to decide what the best overall transformation for a set of batches is. The best overall may be the one that makes all the batches balanced, or at least makes the most of them balanced. This is just our single-batch criterion expanded to several related batches. Consider the five related batches in Table 6.5. Each batch is defined by a "stage" of economic growth, with the stages defined by levels of Gross National Product per capita for about 1957. The batch entries are the number of students enrolled in higher education per 100 000 population, for about 1960. (The exact values of these figures would be different now, no doubt higher on the whole, but the

Table 6.5

Enrollment in Higher Education at Different Levels of Economic Growth

Country	Higher Ed. per 100,000	Country	Higher Ed. per 100,000	Country	Higher Ed. per 100,000
Stage I GNPC 45–64		**Stage III GNPC 108–239**		**Stage IV GNPC 262–794**	
Nepal	56	Iran	90	Mexico	258
Afghanistan	12	Paraguay	188	Colombia	296
Laos	4	Ceylon	56	Yugoslavia	524
Ethiopia	5	Indonesia	62	Hong Kong	176
Burma	63	Rhodesia and		Brazil	132
Libya	49	Nyasaland	3	Spain	258
Sudan	34	Egypt	399	Japan	750
Tanganyika	9	Morocco	40	Jamaica	42
Uganda	14	Surinam	109	Panama	371
		South Korea	397	Greece	320
		Iraq	173	Malaya	475
		Nicaragua	110	Costa Rica	326
		Taiwan	329	Romania	226
		Saudi Arabia	6	Lebanon	345
		Ghana	29	Bulgaria	456
Stage II GNPC 70–105		Syria	223	Malta	142
		Tunisia	64	Chile	257
Pakistan	165	Albania	145	South Africa	189
China		Algeria	70	Singapore	437
(Mainland)	69	Peru	253	Trinidad and	
India	220	Ecuador	193	Tobago	61
South Vietnam	83	Guatemala	135	Cyprus	78
Nigeria	4	Honduras	78	Poland	351
Kenya	5	Barbados	24	Uruguay	541
Madagascar	21	El Salvador	89	Argentina	827
Congo		Philippines	976	Hungary	258
(Leopoldville)	4	Turkey	255	Italy	362
Thailand	251	Portugal	272	Ireland	362
Bolivia	166	Mauritius	14	Puerto Rico	1,192
Cambodia	18	British Guiana	27	Iceland	445
Haiti	29	Dominican		U.S.S.R.	539
		Republic	149	Venezuela	355
Stage V GNPC 836–2577				Austria	546
Netherlands	923	New Zealand	839	Czechoslovakia	398
West Germany	528	Australia	856	Israel	668
France	667	Sweden	401	Finland	529
Denmark	570	Luxembourg	36		
Norway	258	Switzerland	398		
United Kingdom	460	Canada	645		
Belgium	536	United States	1,983		

GNPC = Gross National Product per Capita, U.S. dollar equivalent, circa 1957.

Higher Ed. per 100,000 = number of students enrolled in higher education per 100,000 of total population; primary and secondary schools, adult education and technical training excluded.

Source: Bruce M. Russett et al., *World Handbook of Political and Social Indicators*; Yale University Press, New Haven 1964. Table B.2, pp. 294–298.

patterns would probably be quite similar.) Table 6.6 gives the stems-and-leaves and numerical summaries for these batches. (Incidentally, note that we have used several kinds of stems-and-leaves, plus rounding for the batches with larger numbers but not for those with smaller ones, in order to display the batches conveniently.)

What transformation might make all, or nearly all of these batches balanced? Clearly some correction for upward straggle is called for. Why not start by logging and plotting the summary numbers, since logging so often works out well? The logs are reported in Table 6.7 and plotted in Table 6.8. Since we do not yet know whether logs will be our choice, we use simple box-and-dot plots for the moment. How well do logs work? The most important part of the data is the middle: we look first at the midboxes. Batches II through V look pretty balanced, while batch I still straggles up. This is pretty good; we'll rarely find all the batches balanced. Next we check the extremes, less important than the midboxes (because more likely to fluctuate erratically) but still worth looking at. Here, logging does not seem to do so well: each lower extreme is farther from its batch's lower quartile than the upper extreme is from the upper quartile. We would not worry about one or two unbalanced extremes, probably, but this is a pattern of imbalance. The extremes straggle down for every batch, and some of the

Table 6.6

Stems-and-Leaves for 6.5

Stage I		II		III	
6	3	2	20, 51	9⌡	76
5	6	1	65, 66		
4	9	9		3	99, 97, 29
3	4	8	3	2	23, 53, 55, 72
2		7		1	88, 09, 73, 10, 45, 93, 35, 49
1	24	6	9	8:9	9 :0
0	459	5		6:7	24 :08
		4		4:5	0 :6
		3		2:3	947:
		2	19	0:1	36 :4
		1	8		
		0	454		

stems: tens	*stems*: hundreds, tens	*stems*: hundreds, tens
leaves: units	*leaves*: tens, and units; units	*leaves*: tens and units; units

N =	9	N =	12	N =	30
X_U	63	X_U	251	X_U	976
q_U	49	q_U	166	q_U	223
Md	14	Md	49	Md	110
q_L	9	q_L	12	q_L	56
X_L	4	X_L	4	X_L	3
dq	= 40	dq	= 154	dq	= 167

Table 6.6 Continued

Stage IV		V	
11	9	19⌡	8
10			
9		9	2
8	3	8.	46
7	5	7	
6	7	6	75
5	24453	5	374
4	864500	4	600
3	072355666	3	
2	66366	2	6
1	8349	1	
0	468	0	4

stems: hundreds
leaves: rounded tens

N	36		N	14
X_U	1190		X_U	1980
q_U	500		q_U	840
Md	360		Md	555
q_L	260		q_L	400
X_L	40		X_L	40
$dq =$	240		$dq =$	440

lower extremes will clearly be outliers (and there could be more lower out-liers to find in the stems-and-leaves). Logging may have over-corrected; let's try square roots. Table 6.9 reports the square roots of the summary numbers and Table 6.10 plots them. Compare this plot to that for logs, Table 6.8. The square rooted batches straggle up a bit in the midboxes (to be expected, since logging balances the midboxes) but the straggle is not severe; and the extremes are well balanced for all the square rooted batches whereas they are quite off-balance for the logged version. It also looks like the square root version will have fewer outliers. Overall, square roots seem to do a better job balancing the batches although the decision is close.

We wanted to take a harder look at the square rooted batches, without taking too much time. So we turned the box-and-dot plot of Table 6.10 into

Table 6.7

Logged Numerical Summaries from 6.6

	I	II	III	IV	V
X_U	1.80	2.40	2.99	3.08	3.30
q_U	1.69	2.22	2.35	2.70	2.92
Md	1.15	1.69	2.04	2.56	2.74
q_L	0.95	1.08	1.75	2.42	2.60
X_L	0.60	0.60	0.48	1.60	1.60

Table 6.8

Quick Plot of Logged Higher Education Batches

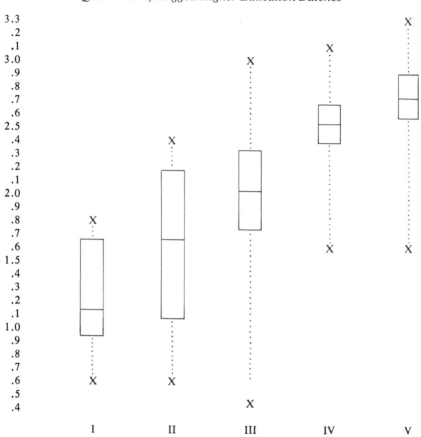

the schematic plot of Table 6.11 with minimal effort in the following way. (We keep 6.10 and 6.11 separate for clarity here but in practice we would just modify 6.10 into 6.11 to save still more time.) First we went back to the square rooted summary numbers in Table 6.9 to check for outliers and adjacent values other than extremes. We found that very little extra calculation had to be done to find the square roots for the schematic plot. For example, we checked the Stage I batch for upper outliers by finding the step value ($6 = 1.5\ dq$) and adding it to the upper quartile to get $7 + 6 = 13$. Since the upper extreme is only 8, there are no upper outliers; X_U is the upper adjacent value; and we don't have to look at any other upper values from this batch. On the other hand, for the Stage III batch we did find that X_U was an outlier. We went back to the raw data stems-and-leaves, found the second-highest value in this batch (399 in raw figures), square rooted it (getting 20)

Table 6.9
Square Rooted Values from Table 6.6

	I	II	III	IV	V
NUMERICAL SUMMARIES					
X_U	8.0	15.9	31.2	34.5	44.5
q_U	7.0	12.9	14.9	22.4	29.0
Md	3.7	7.0	10.5	19.0	23.6
q_L	3.0	3.5	7.5	16.1	20.0
X_L	2.0	2.0	1.7	6.3	6.3
CHECKING FOR OUTLIERS					
dq	4	9.4	7.4	6.3	9.0
STEP	6	14.1	11.1	9.45	13.5
upper outliers are at least:					
	(13)	(27)	(26)	(31.85)	(42.5)
OUT:	none	none	31.2	34.5	44.5
			adj: 20	adj: 28.8	adj: 30.3
lower outliers are at most:					
	(clearly none, I–III)			(6.65)	(6.5)
OUT:				6.3	6.3
				adj: 7.7	adj: 16.1

and found that this was not an upper outlier. So 20 is the upper adjacent value, and we do not have to look at any more upper values for this batch. All in all we found 5 upper or lower outliers and had to look up 5 more values to square root and check; all five extra values turned out not to be outliers so that was the end of our transforming and checking work. We will return to a discussion of the schematic plot shortly. For now, we just note that the adjacent values in batches III to V are also quite well balanced. Let us now turn to another criterion for a good multi-batch transformation.

Table 6.10
Quick Plots of Square Rooted Higher Education

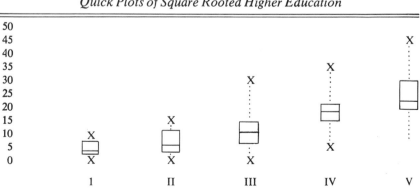

Table 6.11

*Schematic Plots, Square Rooted Higher Education
by Stages of Economic Growth*

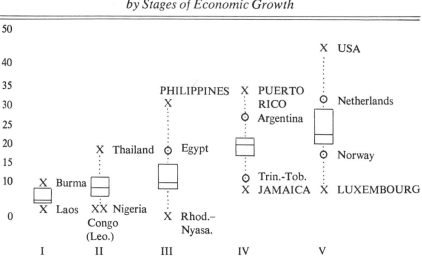

Equalizing Spreads

Instead of trying to make spread even within batches, so that upper and lower halves straggle similar amounts, we would like to try to make spread even between batches, so that each batch midspread is about the same. As we said earlier, we'd like to do both these things, but cannot always do so. Tukey recommends another tool that often suggests a transform that equalizes most of the batch spreads. This tool also can be very much the fastest way to choose a transformation for a large number of related batches.

To equalize the spreads, we need to know how they are related to level. If the spreads tend to increase as levels do, then square roots or logs or one of the negative inverses will help: they will make the spreads of the higher-level batches smaller, just what we need. On the other hand, if the spreads tend to get smaller as levels get bigger then we need some power of the observations (a positive power greater than one); this will draw the higher batch values together and spread out the lower ones, relatively speaking. Here is a rule of thumb that suggests a transform for the former case (by far the more common one) by looking at ratios summing up how much spread changes as level changes. We will not try to justify exactly how the procedure works in detail; pragmatically, the important thing is that this rule of thumb does the job much of the time.

The procedure is illustrated in Table 6.12, using the five higher education batches in raw form again (Table 6.6). First, find the Md and *dq* of each batch from the numerical summary. Next, find the logs of these levels

Table 6.12

Logged Spread and Level; Plot

Logged: Batch	I	II	III	IV	V
Md	1.15	1.69	2.04	2.56	2.74
dq	1.60	2.19	2.22	2.38	2.64

and spreads. For example, for batch I the Md and *dq* are 14 and 40, respectively, in the raw data; log (14) = 1.15 and log (40) = 1.60 are entered in the top of Table 6.12. (By the way, we want the log of the raw data *dq*, *not* the *dq* of logged data, which would be found from Table 6.7 but which is not what we need here.) To see how spread is related to level overall, we plot the logged *dq* on the Y-axis and the logged Md on the X-axis as shown in Table 6.12. There seems to be a fairly steady increase of spread with level, so some transformation that corrects for upward straggle is called for. Which one? First we sum up just how much log *dq* increases as log Md does. Wiggle a bit of string or a ruler around a bit on the plot till you find a line that looks pretty close to most of the points and passes through two of them. The dashed line in the plot shows the line we like the looks of. (Don't worry too much about finding such a line for your own data. If it looks right, it's probably close enough; if you have a terrible time deciding, that probably means that spread is not increasing very regularly with level and transformation is not going to even up the spreads very well whatever you do.)

Having found two points we ask how much the log spread increases as the log level does:

$$\frac{\text{log spread for higher point} - \text{log spread for lower}}{\text{log level for higher point} - \text{log level for lower}}$$

(This is just a slope; more on this in chapter 11.) For our example, the higher point is that for batch V and the lower is that for batch I so taking the ratio:

$$\frac{2.64 - 1.60}{2.74 - 1.15} = \frac{1.04}{1.59} = .65$$

Now turn to the chart below that tells you what transformation is likely to work given the ratio from the log spread/log level plot:

Ratio is about:	Transform to try:
1/2	$\sqrt{x}$
1	$\log x$
3/2	$-\dfrac{1}{x}$
2	$-\dfrac{1}{x^2}$

Our ratio is .65, between one half and one; so square roots or logs should help to even up the batch dqs. The ratio is nearer to one half, so square roots should do a better job than logs. Let's go back to our plots, Tables 6.8 and 6.10, to see. Clearly square rooting does produce more nearly equal midspreads; logging overcorrects, so that the dq actually declines as level in-increases. Logging comes close to making the ranges equal, but ranges are unreliable and much less important than the dq, which looks awful in logs.

The procedure does work, and not only for midspreads and medians. You can use this for any level and spread combination that makes sense to you. For example, you often want to have equal batch spreads in confirmatory work. But the spreads you want to equalize are variances, and the levels you work with are means. No problem: just follow the same procedure as above, using variances and means instead of dqs and Mds.

If you have many related batches to work with, this procedure is certainly the place to start since it is far faster (given a lot of batches) than the informal trial-and-error we began with. Often the transformation that evens up the spreads best also balances the batches best, as square rooting does in our higher education example. This is handy; we want our ideal transformation to do both things, we'd rather not have to decide between a transform good for one goal and another transform good for the other goal. This is also, luckily, pretty common: usually the same process underlies the observations in all the batches (that's why you compare them in the first place, right?) and generates both within-batch straggle and between-batch differences of spread. If the process is common to all the batches then a common transform should work.

Close Choices

So far, things seem pretty easy; we can often get a good multi-batch transformation with either of the approaches described above. But is it always so simple? What if the choice of transformation is close? What if some of the batches don't respond as well to the chosen transform as others do? Right, such problems do come up. For the higher education batches we think that square roots look clearly better than logs overall, but there are some things that logs handle better; and the choice can be much closer. In such cases, it comes down to judgement once again. Sometimes your judgement is helped along because you know that equal spreads are more important, or balanced batches are, for some reason; but most of the time you use your eyes and experience and make a choice.

Sometimes there is a sensible interpretation for one of the possible transforms; the choice becomes easier. For example, we found logging irresistible for over-time population figures because logging fitted so well with a sensible baseline hypothesis of constant growth. If a good interpretation is available, from theory or from your own thinking about the data, by all means try the transformation involved. Even if the theoretical transform fails to fit everything perfectly, it will still be useful. Those failures of fit will be worth discussion, like the dog not barking in the night: why did the expected not happen? For example, in the U.S. and Canada population example we found that the U.S. batch straggled down a bit after logging; we asked why, and that led to some interesting speculations, such as suggestions about the role of declining immigration in the U.S.

On the other hand, if your choice of transformation is based on the data then you'll want to try to come up with an interpretation of your choice. For example, why do square roots work well for the higher education batches? Perhaps a look at the schematic plot (Table 6.11) is in order. Clearly enrollment in higher education is related to levels of economic development, or levels of GNP per capita. This in itself should not surprise you; the wealthier the country, the more highly educated people it needs (to run a more sophisticated economy) and the more it can afford to train. Perhaps the process generating the enrollment figures is, quite simply, wealth and its consequences; then enrollment and wealth will have much the same shape. The *World Handbook* provides the GNP per capita figures to check this out. In any case, it is clear that wealth is not the whole explanation of higher enrollment rates (though it is a large part of the explanation). Within each batch in Table 6.5, the countries are ordered from poorest to richest; and some of our outliers are not unusually poor or rich. For example, Luxembourg is a lower outlier among the most wealthy nations as far as enrollment goes but 6.5 shows it is on the wealthy side in that group if anything. Perhaps Luxembourg's size is important. Luxembourg may be too small to support many institutions of higher education, so that people go outside the country to one of the many institutions in neighbouring nations and aren't counted in Luxembourg's figures. Some of the other lower cases are on the small side too. Size, like GNP per capita, straggles up, which again may contribute to the shape of our batches. The country's age may matter too.

We are used to thinking about cases like Luxembourg as outliers from batches, as cases that cry out for special attention and explanation. We should also get used to thinking of batches as outliers (loosely speaking) when they are very different from the set of batches to which they belong. For example, just as Luxembourg looks very different from the bulk of the batch V countries, batch I looks very different from the rest of the batches: its shape is different, much more markedly upward straggling. From Table 6.8 we see that logging does not balance this batch; something stronger, perhaps the negative inverse, would be needed. That implies quite a difference in shape, since we can get a rough feel for shape differences by seeing how far apart shape fits are on the ladder of transformations. Probably this shape difference is just a simple floor effect. The enrollment figures for the lower half of this batch are very low indeed and could hardly get much smaller. We probably should not make too much of this batch's unusual shape since the batch size is small ($N = 9$) and the figures may not be very accurate; accurate statistics are expensive and the poorer countries like those in batches I and II often cannot afford them. In many ways the shape difference between the U.S. and Canadian population batches was more impressive (Table 5.5). That shape difference was much smaller (the same transform worked tolerably for both batches, though the U.S. batch might look a bit better in square roots than in logs) but the small difference in shape was based on very good data and a good idea of what the processes underlying the shape might be.

By this stage you can do transformations of various kinds, can decide which to do, and can see many of the varied uses of transformation. You will get both more practice and more knowledge of these uses as we go along, for there will be case after case in which we cannot do without transformations.

Summary

Let's briefly recap what we have learned about transformations in the last two chapters. First we have seen that transformations can be used as summaries of the shapes of batches. With summaries of shape, level, and spread we have three pieces of information which tell us a great deal about a batch. This powerful three-part summary is a kind of "troika" in which all three pieces are important. Indeed, sometimes knowing shape is even more important than knowing level or spread: for example, consider income distributions. Some students of revolution and conflict argue that the wealth of a country (level) is not very important by itself because people define themselves as rich or poor in relative terms; further, even the distance between wealth and poverty (spread) is not necessarily important since there are usually persuasive ideologies to justify inequality; what may really provide potential for unrest is heavy concentration of much of the wealth in a very few hands (an extreme straggling upward) or a sudden change in the shape of wealth so that substantial portions of the population gain and lose a lot in relative position. This is one example of ways in which the shape of a batch may have important effects; we have already given an example of ways in which the shape may be an effect of something else (that is, the shape of population batches was traced to a fairly steady growth rate).

When we have a shape and understand it, we can make use of it. For example, if population increases exponentially (as in our first example in chapter 5) then we can extrapolate future population figures by assuming that this kind of growth will continue. Extrapolation will work if we have found the shape correctly (our data might be inadequate and mislead us) and if the mechanisms underlying the shape continue to work in the same way (e.g. if birth and death rates do not change too much). But it's much better if you understand the mechanisms because you feel much more confident about the projections. You can keep an eye on the mechanisms and adjust your predictions as the mechanisms change. Then you will not be like the chicken who ran to the farmhouse door every day at the sound of the bell to be fed — until the day he ran at the sound of the bell to have his head chopped off.

Once a shape is found, and understood as well as possible at the time, the next step is to remove it. This step provides many conveniences for further analysis. For example, it will then be possible to see more; often details of clumping are clearer, and very often the role of outliers is clarified. Apparent outliers may turn out to be just a reflection of the shape of the batch; or outliers may remain outliers after transformation; or extremes that did not look like outliers originally may become so after the batch has been transformed to the standard shape.

Transformation may also underline batch differences in shape. Often no transformation will do a good job for all the batches. If you find that your data are like this, note that what you do not do is find the best transformation for each batch considered independently. If these are related batches we want to compare them; and if they have been transformed in varying ways they will be no longer comparable. Instead, try to get some mileage out of looking at these aberrant batches as outliers from shape. Remember that the data in the batches are often imperfect, so that slight variations in shape may be nothing but chance fluctuations or errors of some sort. Only rather striking shape differences should really "grab" you.

Finally, there is another use of transformation which is very important indeed. We will soon see that many of the confirmatory statistics, especially the most common and most useful ones, are designed for normally distributed data and will work less well or not at all when the data have very different shapes. Therefore when we have a confirmatory question to ask of single-peaked but asymmetric data, we make the data symmetric by transforming it! How much simpler it is to make distributions more nearly normal than to make new statistics for every distribution.

We have stressed symmetry and the use of schematic plots in these last two chapters, because these tend to be the most important issue and the most useful tool. But do not forget that the standard shape has just one major peak as well as symmetry, and the number of peaks in a batch is not easily detected in a schematic plot alone. If your raw data look clumped, it is best to transform the whole batch and look at its stem-and-leaf after transformation; then if the data are clearly multi-peaked you can think about sub-batching. We have one other technical reminder: it is often awkward or impossible to transform batches with zero or negative values (for example, zero has no log). If your data include such values, add some number to all that data, where the number is large enough to remove all zero and negative values. For example, if the lowest value is -50 you would add $+51$ to every value. This will move all the levels up by the same amount but will not affect anything else and will make transformation much more feasible and appropriate.

Some of these uses of transformation are more sophisticated than others and take longer to get used to, but all of them are important and all will become clear to you as you work with data and get to know more about them. So we urge you, for these reasons, to think about shapes and try to understand them. It takes a lot of experience to do this really well, so start soon.

Exploratory and Confirmatory

We have used the picturesque term "straggle" for a trailing off of the data. It is more conventionally called *skewness*. "Shape" is closest to the standard term *distribution*. Transformation is used in confirmatory as well as exploratory work, but in confirmatory work the criteria for "good" transformation may be modified a bit. For example, if you want to transform several related batches before using a confirmatory test like analysis of variance (chapter 10) then you often want batch spreads to be roughly equal, as suggested here; but the spreads you equalize are variances, not midspreads. This is just a difference in emphasis; basically, the procedures and purposes of transformation stay much the same.

Homework

1. Consider the 1967 housing start figures (Tables 6.1 and 6.2). Using the summary points, compare schematic plots for several powers of the data. (You may find it hard to get complete balance.) Then consider all three years: what is happening to shape over these years? Why? Discuss this but do not try to get a good common transformation (why?).

2. Use the plot of logged dq by logged median to suggest a transformation for the female suicide rates and for the male suicide rates (do not actually try the transformation).

3. Return to the metropolitan area sizes (Table 5.16) which you began to analyze in chapter 5. You have logged plots for these data; make plots for the square roots and negative reciprocal versions too. Which transformation does seem best? What new insights into city sizes have you found?

First Review: Batch Analysis

In this section we've brought together several sets of batch data. Each of them is complex enough and interesting enough (we hope) to make them suitable for reviewing most of the things you've learned about batches. Select any *one* of these sets and explore it thoroughly. Since these data come from standard sources, you should expect to find yourselves turning to these sources for additional relevant data where you are led to interesting speculations that need checking out, or generally where it's necessary for pushing an analysis further.

In assignments of this sort, there's a strong tendency for students to try to do some of everything to show that they know how. Such assignments tend to have a very disorganized, helter-skelter sense to them, and are generally not very good as data analyses. Much better is the *organic* analysis, where the paper is organized around a few initial questions or speculations, which may have been suggested by initial exploration of the data, and which are pursued in depth. Such an analysis uses those techniques that are called for by the situation. In short, we suggest that you treat this like a data analysis rather than like a test; write an *essay* based on the data and the ideas you get from thinking about and playing with them. If you feel obliged to show that you can, for example, compute a variance though your analysis didn't require it, put it in an appendix.

The order of your work and the organization of your write-up are your business, but we will make a few suggestions that many students find helpful. First, try to order your analysis "organically" as suggested above. This often means not doing things in the order used in the chapters. The chapters moved (of course!) from easy things to harder things, which may not be a meaningful order for your analysis. For example, often the initial plotting of the batches suggests you should transform before getting deeply into level, spread, or outliers. Second, the order of your work does not have to be linear or tidy. Since you are exploring, you may change your mind as you go; or you may not be able to foresee later steps before earlier ones are done; and this can lead to dead ends, backtracking, missed insights that occur to you in the grocery store line-up, and so on. Fine: that's the nature of the enterprise. When writing up, we strongly urge you to write as you go; the resulting essay will backtrack as your work does, and hence may be a poor piece of composition but a good report of an actual exploration. You can keep things sufficiently clear and organized by having summaries of major ideas from time to time and at the end. If you try to write after all the numerical work and thinking is over (an option people find peculiarly tempting) you will probably find it difficult. Ideas may be forgotten, so analyses must be re-thought; ideas from different parts of the analysis are hard to sort out. Anyway, it's boring to do the same thing for a long time (first just numbers, then just writing).

We have just one final comment on *batching*. So far, we've batched for you, but you may want to do your own batching, perhaps even in this review work. For example, suppose you work on Example 2, Television Around the World. We have divided the countries in this table up into broad regions. This makes sense if you think that region is likely to have some interesting effect on the TV set rate. If you prefer to explore the relationship of TV sets to some other variable, say GNP per capita, you should batch accordingly by size of GNP per capita (for example, you could use the five "stages of growth" batches again; see Table 6.5).

Example 1: Socialization and Fear of People

Many personality theorists look at experience in childhood for explanations of numerous maladaptive adult behaviours. In the opinion of these theorists

Table IR.1
Socialization Anxiety and Fear of Human Beings

High Socialization Anxiety		Moderate Anxiety		Low Anxiety	
Alorese	5	Ainu	6	Bena	7
Ashanti	5	Arapesh	10	Chenchu	2
Azande	10	Baiga	10	Comanche	5
Chagga	9	Balinese	4	Marquesans	7
Chamorro	6	Hopi	8	Siriono	2
Chiricahua	9	Kurtatchi	9	Tikopia	5
Dahomeans	6	Kwakiutl	10	Yagua	11
Dobuans	8	Lakher	7	Yakut	6
Kutenai	6	Lepcha	7		
Kwoma	10	Lesu	9		
Navaho	7	Manus	4		
Paiute	11	Maori	9		
Rwala	7	Ontong–Javanese	6		
Sanpoil	9	Papago	4		
Tanala	7	Pukapukans	6		
Tenino	8	Samoans	5		
Thonga	7	Slave	8		
Western–Apache	8	Teton	0		
		Trobrianders	10		
		Venda	9		
		Wogeo	10		

Source: Whiting and Child, (1962).

Table IR.2

Television Sets/1000 Population by
World Regions (ca 1961)

West Europe (and US and Canada)		South and Central America		Central and Eastern Europe	
US	306.4	Cuba	72.1	E. Germany	90.8
Canada	224.4	Venezuela	34.5	Czechoslovakia	79.1
U.K.	220.3	Argentina	34.4	Austria	41.0
Sweden	176.5	Panama	27.1	USSR	27.5
Denmark	153.3	Mexico	24.9	Poland	21.6
W. Germany	109.0	Brazil	22.1	Hungary	20.5
Belgium	89.4	Uruguay	20.9	Romania	4.7
Netherlands	89.4	Colombia	13.8	Yugoslavia	3.3
Italy	55.8	Guatemala	9.0	Bulgaria	1.4
France	55.6	El Salvador	8.0		
Switzerland	35.3	Peru	7.6		
Luxembourg	31.5	Dominican Rep.	6.0		
Norway	29.6	Costa Rica	5.9		
Ireland	21.3	Nicaragua	3.3		
Spain	13.1	Honduras	2.1		
Portugal	7.6	Ecuador	1.1		
		Haiti	0.5		
		Chile	0.4		

Near East		Far East	
Kuwait	6.2	Australia	142.2
Algeria	6.1	Japan	98
Lebanon	4.9	New Zealand	7.9
Iraq	4.8	Hong Kong	3.0
Egypt	3.4	Thailand	2.9
Iran	1.9	Philippines	1.6
Saudi Arabia	1.4	South Korea	.8
Tunisia	.5	Cambodia	.1
Syria	.2	China	.03

Source: Russett et al., (1964),

an experience like weaning, common to children in every society, involves discomfort and anxiety which may have long term effects. Whiting and Child (1962) look at weaning, toilet training, independence training, sexual behaviour training and socialization of aggression, all of them universal, and all with the potential for producing long term anxiety. What Whiting and Child looked at especially was the severity of socialization, arguing that the greater the parental severity, the greater likelihood of anxiety in the children. We use a summary measure of all the areas called Average Socialization Anxiety for our batching. Societies with anxiety scores of 13 or more are placed in the high batch, those with anxiety scores of 11 or 12 in the moderate batch, and the rest in the low batch in Table IR.1.

Table IR.3

Larger Canadian Cities, 1961: Population and Male in-Migrants

City	Total Population	Movers from Same Metropolitan Area	From Different Part of Province	From Abroad
Calgary	114,817	40,746	25,799	7,621
Edmonton	138,620	54,902	25,848	7,228
Halifax	71,088	25,484	4,426	1,622
Hamilton	168,442	62,875	10,393	8,882
Kitchener	65,972	19,856	7,430	3,123
London	73,188	22,992	9,284	3,646
Montreal	871,282	404,773	36,510	37,049
Ottawa	173,757	65,848	13,846	7,831
Quebec	139,534	50,703	9,145	855
Saint John	38,390	12,913	2,067	519
St. John's	35,702	10,644	1,537	283
Sudbury	47,172	16,533	4,018	1,319
Toronto	775,655	309,995	36,168	66,687
Vancouver	327,494	120,610	16,021	15,891
Victoria	62,409	22,067	3,928	2,358
Windsor	82,256	26,493	3,681	2,033
Winnipeg	198,017	70,915	10,590	8,512

Source: 1961 Census of Canada, Bulletin SX-15 (Catalogue Number 98-529), Table 1. Dominion Bureau of Statistics.

One major way in which long-term effects of socialization anxiety might manifest themselves in adults would be the inability to deal satisfactorily with others. The authors also provide ratings of the various societies on fear of human beings, the higher the rating the greater the fear. Table IR.1 gives "fear of human beings" scores for forty-eight societies plus the society names in case you want to learn more about them. Whiting and Child (1962) provide additional information about these societies and more still is available in the Human Relations Area Files, as indeed are additional ethnographies.

Example 2: Television Around the World

The next table reports the number of television sets per 1000 population, batched by regions of the world. The data came from Russett, et al. (1964), Table 37. Other and more recent data are available in Taylor and Hudson (1972) as well as the *UN Statistical Yearbooks*, so there are many ways of pushing your analyses further.

You will have to decide how to think of these data. For example, does the rate of television sets indicate modernization in the sense of access to high technology goods? or modernization in the sense of exposure to mass media and the rapid dissemination of ideas? or is the number of TV sets per 1000 population an indicator of wealth in general, or of wealth of a privileged group? The interpretation(s) you choose will have some effect on your discussion, and/or may arise from your discussion.

Example 3: Male Migrants into Canadian Cities

The next table gives some Canadian city sizes and figures for three kinds of migrants into the cities. These may be four related batches, since they are all populations or population component figures. Or there may be three related batches of migrants and one different (but relevant) batch of city sizes. Or there may be three related batches of figures on internal Canadian population components and one different batch on people coming from other countries. Take a view and argue for it at some point in your analysis.

Section Two
Moving From Exploration
to Confirmation

You have now acquired a good variety of exploratory techniques for studying batches. You can fit, remove, and discuss major batch features; level, shape, and spread. You can look hard at outliers and at exceptions to overall patterns in sets of related batches. Many ideas can be generated in the process. Now we move to the different, but related and equally important matter of testing ideas after they have been generated. The next four chapters introduce some basic confirmatory tools like random sampling and hypothesis testing, and show how these can be applied to the problem of testing possible differences in levels. You should reread the first chapter soon to remind yourself of the major differences between exploratory and confirmatory approaches.

7
The Random Sample

In previous chapters we used recent statistics from 15 countries to develop a number of ideas about suicide. Will those ideas hold for these countries at other times, or for the hundred or more other countries in the world? A little thought suggests that we would be rash to assume so. On the one hand, the patterns we found may have been flukes based on a set of countries that happen, by chance, to be unusual (we'll talk more about this kind of possibility in the next chapter). On the other hand, the patterns may be misleading because they are usual, but usual only for some kinds of countries. Here the difficulty is that our 15 countries are obviously not a typical cross-section of the world's nations. Instead, they are countries which were selected for particular reasons, one of which being that their suicide statistics are considered fairly reliable (according to WHO); this in turn suggests that they are wealthier and more developed than most. The patterns we saw may not hold at all for poorer countries or for countries from different regions (say Africa) with different cultures and social structures. If we want to make a well-founded guess about patterns for all countries by looking at some countries, we would do better if we had a more representative set to work with. Choosing representative sets brings us to sampling, which is the topic of this chapter.

More formally, *sampling* consists of selecting elements from some *universe* with the intention of making inferences about that universe. The universe can be any collection of objects of interest: all the countries in the world, all the females in Vancouver, all the manufacturing corporations with fewer than 5,000 employees, all protest movements in the 19th century or whatever. Basically, the universe is the set of things you want to know about. So the sample you pick from the universe should be chosen in a way that will give as accurate a picture as possible. A lot of this chapter will be spent describing a method of choosing known as random sampling, and showing how accuracy is related to sample size.

Why Sample?

Clearly it is the universe, the full slice of social reality, that we want to know about. So why, you might ask, don't we just go and look at it? Sometimes we do; the modern census is the most familiar example of this. A decision is made that the population of a given country is the universe you want to know about, you decide what you want to know, and then you go and ask everyone about the things you want to know. (Some writers use the term "population" where we have used "universe." We avoid it here because of the easy confusion with "population" meaning "the total number of people living in a given area.")

Looking at the universe seems like a good idea, and often it is; but there are problems that prevent us from studying complete universes all the time. One problem is expense; it should be clear that complete enumerations of large universes can be very costly in both time and money. Another problem is that of "reactivity," the possibility that what we are studying can be changed or even destroyed by observing or measuring it. In order to "measure" the taste of a cake you must eat at least a part; to measure the life of a light bulb you must burn it out; even measuring a respondent's opinions can significantly alter these opinions. In cases like these, if we study a whole universe then we change or even destroy that universe so that the results we get are no longer true. This is not desirable scientifically and it may be undesirable ethically as well. Finally, we may not want to study the universe itself because we can get a more accurate picture by studying a sample of it. This may sound paradoxical but there are simple and solid reasons for it. Most importantly, it is feasible to do a very high-quality job of data collection and analysis on a sample and often not feasible to be as careful with a census. In the case of the 1971 Canadian census, the requirement that there be a complete enumeration made it necessary to use either mailed questionnaires or many poorly-trained interviewers, or to spend more time and money than was budgeted for. Statistics Canada chose the first option, knowing they were letting themselves in for some error thereby. Similarly analysis of very large amounts of data cannot economically be done as accurately or thoroughly as with smaller amounts of data. It is interesting to note that in the U.S.A., for example, the census is *corrected* on the basis of the Current Population Survey, based on a sample of less than one percent of the population!

Thus we often want to study a universe through studying a sample of it. This is a more familiar procedure than you may realize at first, since "homegrown" sampling is done a lot outside of science. A manufacturer will often try out a new product on a sample of consumers or communities, intending to go into full production should the tryout be a success; this would be a case of generalizing from sample results (the tryout went well) to a universe (the product should sell well in general). Similarly, governments will often try out a new policy suggestion before deciding whether to implement it across the board; for example, both Canadian and U.S. governments have tried out income supplement plans in selected communities. Everyone samples in small ways: we look at the sky to see if we need to take an umbrella (sample the weather to predict whether it will rain that day), we eat a meal at a new restaurant to see if "the food is good there" or we read the synopsis on the back cover of a murder mystery and decide that we will or won't like the book.

Casual sampling is generally better than no data-gathering at all, but clearly it presents problems. What if we hit the restaurant on a bad night or order one of the poorer dishes? What if sample communities are chosen because they are handy, and they turn out not to be typical? Without some careful effort to get a sample that reflects the universe adequately, we could easily be misled. One famous example of failure to effectively sample is the 1936 *Literary Digest* poll. Here, ten million ballots were mailed out and nearly two and a half million returned, on the basis of which the magazine predicted the election to the U.S. presidency of Alfred Landon (who?). Landon lost to F. D. Roosevelt in a landslide. The *Literary Digest* blew it because it failed to realize that its readers were not representative of the voters (the readers were wealthier than most and more conservative; who after all could afford subscriptions to literary magazines during the depression?); and those people who bothered to mail back their mock ballots were not even representative of readers (perhaps the mailers were especially uneasy about Roosevelt and eager to express that by ballot for Landon). Thus the sample the *Digest* got was a very biased sample: one selected in such a way that the data were systematically different from the universe data.

We would like a good sample to be unbiased, to reflect the universe accurately. Then we would be a great deal more confident that the sample results were a good guide to the general universe pattern. The key to getting an unbiased, representative sample is selecting the sample in the right way: selecting it *randomly*.

What do we mean by "random"? Well, we do not mean haphazard or hit-and-miss. Quite the opposite in fact; we mean a sampling procedure with a clearly defined property, ordinarily that each element of the universe we are interested in has an equal chance of being selected for the sample. Such a procedure gives the best chance of getting a representative cross-section of the universe. (We say "best chance" because sampling is, after all, a chance procedure. You could take a random sample and get something very atypical while someone else collected oddments haphazardly and got better results; but though this is conceivable, it is not very likely.) We will soon show you how random sampling can be done very easily.

Suppose we have a random sample, what can we expect of it? Let's get more specific and ask about levels, since levels are of basic importance. We've used levels a lot in exploration and they will be the main focus of the first confirmatory tests we meet. What can we learn about the universe level (which is what we'd like to know) from the sample level (which is what we'll have)? You can see right away that the sample mean will not likely be exactly the same as the universe mean; the sample mean will probably be close to the universe mean (after all, the sample mean is supposed to reflect the universe); and the sample mean may sometimes be far off the universe value (accidents can happen). Obviously we need to get some idea of how misleading a sample is likely to be. So our next step will be to get some samples and examine their relationship to the universe. This will show you how simple random sampling is done as well as illustrating how random samples behave.

Random Samples and Ghosts

The first step in learning about random samples is to get a nice small universe so that it can easily be compared with samples from it. We have chosen data from Whiting and Child (1962) on "fear of others"; specifically, on the extent to which human illness is thought to be caused by others. Agents sometimes thought responsible for illness included other people, both living and dead, as well as non-human spirits. Ethnographies of seventy-five societies were examined and rated by each of two judges on the extent to which illness was attributed to each of the agents. The scores range from "0," a very low degree of attribution to the agent, to "12," a very high degree of attribution. Table 7.1 contains scores for three agents; ghosts (dead people), other human beings (sorcerers, etc.) and spirits (supernatural beings) (see Whiting and Child, 1962, for further descriptions). We will sample from the "ghost" scores, leaving the other two as homework for you.

Table 7.1

Ratings on Fear of Ghosts, Human Beings, and Spirits
for 75 Primitive Societies

		Ghosts	Humans	Spirits
	Abipone	3	9	3
	Ainu	5	6	10
	Alorese	9	5	9
	Andamanese	10	4	10
5	Arapesh	8	10	8
	Ashanti	5	5	8
	Azande	0	10	5
	Baiga	7	10	8
	Balinese	3	4	9
10	Bena	7	7	8
	Chagga	9	9	9
	Chamorro	4	6	10
	Chenchu	8	2	8
	Chewa	8	8	9
15	Chiricahua	8	9	10

Table 7.1 Continued

		Ghosts	Humans	Spirits
	Comanche	2	5	8
	Copper Eskimo	8	7	8
	Dahomeans	7	6	7
	Dobuans	0	8	9
20	Dusun	8	0	9
	Flathead	0	0	4
	Hopi	0	8	9
	Ifugao	8	8	10
	Jivaro	4	10	9
25	Kazak	0	0	8
	Kiwai	4	9	9
	Kurtatchi	4	9	6
	Kutenai	0	6	0
	Kwakiutl	8	10	8
30	Kwoma	4	10	4
	Lakher	0	7	9
	Lamba	9	4	10
	Lapp	8	10	9
	Lepcha	3	7	5
35	Lesu	3	9	3
	Malekula	7	10	7
	Manus	11	4	11
	Maori	9	9	10
	Marquesans	8	7	10
40	Marshallese	9	7	9
	Masai	1	6	3
	Murngin	7	10	7
	Nauru	8	9	8
	Navaho	9	7	10
45	Omaha	7	10	7
	Ontong–Javanese	10	6	10
	Paiute	8	11	10
	Palaung	0	8	10
	Papago	8	4	9
50	Pukapukans	8	6	8
	Riffians	0	9	10
	Rwala	0	7	8
	Samoans	8	5	8
	Sanpoil	3	9	9
55	Siriono	3	2	10
	Slave	0	8	4
	Tanala	9	7	9
	Taos	0	10	8
	Tenino	0	8	8
60	Teton	0	0	10

Table 7.1 Continued

		Ghosts	Humans	Spirits
	Thonga	3	7	7
	Tikopia	6	5	8
	Tiv	0	9	10
	Trobrianders	0	10	9
65	Venda	7	9	7
	Wapisiana	0	10	9
	Warrau	0	3	8
	Western Apache	4	8	9
	Witoto	7	10	9
70	Wogeo	6	10	6
	Yagua	0	11	1
	Yakut	5	6	10
	Yukaghir	3	4	10
	Yungar	0	10	8
75	Zuni	4	10	4
			$\mu = 7.17$	$\mu = 7.95$
			$\sigma = 2.81$	$\sigma = 2.28$

Source: Whiting and Child, (1962) pp. 344–346.

Just in passing, we should make it clear that these seventy-five societies are only our small universe for the purposes of this chapter. They are not the universe of all societies, nor are they all primitive societies or any other easily described universe, nor a random sample of any of these. Whiting and Child used these 75 societies because, at time of writing, they were the only cases whose child-rearing practices had been recorded to the extent that Whiting and Child needed. We will treat these 75 cases as a universe in themselves, and try not to think of them as representative of a larger universe — they probably aren't.

Table 7.2 presents the "Fear of Ghosts" universe in tally form. The shape is not much like the "standard" one we have been stressing, the bell-shaped "normal distribution" we'll meet so often in the confirmatory work to come. Single-peaked? Hardly. The distribution is at least double-peaked (clumping around 0 and at 8) and maybe triple-peaked (some lesser clumping around 3 and 4). Symmetric? Not that either. Trailing off smoothly to either side of the centre? Not with all those zeros. The ugliness of this bumpy shape is a welcome sight because the distributions that we study often *are* ugly (though not often as far from the normal shape as this); and it is important for us to know how samples behave even when they are taken from less-then-perfectly-normal universes. Table 7.2 also reports the mean and standard deviation of the universe.

How will we go about sampling from the mini-universe of societies and their scores on fear of ghosts? The procedure used is similar to one that

Table 7.2

The "Fear of Ghosts" Universe

Rating	Distribution
11	1
10	11
9	~~5~~ 11
8	~~5~~ ~~5~~ ~~5~~
7	~~5~~ 111
6	11
5	111
4	~~5~~ 11
3	~~5~~ 111
2	1
1	1
0	~~5~~ ~~5~~ ~~5~~ ~~5~~

Standard Deviation $= \sigma = 3.5$
Mean $= \mu = 4.7$

would be used in sampling on a large universe, and the patterns we will find illustrate things true of sampling generally. Drawing samples would be quite a chore if we tried to do it by flipping coins, worthless if we tried to do it by guess work. Fortunately there is an effective and easy way: use a set of random numbers already worked out by somebody else! (or something else — computers do the actual work). Table A.1 (p. 377), consisting of 2500 random digits, is a small example. The great advantage of a random number table is that the numbers in it are random in very strict senses: in this table, each digit is equally likely to appear at any given place, as is each pair of numbers, each triplet, etc. If we pull out a chunk of a random number table we get a random selection of numbers. So if we want a random selection from a population we can just link each item in the universe with an index number, pull a set of random numbers from the table, and let the universe items with the associated index numbers be our sample.

Let's try this technique out by drawing a random sample from our mini-universe. First we must link each item in the universe with a number; as you can see in Table 7.1, each item has an index number from 01 to 75 (we've just noted the "fives."). Thus, the society with index number "2" is the Ainu, which has a score of "5" on fear of ghosts; don't confuse the "5" which is the datum with the "2" which is its "house number." Now we can use Table A.1, because every pair of digits in this table corresponds to an index number of one unique member of our universe. Seventy-six to ninety-nine, and 00 (the number corresponding to 100), are simply dropped from our sample; there are no elements in the mini-universe that correspond to them). Next, we take as many pairs of random digits from Table A.1 as we need. They can be taken in any way as long as you decide before looking at the table. We decided to start at the upper left and read from left to right along the rows this time; next time we will have to start somewhere else, or go in a different direction. Otherwise we would get the identical sample each time. We will choose ten samples of size two — the "ghost" scores from ten pairs of societies. Reading across Table A.1 we get 15, 77 (we drop this one), 01, 64, 69, 69, etc. These correspond to scores of 8, 3, 0, 7, 7, etc; so our first sample of size two is (8, 3) and the mean of this sample is 5.5. Turn to Table 7.3 for the samples of size two, their means and the grand mean of sample means, $\bar{\bar{x}}$.

This is an easy method and it works. The digits in the random number table are random, so any row or column or diagonal we read off is random, giving us a random selection of identification numbers, and a random sample.

One last problem about drawing simple random samples: sometimes one or more index numbers will come up more than once in a single sample. This didn't happen in any of the samples of size two, but did in the larger samples. This happens less often when sampling from very large universes, but even so it does happen. What to do? There are two sampling strategies here: sampling with — and without — replacement. When sampling without replacement, a data point can be used only once in any particular sample; if its index number is drawn again the second (or third or nth) drawing is ignored. When sampling with replacement (what we did here), if a data point is drawn several times in the sample, it's included that many times just as if it were an entirely new point. Sampling without replacement is similar to playing a hand of poker; once one person draws the ace of clubs, say, it cannot be dealt again. Sampling with replacement is more like roulette; if 17 comes up on one spin, nothing prevents it from coming up again on the very next spin.

We use "sampling with replacement" because the results are a bit

Table 7.3

Random Samples of Size Two, Fear of Ghosts

Sample Number	Index Numbers Selected from Random Number Table	Data Corresponding to Index Numbers Selected	Means
1	15, 01	8, 3	5.5
2	64, 69	0, 7	3.5
3	69, 58	7, 0	3.5
4	40, 16	9, 2	5.5
5	60, 20	0, 8	4.0
6	22, 28	0, 0	0.0
7	26, 46	4, 10	7.0
8	66, 36	0, 7	3.5
9	66, 17	0, 8	4.0
10	34, 40	3, 9	6.0
			$\bar{\bar{x}} = 4.25$

simpler. In practice, most researchers sample universes far larger than the sample size so that there is little practical difference between "with" and "without."

How Samples Behave

Now we have seen one way to get simple random samples and we are ready to consider the question raised earlier: how accurately will the sample mean reflect the universe mean? Tables 7.3 and 7.4 report some sample means to help explore this question.

But Tables 7.3 and 7.4 both have the old problem of unorganized numbers — it's hard to see anything. So we move to 7.5 where the sample means are stem-and-leafed by the size of the samples they come from. For each sample size we have a batch of means, and these batches can be treated like any others — we can see their distributions in the stems-and-leaves, and their means and standard deviations below the stems-and-leaves. Thus familiar techniques from batch analysis can help us to see some points vital to confirmatory analysis.

Table 7.4

Random Samples of Sizes Five and Twenty

N = 5	Ten Samples of size five, each column a sample									
Sample	1	2	3	4	5	6	7	8	9	10
	8	9	7	0	8	8	8	8	0	8
	5	0	6	4	7	8	8	8	3	7
	0	4	8	7	0	7	3	0	3	2
	4	0	9	8	7	9	0	4	8	0
	8	1	0	7	0	0	9	8	2	0
$\bar{x}$	5.0	2.8	6.0	5.2	4.4	6.4	5.6	5.6	3.2	3.4
									$\bar{\bar{x}} = 4.76$	

N = 20	Five Samples of size twenty				
Sample	1	2	3	4	5
	0 4	10 3	0 4	5 0	9 8
	9 0	0 7	8 7	9 3	3 8
	4 3	7 8	3 3	7 8	3 8
	4 6	7 9	5 3	7 10	6 3
	9 0	7 6	0 6	0 8	4 11
	0 0	0 0	4 8	3 0	0 9
	8 0	8 0	8 8	3 7	7 2
	6 0	8 9	8 0	0 4	4 3
	8 5	1 7	7 9	7 3	0 8
	3 8	8 8	8 6	0 0	9 0
$\bar{x}$	3.85	5.65	5.25	4.2	5.25
					$\bar{\bar{x}} = 4.84$

We see that the means of sample means (4.25, 4.76, 4.86) tend to be close to the mean of the universe (4.69). They are not dead on, but then we can't expect them to be. Sometimes a sample or set of samples will be too high or sometimes too low just by chance. This is inevitable, and we must be prepared to live with it, but we would like to know how serious it is likely to be — how far off a sample mean is likely to be from the mean of the universe. We can get insight into this problem by looking at another feature of the batch displays of Table 7.5: the spread. The eye is struck by a strong "funneling" in the batches: as the count grows from 2 to 20, the spread of the sample means narrows strongly. The *sds* of the means show this pattern clearly, the *dqs* less clearly. Means of samples of size 2 often are far away from their batch centre, means of samples of size 20 are usually closer. In general, the larger the sample, the closer an individual sample mean is to the true value in the universe. This is one of the most important features of random sampling because it guarantees that we can get increased accuracy by taking larger samples.

The previous points are new enough and important enough to reiterate: if you take a lot of random samples, the sample means have a distribution (they are a batch); this distribution of the means has a mean of its own, which tends toward the mean of the universe; finally, this distribution of the means has a spread of its own, which gets smaller as the sample size gets bigger.

We can go further than this and tell you exactly how the spread in the batch of sample means is related to the sample size in the long run. In the long run, if you have an enormous number of samples, it can be shown that the batch of sample means has as its standard deviation, the standard deviation of the universe, divided by the square root of the count of the sample.

Table 7.5

Behaviour of Sample Means by Size of Sample

	N = 2		N = 5		N = 20*
	7 | 0				
	6 | 0		6 | 04		
	5 | 55		5 | 0266		5 | 733
	4 | 00		4 | 4		4 | 2
	3 | 555		3 | 24		3 | 9
	2 |		2 | 8		
stem: units	1 |				
leaf: tenths	0 | 0				
$\bar{\bar{x}}$:	4.25		4.76		4.84
sd of means	1.93		1.25		.77
dq:	2.0		2.2		1.1

*rounded to nearest tenth,
0–4 down, 5–9 up.

This quantity is important enough to have a name of its own; the *standard error* (SE). We will not prove this for you, but we will appeal to your intuition. Look at what the formula says: the sample means will be less spread out as the samples get larger (the denominator increases with N), and they will be more spread out if the universe is more spread out (the numerator is the *sd* of the universe). Both these points are pretty reasonable ones. The samples are supposed to reflect the universe, so if the universe has a big spread, the samples should too. And we expect that big samples are more reliable than smaller ones, so larger N should produce samples that tend to have means closer to the true mean (the mean of the universe).

This general rule is meant to apply to the long run, to very large sets of samples; again, we can't expect it to work perfectly for just a few samples because of the sampling fluctuation. But still, if we look at our examples we find that the rule is not far off. The theory says that samples of sizes 2, 5, and 20 should have means whose S.E.s are 2.50, 1.58, and .79 because the standard deviation of the 75 fear-of-ghosts scores is 3.5, and $3.5/\sqrt{2} = 2.50$, etc. In our examples the *sd*s of 1.93, 1.25, and .77 are really quite close to the theoretical values. We would get much closer if we took more samples, because then we would have bigger samples of the samples themselves!

We have several related levels here, so it is handy to distinguish them with special terms to avoid confusion. At the most basic level, we have the universe and its mean and standard deviation (4.7 and 3.5 in our example). We set off universe parameters by giving them Greek letters, so the mean is symbolized by μ (pronounced "mew"), the Greek equivalent of "m" and the standard deviation is symbolized by σ (pronounced sigma), the Greek equivalent of "s." The usage is standard: Greek letters, in statistics, tend to stand for characteristics of a universe.

At the other extreme we have a particular single sample, and it has a mean and a standard deviation too; we label these x and sd_x or s_x (standard deviation of x, the variable we are looking at).

This single sample is one of many that could be drawn. If we draw more than one, the sample means will have a distribution which we call the "sampling distribution of the mean" which we know will have a mean of μ and a standard deviation of $\sigma/\sqrt{N}$ (the standard error) *in the long run*. We know the level and spread of the sampling distribution of the mean; what about its shape? This can't be guessed at from our results in Table 7.5 as easily as the level and spread can be. It would take more samples to get a good look at shape, because shape is a more complex thing than level or spread. If anything, the Table 7.5 batches of means look like they may straggle down just a bit — which seems plausible given that the universe straggles down a bit, with a big clump of values at the bottom. But if we had a lot of samples, with the samples of fairly large size, we would find the batch of sample means to be normal in its shape even though the universe is not. The bumps and lumps in the universe get "averaged out" when sample means are taken, if the samples are reasonably large and plentiful. This will turn out to be another very important result; in statistics this is referred to as the *central limit theorem*.

It Isn't Only Means

We have only looked at sampling distribution of the mean because that will occupy our attention for several more chapters, but you could look at the sampling distribution of anything else and again you would find that the sample values tend to zero in on the universe value more and more closely as the sample size gets bigger.

We will not illustrate this pattern for other features in the detail that we used for the mean, since the basic idea is the same and the number of extra tables required would be excessive. Take a quick look at Table 7.6, which gives the tallies and standard deviations for our five samples of size twenty. Note that these are standard deviations for the samples; so far we have only seen standard deviations for the universe and for the three batches of means. Here, we see that the standard deviations of the samples tend to be like the standard deviation of the universe: the values 3.4, 3.5, 3.0, 3.5, and 3.4 are quite near the universe value 3.5. (In fact they are unusually close for samples of only twenty cases; just an accident.) The larger the sample, the nearer its standard deviation is likely to be to the universe value (a result we do not illustrate here).

The shapes of the five samples of size twenty tend to look rather like the universe shape too. The larger the sample, the closer the resemblance of its shape to the universe. And so on for all of the many batch features one could calculate.

Table 7.6

Distribution of Samples of Size 20

	1	2	3	4	5
11					1
10		1		1	
9	11	11	1	1	111
8	111	‖‖	‖‖ 1	11	‖‖
7		‖‖	11	‖‖	1
6	11	1	11		1
5	1		1	1	
4	111		11	1	11
3	11	1	111	‖‖	‖‖
2					1
1		1			
0	‖‖ 11	‖‖	111	‖‖ 1	111
sd =	3.4	3.5	3.0	3.5	3.4
$\bar{x}$ =	3.85	5.65	5.25	4.2	5.25

Different Kinds of Samples

We have just illustrated simple random sampling (often abbreviated SRS), in which each element of the universe has an equal chance of ending up in the sample. This is the kind of sampling we assume in all the rest of the book; other kinds of random samples also "work" but they introduce minor complications that we would prefer to ignore here. However, it is important to know that there are other important kinds of samples which are useful and often used.

We may not always want the basic type of sample in which all elements have an equal probability of inclusion (like the U.S. draft lottery). Sometimes it is less expensive or more useful just to have a known probability (greater than zero) for each element. For example, a comparison of religious groups might require a greater probability of inclusion for members of smaller groups (Jews, Jehovah's Witnesses, etc.) so that one can get a reasonable number of them without getting far more of the majority of mainline Christians than are needed. Samples with known (but unequal) probabilities of inclusion for various groups (called strata) are known as stratified random samples.

Another sort of problem, and solution, arises where travel costs become more important in the collection of data. Suppose, for example, you are doing a survey of Newfoundlanders, many of whom live in virtually inaccessible outports. If your sample has, say, one hundred outporters in perhaps fifty outports, the costs of just getting interviewers in and out would be immense. It would be much more economical to define your sample in two stages: first, randomly sample the outports (perhaps five of these) and then sample residents within each outport (perhaps twenty in each), thus cutting ninety percent off travel costs. This sort of two-stage procedure is called a cluster sample. Most large studies use combinations of cluster and stratified samples called multistage samples. Be aware, though, that should you be working with a sample more complex than SRS some formulae may require modification. Consult either a statistician, or a book on sampling.

So far we've been talking as if it were easy to obtain perfectly random samples. All too often, however, we just can't avoid working with biased data. For example, it is very difficult and expensive to get more than 80% or 90% of the people randomly selected for a survey to actually take part. Among typical nonrespondents are people on the move, people with fewer years of school, people uninterested in the research area, etc.; thus the effective sample, the people you get data for, tends to be biased towards residential stability, higher education, concern about the research, etc. Biased data can still be useful as long as we know about how large the bias is so we can allow for it. Kish (1965) provides a very useful discussion of the consequences of non-randomness, different kinds of sampling, and other important topics.

Sample Size

If you are doing a study, how big a sample do you need? It depends on what you are looking for. If the patterns you expect to find are very strong (like big differences between batch means) then a relatively small sample may do; if you are looking for a subtle effect, a larger N will be needed. If you know roughly what kinds of data patterns and what kind of statistics you will work with, you can calculate the necessary N; we will give a small example later.

Sample size also depends on how many things you look at; for example, if you examine the relationship among many variables at once then more cases are needed than for looking at just a few variables.

The necessary N can be a lot smaller than you might expect. National surveys, in which many variables are examined and many of the patterns are weak, can be done quite comfortably with two thousand cases or fewer. To get more would actually be a waste for most purposes: the bigger the sample, the less rapidly $\sqrt{N}$ grows and the less we gain by adding another case. If we have samples with $N = 1600$, the standard error is

$$\frac{\sigma}{\sqrt{N}} = \frac{\sigma}{40}; \text{ if } N = 6400, SE = \frac{\sigma}{80} .$$

Because we use the square root of sample size, we must quadruple the sample (and expense and trouble) to cut the standard error in half. It's a problem of diminishing returns. Researchers very rarely get samples of more than a few thousand, even if they can afford to, unless they have a very compelling reason, such as interest in a special group that can't be easily identified in advance. (If it could be listed in advance the researcher could just opt for stratified sampling, getting as many cases from the special group as needed without getting an overdose of the rest of the universe.)

Combining and Dividing Samples

A random sample can be subdivided into smaller random samples — just break it up randomly. This simple property turns out to be very useful indeed. If you have a large sample, it is often desirable to take a small subsample, explore it, then test your ideas with the rest of the original sample, which is a perfectly good random sample itself. Or you can take a small part for open-ended exploring to get broad ideas, then take a somewhat bigger part to polish these ideas into precision, and test the precise predictions on the remainder. Each of the subsamples is a random sample and reflects the universe as far as its N allows; each is an independent sample, and you can do whatever you like to one and be free to do what you like to another.

On the other hand it can be useful to know that two random samples of the same universe can be combined, making one larger, but still random sample. This is handy if several comparable samples are available and none is big enough for the job at hand. Even if the samples are not exactly alike, a little artfulness can often succeed in merging them effectively.

Overview

The relationship between a sample and its universe depends on two things: how you select the sample and how big it is. If the sample is chosen non-randomly then the sample is likely to be a biased picture of the universe and it is wise to be careful, correcting for the bias as far as possible and being cautious in drawing conclusions. If the sample is probably badly biased but you don't know enough about the bias to correct it, you are safest sticking to exploration. In the long run, this may help you get a fix on the size and kind of bias.

If your sample is selected randomly then you are in the much happier position of knowing what its relationship to the universe is like: the larger the sample, the closer any of its statistics is likely to be to the value for the universe. You now know exactly how this works for one very important statistic, the mean. If a very large number of samples of size N are drawn and their means calculated, the sample means have the same mean, μ, as the universe and they have standard deviation $\sigma/(\sqrt{N})$ (also called standard error).

Bigger samples are more accurate. Bigger samples can also be used more flexibly, for example one can afford to use part of a large sample for exploration. But there always comes a point (varying with the research goals) when a larger N is not worthwhile. Finally, samples can be randomly subdivided or, if comparable, they can be merged, and the results are random samples too.

Homework

1. Table 7.1 presents data on fear of humans and of spirits in Whiting and Childs's seventy-five societies. For either one of these, select ten random samples of size 4 and ten samples of size 10. Discuss what you find, remembering to bring in:

> universe mean and standard deviation (see Table 7.1), how you drew your sample, e.g. where you started in Table A.1, which direction you went in, etc.;

the means of each of the samples, standard deviation of the two batches of sample means, and standard errors.

The sampling procedure is easy but a little dull; working with a friend is suggested.

We will be using means, variances and standard deviations a lot in this set of chapters. This might be a good time to review chapter 3.

8

Confirmatory Statistics

In this chapter we continue our search for ways to generalize the ideas gained from exploratory work. In chapter 7 we learned about the random sample, on which all confirmatory work is based. In this chapter we begin to show how such samples are used to make decisions about patterns in the universe as a whole. We will discuss the procedure in general and will describe one very simple case in particular.

Confirmatory work begins with random samples and ends with con-conclusions about the universes from which the samples come. The conclusions can be wrong; for example, we have seen that a sample mean can, by chance, be far from the mean of the universe, and hence can be really misleading. But the golden thing about samples is that we know *how likely* it is that a sample result has seriously misled us; individual samples can be very unpredictable, but the samples in the long run behave very predictably. Here we discuss how our knowledge about sample means can be used to test a simple hypothesis. First we'll consider a hypothetical example using very little in the way of new ideas; then we'll discuss some of the new issues and concepts raised.

An Example

Suppose we are interested in a new teaching method which its designers claim will increase IQ in children. Further, let us say that we selected, randomly, 100 children for our test, testing them only after they had gone through the process at which time they were found to have a mean IQ of 107. (We preferred not to test them beforehand because that alone could raise their later IQ scores by giving them practice.) IQ is a much-studied variable, so we know what the universe is like; for this IQ test and children of the age studied, the universe of test scores has a mean of 100 and standard deviation of 14, and the shape is normal. The children exposed to the new method do score higher than the mean for all children (107 is bigger than 100). But that could be an accident. The problem is: can we conclude that the process has increased the IQ scores, or is it reasonable to attribute this difference of 7 points between the sample and the universe simply to sampling fluctuation?

First things first: we note that the children were randomly sampled. So we are not observing higher scores just because of some bias (as would happen if, say, the test had been done on good students or if the students had been pretested). The students were originally selected to be representative of the universe, not to be a smarter part of it. But the random selection, as we know now, does not guarantee perfect representation; as we saw from the samples in chapter 7, a sample will almost never have a mean that's exactly μ, thus a mean greater than μ would be expected about half the time just by chance. Hence, we have as yet no reason to conclude that the higher IQs were due to the new teaching method. This brings us to our *null hypothesis*, abbreviated H_0, that the teaching method really had no effect. If so, the 100 children are still (even after experiencing the new method) a random sample from the universe and the apparent gain of 7 IQ points can simply be attributed to an accident of random sampling. Now this is always possible; a random sample of this universe could have a mean of 107, or 50, or 200 or whatever. But some of these possibilities are pretty unlikely. What about our result: could it be just a fluke?

To answer that, we first need to know what means of random samples from this universe are like. That's easy after chapter 7. Our $N = 100$, $\mu = 100$, $\sigma = 14$. If we take lots of samples of size 100, their means have mean 100 and standard error

$$\frac{\sigma}{\sqrt{N}} = \frac{14}{10} = 1.4$$

and their shape is normal. Our null hypothesis says that our sample mean is part of this batch. If so, it is a rather unusual member of the batch; it is five standard errors away from the mean: ($7/1.4 = 5$, and our sample mean is 7 points above the mean of the universe). In the exploratory chapters we developed rough rules of thumb for deciding when a case is unusual. Outliers were cases at least $\frac{3}{2}$ dq beyond the quartiles, or about 2 dq beyond the median (assuming the median to be about half-way between the quartiles). Now in this example, using rough confirmatory equivalents (mean, not median, and S.E., not dq) we find that our sample's mean is five spread units from the centre. Even remembering that the confirmatory and exploratory measures are not exactly the same, we can see that our sample's mean is surely an outlying value in the batch of all means of samples of 100 from the universe. If it turns out to be part of that batch it is surely a very unusual case.

In fact, it is so unusual that it does not look like a member of this universe at all. While we must remember that it always could be, it seems much more plausible to say that our sample is not, as H_0 asserts, a random selection of children: in short, we feel obliged to reject H_0. If we do, we are left with a tentative conclusion that the new teaching method worked, making the children's IQ scores higher than one could expect for a typical set of

100 children. This is the *alternate hypothesis* (H_1) in our example. We entertain it tentatively, rather than claiming we have proven it, because H_0 still may be true; and even if H_0 is false, the difference may be due to something other than the teaching method.

Again (as in chapter 7) we have several related layers to keep straight. Perhaps a few diagrams will help. H_0 asserts that our 100 children are a sample from this universe:

IQ SCORES FOR ALL UNTREATED CHILDREN

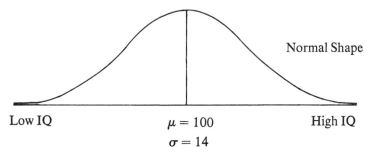

Normal Shape

Low IQ $\mu = 100$ High IQ
                $\sigma = 14$

(This diagram is like a stem-and-leaf turned on its side.)

If so, then the sample mean belongs to the sampling distribution of means of all samples of size 100 that could be taken from this universe:

H_0 DISTRIBUTION OF SAMPLE MEANS, $N = 100$

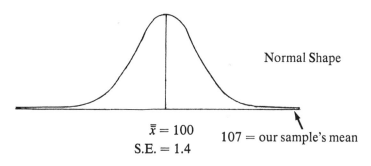

Normal Shape

$\bar{x} = 100$ 107 = our sample's mean
S.E. = 1.4

If H_0 is true, our sample mean fits in about where the arrow points — and it looks pretty odd. (We will show no diagrams of the sample itself. For the purposes of this chapter, we only need to know $\bar{x}$ and N; everything else about the sample is irrelevant.)

Thus, hypothesis testing is a lot like looking for outliers in exploratory work. Begin by assuming that the variables you are interested in are not related (in this case, that the teaching method doesn't raise IQ). Then figure out what things would be like if this null hypothesis, H_0, were true (e.g. if the teaching method does not raise or lower IQ, the children exposed to it should be like a random sample from the universe; specifically, their mean

IQ will be a fairly typical member of the batch of means from samples of size 100). If the results look plausible assuming the H_0 situation, then you can't reasonably reject H_0; but if your results are very unusual, an outlying value, you can reject H_0 as unlikely.

But this broad sketch is not enough. We have been using phrases like "very unusual case," loose impressionistic phrases. That's fine for exploration, where rules of thumb and intuitive interpretations are routine and useful. It won't do for confirmatory where we want to know exactly where we stand; we need more precise results usable for conclusions (not insights) and public (not private) communications. For this reason it's necessary to know exactly how unusual a case we have. Happily, as we will see later in this chapter, this is not very hard.

But before considering this let's try to look systematically at the elements of hypothesis testing.

The Logic of Testing

To help illustrate some of the basic steps in the hypothesis-testing strategy, an analogy to the courtroom may be useful. Consider that in both confirmatory work and the courtroom we want to compare some strongly held hypothesis to suitable evidence in an appropriate way and come to a reasonable conclusion about whether the hypothesis is acceptable or not. Now it is time to look a little harder at what this goal implies. How do we make reasonable conclusions, what do we make them about, what is "reasonable," what sort of evidence do we need to work with? Let us examine some of the basic and familiar elements of criminal courtroom procedure and then compare this procedure with the process of confirmation in data analysis.

1. The charge must be carefully specified. Before the trial even begins, the defendant must be indicted; that is, there is a specific accusation that the defendant committed an act or acts at a specific time or times. Thus the defendant is not required to defend himself against an amorphous charge; if it's often difficult to find an alibi for a single specific time and place, imagine the problems of the defendant if the time and place aren't even specified!

2. A major element in our legal system is the assumption of innocence; a defendant is assumed innocent until proven guilty, even though the prosecution clearly believes the defendant guilty. After all, there are large monetary costs in any trial, large social costs in glutted court calendars and large professional costs to the prosecutor who tries too many cases that result in acquittals. The burden of proof rests with the prosecution and if, after the trial, the result is ambiguous, the defendant is found "not guilty." There is no verdict of "innocent," unless the local "Perry

Mason" manages to fasten the guilt clearly on someone else; rather, the verdict just states that the defendant was not demonstrated to be guilty.

3. The criminal trial is based on the adversary system; competition between defense and prosecution together with rules of evidence. In this way, it is hoped, only proper, unbiased evidence will result.

4. In order to convict, the evidence should be conclusive "beyond a reasonable doubt." The value to society of this requirement is that more harm accrues from convicting an innocent person than from failing to convict a guilty person. Indeed, a familiar rule of thumb is, "better a hundred guilty men go free than one innocent man be convicted." It is expected that we will make some mistakes (no decision is without some risk of error); and we see here that one sort of error, finding a guilty person not guilty, is strongly preferred to the other sort of error, convicting the innocent.

Table 8.1

The Possible Courtroom Decisions

		Verdict	
		Innocent	Guilty
Real State of Affairs:	Innocent	Justice	Error Type I or α
	Guilty	Error Type II, or β	Justice

We can see this line of thought in table form in Table 8.1. This sets out the possible decisions: the court may decide that a man is guilty when he really is, or is not, and may decide that he is innocent when he really is, or is not. If the verdict and truth correspond, the process of justice has worked as it was supposed to and an appropriate decision has been made. But unfortunately errors do happen. In one type of error (Type I error or α error in the table) the accused is innocent but is found guilty; in the other (Type II error or β error) the accused is guilty but found innocent. One way to restate the rule of thumb mentioned earlier is, "Try to have 100 Type II errors for every Type I." If you decide on a verdict of "guilty" you risk the first kind of mistake, and if you choose a verdict of "not guilty" you risk the second kind of mistake; there is no choice you can make which avoids mistakes entirely. There is always some risk in decision, and you can't even escape the risk of error by making no decision because non-decision (here a "hung jury") is itself a kind of decision with risks and costs of its own. If the person is guilty, then he has been set free incorrectly; if the person is innocent, the trial has failed to clear him, and the social costs for him may be immense.

In short, then, the familiar courtroom procedure has four important attributes. These are: an explicit accusation prior to the trial, assumption of the opposite state of affairs from that which the prosecution believes, the reliance on unbiased evidence through the adversary system, and the necessity that guilt (the prosecution's cherished belief) be demonstrated beyond a reasonable doubt. With minor variations the process of testing hypotheses with confirmatory statistics can be seen to possess these same four attributes.

In the same way that an explicit accusation is made prior to the trial, for example, the researcher is obliged to make a careful and explicit prediction prior to looking at the test data, usually prior to collecting it. Unlike the indictment, however, the hypothesis can vary in degree of specificity. Consider predictions involving means, for example. When little is known about the effects of a treatment, the hypothesis may simply be that two (or more) universes have different means for some attribute under consideration: perhaps children from urban areas are less able to resist pressure to conform than children from rural areas, perhaps the reverse. We expect a difference, but it's not clear which way the difference will go. This form of test is known as "two-tailed." If more is known, the direction of the relation may be specifiable: for example, on the basis of theory and other data first-born children can be predicted to have higher IQs that later-borns. This is a "directional hypothesis," which is tested by a one-tailed test.

The assumption of innocence, too, has a direct analogue in hypothesis testing. Here, the researcher formulates each problem in terms of a null hypothesis (H_0) which specifies that there is no difference between the various populations or treatments; like the assumption of innocence, this is clearly not what the researcher believes. This null hypothesis is held until it is disproven in favour of our preferred expectation, the alternative hypothesis (H_1). Again as in the court, failure to disprove H_0 is not the same as proving H_0.

The research process, however, does not make use of an adversary system to obtain unbiased evidence; instead, we depend for unbiased data on an element of our methodology, the random sample. We have just learned about many of its important properties. The adversary system also attempts to prevent unwarranted deductions from the evidence; in social science research, publication serves this function.

Finally, while we prefer not to make any errors, we are particularly averse to Type I errors, again like the court (see Table 8.2). We do not want to make Type I errors too easily because they affect our actions more; if an alternative hypothesis is accepted, it may often be assumed in subsequent research. If it has been accepted because of a Type I error, that error will be compounded in the subsequent research and decisions. However, if we make a Type II error we just sigh deeply and go on looking. After all, in research as in the courts and in life generally, there is no way to avoid these risks; once again, making no decision is a decision too. If we refuse to say whether a null hypothesis is rejected or not then we may in effect have made a decision to do nothing, which is sometimes the most costly error of all.

So in both cases, the courtroom trial and the statistical test, we put most of our effort into minimizing errors of Type I; but what we really would like to get is as little error of either kind as possible. How can we avoid both kinds of errors and get as much justice or accurate knowledge as possible? One major strategy is to use evidence-evaluation procedures that get the most out of the evidence, that let us make better and better decisions on the basis of the same amount of data. For example, consider the use of more and more powerful forensic techniques in the courts. Faced with a hand print, Sherlock Holmes had to make do with broad measures like hand size in showing who was at the scene of the crime, and errors were quite likely; many people have size 8 hands, so a size eight hand print might or might not have been left at the scene by the (size eight) suspect. Nowadays much more exact devices such as fingerprinting can be used. When the techniques are more exact the decisions are less risky. In particular, we can keep the risk of convicting an innocent man low (i.e. avoid Type I errors) while at the same time reducing the risk of acquitting the guilty (i.e. bringing down the rate of Type II errors).

A similar pattern is found in statistics: some statistical tests are able to make finer distinctions than others, some can reduce the risk of rejecting the null erroneously while not increasing the risk of erroneously failing to reject it. We speak of these tests as having greater *power* compared to other tests. To put this more exactly,

α is the chance that we will reject H_0 when H_0 is true

β is the chance that we will not reject H_0 when it is false

$1-\beta$ is the *power of the test* (that is, its power to correctly reject the null hypothesis).

Various confirmatory tests differ in power and we can usually choose the highest power test. (The tests we emphasize in this book are quite powerful, which is one reason for their popularity.)

Table 8.2

The Possible Test Decisions

		Decision on Null Hypothesis	
		Accept	Reject
In Reality Null Hypothesis is:	True	Correct Decision	Type I (α) Error
	False	Type II (β) Error	Correct Decision

More powerful tests often are based on more stringent assumptions about the batches of data tested; the spreads should be similar, the shapes symmetric, the counts (nearly) equal, and so on. Fortunately the tests we examine in this volume are quite *robust*; in statistics, this means that the data being examined do not need to satisfy these assumptions totally. For each of the tests we examine we will consider, at least briefly, its theoretical assumptions as well as the extent to which they may be violated. Finally, we can almost always increase power by increasing sample size.

Before going further, let's sum up the major steps in hypothesis testing as we have them so far:

1. A null hypothesis, H_0, is constructed which we expect and hope to reject in favour of the alternative hypothesis H_1. H_1 may be quite loose. For a comparison of two means, H_1 may just assert there is some difference (two-tailed test); H_1 may also specify a direction, in which case we have a one-tailed test.

2. A statistical test is chosen, keeping its assumptions and robustness in mind. Naturally you pick the most powerful one appropriate to the data, thus minimizing Type II error.

3. It is decided whether to accept or reject H_0. To do this, compute the test statistic for your data. Then find out how likely it is that you could get such a statistic (or one even more extreme) if H_0 is true. This likelihood (or probability) is found in the statistical table that goes with the particular test used.

Most of this is pretty simple once you get over the initial shock of having to disprove the null hypothesis rather than proving H_1, the one you probably believe in. However, some of the process has not been discussed very much so far, step 3 in particular.

Much of step 3 goes beyond this chapter and into all the other confirmatory chapters in this book, for all the other confirmatory chapters boil down to figuring out how probable the observed data are, if H_0 is really true. Different kinds of data and hypotheses require different tests so there are many ways to do the computations. The basic logic is usually the same, though. You might find it useful to read this general discussion of testing again after a few more chapters, when you know more tests and can see how the basic logic is used repeatedly. For now, let's return to our example and do a test on it.

Children's IQs Continued

Now we can return to our original example of testing a process that purported to raise IQs in children. You will recall that the mean IQ of children taught in the new way is 5 SEs above the mean of the means of all samples of that size. How likely is it that our batch mean would be so far away from this grand mean? We may ask this question in a different way: what proportion of the sample means are as high as our batch mean or even higher? If it's a very small fraction, then this is an unusual case. The probability of getting a sample with a given property (e.g. a sample five or more SEs above the mean) is just the proportion of all samples that have that property. Again, we often got a rough feel for probability in exploratory work; where a stem-and-leaf had just a few cases (usually at the extremes), cases were viewed as unusual, while where the cases were thick (usually the middle) they were seen as quite typical.

Now for a normal distribution we can get at the same sort of idea in a much more formal way. The exact proportion of cases in any part of a normally distributed batch has been worked out to as many decimal points as you are ever going to need. Table A.2 (p. 378) gives these values for the "standard normal distribution," called Z for short, a hypothetical batch with infinitely many cases, perfect normal shape, mean of zero and standard deviation of one. This table is invaluable, so let's spend a minute learning how to read it. The numbers down the left hand side give the values of Z to one decimal place, and the numbers across the top give the second decimal place. Thus where the row labelled 1.2 and the column labelled .06 intersect, we find information about a Z of 1.26. That information is the proportion of Z cases as far away from the mean as 1.26 or farther, that is, the *probability* of getting a Z-value as big as 1.26 or bigger, and that value is seen to be .1038, about one-tenth. Normal distributions are perfectly symmetrical, so this table is fine for both halves of Z; the half above the mean (zero) and the half below. For example, the probability of a Z value as small as -1.26 or smaller is also .1038.

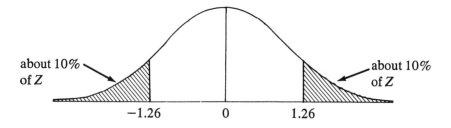

about 10% of Z about 10% of Z

-1.26 0   1.26

But, you ask, what good is Z to us? We're thinking about an example where the H_0 distribution of sample means is normal but its mean is 100 and its *sd* is 1.4. No problem at all: just think back to standardization. If we remove level and spread from a batch, as follows:

$$\frac{\text{observation} - \text{level}}{\text{spread}},$$

we get a new batch with new level of zero and new spread of one but nothing else changed; the shape is the same, so the probabilities are the same too. So we can standardize our H_0 distribution (in confirmatory terms, of course) by finding

$$\frac{observation - 100}{1.4},$$

which has a mean 0 and *sd* 1, just like Z; and it will still be normal. In fact, it is Z! That's why Z is called the *standard* normal distribution. Any normal distribution becomes Z when standardized. So the Z table is the only normal table that we need (very handy)!

Back to our example. We want to know how likely it is that we would get a sample of 100 with mean 107 if H_0 is true. We know the sampling distribution of the mean is normal, with mean 100 and SE 1.4, if H_0 is true. So let's standardize and turn to the Z table, thus:

$$Z = \frac{107 - 100}{1.4}$$

$$= 5.00$$

as we noted before. The probability of a value as big as this or bigger is about .0000003, which is pretty small! This means that the probability of our result or one more extreme if H_0 is true is about three in ten million. This is so small that we just can't believe H_0 is true; it's too unlikely, hence the decision is to reject H_0. We say that the mean IQ of the specially trained sample of children is *significantly* greater than 100, the μ under the null hypothesis; that is, H_0 could still be true but it's too unlikely for us to hold to.

The Basic Z-test Procedure

We have discussed this example at length, with a discussion of hypothesis testing in general thrown in; of course, this is not what you usually have to go through to do a simple Z-test! So let's review the process step by step as it would routinely be done.

First, what do we need for a Z-test? We must be interested in some variable x which is measured numerically (in order that means and so on can be found). We must know the universe mean and the standard deviation of x, that is, μ and σ. We must assume that the shape of this universe is normal, or we must have a fairly large sample, at least 30 or 40 cases; the normality assumption can be violated fairly freely for large samples. This robustness with respect to normality has been proven empirically by looking at samples drawn from non-normal universes. We also need a random sample, size N, for which x has been measured to give us the sample mean, $\bar{x}$.

How do we treat these components? Our basic question is, how different are $\bar{x}$ and μ? So our two hypotheses are:

$H_0: \bar{x} = \mu$

$H_1: \bar{x} \neq \mu$ if the test is two-tailed,

   or $\bar{x} > \mu$ if the test is one-tailed and we expect that x will be bigger than μ.

   or $\bar{x} < \mu$ if the test is one-tailed and we expect that x will be smaller than μ.

We must decide whether H_1 will be one-tailed or two-tailed before doing the rest of the test. We must also decide beforehand on an α-level, or how unlikely our sample results must seem before we decide we can't accept H_0. Usually people use $\alpha = .05$, or $\alpha = .01$ if they want to be very careful. Decisions about α, and about whether the test is one- or two-tailed are made in advance to avoid temptation; if you have strong feelings about a topic it is hard to avoid bending the confirmatory rules in the direction of the results you would prefer.

Then we are ready to compute a Z score.

$$Z = \frac{\bar{x} - \mu}{\sigma / \sqrt{N}}$$

That is, we compare the observed difference of the means $(\bar{x} - \mu)$ to the standard error of means of size N if H_0 is true $(\sigma/\sqrt{N})$. We can then look up Z in our normal Table A.2. As we argued before, as Z gets more extreme we are more sure that the difference $\bar{x} - \mu$ is no accident. The Z-table tells us just how sure we can be, because this table gives the probability of getting a Z of a given size or one even more extreme. Finally, if this probability is α or less, we decide to reject H_0. If this probability is greater than α, we decide we can't reject H_0.

Hypothesis testing can give us very precise information, but at a price. To get precise results you have to first make precise assumptions (here we assumed a normal distribution for IQ scores with a mean of 100 and sd of 14). Then you have to use mathematically tractable measures (here, mean and standard deviation) which sacrifice a great deal of resistance. Finally, you have to feed in suitable data (a good random sample). These are much stronger demands than exploratory analysis called for, but they produce results that are needed.

Using the Z-table: An Easier Way

Many people are initially turned off by the Z-table; it's too full of numbers, far more than we are likely to need. If this bothers you, take a look at Table 8.3. To use this table, just decide on an α-level, and whether the test is one- or two-tailed. Look up the appropriate row and column in Table 8.3 to find the *critical value*, or the least extreme Z-value needed to make H_0

Table 8.3

Critical Values for the Z-test

	α – Levels			
	.05	.01	.005	.001
One Tail	1.645	2.326	2.576	3.090
Two Tails	±1.960	±2.576	±2.805	±3.291

unacceptable. For example, consider a one-tailed test with $\alpha = .05$. Let's say we expect $\bar{x}$ will be smaller than μ ($H_1 : \bar{x} < \mu$). The big Z-table (Table A.2) tells that five percent of the Z-values are less than or equal to -1.645 if H_0 is true:

 H_0 Distribution

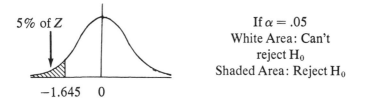

5% of Z

-1.645 0

If $\alpha = .05$
White Area: Can't
reject H_0
Shaded Area: Reject H_0

So if our Z works out to -1.645 or less, we will reject H_0. Thus -1.645 is the *critical value* of Z here: we reject H_0 for any Z this far from zero or farther. Knowing this *CV* (critical value) we don't need the large Table A.2.

The tables you will see for other tests are more like 8.3 than A.2: they just provide critical values for selected significance levels. They tell you how extreme your statistic must be in order to be the kind of thing that happens only (say) five percent of the time if H_0 is true ($\alpha = .05$).

Another Example

Consider the following (hypothetical) problem. A social psychologist is doing research on conformity, using a measure which has been validated on urban males and found to have a mean μ of 3.1 and standard deviation σ of 4.8. The researcher next turns to a random sample of 500 rural males and finds that they have a mean $\bar{x}$ of 3.5. What should he conclude? We can simply do the Z-test step by step as before. The first part is just like the previous example: we know μ, σ, $\bar{x}$, N. We do not know whether the population is normal but the N is so large that this almost certainly won't matter. The sample is random. Fine: we have all we need for a Z-test.

Next we set up H_0 and H_1. Here there is an important change from the previous example. Was there any reasonable way that we could have very confidently predicted that rural males would score higher on this test? Not so far as we know. Therefore, we must use a two-tailed test because we could not confidently have predicted the direction of the difference; it was, of course, easy once we had seen the results, but the decision should be made ahead of time and on compelling grounds. For a two-tailed test we have the following hypotheses:

$$H_0: \bar{x} = \mu$$
$$H_1: \bar{x} \neq \mu.$$

Let's use $\alpha = .05$. For a two-tailed Z-test at the 5% level, the critical values are ± 1.96. Now we can compute the observed Z:

$$Z = \frac{\bar{x} - \mu}{\sigma/\sqrt{N}}$$

$$= \frac{3.5 - 3.1}{4.8/\sqrt{500}} = \frac{.4}{4.8/22.36} = \frac{.4}{.215}$$

$$= 1.86$$

In diagram form again, if H_0 is true then $\frac{\bar{x} - \mu}{\sigma/\sqrt{N}} = Z$ is part of the Z-distribution:

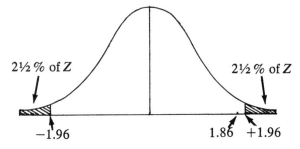

Our observed Z does not look like an especially unusual member of this batch; it is between the two critical values, so we know we could get a value like 1.86 more than 5% of the time just by chance when H_0 is true. In other words, the observed value of Z is less extreme than either critical value. Therefore, we can't reject H_0; we are unable to conclude, at this level of significance, that rural males differ from urban males as regards conformity. The results are, however, suggestive and would appear to be worth further research. We don't reject H_0 but we do keep thinking about conformity, urban and rural.

Sample Size

In the previous chapter, in discussing how large a sample should be, the answer was left rather vague. We are now in a position to tighten this up a bit. In order to estimate minimum sample size for a Z-test problem we must know one thing about the universe, its standard deviation, σ; and we must make two decisions, the smallest difference you are interested in, that is, $(x - \mu)$; and the significance level at which you wish to detect this difference. For example, suppose in our IQ example we wanted to be able to detect an IQ gain of five points, at the .01 level (one-tailed, as it's only a gain we are interested in).

$$Z = \frac{\bar{x} - \mu}{\sigma/\sqrt{N}} \text{ gives us for } \alpha = .01$$

$$\bar{x} - \mu = 5$$
$$\sigma = 14$$

So: Z must be at least 2.326 (see Table 8.3).

$$2.326 = \frac{5}{14/\sqrt{N}} \text{ and we just solve for } N$$

$$\frac{32.564}{\sqrt{N}} = 5$$

$$\sqrt{N} = 6.513$$

$$N \simeq 43$$

Here our omnibus formula plus a little high school algebra gives pretty strong results. The same idea can be applied to other tests.

Homework

1. To find the two-tailed critical values in Table 8.3, we found values of Z that marked off an interval symmetric around 0 and including $1 - \alpha$ of the Z-distribution. Find Z-values symmetric around 0 and including the following proportions of the distribution: .50, .75, .999. For what α-levels are these the critical values?

2. A test of reading achievement is scored so that the universe mean and standard deviation are 50 and 10, respectively. What proportion of the students score:

    a. less than 43? more than 47?
    b. between 56 and 62? between 48 and 81?

What scores are in the lowest quartile? the lowest decile? the second lowest decile?

3. On a standard test of mathematical skills, the mean score is 100 with a standard deviation of 10. A teacher tries out a new teaching method with a class of 30 randomly selected students and finds their mean performance is 103.

    a. Can he conclude that the new method is more effective than usual methods?

    b. How large a sample of students would we need to reliably detect a difference of this size (103 vs. 100) at the .02 significance level? the .001 level?

4. Here is a harder question; it is open-ended, and part of the problem is to define the problem: to describe how a broad question can be turned into a Z-test problem, and to point out the assumptions made in doing so.

    Suppose that you are interested in fear of spirits. Before looking at the available data (Table 7.1) you decide that you are especially interested in fear of spirits in North American primitive societies as compared to fear of spirits in all 75 societies. Discuss how you might go about setting up a Z-test. Consider in detail: nature of the universe, randomness of sample, definition of H_0 and H_1, and so on.

9

When σ Is Not Known

The previous chapter (we hope!) made hypothesis testing look fairly easy. It does mean getting used to a new way of thinking, but that's mainly a matter of practice. The procedural details are simple and straightforward. If we know the universe mean and standard deviation, μ and σ, we can always tell how likely we would be to obtain a sample mean at least as extreme as a given $\bar{x}$ if sampling that universe. If the probability of this event is small, then we would reject the null hypothesis ($\bar{x} = \mu$) in favour of the alternative ($\bar{x} \neq \mu$ if two-tailed; $\bar{x} > \mu$ or $\bar{x} < \mu$ if one-tailed). If the probability is not small, then we tentatively retain the null hypothesis. To find the probabilities, all we need to do is compute the ratio:

$$Z = \frac{\bar{x} - \mu}{\sigma/\sqrt{N}}$$

and look it up in a Z-table; this turns Z scores directly into probabilities.

Unfortunately, like many problems that are easy to solve, this situation rarely occurs in the real world because we only rarely know the true variance of a universe. Our knowledge of a universe is not often so complete. Therefore, we must decide what to do in the more typical situation which is like the Z-test but with one piece of information missing: there is an $\bar{x}$, and a μ to compare it to, but we do not know σ. Now we have already suggested in chapter 7 that sample values tend to reflect universe values, and this is true for standard deviations as well as for means (although we discussed means more thoroughly). So why not use the sample standard deviation to estimate the universe value, σ? This is in fact just what we do. In symbols,

$$\hat{\sigma} = sd = \sqrt{\frac{\Sigma(x_i - \bar{x})^2}{N-1}}$$

This says that the estimated standard deviation of the universe, $\hat{\sigma}$, equals the standard deviation of the sample. (Statisticians often use "$\wedge$," called a "hat," to denote an estimate.)

The test created in this way is called the t-test, and the formula for calculating t-values looks nearly identical to the formula for calculating Z-values:

$$t_{N-1} = \frac{\bar{x} - \mu}{\hat{\sigma}/\sqrt{N}} \quad \text{where} \quad Z = \frac{\bar{x} - \mu}{\sigma/\sqrt{N}}$$

157

Comparing the t-formula to the Z-formula shows that the basic idea is the same: the size of a difference (the top part) is compared to the size of sampling fluctuations one can expect if H_0 is true (the bottom part). Still, there is a difference between the statistics which should be explained.

A feature in the t-formula but not in the Z-formula is the subscript "N–1" appended to the t. This refers to the number of *degrees of freedom* or *df*, which is N–1 here. Why this extra complexity? Well, we have a less simple problem now because we have less certainty in our formula. In the Z-test only *one* thing was an estimate: $\bar{x}$, which is an estimate of μ when the null hypothesis is correct. All of the uncertainty in the case of the Z-test arose from the sampling variability of the $\bar{x}$ estimate. But things are different now: we have an estimate not only in the numerator ($\bar{x}$), but also in the denominator ($\hat{\sigma}$). This extra element of uncertainty has to be accommodated somehow, and we do so by using different tables for different *df*; since *df* is equal to the count minus one, this amounts to having different tables for different sample sizes.

To get a feeling for what is happening, consider the following two hypothetical batches:

A		B	
10	$sd_A = 1.41$	9	11
12		9	11
		9	12 $\quad sd_B = 1.43$
		10	12
		10	13

Which batch gives us the more secure feeling, the feeling that our estimates of mean and standard deviation are more soundly based? Clearly batch B, not batch A, even though batch A has the smaller standard deviation. The difference in the size of the two batches seems to matter to our intuition, and intuition and mathematics are in agreement here. Thus, if we calculate a t-value for a small batch like A and one for a larger batch like B, we would want to be a good deal more cautious about the t-value from the smaller batch. In other words, we want to see a much bigger discrepancy between $\bar{x}$ and μ before rejecting the null hypothesis; that is, we want to have a larger (more extreme) critical value.

Have a look at Table A.3 (p. 380), a table of critical values for t, and you will see that this is happening. The first column of figures on the far left gives degrees of freedom, or $N - 1$. The double line of figures at the top gives α-levels, either one-tailed (upper row) or two-tailed (lower row). If you look from left to right across any row, the critical values increase in size. This is familiar from working with Z: to reduce α, or the risk of wrongly rejecting H_0, we have to use a more extreme critical value so we have less chance of a Type I error. (By the way, t is symmetric, like Z, so these values do for either positive or negative t.) The novelty here is what happens within any column, that is for a fixed α but differing degrees of freedom. As $N - 1$ gets larger and larger, increasing our confidence in the estimate of universe standard deviation, the entries in the table get smaller and smaller. H_0 can be rejected more and more easily because the accuracy of our estimate of σ increases as $N - 1$ does. At some point we get very accurate estimates indeed, so accurate that we might as well assume that our estimate is the same as σ. What then? Why, we can go right back to the Z-test! Look at the last row of the t-table, where the dfs are infinitely large, so our estimate of σ should be perfect: the values for t are exactly the same as the values for Z! They have to be, because the only real difference between t and Z, the uncertainty about σ, has disappeared. When $N = 30$ (or 40 or 50, depending on how conservative you wish to be), the Z-values and t-values are "close enough" that the Z-table may be used rather than the t-table. It is sometimes convenient and the error introduced is small.

There is one other parallel to Z-testing which should be remembered: the t-test is appropriate for *normal* data. If the sample size is small, it is wise to stem-and-leaf the batch and see whether it looks roughly normal; if it doesn't, transform it. But if the sample size is large, then you don't have to worry. (Remember, if N is large then $\bar{x}$ is distributed normally even if individual observations aren't.)

Let's try an example: an artificial one so that we can keep things simple, but not an unrealistic one. As the Dean is reviewing the lists of final grades, he comes to Professor Aardvark's grade list, and he remembers that last year Aardvark's grades were much higher than those of his colleagues. At that time he didn't know whether Aardvark graded more "tenderly" or had a smarter class, so he planned then to test this year's grades against a mean (μ) of 65%, the theoretical "average." If this year's grades are also very high, he may decide to have a few words with Professor Aardvark.

To turn this vignette into a statistical example, we first identify the components. We know μ, which is 65 or the mean grade for students in general. We don't know σ (presumably because no one has bothered to calculate it), so we can't do a Z-test. Our sample is Aardvark's 10 students, whose grades are stem-and-leafed below:

9	4	$N = 10$
8	63	$\bar{x} = 72$
7	15	$sd_x = 12.36$
6	249	
5	88	

stem: tens   *leaf*: units

Now we have all the components we need for a t-test. Before doing one, is it appropriate to do so? Do the data meet the assumptions that should be met for a t-test to be appropriate? First, we look for normality: the sample is small, just ten, so we'd better examine the data. The stem-and-leaf looks all right; it's not perfectly symmetric and bell-shaped but doesn't diverge wildly and there is no serious straggling or clumping or straying values. Checking for random sampling, our second assumption, is trickier, since it depends on how students were chosen for the class and we don't really know. Let's tentatively assume students choose classes at random (not an entirely false assumption!) and go on, remembering that this assumption may need to be checked. We set up our hypotheses:

$$H_0: \bar{x} = \mu = 65$$
$$H_1: \bar{x} > \mu = 65$$

Note that our alternate hypothesis is one-tailed; the Dean had predicted on the basis of last year's grades that these would be higher than average. Next we compute t for our data:

$$t_{N-1} = \frac{\bar{x} - \mu}{sd_x/\sqrt{N}} = \frac{72 - 65}{12.36/\sqrt{10}}$$

$$t_9 = 1.79$$

From our t-table we see that a one-tailed test for nine degrees of freedom and $\alpha = .05$ has a critical value of $t = 1.833$. Our value is not quite extreme enough to reject H_0 (i.e. to chew Aardvark out), but the Dean will probably keep his eye on him carefully. (You can see that this isn't a real life example; in real life, the Dean would probably chew Aardvark out anyway.)

In summary, then, when we are faced with a Z-type problem, but where we don't know the true universe variance, we can test our hypotheses by means of the t-statistic. The t-statistic looks very much like the Z but uses the sample standard deviation in the denominator instead of the (unknown) standard deviation of the universe. Since the accuracy of the substitution depends in large part upon the number of observations we have, we take this number into account via the degrees of freedom of our sample. The greater the df, the more *powerful* the test will be, i.e. the more likely we are to decide correctly when H_1, the alternate hypothesis, is true.

Some Wrinkles

How Can You Find Out What μ Is?

The one-sample t-test is pretty simple, and so are the complications we are about to consider. First, while we must always have a value for μ in order to do the test, there are a number of different ways of finding it. Sometimes μ is known from extensive previous evidence: mean IQ is known to be 100 for many tests. Sometimes μ is a standard which is fixed arbitrarily; for example, in some schools 65 is defined as the proper mean grade and instructors are responsible for making their means as close to that as possible, and spot-checked to see that they are not straying too far from $\overline{x} = 65$ ("grading on a curve" is a more elaborate version of this). Often μ is known even though σ is not; many common sources of data publish means but not variances (for example, censuses often give means only; and the distributions given are usually not detailed enough to allow accurate calculation of variances). Finally, there are times when you can reason out a meaningful μ, as in the next example.

Working with Two Matched Samples

The simple t-formula above was described for one sample, whose mean $\overline{x}$ is compared to μ. The formula can also be used for two samples at once if the samples are *matched*. Consider Table 9.1, from Robert Zajonc's "The Attitudinal Effects of Mere Exposure" (1968) pp. 4–5. Zajonc discusses the relationship between familiarity with things and liking them, using a variety of data. To gather the data in Table 9.1, Zajonc and colleagues gave a list of antonym pairs to 100 students and asked them to judge which member of

Table 9.1

Preference and Frequency of Antonym Pairs

Preference	Word	Frequency	Preference	Antonym	Frequency	(More Preferred–Less)
100	Able	930	0	Unable	239	691
100	Better	2354	0	Worse	450	1904
99	Peace	472	1	War	1118	−646
99	Responsible	267	1	Irresponsible	30	237
99	Smile	2143	1	Frown	216	1927
98	Friend	2553	2	Enemy	883	1670
98	Moral	272	2	Immoral	19	253
97	Important	1130	3	Unimportant	40	1090
97	Profitable	57	3	Unprofitable	12	45
96	Live	4307	4	Die	1079	3228
96	Superior	166	4	Inferior	40	126
93	First	5154	7	Last	3517	1637
91	Always	3285	9	Never	5715	−2430
90	Agree	729	10	Disagree	38	691
78	Long	5362	22	Short	887	4475
67	Infinite	71	33	Finite	2	69
52	Play	2606	48	Work	2720	−114

Source: Zajonc, Robert B., "*The Attitudinal Effects of Mere Exposure*", Journal of Personality and Social Psychology 9:2 pt. 2, 1968. ©1968 by the American Psychological Association. Reprinted by Permission.

each pair had the more pleasant meaning. 100% of the students thought "able" more pleasant than "unable," while 52% preferred "play" to "work," with the other preferences in between. Table 9.1 also includes frequencies of usage for each word; the frequencies were taken from a standard reference. Now if frequency and favourable meaning are linked, the preferred halves of the antonym pairs should be more frequent; so if we find the difference between the frequencies of each pair of antonyms, subtracting the frequency of the less preferred word from that of the more preferred, these differences should, on the whole, be greater than zero. Because we have two sets of matched data, we can reduce them to one set of differences and do a t-test.

Before doing so we consider whether the data satisfy the assumptions that must hold if the t-test is to be appropriate. Are the 17 word pairs in Table 9.1 a random sample? Our source is not clear on this point, so we will have to hope for the best and make a mental note to be cautious. We can see that these pairs are not a sample of words, since many words do not have opposites: does that matter? Are the 17 differences in frequency roughly normally distributed? We have to give this careful attention since an N of 17 is not large enough to allow much leeway here. Note that N is 17 and not 34; we will do our test on 17 differences, not 34 separate words. Similarly, we check normality for the differences, not the original frequencies. For the raw data the differences are found in Table 9.1, then stemmed-and-leafed and plotted in Table 9.2. The plot alone does not look terrible, although there is upward straggle in both the midbox and the extremes, suggesting that transformation is worth trying. The stem-and-leaf looks worse than the plot, for the stem-and-leaf shows two peaks (rather than the

Table 9.2

Checking Normality of Differences
of Word Frequencies

4	5	X_U	4500		X
4					
3					
3	2				
2					
2					
1	9976	q_U	1700		
1	1				
0	717	Md	700	$\overline{D} = 874$	
0	23010	q_L	0		
−0	1				
−0	6				
−1					
−1					
−2	4	X_L	−2400		X

stems: thousands   *leaves*: hundreds

desired single peak), and the lack of symmetry. There is no big problem; we can just transform the data. It is best to transform the original frequencies rather than the differences of frequencies (among other things, the differences have negative values). The logs of the original frequencies are found in Table 9.3, and the differences of logged frequencies are found in 9.3 and stemmed-and-leafed and plotted in Table 9.4. The plot does not look much improved after logging; the midbox still straggles up in the same way and the upper outlier has been replaced by a lower outlier. But perhaps the overall symmetry is better, in that we have no systematic straggling. As a final check of overall symmetry we considered the mean versus the median. For the logged data, Md $= .68$ and $\overline{D} = .67$; for the raw data, Md $= 700$ and $\overline{D} = 874$; the median is clearly much nearer to the mean for the logged data. In the stem-and-leaf we see a very clear advantage for the logged version: it comes much closer to being single-peaked. All in all, logging seems preferable. The results are not quite ideal, but they do not have to be since rough normality is sufficient for a t-test. We will proceed to do a t-test on the differences of logged word frequencies.

Table 9.3

Analysis of Logged Frequencies

Logged Frequency			
Preferred	Opposite	$(P - O) = D$	D^2
2.97	2.38	.59	.3481
3.37	2.65	.72	.5184
2.67	3.05	$-.38$	.1444
2.43	1.48	.95	.9025
3.33	2.33	1.00	1.0000
3.41	2.95	.46	.2116
2.43	1.28	1.15	1.3225
3.05	1.60	1.45	2.1025
1.76	1.08	.68	.4624
3.63	3.03	.60	.3600
2.22	1.60	.62	.3844
3.71	3.55	.16	.0256
3.52	3.76	$-.24$	.0576
2.86	1.58	1.28	1.6384
3.73	2.95	.78	.6084
1.85	.30	1.55	2.4025
3.42	3.43	$-.01$	.0001
		$\sum D = 11.36$	$\sum D^2 = 12.4894$

$$\overline{D} = .67$$

$$\text{VAR(D)} = \frac{12.4894 - 7.5912}{16}$$

$$= .3061$$

$$\text{sd}_D = .5533$$

Table 9.4

*Checking Normality for Differences of
Logged Word Frequencies*

14: 15	5:5	X_U = 1.55		X
12: 13	8:			⋮
10: 11	0:5	q_U = 1.00		⋮
8: 9	:5			⬜
6: 7	028:28	Md = 0.68	$\bar{D}$ = 0.67	⬜
4: 5	6:9	q_L = 0.46		
2: 3				⋮
0: 1	:6			⋮
−1:−0	:1			⋮
−3:−2	8:4	X_L = −0.38		X

If being preferred or not preferred makes no difference to word frequencies, then the differences should be zero overall; so our H_0 is that the true mean of the differences, μ, is zero. (Note that μ does not come from data, but from the nature of H_0). On the other hand our H_1 is based on the argument that liking and familiarity go together; this is a common assertion, so a one-tailed test is reasonable. Thus our hypotheses are:

$H_0: \bar{D} = \mu = 0$ (where D is found by subtracting the log of the fre-
$H_1: \bar{D} > 0$ quency of the opposite from the log of the frequency
                  of the preferred word).

Our last decision is which α to use; let's try .01 for a change.

With assumptions checked out and the basic decisions about H_1 and α made, we are finally ready to compute. From Table 9.3 we find:

$$df = N - 1 = 16$$
$$\bar{D} = .67$$
$$sd_D = .5533$$

And from Table A.3 we find that the critical value of 16 *df*s and α = .01 (one-tailed) is 2.583. Finally we do the test, still using the basic t procedure applied to differences:

$$t_{16} = \frac{\bar{D} - \mu}{sd_D/\sqrt{N}} = \frac{.67 - 0}{.5533/\sqrt{17}} = 4.99$$

so we can easily reject H_0.

There are two things worth discussing: why are the more likeable words more frequent in general, and why are there exceptions to this rule? Zajonc argues that it is familiarity which leads to liking, perhaps because lack of familiarity produces mild discomfort from uncertainty as to know how to respond. We have tested for the opposite causal possibility, liking leading to frequency of use; this is also plausible since people probably enjoy writing and reading about pleasant things. The discrepancies are three cases for which the less preferred word is more frequent: war vs. peace, never vs. always, and work vs. play. The work vs. play case is not striking; work is only a little more frequent and only a little less popular. We confess to puzzlement over "never"; why should it be more frequent than "always"? Pessimism, perhaps? ("Mark my words, it'll never fly!") The greater frequency of war vs. peace is sadly easy to understand; war is typically more common in the news and in our fears.

Matching is often appropriate when one has scores before and after some treatment, when one has subjects identical on all salient variables but one, and so on; and matching lends itself to powerful statistical tests. The process does have some problems (for example, you can't always get close matches for all the cases you would like to use).

But what if we just have two batches, not matched? We might have a randomly selected group of women to compare to a randomly selected group of men on some variable, for example. There is a special form of the t-test that will handle this. However, learning this special form is not really necessary; in the next chapter we are going to show you how to compare the levels of several batches, and the technique we will learn there works for two batches as the simplest case.

Working with Grouped Data

Sometimes N is much larger than the number of possible scores on the variable we're examining, so that data reporting and analysis is faster if we work with groups of equivalent values instead of individual values. For example, students at a Canadian university were asked several questions as part of course evaluations; one question was:

Overall, my opinion of this course was

| 1 | 2 | 3 | 4 | 5 |

a very poor course   an excellent course

You have probably seen this "Likert" type of question format before.

In one course (*not* one of the authors'!) there were 36 student ratings: six students circled 1, twelve circled 2, and so on. Instead of working with the 36 individual replies we can work with the five possible ratings and their frequencies:

Rating	Frequency
(poor) 1	6
2	12
3	9
4	6
(excellent) 5	3
	$N = 36$

Results from the total course survey showed that the average course rating (the mean for all students' ratings of all courses) was 3.0. This particular course was clearly lower than average. How could the instructor decide whether his course's rating is significantly lower than average?

Before proceeding we check the assumptions. The ratings are not normally distributed but an N of 36 is large enough to make up for this. The assumption of random sampling may not hold, as it didn't in the Aardvark example; but there's no obvious reason why this course should get unusually critical students. The instructor decides on a 5% significance level and a two-tailed test (presumably he was sadly surprised by the results).

Now we need $\bar{x}$ and sd_x from the grouped data. To speed things up, we compute values we need and then just multiply by their frequency. To find the mean we need the sum of the x values:

x Value (Rating)	Frequency	x times frequency
1	6	6
2	12	24
3	9	27
4	6	24
5	3	15
	$N = 36 =$ total number of students replying	$\Sigma x = 96$

$$\bar{x} = \frac{96}{36} = 2.67$$

To find sd_x we need the Σx just found plus Σx^2 found similarly:

x^2	Frequency (f)	fx^2
1	6	6
4	12	48
9	9	81
16	6	96
25	3	75
		$\Sigma fx^2 = 306$

$$\text{VAR} = \frac{\Sigma x^2 - (\Sigma x)^2/N}{N - 1} = \frac{306 - 9216/36}{35} = 1.429$$

$$sd = 1.20$$

And so

$$t_{35} = \frac{\bar{x} - \mu}{sd/\sqrt{N}}$$

$$= \frac{2.67 - 3}{1.20/\sqrt{36}}$$

$$= -1.65$$

The t-table gives a *CV* of 2.042 for 30 *df*s for a two-tailed test (we have 35 *df*s but the table does not give this value; choosing 30 instead of 40 from the table is more conservative, a slightly tougher test). So we reject H_0 only if our t is greater than $+2.042$ or less than -2.042:

```
..............|−2.042........0........+2.042| ..............
              |                              |
reject H₀     |_____|     reject H₀
```

don't reject H_0

Our t-value is not extreme enough to reject H_0, so perhaps the low ratings in this course should not be taken too seriously, since they are not significantly different from an "average course" rating.

Many older statistics books devote a good deal of space to modified formulae for efficient calculation from grouped data. However, these formulae are not as important these days; if you do have large amounts of data, grouped or not, you usually analyze it by computer. So we will not give any more grouped data examples although you should be aware that computational short-cuts for them are available if you happen to need them. Such short cuts have been worked out for all the standard confirmatory procedures, not just the t-test.

Ordinal versus Numeric Data

In the course rating example just concluded, the data present a mild problem that we have not discussed before. We usually assume that when we have scores of 3, 4 and 5, say, the "5" is higher on what is being measured than the "4" (i.e. the data have order properties). Furthermore, we usually assume that the difference between a "5" and a "4" is about the same as that between a "4" and a "3" (the "interval" property). Data with both properties are called interval or numeric data and most statistics are designed for such data. Data with order properties but not interval properties are called ordinal, and such data are often not good enough for classic confirmatory procedures like the t-test.

Now, are the course ratings interval or just ordinal? They have order properties: a rating of 1 is worse than one of 2. But the interval property is probably absent: we can't be sure that 1 is worse than 2 in the same degree as 4 is worse than 5. The ratings are just ordinal. Yet we did a t-test: why? Pragmatic investigations have shown that ordinal data can be treated like interval data pretty safely if the data have a fairly smooth distribution, N is fairly large, and the test is robust. All these "ifs" hold in our example.

One Last Wrinkle: Proportions

So far in our treatment of statistics, we've looked at counts, at rates, and at scores. One important omission has been proportions. There are many important questions where the answers involve percentages: what proportion of eligible voters would support which party in an election? what proportion of males never marry? etc. The most familiar instance of this is the public opinion poll, though this is perhaps not the best example since it rarely uses truly random samples. Still, it will do for an illustration.

Suppose parliament is faced with a free vote in the legalization of marijuana. Many of the Members of Parliament without strong personal views may wish to go along with the majorities in their constituencies, if they can find out what the majorities want. Clark Kent, MP (Metropolis), decides to hire Truth, Ltd. to sample his riding and report back to him. If there is clear evidence of a majority for or against legalization, Kent plans to vote with the majority; if there isn't clear evidence of a majority either way, if it is "too close to call," Kent plans to come down with a 24-hour virus on voting day rather than decide which half of his riding to offend. Truth, Ltd. interviews 800 voters and reports 52% opposed to legalization and 48% in favour (the issue had been so hotly debated that no one is undecided). Now what?

Some of the testing is easy enough. We can see that Kent wants to do a two-tailed test. If μ really is .50, he does not want to make a decision at all; he'll dodge. But if there is a detectable majority either way, he wants to go with it: if more than 50% of the riding opposes legalization he will too, and if less than 50% oppose it he'll vote for it. Thus

H_0: $\mu = .50$ (decision: get sick!)
H_1: either $x > .50$ (decision: vote against legalization)
or $x < .50$ (decision: vote for legalization)

We can also set a reasonable α-value: since a politician must get off the fence more readily than a scientist (the former is expected to decide whenever he can, the latter to decide only when he is pretty sure about things), we select $\alpha = .10$ or a somewhat looser standard than usual in research situations. Now Kent does a test.

Are you thinking that he doesn't have the information to do a test? He doesn't know σ and doesn't have the information to compute $\hat{\sigma}$? Well, there's a very handy fact about proportions and percentages: if you know the mean, you know σ (not $\hat{\sigma}$!) as well. If your universe consists of people in one of two categories, for example, those who favour or are opposed to legalization of marijuana, then you have two proportions, p and q (where $p + q = 1.0$). A little algebra shows that the variance here is just pq. So under the H_0: $\mu = p$, $\sigma^2 = pq$ and we can do a simple Z-test. Turning to Table 8.4, we find a $CV = 1.645$. Thus:

$$H_0: \mu = .50$$
$$H_1: \mu \neq .50$$
$$\bar{x} = .52$$
$$\mu = .50 \quad \sigma^2 = .25$$
$$N = 800$$
$$CV = \pm 1.645$$

$$Z = \frac{.52 - .50}{\sqrt{.25/800}} = \frac{.02}{.0177} = 1.130$$

The Z score is between the critical values, meaning that we can't reject H_0, so Kent is likely to be very sick when the bill comes to a vote.

Several general cautions apply to reading poll results as you usually see them, very briefly reported in newspapers. First, remember that commercial firms have to keep costs down; they use cluster sampling at best, and their results can't always be relied on to the last decimal place. Some polls are more carefully accurate than others but it is hard to tell about this from brief reports. Moreover, most large polls give results accurate to within, say, four or five percent for the whole sample. If the results are given for subsamples (e.g. the percentage approval for men, or Jews, or the urban northeast), then the N is reduced, and so is the accuracy of the results. Finally, you should be especially careful in reading polls for forecasting, for example pre-election polls. Everyone has seen examples of embarrassing failures with all the big pollsters reporting an edge for party X up to the eve of the election, won by party Y. Usually the thing to watch for is either a trend (for example, one party is behind but increasing its share of the vote in successive polls, with greater increases occurring in more recent polls), or a large proportion of undecided voters (who often swing elections with last-minute decisions). The relationship between pre-election polls and election results is pretty complicated; so either learn a lot about it, or take the poll indications as little more than a very broad guide.

Homework

1. In our society, children are almost uniformly toilet-trained substantially later than they are weaned. Such an ordering seems "natural" to us. You might be interested in looking at the timing of these two stages in a number of primitive societies as recorded in Table 9.5 (all societies in Whiting and Child (1962), for which stable estimates of ages at the start of weaning and toilet training are provided). These data can be used in a t-test; lay the problem out as a t-test, making sure to discuss all important assumptions.

Table 9.5

Weaning and Toilet-Training

Society	Age at Weaning	Age at Toilet Training	Society	Age at Weaning	Age at Toilet Training
Alorese	2.3	1.8	Marquesans	0.5	1.0
Balinese	2.7	3.0	Navaho	2.0	2.2
Bena	1.8	4.7	Ontong–Javanese	3.0	1.2
Chagga	2.7	0.8	Papago	2.3	1.9
Comanche	1.5	1.2	Pukapukans	1.5	1.7
Dahomeans	2.5	2.0	Siriono	2.3	2.8
Hopi	2.0	1.5	Slave	2.0	1.7
Kwakiutl	2.0	1.5	Tanala	1.7	0.3
Kwoma	2.5	3.0	Tenino	2.0	2.2
Lepcha	2.8	2.2	Teton	2.7	2.2
Lesu	2.2	2.0	Western Apache	1.3	2.7
Manus	2.5	1.2	Wogeo	2.8	2.0
Maori	1.3	2.2			

Source: Whiting and Child, (1962).

2. Davis and Havighurst (1946) estimate that toilet training begins at about eight months (0.67 years) in North America. This estimate is roughly contemporary with those listed above for primitive societies. Is the age at the start of toilet training significantly different in the primitive societies as compared to the Davis and Havighurst figure for North America?

3. Your instructor may assign an example based on a current poll.

10

Comparing Several Batch Levels

Our experience so far with hypothesis testing about levels has been peculiar. First, we spent a fair amount of time learning to deal with the Z-test only to find out that the Z-test is rarely useful because we're very unlikely to know σ. Consequently, we found we needed to learn the t-test. Now we know how to test a single mean against a theoretical expectation, and how to compare the means of two matched batches. Ironically, although we've begun to understand hypothesis-testing logic we really haven't gotten very much "forrader" in terms of widely useful tests. Most of the interesting questions involving batch levels deal with several differences: the effects of half a dozen different teaching methods on reading skills, the effects of being in different age cohorts on propensity to commit suicide, the effects of different work situations on union involvement, the effects of living in various neighbourhoods on delinquency rates, and so on.

In each of these examples, we have one variable, such as reading skill, suicide rates, etc., that we want to explain. This is the *dependent variable*. And we have another variable, like teaching methods, age group, etc., which we believe affects the first: for example, teaching method may have an effect on reading skill. This is the *independent variable*. We will learn how to work with various kinds of independent and dependent variables. For now we are interested in cases where the independent variable is categorical and the dependent variable is numeric. A categorical variable (or nominal variable) is a batching variable, a set of related categories into which cases can be sorted. Preferably the sorting is unambiguous: each case belongs in one and only one category. The world regions used in review example II (following chapter 6) are one example of a categorical variable. The age groups used in the suicide rates example (chapters 2 to 4) are another. But the age groups have something the world regions do not have: an order (from youngest to oldest). In batch analysis, or in confirmatory equivalents, the batching variable can be categorical or ordinal. The dependent variable is numeric. Sometimes cases are borderline, for example, the "fear of ghosts" could be seen as ordinal or as numeric. In chapter 9 we said the distinction matters because theoretically, at least, ordinal variables should not be analyzed with tools that take more than order into account; but a number of pragmatic investigations have shown that you will not be misled if you define "numeric" pretty freely.

Let's return to our current problem: categorical independent variable, numeric dependent variable. To see the effect (if any) of the independent on the dependent variable, we see whether the level of the dependent variable is different from batch to batch depending on the "value" of the independent variable. For example, in the suicide data we found that suicide rates were different by age group (with older groups having higher levels of suicide) so we concluded that age has an effect on suicide; if the levels had been pretty much the same for all age categories we would have concluded that age is unrelated to suicide.

For such examples, there are more than two batches so the t-test will not do. On the one hand, we cannot boil the multiple batch differences down to one difference and compare it to the t distribution. On the other hand, if we look at every pair of batches we can use a form of the t-test; but it costs too much to do so, since it takes a lot of time and wastes a lot of statistical power. We need a new approach. Fortunately, we will find that our new approach will turn out to be far simpler than the direct approach used in both the Z-test and t-test.

In the t- and Z-tests we used the same basic idea: to decide whether two means ($\bar{x}$ and μ) are different, compute the observed difference and compare it to a measure of how large such differences are likely to be when the two means are "really" the same, when they appear different just because of sampling fluctuations. We compared observed and chance differences in a ratio:

$$\frac{\text{difference of means}}{\text{"chance" difference}} = \frac{\bar{x} - \mu}{\text{SE of } \bar{x} \text{ if } H_0 \text{ true}}$$

$$= \frac{\bar{x} - \mu}{\sigma/\sqrt{N}} \text{ for } Z$$

$$\text{or} = \frac{\bar{x} - \mu}{sd_x/\sqrt{N}} \text{ for } t$$

If H_0 is true and $\bar{x}$ differs from μ only because of sampling fluctuations then the ratio probably will not be very large (positive or negative); if H_0 is false the ratio is quite likely to be large.

Now we can adopt the same basic idea for comparisons between several means (not just $\bar{x}$ and μ). Again we use a ratio; but now the top part should tell us how different the several means are from each other. Well, we know how to sum that up: the variance of the category means tells us how different they are, how spread out they are as a batch. For the bottom of the ratio we need a measure of how big the top will be if H_0 is true and the category

Table 10.1

The Original Sample of Pellagra Sufferers:
Distribution of Relief

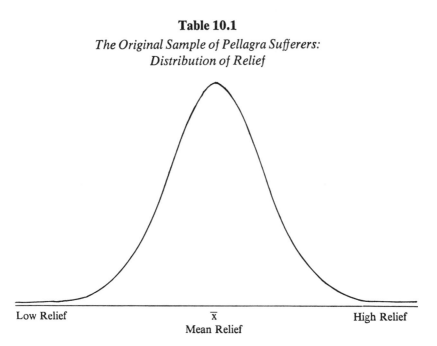

Low Relief   x̄   High Relief
Mean Relief

means differ because of sampling fluctuations alone. This turns out to be easy too: it's based on the variance within the categories, just as the denominator for the one-sample t ratio is based on the variance in the sample. This technique is called *analysis of variance* or "anova." Let's see how this works for a simple hypothetical example to convince ourselves that it makes sense, and then go through a real example in detail.

Anova Thinking

Suppose we are attempting to treat the disease pellagra, and we have two experimental drugs we want to test, "curit" and "stopit." We want to compare the effects of these drugs on untreated sufferers, but since some people recover simply as a result of thinking they've been treated, we have a *placebo*, perhaps a sugar pill, that we give to our untreated group. So we take a random sample of sufferers that we divide into three random subsamples: a "curit" group (c), a "stopit" group (s) and a placebo group (p) (naturally the doctors, patients, and experimenters must not know which people are getting which until the data have been collected). How can we compare the three treatments, which form three categories of our independent variable "type of treatment"? Let us consider how the three batches are related. In the first place all three groups were selected randomly from the same original sample of patients; that sample as a whole has a mean and variance in terms of relief from pellagra. Let us suppose that the distribution looks like the one in Table 10.1. (We are assuming a normal distribution.) Now each of the three subsamples will have a distribution too, with mean and variance of its own. What will the three distributions look like? This has to depend in part on the effects (or lack of effects) of the three treatments. For example, suppose that all three treatments are ineffective; then the three distributions of relief will tend to look like smaller versions of Table 10.1 because they will just be three random samples from the original sample portrayed in Table 10.1. We would not expect the groups to look identical because there will usually be some random fluctuations, but they will be close most of the time, so we expect something like the top of Table 10.2. The curit, stopit, and placebo distributions are shown one underneath another to allow comparison. Each distribution is roughly normal and has roughly the same spread; the means will vary a little bit (the placebo mean relief being highest here) but essentially the three treatment groups look the same. If we combine them, as at the bottom of Table 10.2, we get a combined distribution just like the three separate ones (similar level, spread, and shape) with the only difference being a larger number of cases. This combined distribution looks like the original sample's distribution in Table 10.1. In short, the three treatments do not differ so the differences between them are no more than one would expect from the random allocation of sufferers to the groups.

Now let us see what happens when the treatments do have different effects. We will get something like Table 10.3 perhaps, where the mean relief from curit is clearly greater than the mean relief from stopit or placebo. Again, we show the three groups pooled together in the bottom of Table 10.3. Now one striking thing about this comparison is that *the variance around $\bar{x}$ (bottom picture) is large compared to the variance around subsample means (top picture)*. This is quite different from Table 10.2 where the pooled distribution has about the same variance as the three subsamples. Where does the "extra" variance in Table 10.3 come from? Clearly from the separation of the means of the subsamples. The stopit and placebo samples have lower means than the curit sample, so overall the observations are quite spread out compared to spread within subsamples. When the three samples had closer means (as in Table 10.2) the variance around $\bar{x}$ was a lot smaller. To generalize this, we can say that overall (or total) variance will be great compared to subsample variance if the subsample means are far apart.

We can make this insight more precise because a useful and easily proven relationship exists among the variances; the total variance can be broken down into two components, one describing the "average" variance within the subsamples (the "within groups" term) and the second describing the variances of subsample means around the grand mean (the "between groups" term). These components are very similar to variances. A simple proof of this relationship can be found in the appendix at the end of the

Table 10.2

Typical Results for Ineffectual Treatments

CURIT DISTRIBUTION

```
                              c
                           c  c
                        c  c  c
                     c  c  c  c
                     c  c  c  c
                  c  c  c  c  c
                  c  c  c  c  c
               c  c  c  c  c  c
            c  c  c  c  c  c  c
      c  c  c  c  c  c  c  c  c  c  c  c  c
```

PLACEBO DISTRIBUTION

```
                              p
                           p  p
                        p  p  p
                     p  p  p  p
                     p  p  p  p
                  p  p  p  p  p
               p  p  p  p  p  p
            p  p  p  p  p  p  p
      p  p  p  p  p  p  p  p  p  p  p  p  p
```

STOPIT DISTRIBUTION

```
                     s  s
                  s  s  s
               s  s  s  s
               s  s  s  s
            s  s  s  s  s
            s  s  s  s  s
         s  s  s  s  s  s
      s     s  s  s  s  s  s  s  s
```

LOW RELIEF   HIGH RELIEF

CURIT, STOPIT, AND
PLACEBO COMBINED

```
                        c
                        c  c
                     c  c  c
                     c  c  c
                  c  c  c  c
               c  c  c  c  c
               p  p  p  c
               p  p  p  c
            p  p  p  p  c
         s  p  p  p  p  c
      s  s  p  p  p  p  c
   s  s  s  p  p  p  p  c
s  s  s  s  p  p  p  p  c
```

LOW RELIEF   HIGH RELIEF

Table 10.3

Possible Results for an Effective "Curit"

CURIT DISTRIBUTION

```
                              c c
                            c c c c c
                          c c c c c c c
                        c c c c c c c c c
                        c c c c c c c c c
                      c c c c c c c c c c c
                    c c c c c c c c c c c c c
 c    c    c c   c c   c c c c c c c c c c c c   c   c   c
```

PLACEBO DISTRIBUTION

```
                                  p
                                p p p p
                              p p p p p p
                            p p p p p p p p
                          p p p p p p p p p
                          p p p p p p p
                          p p p p p
 p   p   p   p p   p p   p p p p   p p   p p   p   p   p
```

STOPIT DISTRIBUTION

```
                        s s
                      s s s s s
                    s s s s s s s
                  s s s s s s s s s
                  s s s s s s s s s
                s s s s s s s s
                s s s s
 s   s      s s   s s s   s s s s   s s s   s s   s   s
```

LOW RELIEF   HIGH RELIEF

CURIT, STOPIT, AND PLACEBO COMBINED

```
                          c c c
                        p c c c c
                      p p p c c c c
                    p p p p p c c c
                    s s p p p p p c c
                s s s s p p p p p p c c
              s s s s s s p p p p p p c c
            s s s s s s s p p p p p p c c
          s s s s s s s s p p p p p p c c
        s s s s s s s s s p p p p p c c c
      p s s s s s s s s s p p p p c c c c
 s  s p s s s s s s s s s p p p c c c c c c
```

LOW RELIEF $\overline{x}$ HIGH RELIEF book (p. 374). Now the "between groups" term tells us how different the batch means are. What about the "within groups" term? Since this is approximately the average variance within treatment groups (the average of the variance of c's only, p's only, s's only) it does not depend on differences between treatments; it tells us what variability to expect if H_0 is true and the treatments do not differ. But this brings us right back to the ratio idea in the introduction:

$$\frac{\text{difference of means}}{\text{"chance" difference}} = \frac{\text{"between" terms}}{\text{"within" term}} \cong \frac{\text{observed variance}}{\text{variance if } H_0 \text{ true}}.$$

If this ratio is very large then the means are more different than one could reasonably expect, given H_0. So if the ratio is big enough, we'll reject H_0 and decide that the independent variable probably does have an effect. Again, we'll find out what "big enough" means by looking at a table of critical values. We are asking the same kind of question as for t- or Z-tests, and asking it in the same way. However, with our new approach we can now ask this question of as many means as we wish. We are still looking at differences between means, because as the means become more different, the "between" component must increase, but one test makes all of our comparisons simultaneously.

There is one difference from the t or Z case: we don't have to worry about one- or two-tailed tests here. We only reject H_0 when we get significantly large ratios. Negative ratios are impossible (the top and bottom parts must both be positive, being like variances, i.e. sums of squares). Thus we have a kind of omnibus test for any kind of difference between the means, because any substantial differences between them will make their variance big.

Now that you've seen what we are after, let's go through the formulae used to compute the ratio.

Computations for the Analysis of Variance Ratio

We need two variance analogues for our ratio: "between groups" and "within groups." What should they look like? Well, that familiar quantity, the simple variance of a batch, is:

$$\text{variance} = \frac{\Sigma(x - \bar{x})^2}{N - 1} = \frac{\text{sum of squares}}{\text{degrees of freedom}}$$

Or, in computational form, we have

$$\text{variance} = \frac{\Sigma x^2 - (\Sigma x)^2/N}{N - 1}.$$

The "between" and "within" parts of our ratio are very similar:

for "between," we have $\dfrac{\text{Between sum of squares}}{\text{between } df}$,

and for "within" $\dfrac{\text{Within sum of squares}}{\text{within } df}$.

These are called "mean squares," or "MS" for short. Then our test ratio will be

$$\frac{\text{Mean Square between}}{\text{Mean Square within}} \text{ or } \frac{MS_B}{MS_W} .$$

So we need sums of squares and degrees of freedom for top and bottom, between and within. The total variance is also computed from sums of squares and degrees of freedom, and it gives us a useful arithmetic check since these pieces must add up:

Total sum of squares = between SS + within SS
Total df = between df + within df.

Let's work out the degrees of freedom first. We have N observations in all (N items in all the groups together), so the total df is equal to $N - 1$ (just as for any simple variance). The df for the between groups "variance" is very similar: the number of groups (K) minus 1. And if we have $N - 1$ dfs altogether, with $K - 1$ for between groups, then we must have $N - K$ for the within group df since $(K - 1) + (N - K) = N - 1$, as it should.

To get sums of squares we need convenient computing formulae (as we did even for the simple one-batch variance). We get the least wear and tear if we do three computations (A, B and C) which serve as efficient building blocks: they are fast and easy, and fit together to make the "within group" and "between group" estimates we want. We give both formulae and verbal descriptions for each one. First,

$$A = \Sigma x_{ij}^2$$

where "i" indexes the groups and "j" the observations within the groups, so the formula says: take every observation in every group, square each one, then add them all together.

$$B = \frac{(\Sigma x_{ij})^2}{N}$$

That is, take the sum of all the observations, square it, then divide by the count, N.

$$C = \sum_i \frac{\left(\sum_j x_{ij}\right)^2}{N_i}$$

To get C, take the sum in each separate group, $\sum_j x_{ij}$, square each sum, and divide by the count in that group, N_i ($\sum N_i = N$). Then add up these group figures. Now we are in business.

A and B should look familiar: they are the same sums we use in the computational form of the variance. The total sum of squares is $A - B$,

$$\text{Total SS} = A - B$$

which is just the numerator in the formula for the variance. The other two sums of squares are just as easy:

$$\text{between SS} = C - B$$
$$\text{within} \quad \text{SS} = A - C$$

All three of these sums of squares must be positive; if they are not, you have made an error! They must also add up: $(C - B) + (A - C) = A - B$.

This gives us all we need for the two mean squares we need as variance analogues for our ratio:

$$\frac{\text{between}}{\text{within}} = \frac{\text{between SS/between } df}{\text{within SS/within } df} = \frac{\text{between MS}}{\text{within MS}}$$

This ratio is called the F-ratio. None of this is hard, but there's a certain amount of detail to keep straight so we use an analysis of variance summary table. First we use it to summarize the computations using A, B, and C:

Table 10.4

Analysis of Variance Summary Table

Source of Variance	Sum of Squares	df	Mean Squares	F-ratio
Between Groups	$C-B$	$K-1$	$SS/df = MS_B$	$\dfrac{MS_B}{MS_W}$
Within Groups	$A-C$	$N-K$	$SS/df = MS_W$	
Total	$A-B$	$N-1$		

The F-ratio contains two variance estimates, unlike the t-test where there was only one, and two df figures instead of one. For each pair of dfs we could generate an entire table similar to the Z-table 8.3, but ordinarily F-tables just provide CVs for popular levels of significance. Table A.4 gives CVs for $\alpha = .05$. To use Table A.4, find the column with the df for the numerator (between) and the row with the denominator (within) df: the CV is at the intersection of that row and column. For $\alpha = .05$ the critical value for $F_{10,10}$ is 2.98; that is, we would get an F-ratio bigger than 2.98 five percent of the time if H_0 is true and we reject H_0 at the .05 level if we get such a value. In short, the F-table, like the t-table, gives us a critical value; we simply compute our ratio and compare it to the CV. If our ratio exceeds or equals the CV we reject H_0. If not, we don't.

Now we're ready for a real example. First we apply the formulae just given; later we will go briefly into the assumptions made in doing an analysis of variance. Please note that, in practice, you check the assumptions first! If the data do not meet them, the test is likely to be misleading.

A Worked Example

An observer sat in an elementary school classroom observing and coding interactions between the teacher and the pupils. Among the types of inter-action observed was the mean frequency of criticism of each pupil by the teacher per session. We have sorted the students into three categories by IQ: low (IQ less than 90), medium (IQ from 90 to 110), and high (IQ over 110). Our observations in each IQ group are the mean number of times that each student in the group was criticized. The data are presented in Table 10.5, in the form of square roots of the original observations (we will return to why we used square roots after we have gone through the ex-ample). Does a child's IQ have any effect on how likely the teacher is to squelch him? According to H_0, no; the rate of criticism is the same for each of the three IQ categories in general:

$$H_0: \mu_{\text{low}} = \mu_{\text{medium}} = \mu_{\text{high}}$$

The sample means may differ a bit because of sampling fluctuations. H_1 is more complicated since it includes any inequality among the means. Per-haps all three are different, perhaps one is quite different from the other two; we do not usually write it down explicitly.

Let's compute A, B, and C. We've made a start in Table 10.5 by adding up x and x^2 values for each of the three groups. So A, the sum of the squared values, is just

$$A = 129.78 + 191.93 + 62.62 = 384.33$$

For B we sum all the values, square the sum, and divide by N, or

$$B = \frac{(34.0 + 52.5 + 21.0)^2}{45}$$

$$= \frac{11556.25}{45} = 256.81$$

For C we first square each group's total and divide the squared total by the group's size, getting

$$\frac{(34)^2}{13}, \quad \frac{(52.5)^2}{18}, \quad \text{and} \quad \frac{(21)^2}{14}.$$

(Note that each group's squared total is divided by its own count.) Then C is the sum of these values:

$C = 88.92 + 153.13 + 31.5 = 273.55$

All we need now to construct a summary table and do our test is the degrees of freedom. The total count is 45, so total $df = 44$. The number of groups is $K = 3$ so the "between" df is $K–1 = 2$, and $N–K = 45 - 3 = 42$, the "within" df. This gives:

Source of Variance	Sum of Squares	df	Mean Squares	F-ratio
Between IQ Groups	16.74	2	8.37	3.17
Within IQ Groups	110.78	42	2.64	
Total	127.52	44		

For example, the values in the "Between" row were found by plugging our values in the formulae given earlier:

Between SS $= C–B = 273.55 - 256.81 = 16.74$

$$\text{Between MS} = \frac{\text{Between SS}}{\text{Between } df} = \frac{16.74}{2} = 8.37$$

Having found all the SS and df values separately we can check our arithmetic easily:

$16.74 + 110.78 = 127.52$
$2 + 42 = 44$

So we finally have an F-ratio for our example: 3.17. We look at our $\alpha = .05$ table of F-values, Table A.4, and find that the critical value for 2 and 42 dfs is 3.22. Our value, 3.17, is not quite as extreme as this so we can't reject H_0; the observed differences among the group means are almost but not quite large enough compared to chance differences one could reasonably expect if H_0 is true. But the F is so close to significance at the standard 5% level that we can't help wondering if perhaps H_0 is wrong and there is some connection between child's IQ and criticism received. We don't reject H_0 but we do go back to exploratory thinking to see if we should study this problem further.

We can start by exploring the batches we have. The values in Table 10.5 are plotted schematically in Table 10.6. In the middle of each box, the horizontal line is the median and the "X" is the trimean. Both levels suggest that the children with high IQs get fewer "shots," perhaps because they are more academically successful and hence more likely to please the teacher. The low and medium IQ children get about the same amount of criticism on the whole. Perhaps the low IQ children get a bit less; this is not strongly indicated, but if it is true then maybe the teacher does not expect as much of the least bright children and ignores more than criticizes their failings. Well, this all makes sense but we weren't able to support it: why not? Table 10.6 makes one possibility clear; there is a near upper outlier in the high IQ groups. This value probably pulled up the nonresistant mean,

Table 10.5

Criticism by IQ

Low IQ (under 90)	Medium IQ (90–110)	High IQ (over 110)
2.3	3.8	0
4.4	1.6	1.8
4.9	3.5	0
2.0	2.1	2.3
4.7	4.9	1.8
2.2	2.0	2.9
1.2	3.4	1.2
5.5	2.4	1.6
0	4.8	5.4
1.5	1.2	0
0	4.9	0
1.6	2.0	1.2
3.7	2.6	0
	4.2	2.8
	0	
	5.4	
	2.0	
	1.7	

Group 1: $N_1 = 13$	Group 2: $N_2 = 18$	Group 3: $N_3 = 14$
$\sum X = 34$	$\sum X = 52.5$	$\sum X = 21$
$\sum X^2 = 129.78$	$\sum X^2 = 191.93$	$\sum X^2 = 62.62$

(Data from an unpublished study by Sally Luce; transformed by taking square roots.)

making the group means more alike. With the very high value (5.4) dropped, the mean for the high IQ batch goes from 1.5 to 1.3. Furthermore, the variance goes from 2.39 to 1.23. Thus this one case both makes the group means more alike and makes the "within" value larger. Well, if the high IQ mean has been distorted by the upper outlier, is there some reason for the

Table 10.6

Schematic plots of "Criticism" data

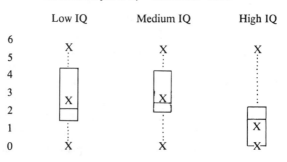

outlier being so unusual? We looked back at our data source and found this child had an IQ of 112; he is near the boundary line between the medium IQ and high IQ groups, and may perhaps be more similar to students in the medium group.

All in all, our failure to get a significant result may be a result of one slightly misclassified case; we almost got a significant result, and the pattern we found in exploration made sense. So we conclude that we should collect more data to clarify the possible link between IQ and criticism.

Analysis of Variance Assumptions

The analysis of variance, like all confirmatory tests, is based on some assumptions about the nature of the data. There are three assumptions, the first of which is a familiar one.

Assumption 1: Normality. Each group's values should be drawn from a normally distributed universe. Of course, we don't have the universes at hand, so we check whether this assumption is met by looking at the shapes of our batches. In our example, the original values did not look normal. The original values are stemmed-and-leaved and plotted in Table 10.7, which shows a lot of upward straggle. We coped quite easily by taking square

Table 10.7

The Untransformed Criticism Batches

Low IQ		Medium IQ		High IQ	
3		3		3	
3	1	3		3	
2		2	59	2	9
2	42	2	34	2	
1	9	1	58	1	
1	3	1	22	1	
0	55	0	67	0	588
0	410203	0	34414043	0	0303130010
stems: tens		*leaves*: units		(rounded data)	

roots, which produced the tolerably normal batches plotted in Table 10.6. The shapes aren't perfect but they are single-peaked and quite symmetric around the trimean, which is usually good enough.

Analysis of variance is robust with respect to the normality assumption; the data don't have to meet it exactly, or even very closely if the data are plentiful, with many cases in each group. We transformed our data because the group sizes were not all that large. It is hard to give exact rules here, because the amount of non-normality you can safely work with depends on group sizes and both can vary a lot. In many cases you can correct non-normal data by transformation. If you are unsure whether to proceed or not, consult an expert.

Assumption 2: Equal Variances.   Each of the groups should be drawn from populations with equal variances; again, in practice we check out the batches we have. There isn't much need for concern if the groups are approximately equal in size: if they are, the variances can be moderately unequal without messing up the anova test. But if the group N's are substantially unequal, then unequal variances can produce misleading results. We had slightly unequal group N's in our example so we will check out the group variances (not too hard with the Σx and Σx^2 values from Table 10.5 and the fast formula for variances). Note, by the way, that we check variances for square rooted data since we just decided to use square roots to help satisfy the normality assumption. From low to high IQ the variances are: 3.405, 2.282, 2.394. This isn't too bad; in this case the variances would have to differ by a multiplicative factor of about three or more before the difference would begin to make itself felt. Again, there is no simple rule for how much difference you can tolerate; so as before, when in doubt, consult an expert. On the whole though, your own eyes are a good guide; for example, we only have to look at Table 10.6 to see that our batches are roughly normal and roughly alike in spread.

If you have unequal groups with clearly unequal variances, transformation can help again! Think back to the rule of thumb, described in chapter 6, for picking a good transformation for several batches, log spread plotted against log level. That procedure often suggested a transform that would equalize batch spreads (and hopefully even up spread inside batches too, leading to symmetry). Surely we can use it here for the same purpose. Log of standard deviation versus log of mean would be most appropriate. As long as the batch spreads rise or fall fairly regularly with batch levels, this is likely to work.

Assumption 3: Independent Observations.   Roughly, this implies that each value is a separate piece of information, not affected by the others. Randomly sampling cases and randomly assigning them to treatment groups guarantees this; indeed, this is one reason why analysis of variance is so popular with experimentalists, who can and do randomly assign people to groups. Non-experimental studies have to randomly sample within groups defined naturally (like our IQ groups, over which we have no control) and hope for the best. This assumption applies to how the data were gathered and can't be checked by looking at the data, as the other two assumptions can; a more detailed discussion of it really belongs in a course on research design.

In summary, there are three assumptions that must be met if analysis of variance is to be done appropriately; if they're not met, the analysis can be very misleading. Fortunately anova is robust with respect to the first two assumptions which need not be met exactly and can be somewhat bent safely if conditions are right.

Normality tends not to matter much if the group N's are large. If they are small, transform the data to roughly normal shape. If this can't be done (e.g. if some groups straggle up and some down), be very cautious; treat anova results as merely suggestive and do exploratory work to find out why the shapes differ.

Equal variance tends not to matter much if the group sizes are equal. If group sizes and group variances are both clearly unequal, transformation may help; if if doesn't, be very cautious. If the largest variance is less than three times the smallest, relax.

Independence is hard to get around. Think ahead when gathering the data to be sure this assumption is met. If you collect your own data you can clearly avoid possible future grief by a few simple precautions: make the observations independent, randomly sample a roughly equal number of cases for each group or category of the independent variable, and get as many cases for each group as you can afford. Then you will not have to worry about anova assumptions. These precautions are easy to take if you are doing an experiment. We have stressed that confirmatory statistics are relatively rigid, requiring standard procedures and assumptions which must be taken seriously. Here we see that the analysis of variance assumptions are indeed important, but not paralyzingly stiff; mild violations of them are tolerable. The test is quite robust which is one of the reasons for its usefulness.

Summary

You can use analysis of variance if you want to look at the effect of one variable (the "independent" variable) on another (the "dependent") and the variables have the right levels of measurement. The dependent variable has to be quantitative (otherwise how can you compute means?) and the independent variable has to be a set of categories or something that can be sensibly turned into a set of categories (otherwise how do you get your batches?).

The test is appropriate if the data meet the three basic assumptions, which, as we just saw, are not very restrictive in practice. You can't use anova blindly, since you often need to adjust your data by transformation beforehand; but you can use it a great deal. Very few problems are hopelessly unsuitable.

The basic idea behind the test is simple and familiar; even the mathematics (in the appendix) is simple if you know a bit of algebra; and certainly the computations are simple; in fact, you end up doing no more work than you would do for a t-test. Analysis of variance has a reputation for difficulty that it does not deserve, and a reputation as a high-powered technique that *is* deserved. A few simple modifications give the basic approach remarkable flexibility. If you wish to learn more, or to find just the right version for a particular problem, there are many good standard sources such as Hays, *Statistics for Psychologists*.

Exploratory and Confirmatory

This chapter is a particularly good example of the interdependence of the two statistical approaches. Exploratory techniques are useful in making sure that the confirmatory anova can be safely used; exploratory methods also help in adjusting the data (usually by transformation) if necessary. After an anova analysis is finished, exploration starts again. If the test was not significant (as in our example), why? If the test was significant, then what happened, that is, which group means are higher or lower and why? (The anova only tells us there is some significant difference, not what the difference is.) On the other hand, the anova is often done to test ideas that came from previous exploration of other data in the first place.

Our batch explorations suggested that level, spread, shape and outliers are all important. Anova as described here deals only with level. There are confirmatory tests for differences of variance and shape as well. You should not be too surprised to hear that the F-test can be adapted as a test for differences of batch variances (the Cochran "C-test" is one such adaptation) and there are tests for differences of shape. We don't propose to go into these in this course, but we do want you to know that tests are available if you need them.

Homework

1. The homework data are taken from "CANFAM," a larger set of data on decision-making in the Canadian family, collected by L. Pettit and I. Pool.

The dependent variable is a family power index in the tradition begun by Blood and Wolff in their study of American families, *Husbands and Wives*. Each woman studied was asked "Who makes the final decision in your family about . . . ," where a number of topics of decision were listed. Here we selected decisions about: luxury items, necessities, recreational activities, size of family, and method of contraception used. For each topic, we gave a score of 1 if the wife usually made the decision; a score of ½ if both husband and wife made the decision; and a score of 0 if the husband usually decided. Next we found the mean score on all the topics for which the wife gave a definite answer, which gave a wife's power index running from 0 to 1.00. (Feel free to criticize the index, especially if this helps in your discussion.)

For the independent variable we chose an age/residence classification which may be a guide to the woman's early socialization:

Category	Definition
1	born 1890–1900; married and living in a town or city when 25–35 (*urban*)
2	born 1890–1900; married and living on a farm when 25–35 (*rural*)
3	born 1920–1930; urban (see 1)
4	born 1920–1930; rural (see 2)
5	born 1940–1950; urban
6	born 1940–1950; rural

Having chosen independent and dependent variables, we randomly selected 42 of the women studied, choosing seven from each of the six groups defined above. The data are presented in Table 10.8. Do an anova for this table, remembering to do the related exploratory work as well.

Table 10.8

*Age, Residence in early married life,
and Power for Wives*

Categories: Age and Residence					
1	2	3	4	5	6
.75	.50	.67	.50	.40	.60
.50	.50	.17	.50	.63	.70
1.00	.50	.50	.33	.33	.38
.63	.17	.50	.00	.63	.50
.50	.75	.50	.50	.50	.60
.38	.33	.50	.40	.70	.50
1.00	.25	.50	.17	.38	.40

Source: CANFAM, unpublished data collected by L. Pettit and I. Pool.

Table entries: an index of wife's power (low of .00, high of 1.00).

Second Review: Confirmatory Comparison of Levels

It is now time for you to review your new tools: confirmatory techniques to test differences between levels. As you come to each problem, do not forget to go through the necessary steps in the right order. First, decide what kind of test is suitable: *t*-test, analysis of variance, or another. Second, check to see if the test assumptions are met (and if they aren't, do something about that). Third, do the test (don't forget to specify α, H_0 and H_1 in advance). Finally, discuss the results, using exploratory tools and thinking as seems appropriate. You do *not* have to use every exploratory or confirmatory tool you have learned; use what you need.

Do Example 1 and *either* Example 2 *or* Example 3.

Example 1. The data in Table IIR.1 come from a recent study by Atkinson and Polivy on the effects of unprovoked verbal attack. Randomly selected subjects first filled out a large number of items, some of which were self-reports of hostility (scores increase as hostility increases). After a long wait, the experimenter came to collect their responses, while behaving in a very abusive manner. The experimenter said, among other things, that the subjects couldn't even fill out a simple questionnaire properly, that they should do it again and *this* time do it properly! The data here are the hostility scores before and after this treatment. Do they differ? Also, do males and females differ? These questions can be approached in various ways. Clearly describe your reasons for setting up the problems as you do.

Example 2. In example 1 we described one part of the Polivy study for males and females; here we describe four parts of the study, giving data only for the male subjects in Table IIR.2. In the first part, subjects were just insulted as described above; so the data in batch 1 of Table IIR.2 are the same data as for males above. In the second part, other subjects weren't insulted but after the long wait were given an apology and an explanation for the experimenter's behaviour (an explanation meant to arouse empathy with the experimenter). In the third part, subjects were insulted and then given a chance to retaliate against the experimenter by recommending a bad grade for her. In the fourth part, delay was followed by both an apology and a chance to retaliate. Subjects were randomly assigned to the four treatments, so they should start off without any significant differences in level of hostility. Do they differ after these different treatments? If so, in what way and why? If not, why?

Table IIR.1

Hostility Before and After Being Insulted

Female Subjects		Male Subjects	
Before	After Insult	Before	After Insult
51	58	86	82
54	65	28	37
61	86	45	51
54	77	59	56
49	74	49	53
54	59	56	90
46	46	69	80
47	50	51	71
43	37	74	88
		42	43

Source: These data appear in another form in Atkinson and Polivy, Journal of Abnormal Psychology, 1976. © 1976 by the American Psychological Association. Reprinted by permission.

e.g. The first pair of figures under "Female Subjects," or 51 and 58, means that one female subject got a hostility score of 51 at the start of the experiment and a score of 58 after being insulted and told to answer the questions over again.

Table IIR.2

Male Hostility After Delay

Insult No Retaliation	Apology No Retaliation	Insult Retaliation	Apology Retaliation
82	53	69	80
37	67	51	55
51	38	77	54
56	68	30	42
53	99	89	41
90	49	76	58
80	33	55	60
71	47	57	50
88	32	55	67
43	50	52	59

Source: Atkinson and Polivy, Journal of Abnormal Psychology, 1976. © 1976 by the American Psychological Association. Reprinted by permission.

A brief sketch of the theory behind the experiment may be helpful. Apology with an empathy-arousing explanation is supposed to reduce hostility by making the insult understandable and making the subject feel closer to the experimenter. A chance to retaliate is also supposed to reduce hostility, but by a different mechanism: catharsis rather than empathy. Getting a chance for revenge should help people to "work it off" so they end up less hostile.

Example 3. The data in IIR.3 are from the same experiment as those in IIR.2, the only difference being that we give female subjects' scores on a measure of depression instead of male subjects' scores on a measure of hostility.

For more background reading you might like to consult the authors' report: C. Atkinson and J. Polivy, "The Effects of Delay, Attack and Retaliation on States of Depression and Hostility" (Atkinson and Polivy, 1976).

Table IIR.3

Female Depression After Being Insulted, With and Without Apology or Retaliation

No Apology No Retaliation	Apology No Retaliation	No Apology Retaliation	Apology Retaliation
66	70	141	57
78	73	64	60
89	68	73	41
75	52	59	49
96	69	77	39
70	107	72	69
57	57	78	57
52	42	51	122
41	55	78	46
69	44	41	39

Source: Atkinson and Polivy, Journal of Abnormal Psychology, 1976. © 1976 by the American Psychological Association. Reprinted by permission.

Section Three
X by Y Analysis

The first sections of this book have dealt with batches. We've learned quick and easy ways of analyzing and comparing batches, ways of noting and removing batch features, and most importantly, learning to go further by trying to understand the nature of the process that produced the batches. We've also learned how to test some of our insights by means of confirmatory procedures. But everything we've learned is set up to treat the simplest collections of numbers, those with no influence on one another, with no connection beyond their common origin in the process being investigated.

Now we move to a new form of data: numbers that are somehow linked together. Usually, the numbers are linked because they relate to the same unit; for example, one person (one kind of unit) has an age, an income, a political preference and so on. Thus age, income, and politics are numbers linked person by person.

Let's clarify this rather abstract distinction by looking at some numbers. One nice thing about the mental illness figures of Table 11.16 (p. 215) is that they can be looked at as batch data *or* as linked data (also known as X by Y data), thus giving a chance to compare the two. These male and female mental illness rates come from a study by Gove and Tudor which argued that women are more likely to be mentally ill than men because female roles in modern industrial societies are more frustrating and less rewarding than male roles. Each row in Table 11.16 gives the results of one post-World War II community survey (using interviews) for men and for women. Here we see one kind of batch idea; the sets of survey results were divided into two batches (one male, one female) and a batch summary (percentage ill) was computed. In analyzing these data, one familiar approach involves looking at the whole table as a set of two batches: one batch is the female rates, one batch the male rates. Briefly, it is easy to see that the level for the female batch is well above the level for the male batch (you could follow this up with schematic plots). Looking at batch levels alone can take us a fair way with this set of numbers. It also seems natural to make use of the fact that each community studied gives both a male and a female rate; that is, we can compare the male and female rates and see at a glance that the rate of mental illness is higher among women in every study. This is consistent with Gove and Tudor's argument: the level of mental illness for women is higher than the level for men in many different studies. Some process (they say sex

191

role experience) is acting differently on men than on women and yielding different rates.

But we can ask a new, more sophisticated question that is possible because the male and female rates are paired. This means we can ask about relationships between male and female rates: not only, "Is one batch higher overall?" but, "Is each observation related to its mate? Do they vary together?" A longer look at Table 11.6 suggests that female and male rates do in fact rise and fall together: where one is low, the other is, and where one is high the other is. Maybe the higher rates come from studies done in more stressful places (inner cities?) or perhaps from studies with a more inclusive definition of mental illness. If we follow up ideas like these we may learn some things about illness rates that go beyond the Gove and Tudor argument.

To follow this new line of attack we need new approaches, called *X* by *Y* techniques, which the next set of chapters outlines. As usual, the exploratory version comes first and the analogous confirmatory technique follows. In addition to the *X* by *Y* techniques, another tool useful for working with two categorical variables will be described in this section (the chi-square test in chapter 14).

11

X by *Y* and Straight Lines

This chapter begins with a very simple example; one where the simplest *X* by *Y* technique works in the simplest way. After the technique has been described and illustrated we will discuss it broadly and then go through a more complex example to round out your knowledge of the technique.

Seeing an *X* by *Y* Pattern

Consider the data in Table 11.1, due to Angell (1951), reporting integration, mobility, and heterogeneity for fifteen U.S. cities. In this study, integration was defined as a combination of crime rates and welfare effort; mobility was the number of persons moving in or out of a city, relative to its population; and heterogeneity was defined to be the number of non-whites and foreign-born whites relative to the population. Clearly these are *X* by *Y* data because

Table 11.1

Integration and Mobility for Selected
U.S. Cities

City	Integration	Mobility	Heterogeneity
Rochester	19.0	15.0	20.6
Worcester	16.4	13.6	22.1
Milwaukee	15.8	17.6	17.4
Buffalo	15.2	14.7	22.3
Reading	14.2	19.4	10.6
Cleveland	14.0	18.6	39.7
Peoria	13.8	35.1	10.7
Trenton	13.0	15.8	23.5
Toledo	12.7	21.6	19.2
Baltimore	12.0	12.1	45.8
Akron	11.3	22.1	20.4
Tacoma	10.9	31.2	17.8
Spokane	9.6	38.9	12.3
Indianapolis	8.8	23.1	29.2
Portland (Ore.)	7.2	35.8	16.4

Source: R. C. Angell, *American Journal of Sociology* 57, 1951. Published by the University of Chicago. © 1951 University of Chicago.

the values for the three variables are linked: all three scores in any one row come from the same city. To begin our exploration, we need to decide which two variables we will study; we choose integration and mobility because they seemed to be related (going down the columns, it looks like mobility increases as integration decreases). Obviously this is a matter of judgement and other choices of two variables to work on could have been made. Further, we have to decide which variable is X, the independent variable useful in predicting the other, Y. Again this is a matter of judgement. Let's assume that integration and mobility are related because higher levels of integration make a city pleasanter to live in so that fewer move out; that is, mobility declines as integration increases. Then mobility is dependent on integration, and integration will be X, the independent variable, while mobility will be Y. You could reverse the dependent and independent variables here and still make a very plausible case, that is, a decline in mobility might lead to a rise in integration. (Perhaps high levels of mobility disrupt informal social control mechanisms?)

With X and Y chosen our next step is to plot them so we can see their relationship. Table 11.2 plots integration as X and mobility as Y (note that the X-axis is horizontal and the Y-axis is vertical, as is conventional). Without any statistical help at all, just using your eyes, you can easily see a lot. Something is going on; these points aren't randomly scattered about, they form a loose pattern. Very broadly, they sweep from higher on the left to lower on the right; again, mobility generally declines as integration increases. A straight line from upper left to lower right would capture the

Table 11.2
Mobility and Integration

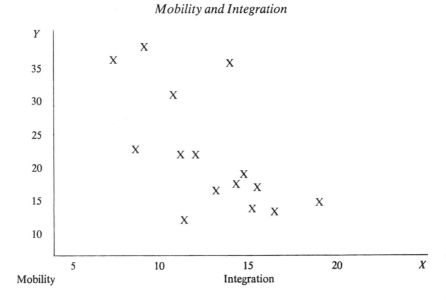

pattern fairly well. Try it: wiggle a thread or pencil around on the plot until it looks right. Then compare your intuitive try to the line in Table 11.3 found by the technique we'll describe shortly. Chances are that these lines are much the same, and they should be: the technique just gives a precise numerical summary of a trend that you can usually see plainly, if not exactly.

A linear pattern (like the one in Table 11.2) is the simplest pattern one can find in X by Y data, and also one of the most common patterns. The rest of the chapter will show how to find resistant summaries of such patterns easily, and how to go beyond the summaries by looking at residuals from them. Just as the mean or trimean is a numerical summary of level, a straight line equation is the numerical summary of a linear pattern.

The equation of a straight line looks like this:

$$Y = bX + a, \text{where}$$

Y is the dependent variable: the variable you try to predict or explain;

X is the independent variable: the basis of prediction (sometimes but not always the "cause" of Y);

b is the slope: the number of units Y changes for every unit change in X;

a is the intercept or constant: the value Y has when X is 0.

In our example, we want to find values for b and a which will make

$$\text{mobility} = b \text{ (integration)} + a$$

a good summary of the relationship between the two variables. Finding a line would be easy if we had just two points, but in fact we have fifteen in our example and often we have more. A convenient first step is to find just three *summary points* that sum up the main pattern of the data; then we find the line fit from the summary points.

Finding Three Summary Points

We would like to find three points that sum up the overall trend of the data, points that reflect most of the cases while not being deflected by atypical ones: *resistant* summary points. If we base our line on resistant summary points, the line will be a resistant fit. Tukey suggests that we break up our data into thirds on X, giving us three batches of points which can be summarized with our familiar batch tool, level.

First let's see how to break up the data into thirds on X. This requires ordering the data points on X. Table 11.1 has already been ordered on our X, integration. In table form, one can just draw two lines to mark off the thirds clearly and easily. This also has been done in Table 11.1: the cases Rochester through Reading are the top third on X (they are the five highest

Table 11.3

The Exploratory Line

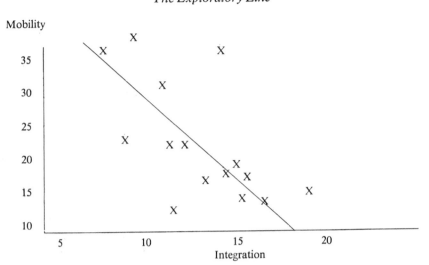

on integration) and so on. Table 11.4 shows the thirds graphically: here two vertical lines have been drawn to mark off the thirds. For example, the five points to the right of the right hand vertical line are the five points highest on *X*, or Rochester through Reading again. These thirds let us summarize what happens when *X* is high, medium, or low, which should be enough to give us the overall picture without drowning us in detail.

Table 11.4

Constructing the Line

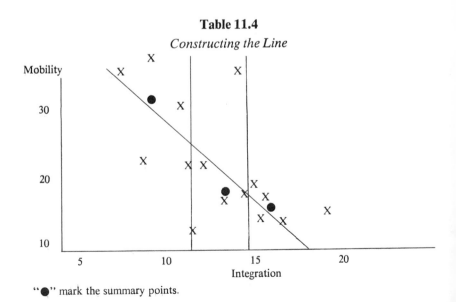

"●" mark the summary points.

Finding the thirds is not always as easy as it is in the present example. The following *rules of thumb for thirds* should always be checked:

1. Each end third should have *at most* one third of the points. (Otherwise there will not be enough points in the middle third; the middle third is the least important one for straight lines, but very important when we get to curves in the next chapter.)
2. Each end third should have a range on *X* which is less than half the total range on *X*. (In the second example in this chapter, we will see some of the problems that can arise when this rule is violated. Sometimes *X* needs to be transformed to conform to this rule.)
3. When there are several points with equal *X* values, they should all be treated in the same way: they should all go in the same third.
4. Get as many points into each end third as possible while still satisfying the first three rules of thumb. (The end thirds are especially important, and estimates using more cases are more reliable as we have seen.)

Are these rules met in our example? We note that the count is 15 so by rule 1, each extreme third can have at most five points. The top and bottom five are marked off by horizontal lines in Table 11.1. By rule 4, we would like to leave all five points in each of the end thirds; can we? First check rule 2. The total range on *X* is $19.0 - 7.2 = 11.8$ and the range of the upper third is $19.0 - 14.2 = 4.8$ while that of the lower third is $11.3 - 7.2 = 4.1$. Both end thirds have ranges that are less than one half the total range; rule 2 is satisfied. Finally we note that rule 3 is satisfied too; no two of the cities have the same *X* value. In the next example we will show what to do when the rules are not met so easily.

Having found the thirds, we want to summarize them. For each third we need a typical *X* value and a typical *Y* value. For example, the plot in Table 11.4 shows that *X* values are low and *Y* values high in the low third on *X,* while *X* values are high and *Y* values low in the high third on *X* — that's the kind of thing we want to capture in a simple numerical summary. But isn't this just a batch problem? In the top third on *X,* or the first five cases in Table 11.1, we have a batch of five *X* values and a batch of five *Y* values; we can just find the level of each. In this example, with five cases per third we can use trimeans (with fewer cases, medians would be used). For our example the high, medium, and low summary values are:

$$X_H = 15.8 \qquad\qquad Y_H = 15.6$$
$$X_M = 13.1 \qquad\qquad Y_M = 18.7$$
$$X_L = 9.7 \qquad\qquad Y_L = 30.3$$

Each pair of summary values is a summary point: X_H and Y_H, X_M and Y_M, X_L and Y_L. These three points are plotted in Table 11.4 as large filled-in circles. They do seem to summarize the thirds: each summary point is in the midst of the points in its third. Note that a summary point does not have to be an actual data point. None of the summary points coincides with a data point in our example, although this can happen. Note also that these are resistant summary points (because they are based on resistant levels): look hard at the middle third and you will see that the one atypically high value on *Y* does not pull the summary point up unduly.

So far we have done nothing elaborate; we have just divided the data on *X* and summarized *X* and *Y* for each part with a basic batch tool, level. But there are several common errors to watch out for:

1. Do not find the highest and lowest thirds for *Y* by ordering the *Y* values on *Y* itself; keep them together with their associated *X*'s.
2. Once you have found the thirds, the *X* and *Y* values within each third are summarized separately. Don't just take the *Y* paired with the summary *X* (if there is one).
3. Y_M should lie between Y_H and Y_L: if it doesn't, a linear fit will do a poor job of summarizing the data.

Finding a Line From the Summary Points

Now we are ready to find a line equation using the summary points. First *b* is found, then *a*. You may recall that we can find the slope of a line from any two points on the line: call them (X_1, Y_1), and (X_2, Y_2). We just find the "rise over the run" or the amount *Y* changes, $(Y_2 - Y_1)$, divided by the amount *X* changes, $(X_2 - X_1)$. Here the two points are the high and low summary points:

$$b = \frac{Y_H - Y_L}{X_H - X_L} = \frac{15.6 - 30.3}{15.8 - 9.7} = \frac{-14.7}{6.1} = -2.41 \cong -2.4$$

which is just the slope of the line connecting the high and low summary points. (We use the two end points to find *b* because those points give the best summary of the overall slope of the data.) To convince ourselves that the "*bX*" part of the line does indeed fit slope for us, let's treat $Y = bX$ as a fit temporarily. As with any fit, residuals can be found:

$$\text{temporary residuals} = \text{observation} - \text{fit}$$
$$= Y - bX.$$

Table 11.5, an example of the handiest kind of work sheet for *X* by *Y* work, gives *bX* and $Y - bX$ in the third and fourth columns respectively.

The fourth column is computed just to let us see what the *bX* part of the line does; it is not normally included in the worksheet. The $Y - bX$ values can be more easily seen in Table 11.6, where they are plotted on the *Y*-axis with *X* on the *X*-axis. The temporary residuals have little if any slope; they may have a slight tilt upward going from left to right, but compared to the original plot it's negligible. Using another decimal place in *b* might

Table 11.5

Basic Work Sheet (Angell Data)

		$Y = -2.4X + 53$		
X	*Y*	*bX*	*Y − bX*	*Y − (bX + a)*
19.0	15.0	−45.6	60.6	7.6
16.4	13.6	−39.4	53.0	0.0
15.8	17.6	−37.8	55.5	2.5
15.2	14.7	−36.5	51.2	−1.8
14.2	19.4	−34.1	53.5	.5
14.0	18.6	−33.6	52.2	−.8
13.8	35.1	−33.1	68.2	15.2
13.0	15.8	−31.2	47.0	−6.0
12.7	21.6	−30.5	52.1	−.9
12.0	12.1	−28.8	40.9	−12.1
11.3	22.1	−27.1	49.2	−3.8
10.9	31.2	−26.2	57.4	4.4
9.6	38.9	−23.0	61.9	8.9
8.8	23.1	−21.1	44.2	−8.8
7.2	35.8	−17.3	53.1	.1

	Y			*Y′*
3	596		1	5
3	1		1	
2			0	89
2	223		0	03140
1	585996		−0	2114
1	42		−0	69
			−1	2
			−1	

stem: tens   *stem*: tens
leaf: units   *leaf*: units

get out the last little bit of slope, but these values are untilted enough for most exploration purposes. It's easy to see that fitting *bX* does take care of slope. If it obviously doesn't — if, when you plot $Y - bX$ by *X*, you see any clear slope — then you've made a mistake.

$Y - bX$ residuals have no slope but do have one interesting feature: level. And that's what we use to find *a*. We could find *a* in several ways, but the easiest way is to carry on with our summary points: find $Y - bX$ for each summary point and take the mean of the three values. For our example,

$$a_H = Y_H - bX_H = 15.6 - (-2.4)\,15.8 = 53.5$$

$$a_M = Y_M - bX_M = 18.7 - (-2.4)\,13.1 = 50.1$$

$$a_L = Y_L - bX_L = 30.3 - (-2.4)\,9.7 = 53.6$$

$$a = \frac{a_H + a_M + a_L}{3} = 52.4 = 53$$

Table 11.6

Temporary Residuals from Partial Fit

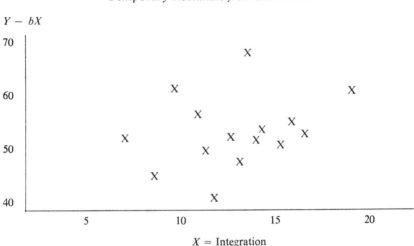

X = Integration

We've chosen to round up to 53 rather than down to 52 because 53 turns out to be a slightly better fit. This gives us the equation

$$Y = -2.4X + 53$$

as an approximate numerical summary of the linear relationships. Again, the procedure can be seen in Table 11.4. The line $Y = -2.4X + 53$ takes its slope from the top and bottom summary points, running parallel to the line passing through those two points. The line runs a bit below the end summary points because its level is based on all three summary points and the middle one pulls the fitted line down a shade. (In our example the three summary points are a little curved but not much. We'll learn in the next chapter what to do when there's too much curviness to ignore.) To plot the line, you can either draw it by eye using the summary points (a rough method but usually good enough once you have become used to line fitting) or you can solve the line equation for two convenient values of X (two well-separated values that make arithmetic easy).

The equation for the line is easy to find from the summary points, and we can see (in Table 11.3 or 11.4) that the exploratory line is a reasonable summary of the data pattern. Now, what is this numerical summary good for?

Uses of the Line Fit

The three main uses of the exploratory line fit are summarizing, predicting, and removing.

Summarizing: It is a simple use of lines but a very important one; don't underestimate it. For example, we summed up part of Table 11.2 with this brief description of the line from Table 11.3:

$$Y = -2.4X + 53$$

or   Mobility $= -2.4$ (integration) $+ 53$

This says that mobility would be fifty-three in a hypothetical city with zero on the integration index ($a = 53$); it also says that mobility goes down as integration goes up ($b = -2.4$). Earlier we speculated that increasing integration means increasing satisfaction in a city and as a result people are less likely to move out. Note how economical the line is: two numbers, *a* and *b*, say everything that the line says and much of what the data say. This economy is especially useful if we want to make a lot of comparisons, for example, if we want to compare the relationship between integration and mobility in several different countries. The comparison could be summed up very compactly with several sets of *a*'s and *b*'s. (This is like using numerical summaries to compare several batches.)

Predicting: Our line gives us a way (maybe imperfect) of predicting *Y* from *X*. So if we know an *X* value but not a *Y* value we can make an educated guess of what *Y* should be like. You are probably most familiar with projections based on past performance or trends, like population projections: one finds a line summing up the relationship of population to time so far and predicts what is likely to happen next.

Removing: Once we have a numerical summary of the linear relationship between *X* and *Y* we can remove this linear fit from *Y*:

$$Y - bX - a = Y - (bX + a)$$

These residuals are used for two important things: evaluating the line fit and going beyond it. These uses are so important that we will move now to a separate section on residuals from lines to clarify what such residuals are and how they are used.

Residuals from a Linear Fit

We have already seen what residuals from a linear fit are numerically: $Y - bX - a$. But it's easier to understand the residuals when they are shown graphically. Let's have a look at the points in the low third on *X* as shown in Table 11.7 (we show just one third to avoid unnecessary complication of the picture). This plot is like the previous ones except that residuals are shown numerically and graphically. Beside each point is its numeric residual, taken from the work sheet in Table 11.5. Graphically, each residual is the vertical distance between the point and the line, shown as dotted vertical

Table 11.7

A Close-Up View of Some Residuals
(Low Third Only)

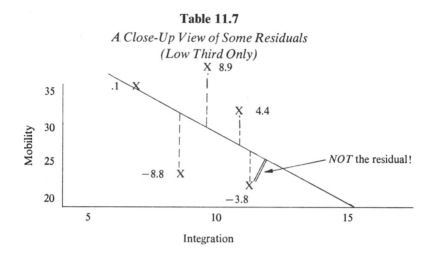

Table 11.8

Relationships and Residuals

A Weak (inverse) Relationship (*X* predicts *Y* poorly)

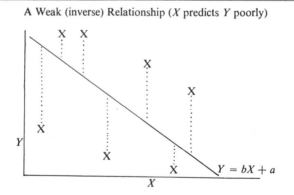

A Strong (inverse) Relationship (X predicts Y well)

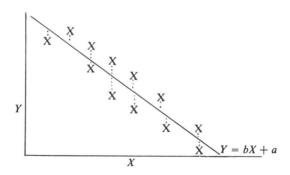

lines. One point is right on the line and hence has virtually zero residual (0.1); one point is well above the line and has a large positive residual (8.9); one point is well below the line and has a large negative residual (−8.8). The plotted point is the observed value and the line gives the predicted or fitted value for the same *x*, so the point-to-line distance is the same as "observation − fit" or the residual.

The only trick here is that your eyes may not be quite used to it. When starting, it is awfully tempting to think that the residual is the distance from the point to the line by the shortest route, like the double line shown for the point with residual −3.8. The double line is not the residual; it connects with our fitted line at a point with an *X* value different from the one we are interested in, the one for the point with residual −3.8.

With the line fit, $Y = bX + a$, we can find numeric residuals easily; with the residuals we can evaluate the line fit. Evaluating the line fit means finding out how good a fit is, how closely it predicts *Y*. If *X* and *Y* are weakly related we get something like the top plot in Table 11.8: the points are widely scattered and don't fall into a clear linear pattern, so the residuals from a line fit are big. For most of the points, the observed and predicted *Y* are far apart. On the other hand if *X* and *Y* are strongly related in a linear way then their values fall into a tidy pattern like that in the bottom plot of Table 11.8: the points are close to the fitted line and the residuals are small. In general, the greater the spread of the residuals, the worse the fit is: the more poorly the line predicts *Y*, and the more variation in *Y* there is left to explain. But spread alone won't be useful for evaluating fit because of problems of scale; the data could be big or small to begin with. For example, residuals for a population *Y* in the millions will be larger than those for a mobility index *Y* in the tens even if the population *Y* is much better predicted. We compensate for the scale factor, the original spread of *Y*, by using

$$\frac{dq \text{ residuals}}{dq \text{ original } Y}$$

as our general guide to how good a fit is. In our example, from the stems-and-leaves in Table 11.5, we find:

$$\frac{dq \text{ residuals}}{dq \text{ original } Y} = \frac{8.2}{16.2}$$

and the ratio is $\frac{8.2}{16.2} = .51$. This is in between the best possible fit (where *Y* is predicted almost exactly, residuals are mainly zero, and the ratio is zero) and the worst (where *X* doesn't help at all in predicting *Y* and the ratio is 1, and may even be more if you have really bad luck).

Another way of looking at the ratio is to focus on one major question: why is one *Y* value higher or lower than another? Why does mobility vary from city to city? We hope our line will explain part of this variation, and if it does then the amount of variation should decrease when the effects of integration (X) are removed.

So removing the line gives residuals useful in evaluating the line. If the line isn't a perfect fit for Y (and it hardly ever is) we want to go further and attempt to explain some of the still unexplained part of Y. But that just means explaining the residuals. The equation for the line is an economical summary statement of what we "know" about the relationship between the variables X and Y; the residuals are the part we don't yet know, so having "cleared away the underbrush" we can now look hard at what still needs to be explained without being distracted. New variables can be suggested. Since these residuals have had an "X" effect subtracted, we sometimes say we have "controlled" for X; the residuals indicate activity in Y that has nothing to do with X (nothing we can get at with a straight line, anyway). In the Angell example we could start by looking hard at the $Y - bX - a$ residuals in Table 11.5.

It is always a good idea to make the data patterns as visually clear as possible. Here, we could look hard at a familiar tool: the stem-and-leaf of the residuals (which we need to find the dq ratio anyway). None of the residuals are outliers, but the 15.2 residual for Peoria seems a little different from the rest of the residual batch; why is Peoria's mobility index so much higher than one would expect from Peoria's integration score and the overall relationship summed up in our line? If we carry on in this way, we are back to familiar batch exploration tools. We made a fit for a striking aspect of the data (the relationship between X and Y); we removed it (found $Y - bX - a$); and, treating the residuals exactly like any other batch of numbers, we started looking for ideas about unexplained parts of the data.

We can also take advantage of the X by Y character of the data a bit more by plotting the residuals: make another X by Y plot, but this time use $Y - (bX + a)$ instead of the original Y. The residuals can also be seen graphically in a plot like the one in Table 11.3, where the points can be compared to the line fit, but many people find this a bit hard at first; your eyes may not be used to comparing the points to the line vertically, as in Table 11.7. Plotting the residuals against X avoids possible confusion. You can make the residuals plot even clearer by labelling the larger residuals with any information that may help explain them. Finally, the residuals plot often shows a pattern of some sort that demands a better fit. For example, if the residual plot has some slope or level in it then the line fit probably needs to be improved; or the residuals plot may show a curve more clearly than the original X by Y plot did. As the next example shows, residual plots may lead to important insights.

What We've Learned So Far

With the help of Angell's data we've learned how to fit an exploratory straight line. Divide the data into thirds on X; summarize each third with a resistant level; then use the two end thirds to find the slope, and subsequently make use of all three to find a. This produces a simple linear summary of the relationship between X and Y. By finding residuals $(Y - bX - a)$ we can evaluate the straight line fit and try to add new ideas to it.

The X by Y numerical summary of a relationship (a line) has the same properties as exploratory numerical summaries for batches. The exploratory straight line is quickly found, resistant, and conforms with what your eyes tell you. Fits and residuals crop up again, and indeed these concepts are especially important and clear for X by Y data. The residuals from the linear fit, $Y - (bX + a)$, deserve detailed attention because they are the potential source of new insights beyond the line.

Now we will go through one other example which illustrates two new things: a direct instead of an indirect relationship, and an experience with data where there are complexities in finding thirds. Nothing else is new; the basic line-fitting routine is the same as before.

Another Example: Civic Voting

Consider Table 11.9, adapted from an M.A. thesis by A. Ewing (1972) on civic voting in Vancouver, B.C. The unit of observation here is the "district" or area of Vancouver; these areas are distinct in the eyes of long-term residents of the city and the areas are known to most Vancouverites by name. The areas are grouped as East Side, or West Side, also a familiar local distinction. For each of the 24 districts we have the following information: mean income in 1961 (from the 1961 census); and, for the 1964 civic elections, percentage of eligible voters casting ballots, or turnout (TO).

We would like to try to "explain" voter turnout (Y) on the basis of income (X). It's easy to see that those districts with higher incomes tend also to have greater turnout. No surprise about this; there are several arguments in the literature about why this might be. First, people with higher incomes are generally more highly educated and well-informed about politics, so they are more likely to understand the election issues and take an interest in them, implying that they will come to a voting decision more easily and carry it out more often. Second, people in higher income areas are probably paying higher municipal taxes which may make them feel more concerned about how the money is spent, or make them value municipal politics more because it costs more. (On the other hand, their taxes may not be as much of their disposable incomes as the taxes paid by the poorer people are of theirs.) These explanations stress individual characteristics; one could stress political systems instead. For example, it is possible that municipal (and other!) governments are more oriented to the interests of the rich than the interests of the poor; so the poor may stay home because they correctly perceive that the election outcome will make little or no difference to them, while the wealthy go to the polls to fight out their intraclass differences. We haven't come close to exhausting the speculations about the relationship between income and turnout.

Let's examine the relationship with our new technique. The plot in Table 11.10 suggests that we do indeed have a relationship between X and Y, with Turnout (Y) increasing as Income increases: a direct relationship. The plot has a few extra features that we will discuss in a moment. To start our numerical analysis of the relationship, we order the areas on X as in Table 11.11, a standard work sheet. Next we find thirds. With 24 points, we would like to get eight into each third. Each end third must have a range less than

$$\tfrac{1}{2}(8477 - 2751) = 2863$$

Clearly, this rule is *not* met; the top eight points have an income range of almost 4000. To see the problems this raises, consider the plot of the raw

Table 11.9

Vancouver Municipal Voting

District	Mean Income (1961)	Turn-Out 1964
East Side		
1. Strathcona	2751	24
2. Woodland	3315	26
3. Mt. Pleasant	3422	30
4. Grandview	3864	42
5. Riley Park	3865	38
6. Kingsway	3865	38
7. Cedar Cottage	3974	40
8. New Brighton	4003	39
9. Fraserview	4173	42
10. Collingwood	4186	38
11. Sunset	4299	40
12. Little Mountain	4383	43
13. Newport	4594	41
West Side		
14. Burrard	3589	27
15. Kitsilano North	3785	34
16. Fairview	3786	30
17. West End	4233	33
18. Kitsilano South	4558	41
19. Marpole	4640	40
20. Dunbar	5701	58
21. Pt. Grey	5908	48
22. Arbutus	6267	55
23. Kerrisdale	7066	59
24. Shaughnessy	8477	52

Source: Ewing, (1972).

Table 11.10

Turnout by Raw Mean Income
Vancouver, B.C.

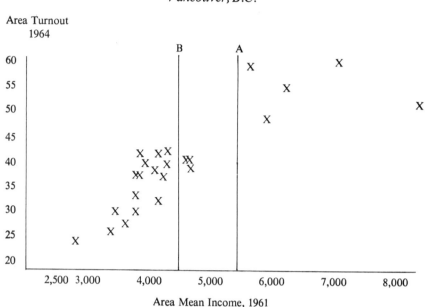

data in Table 11.10. One vertical line, *B*, marks off the top eight cases whose range we just found to be too great. In the plot we see how widely spread these cases are compared to others. If we use these eight for the top third, then the top summary point will have to summarize about half the picture by itself. The second vertical line in the plot, *A*, marks off the top five cases. If we use these for the top third, moving the three cases between *A* and *B* into the middle third, we can satisfy the range rule, but at the cost of basing our high summary point on only five cases, and atypical-looking ones at that. If we could satisfy the range rule by moving one point into the middle we probably would, since the top third would not lose much data and we would save ourselves a bit of transformation work, but in this case the range rule cannot be met unless all three points between *A* and *B* are moved into the middle. If we work with the raw data we're stuck: either the top summary point is based on too few points, or it is called on to summarize too much of the overall pattern.

So why stick with the raw data? The problem is simple and familiar: there is too much upward straggle in *X*. Let's use some transformation from the left-hand side of the ladder of transformations: square roots, logs, and so on. A little trial and error shows that negative reciprocals are needed; to keep the numbers from getting too awkwardly small we used $-1000/X$ instead of $-1/X$. The transformed data **are** also shown in the worksheet

Table 11.11. Now the total range is $-.12 - (-.36) = .24$, and the upper eight points have a range of $-.12 - (-.22) = .10$, no longer too much. Our lower points satisfy the range rule too. However, the lower third does present problems with the rule for values tied on X. If we look at the transformed data, it seems that there are five cases tied at $-.26$ and all will have to go into the middle third (if we put them in the low third, the low third will have nine points and should have at most eight). However, if we look at the original income figures we can break some of the ties: only areas 5 and 8 are really tied. They should be treated alike, so both go into the middle third, leaving us seven points for the low third. Again we mark off the thirds with two horizontal lines across the worksheet, to make it easier to find the summary points.

Once again each third has enough points to make a trimean summary of the X and Y levels useful:

$$X_H = -0.18 \qquad\qquad Y_H = 49.4$$

$$X_M = -0.243 \qquad\qquad Y_M = 39$$

$$X_L = -0.28 \qquad\qquad Y_L = 30$$

$$b = \frac{Y_H - Y_L}{X_H - X_L} = \frac{49.4 - 30}{-0.18 - (-0.28)} = \frac{19.4}{0.10}$$

$$= 194 \simeq 190$$

There's no compelling reason here for taking $b = 190$; we could as easily have taken $b = 200$ or 195 or 194. Convenience, judgement and accessibility of electronic aids will usually determine this choice for you.

Next we estimate a from the three summary points:

$$Y_H - 190X_H = 83.6$$

$$Y_M - 190X_M = 85.2$$

$$Y_L - 190X_L = 83.2$$

The mean of these is 84, which we round to 85 for a little more convenience. Thus our numerical summary of the linear pattern is:

$$Y = 190X + 85$$

Table 11.11 shows the residuals from this fit in the last column; Table 11.12 shows the line, summary points, and data points.

What does the line fit mean, how good a fit is it, and how can we go further? First, and most important, b is positive; higher income goes with higher turnout, as we can see from the plots as well as from the equation. This doesn't necessarily mean that there is a causal relation between income and turnout. However, as we have seen there are quite a few causal explanations of why this might be the case. We also see that $a = 85$, which means

Table 11.11

Work Sheet, Income and Turnout in Vancouver

District	1961 Income	$X = \dfrac{-1000}{\text{Income}}$	$Y = \text{TO}$	$bX = 190X$	$Y' = Y - bX - a^*$
1.	2751	−.36	24	−68	7
2.	3315	−.30	26	−57	−2
3.	3422	−.29	30	−55	0
14.	3589	−.28	27	−53	−5
15.	3785	−.26	34	−49	−2
16.	3786	−.26	30	−49	−6
4.	3864	−.26	42	−49	6
5.	3865	−.26	38	−49	2
6.	3865	−.26	38	−49	2
7.	3974	−.25	40	−48	3
8.	4003	−.25	39	−48	2
9.	4173	−.24	42	−46	3
10	4186	−.24	38	−46	−1
17.	4233	−.24	33	−46	−6
11	4299	−.23	40	−44	−1
12.	4383	−.23	43	−44	2
18.	4558	−.22	41	−42	−2
13.	4594	−.22	41	−42	−2
19.	4640	−.22	40	−42	−3
20.	5701	−.18	58	−34	7
21.	5908	−.17	48	−32	−5
22.	6267	−.16	55	−30	0
23.	7066	−.14	59	−27	1
24.	8477	−.12	52	−23	−10

$^*a = 85$. In district 1, for example, $Y - bX - a = 24 - (-68) - 85 = 7$.

Y is predicted to be 85 when X is zero; here that means that 1964 turnout is predicted to be 85% for a hypothetical district of very, very wealthy people (so wealthy that -1000/income is .00). So, this fit would predict that even very well-off people would not all vote; there are always a few people who can't make it or are just not interested. (Actually, other data suggest that turnout drops off among the rich; perhaps they have other, more effective ways to make inputs to governments.)

This fit appears to make a lot of sense. How strong is it? Well, we use the same test as before:

$$\frac{dq \ Y \text{ residuals}}{dq \text{ original } Y} = .61$$

suggesting a moderate fit, in line with the visual impression from the plots. Thus our first attempt has explained quite a bit of Y but by no means all; some of Y, the residuals, still has to be thought about. That's what we'll try to do next.

Table 11.12

Turnout and Transformed Income Plot,
With Fit

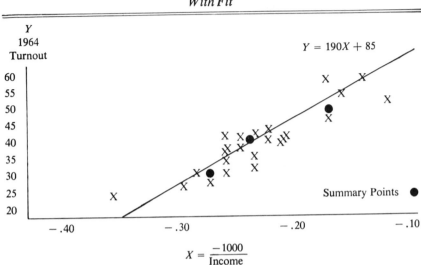

$$X = \frac{-1000}{\text{Income}}$$

While looking over the residuals in Table 11.11, it seems the positive and negative residuals come in clumps; for example, areas 4, 5, 6, 7, 8, and 9 all have positive residuals; and their low area numbers tell us they are East Side areas. On the other hand, a lot of the high numbered areas, or West Side areas, have negative residuals. Is there a meaningful pattern here? Let's

Table 11.13

Residuals

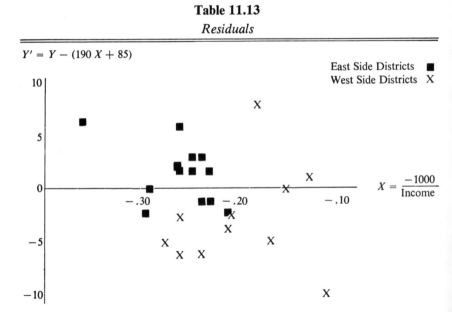

do a residual plot including East-West information to check this possibility further. Table 11.13 plots $Y - bX - a$ against X, using crosses for West Side areas and filled-in squares for East Side areas. Something is happening here! Most of the West Side areas have lower turnout than predicted from their income, while most of the East Side areas have higher turnout than predicted from their income. Note that this does not mean that the East Side areas have higher turnout; they don't, as Table 11.9 makes clear. East Side districts have lower turnout than West Side ones but not as much lower as predicted from the East-West difference in income. Perhaps this distinction between raw data (East Side turnout lower) and residuals (East Side turnout higher than predicted) will be a bit clearer in Table 11.14, a plot of income and turnout just like Table 11.12 except that the East Side has been marked by squares as in the residuals plot. (This change can be made easily with tracing paper.) Turnout and income are related for both East and West areas. The wealthier West areas have higher turnout, overall. But it is also true that the East areas have higher turnout than West areas of comparable income. Income affects turnout, and so does an East-West difference of some kind. How can we explain and fit the East-West difference we have found by examining the income residuals?

Table 11.14

Income and Turnout

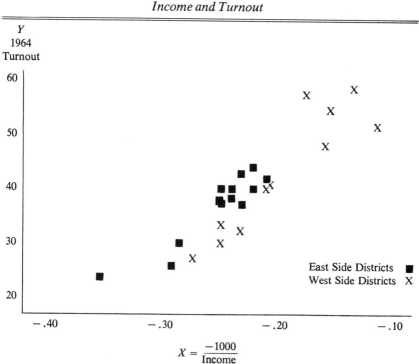

Table 11.15

Residuals from Table 11.11 in East-West Batches

Y'(East)	$Y'' = Y'$(East) $-$ Md	Y'(West)	$Y'' = Y'$(West) $-$ Md
7	5	-5	-3
-2	-4	-6	-4
0	-2	-2	0
6	4	-6	-4
2	0	-2	0
3	1	-3	-1
2	0	7	9
2	0	-5	-3
3	1	0	2
-1	-3	1	3
-1	-3	-10	-8
2	0		
-2	-4		
Md = 2		Md = -2	

Stem and Leaf and Summary of Second Residuals

0	59	N	24	
0	40100 10002 3	X_U	9	
-0	42334 34413	q_U	1	
-0	8	Md	0	$dq = 4$
		q_L	-3	outliers: Shaughnessy
		X_L	-8	adjacents: Dunbar, Strathcona

The explanation may lie in the special features of the 1964 election, or it may lie in long-run differences between the two areas; Ewing notes in his thesis that East and West have traditionally had somewhat different sub-cultures, and are seen as different by politicians who often plan campaigns with those differences in mind. Our data don't let us examine East-West differences, but we can speculate: for example, do the East side districts have less turnover (poorer people tend to be less geographically mobile) so that their residents are longer-term residents with more knowledge of civic politics? Ideas like this would be worth pursuing if other elections showed the same pattern, with East Side districts showing more turnout at equal levels of income.

At any rate, this East-West difference looks important, so how can we express it? Easily! Remember, the residuals are just a batch with no slope and with level about zero. In batch terms, we have found two sub-batches; let's break them up. This has been done in Table 11.15. The median for the East sub-batch was found and subtracted from each element of that batch. Result? The East sub-batch now has zero level. The same thing was done with the West sub-batch. We are now left with a second set of residuals, Y'', which are unaffected by area of the city. How well have we done with this fit? The *dq* ratio should give us an indication.

$$\frac{dq\ Y''}{dq\ Y} = \frac{4}{8} = .5$$

The previous *dq* ratio was .61 and we've improved a bit on that, though not an enormous amount. It looks like both income and side of the city are important for understanding turnout, with perhaps income rather more so.

In summary, our first fit was

$$1964\ \text{Turnout} = 190\ (-1000/\text{income}) + 85$$

meaning that higher income goes with higher turnout, though even the wealthiest people may not all turn out. With a *dq* ratio of .61, this fit is pretty good. Then we tried an area fit for residuals: holding income constant, the East Side turnout is the West Side turnout plus 4 percent. The two layers of fit together have a *dq* ratio of .5, an improved fit though still far from a perfect one.

Residuals versus Original *Y*

A peculiar thing has happened in this example. The residuals behave in a way opposite to the original data. Consider *Y* or 1964 Turnout. The East Side has much lower turnout than the West Side. But if we look at *Y'*, or the residuals of turnout from income, the East has higher turnout residuals. The apparent relationship between one variable and another (here, city area and turnout) can be dramatically changed by controlling for a third variable (here, income). The West Side does turn out more on the whole, perhaps because it is a wealthier area; but it does not turn out quite as much more as we would expect given its income. Looking at East-West and at income tells us more about turnout than looking at either one alone.

Since *Y'* is a very different affair from *Y*, we need different ways of talking about *Y'*. If you've been reading carefully, you'll have noticed that we used several ways of describing the residuals from a fit, with all the phrases meaning much the same thing. Here we list some of the commoner ones.

Y' is: the set of residuals from a fit of *Y* to *X*
   the part of *Y* not explained by *X*
   Y with effects of *X* removed
   Y with *X* controlled (or held constant)
   the difference between *Y* and what we predict it is, given *X*.

Use whatever phrasing you find most comfortable. You will find all of these, and variations on them, in the literature.

Voting in Vancouver: A Summary

This example has turned out to be fairly complex, much more so than the first example of mobility and integration. First, the data required transforming. This was simple enough and made finding an exploratory line very straightforward. We will find other uses of transformation when we get to curvy line fits.

We also had a pair of tied values on the borderline between the low third and the middle third; we put both in the middle third.

Most importantly, this example showed the power of looking hard at the residuals from the linear fit, and how useful simple and familiar techniques like sub-batching can be. You will not always want to sub-batch, of course; the techniques used on a set of residuals depend on what you see in the residuals. A plot of residuals by *X* is always worth trying, but the most important thing is looking hard and thinking about what you see.

A straight line is the simplest line, and a straight line fit is easily made. Finding *a* and *b* is mostly a matter of using familiar tools like medians and trifling arithmetic like subtraction. You have to remember a few rules of thumb but the reasons for them are so obvious that the rules are easy to keep in mind. Once you have your line you have a very powerful gadget indeed. It summarizes, it predicts, it can be removed easily to leave interesting residuals. Transformation will help if the range rule gives trouble.

Exploratory and Confirmatory

In standard confirmatory statistics, fitting a straight line is called "linear regression." The general strategy is the same: fit a line, evaluate the fit, find residuals, try to explain them. Plots (usually called "scatterplots") are used in the same way as well. The main difference is that a more rigorous, less resistant technique for finding the line is used. We will say no more about this here since confirmatory regression has a chapter of its own, and we will point out the parallels to exploration there.

Homework

Do an exploratory straight line analysis of the *X* and *Y* of your choice. Either do an analysis of the Gove and Tudor data in Table 11.16 or take any pair of variables from Table 11.17. (Hint: 1973 abortions or abortion rates look like promising *Y*'s.) Give reasons for your choice for a start; why did you think that *X* and *Y* would be related?

Then plot *X* and *Y* and note what you see. Start finding your line: find thirds on *X*, make sure they fit the rules, transform if necessary. When the thirds are OK, find summary points, then *b*, then *a*, then $Y - bX - a$, the residuals. Evaluate your fit. Plot residuals by *X*.

Discuss as you go. Is the relationship inverse or direct? Why? Is it strong or weak? Why? What are the residuals like and what might explain them?

Table 11.16

Sex and Mental Illness

Mentally Ill (Per Cent)	
Male	Female
13.1	26.3
14.9	34.2
14.9	33.3
15.6	22.9
18.2	25.3
18.4	38.0
20.3	38.9
21.0	34.0
21.2	35.5
22.0	43.0
22.0	40.0
31.0	54.0

Source: Adapted from Table 1 (p. 819) of Gove and Tudor, (1973), *American Journal of Sociology*, published by the University of Chicago. © 1973 University of Chicago. This table includes all studies from part A of the original table for which exact percentages for both sexes are given.

Table 11.17A

Canadian Abortions and Abortion Rates, 1972 and 1973

	Therapeutic Abortions		Abortions per 100 Live Births	
Province	1972	1973	1972	1973
All Areas*	38,853	43,201	11.2	12.6
Newfoundland	133	193	1.0	1.6
P.E.I.	45	41	2.2	2.2
Nova Scotia	837	932	6.2	7.0
New Brunswick	183	341	1.6	3.0
Quebec	2,647	3,141	3.4	3.7
Ontario	20,272	22,603	16.2	16.3
Manitoba	1,178	1,259	6.8	7.4
Saskatchewan	1,043	1,219	6.7	8.2
Alberta	3,887	4,047	13.3	13.6
B.C.	8,179	9,176	23.7	26.7
Yukon	48	76	10.6	18.1
N.W.T.	44	51	3.6	4.2

Source: Statistics Canada.

Note: These figures do not include Canadian residents who obtained abortions in the United States. In each year, about 6,000 Canadian residents obtained abortions in New York State.

* Includes patients for which province of residence was not reported.

Table 11.17B

Hospitals in Canada with Therapeutic Abortion Committees (TACs) 1974

Province	Number of Hospitals	Hospitals with TAC
Newfoundland	48	6
P.E.I.	12	2
Nova Scotia	56	12
New Brunswick	41	7
Quebec	281	27
Ontario	357	108
Manitoba	108	9
Saskatchewan	147	10
Alberta	164	24
B.C.	130	52
N.W.T.	8	1
Yukon	7	1
Canada	1,359	259

Source: Geekie, Canadian Medical Association Journal, 111(5) 1974, pp. 475–477.

Note: To be empowered to set up a TAC and conduct abortions, a hospital must either be accredited by the Canadian Council on Hospital Accreditation or receive special approval from the Minister of Health in the province in which it is located.

12
Unbending

Data Can Be "Curvy"

Many of you may have been thinking, as you were reading and working through the last chapter, that this was all a "put-up job." Our straight line fits worked reasonably well only because the data were essentially linear. You might also wonder how often we actually have linear data to work with; the answer to this is, surprisingly often. But even when the data are substantially non-linear, we can often cope easily, by using transformations. Let us return to some simple data we first looked at in chapter 5, Canadian population from 1851–1961, in Table 12.1.

Table 12.1

Canadian Population, 1851–1961
(in millions)

Census Number	Census Year	Population (millions)
1	1851	2.44
2	1861	3.23
3	1871	3.69
4	1881	4.32
5	1891	4.83
6	1901	5.37
7	1911	7.21
8	1921	8.79
9	1931	10.38
10	1941	11.51
11	1951	14.01
12	1961	18.24

Source: Statistics Canada.

This time, we will treat these data as X by Y data where X is time and Y is population. To keep the arithmetic easy we use census number in place of census year: or 1, 2, 3, etc., in place of 1851, 1861, 1871, etc. The relationship is plotted along with the summary points in Table 12.2. The plot clearly shows that there is a strong relationship between time and population size; equally clearly, the relationship is not linear. The middle summary point is below the line between the other two. It doesn't look like much, but we

Table 12.2

Canadian Population by Census, 1851–1961

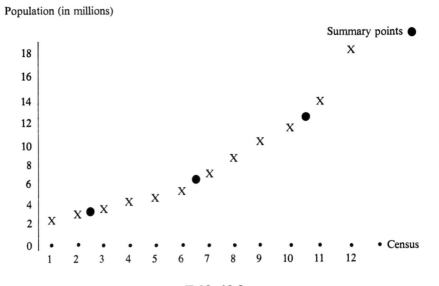

Population (in millions)

Table 12.3

Population (in logs of millions)

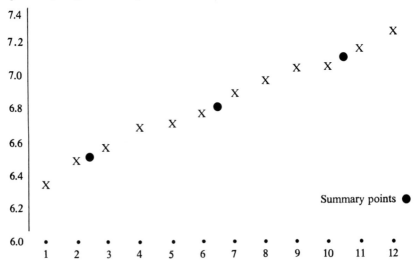

will soon see that this departure from linearity is pretty important. Population does not grow steadily with time, growing by the same amount for every time interval; instead, it grows faster and faster as time goes by. Since

Table 12.4

Worksheet for Equation Y = .071X + .36

X	.071X	Y	Y' = Y − .071X − .36
1	.071	6.39	−.04
2	.142	6.51	.01
3	.213	6.57	.00
4	.284	6.64	.00
5	.355	6.68	−.04
6	.426	6.73	−.06
7	.497	6.86	.00
8	.568	6.94	.01
9	.639	7.02	.02
10	.710	7.06	−.01
11	.781	7.15	.01
12	.852	7.26	.05
		$dq = .435$	$dq = .035$

$$dq \text{ ratio} = \frac{.035}{.435} = .08$$

Median Summary Points

$$X_L \quad 2.5 \qquad X_M \quad 6.5 \qquad X_H \quad 10.5$$
$$Y_L \quad .54 \qquad Y_M \quad .80 \qquad Y_H \quad 1.11$$

$$b = \frac{1.11 - .54}{10.5 - 2.5} = .071$$

a: $a_H = 1.11 - .071 (10.5) = .365$
$\quad a_M = .80 - .071 (6.5) = .339$
$\quad a_L = .54 - .071 (2.5) = .363$

$$a = \frac{a_H + a_M + a_L}{3} = .36$$

the data are curved, no straight line fit can do them justice and we will have to do something new.

Let's try *transforming* the population values. In chapter 5, we saw that logging is a natural choice because logging will make population batch data symmetric when the rate of net growth is constant; perhaps logging will help with our X by Y problem too. The logged population figures are found as part of Table 12.4, and they are plotted in Table 12.3. The three summary points are almost perfectly in line; that's more like a straight line! Therefore, we can use our familiar line-fitting technique for straight lines after all, once transformation has straightened the data out. Table 12.4 also gives the numerical work for finding *b* and *a* using logged populations:

$$Y = bX + a$$
logged population = .071 (Census number) + .36

From the plot in Table 12.3 or from the *dq* ratio in Table 12.4

(*dq* ratio = .08) we can see that the fit is very good indeed. This is slightly misleading as several of the estimates are "off" by 10% or more when we translate from logs back to populations (an error of about 2½ million in 1961), though how much of this is "translation error" that we could reduce by using more accurate log tables is difficult to say without trying. Even so, the fit is very good.

What does the fit mean? Well, the population grows by a constant amount in logs: it grows by about .071 from census to census (a figure quite close to the .08 growth in logs that we found in chapter 5 using a different approach to the data). Adding logs corresponds to multiplying raw numbers, so the population grows by a constant proportion in raw numbers. As we've argued before, this makes a great deal of sense. We could push the interpretation further by looking at the larger residuals; for example, why was the population smaller than predicted in the sixth census, that for 1901? Why was it larger than predicted in the twelfth census, or 1961? Economic conditions and migration patterns might help explain these slight departures from a simple basic pattern of steady growth rates.

When to Unbend

We've just seen that it can be very easy to handle a curve by transformation. Now we need to know some useful practical details like: when should you make a curve fit instead of a straight one? and how do you decide which transformation to use?

First, how much curvature do we tolerate before we decide that the linear fit won't do and transforming should be tried? This really depends on many things; how many points there are, how close the points are to the best-fitting line, etc. As a result, we can only provide some very loose rules of thumb. One rule emphasizes the amount of curvature in the summary points. To see how this works, consider the three summary points for the untransformed population data:

$$X_L \quad 2.5 \qquad\qquad Y_L \quad 3.46$$

$$X_M \quad 6.5 \qquad\qquad Y_M \quad 6.29$$

$$X_H \quad 10.5 \qquad\qquad Y_H \quad 12.76$$

Now instead of computing one slope, compute two: from the low summary point to the middle, and from the middle point to the high. The two slopes are:

$$b_{LM} = \frac{6.29 - 3.46}{6.5 - 2.5} = .71; \quad b_{MH} = \frac{12.76 - 6.29}{10.5 - 6.5} = 1.62$$

These two slopes tell us the same thing as the plot in Table 12.2: the second part of the curve is increasing faster than the first. If the line were straight, then b_{LM} and b_{MH} would be roughly the same. The advantage of looking at the two slopes instead of just at the plot is that we can use the slopes to give us a simple numerical summary of how curvy the line is if b_{LM} and b_{MH} have the same sign. The easiest way to do this is a ratio: put the smaller slope (smaller in absolute value) over the larger one. In our example, this means $\frac{.71}{1.62} = .44$. If this ratio is one or very nearly one, then the two slopes are about equal and a straight line will do; if the ratio is much less than one, then the slopes are unequal and perhaps fitting a curve should be tried. Here is one crude rule of thumb for decision:

If the slope ratio is	You should:
0.9 to 1.0	leave the data alone and make a linear fit.
0.5 to 0.9	consider a curve fit, depending on the situation (see below).
under 0.5	transform X or Y or both to straighten the data out; this is too much curve to ignore.

(Use only if b_{LM} and b_{MH} have same sign.)

Where the slope ratio is between .5 and .9 you have to use your judgement. Several issues may be important in the decision:

1. The number of data points: the more points you have, the more fits — including curve fits — you should be willing to try.
2. The strength of the relationship: if you look at the plot of X and Y and find that the data are all over the place, with a very weak relationship between X and Y, you usually go for a simple linear fit instead of a more complicated curve fit. But if the relationship is very strong, it's worthwhile to fit it as closely as you can by transforming as required.
3. The amount of sense a transformation makes. If there is a natural explanation for transforming, if the slight curve in the data seems to be there for a reason you understand, then treat it more seriously than something that may be just an accident as far as you can tell.

In the population example, the case for transformation is very clear-cut: the slope ratio of .44 is less than .5, the plot in Table 12.2 makes it clear that the relationship is strong, and the curve makes very good sense. The number of data points is a bit small but this poses no problem with such clear-cut data.

We cannot overemphasize the importance of plotting and judgement here. The slope ratio rule of thumb is often helpful, especially when you are just getting started, but it is not foolproof and should not be used automatically. Always make a plot like Table 12.2, showing data points and summary points; often the plot is the clearest guide to whether unbending will be worthwhile or not.

Choosing Transformations

The choice of transformation will not always be as obvious as it was for the familiar population data. Faced with a curve we know less well, how do we decide which transformation to use? Tukey suggests a table like 12.5 which shows four basic curves, gives verbal descriptions of them, and indicates which side of the ladder of transformations should be used for X and/or for Y to straighten out that curve. For example, the population data have $b_{LM} < b_{MH}$, with both positive; and we saw that logging Y worked out nicely. Taking some power of X would have worked too, but would have been rather silly in this particular case.

Table 12.5

Appropriate Transforms for Various Curves

Curve	Verbal Description	X Transform	Y Transform
	$b_{LM} > b_{MH}$, both positive	log x, $-1/x$, etc.	y^2, y^3, etc.
	$b_{LM} > b_{MH}$, both negative	log x, etc.	log y, etc.
	$b_{LM} < b_{MH}$, both positive	x^2, x^3, etc.	log y, etc.
	$b_{LM} < b_{MH}$, both negative	x^2, etc.	y^2, etc.

Source: Tukey (1970). Adapted from p. 9-4b

Still using the population data, a little thought will show you why transformations can unbend a curve. The population curve involves a more rapid growth of high Y values than of low Y values; that is, the higher two Y summary values differ more than the lower two. Some correction for upward straggle in Y will even this up so that Y grows evenly with X. Alternatively, we could think about X. The three summary points would be straighter if the middle point were more to the left, that is, if the lower X values were squeezed together and the higher ones spread out; this suggests a correction for downward straggle, or some power of X, which is just what the chart indicates.

You can use this table to suggest the correct side of the ladder for straightening by transforming X; for transforming Y; or for straightening by transforming both X and Y. You don't often transform both X and Y because that is more work and harder to interpret; but sometimes you may feel it's worthwhile because transforming both variables improves the fit. For example, you might find that log X undercorrects and the negative reciprocal of X overcorrects but log X along with square root of Y is just right. As always, feel free to follow your judgement.

When Are the Data Unbent?

How do you know when you have pretty well straightened out the line? How do you know which transformation to use? As so often before, we suggest that you make life easy for yourself by deciding on the basis of the summary points; there are only three of them, so how long can this take? Try a transform on the summary points, find the new b_{LM} and b_{MH}, and go ahead with the transform when you get two slopes that are nearly equal.

Suppose we are trying this with our population figures. We would start from the raw data summary points, then log the Y summary values:

Raw X	Raw Y	Log Y
X_L 2.5	Y_L 3.46	.54
X_M 6.5	Y_M 6.29	.79
X_H 10.5	Y_H 12.76	1.11

(These logged Y values are not exactly the same as those we used earlier, which were medians of the logged Y rather than logs of Y medians. It is more accurate to transform first and then find the summary values, but you don't want to bother transforming all the values until you are sure the transform is pretty good.)

Next we check the two slopes:

$$b_{LM} = \frac{.79 - .54}{6.5 - 2.5} = .063 \qquad b_{MH} = \frac{1.11 - .79}{10.5 - 6.5} = .080$$

$$\text{ratio} = \frac{.063}{.080} = .79$$

The two slopes are not equal, but neither are they dramatically unequal; they are in our discretionary range. On the one hand, we might like to try to fit the curve a bit more exactly: when logs are used the curve still has b_{LM} a little lower than b_{MH}, so perhaps the curve is undercorrected and negative reciprocals would work better. On the other hand, the log transformation is so natural and so easily interpreted for these data that we would rather use it even if it does not flatten out the curve perfectly.

Another Example: Wealth and Literacy

Unbending with transformation is pretty easy, with no new major tools, but it does involve some unfamiliar rules of thumb; so we will go through another simple example that also happens to illustrate a slightly different use of logging. Table 12.6 presents Gross National Product per capita and adult literacy rates (percent) for 22 countries or areas. If your review example after chapter 6 was higher education by economic stages, you may find this example especially interesting. Once again the data are taken from the *World Handbook of Political and Social Indicators*, though this time we have used only every fifth case from their Table B.2. Remember, we have suggested that sampling a small number of cases to explore makes a lot of sense; you can get useful ideas without investing too much time.

The raw data are plotted in Table 12.7. Without using any rules of thumb at all, just our eyes, we can see that this is a very difficult plot to work with. Too many cases are packed into the left side of the plot, so that their pattern and deviations from the pattern are hard to see. The overall pattern of all the points is unclear. Is there a single curve, rising very sharply on the

Table 12.6

Wealth and Literacy

Country	GNP per Capita	Adult Literacy Rate (%)	Log (GNP per Capita)
Nepal	45	5.0	1.65
Burma	57	47.5	1.76
Uganda	64	27.5	1.81
South Vietnam	76	17.5	1.88
Thailand	96	68.0	1.98
Haiti	105	10.5	2.02
Indonesia	131	17.5	2.12
South Korea	144	77.0	2.16
Ghana	172	22.5	2.24
Peru	179	47.5	2.25
El Salvador	219	39.4	2.34
British Guiana	235	74.0	2.37
Hong Kong	272	57.5	2.43
Panama	329	65.7	2.52
Lebanon	362	47.5	2.56
Singapore	400	50.0	2.60
Argentina	490	86.4	2.69
Iceland	572	98.5	2.76
Czechoslovakia	680	97.5	2.83
France	943	96.4	2.97
New Zealand	1,310	98.5	3.12
Canada	1,947	97.5	3.29
(U.S.A., not part of sample:	2,577	98)	

Source: Russett et al., (1964), pp. 294–298. Used by permission.

Table 12.7

Wealth and Literacy, Raw Data Plot

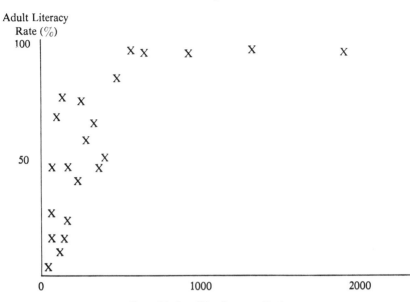

Gross National Product per Capita

left and very slowly on the right? Or are there two different patterns, one for highly developed countries with literacy rates close to 100% (right half) and one for underdeveloped countries with lower and more variable rates (left half)? Either of these possibilities could make sense.

The rules of thumb back up our visual impressions here. In Table 12.6 we have drawn two horizontal lines to mark off the top seven and bottom seven values on X (GNP per capita) to help with the arithmetic. Consider the old basic range rule. In raw figures, the upper third of X has range $1947 - 400 = 1547$, far more than half of the total range $1947 - 45 = 1902$. Thus some correction for the upward straggle of X is called for before trying even a basic linear fit. Clearly such a correction will help a lot with our visual problems by spreading out the overcrowded values on the left. Or consider the newer rule of thumb, the slope ratio for checking for a curve. Using medians for speed, the summary points are:

$$X_H = 680 \qquad X_M = 222 \qquad X_L = 76$$
$$Y_H = 97.5 \qquad Y_M = 52.5 \qquad Y_L = 17.5.$$

So the slopes and slope ratio are:

$$b_{LM} = \frac{52.5 - 17.5}{222 - 76} = .240; \quad b_{MH} = \frac{97.5 - 52.5}{680 - 222} = .098;$$

$$\text{and} \frac{b_{MH}}{b_{LM}} = .41.$$

This ratio, well under half, indicates "too much curve to ignore," and our chart of suggested transforms points to powers of Y or something like logs for X. Our visual inspection of the plot also suggested that some curve fit might work. Since we have to correct upward straggle in X anyway to fit the range rule for thirds and spread out the cases on the lower end of X, we might as well try that instead of powers of Y. Logging is usually a good starting point so we get new summary points with the old X values logged (the Y values are unchanged):

$$\log X_H = 2.83 \qquad \log X_M = 2.35 \qquad \log X_L = 1.88$$
$$Y_H = 97.5 \qquad\qquad Y_M = 52.5 \qquad\qquad Y_L = 17.5$$

$$b_{LM} = 74.5 \qquad b_{MH} = 93.8$$

$$\frac{b_{LM}}{b_{MH}} = .79.$$

This is in the discretionary range. What might do better? If anything, the logging has overcorrected slightly, since the curve now increases more quickly where X is higher, rather than where X is lower as before. We could try a milder correction for the upward straggle in X, square roots:

$$\sqrt{X_H} = 26.1 \qquad \sqrt{X_M} = 14.9 \qquad \sqrt{X_L} = 8.7$$

$$Y_H = 97.5 \qquad\quad Y_M = 52.5 \qquad\quad Y_L = 17.5$$

$$b_{LM} = 5.65 \qquad\quad b_{MH} = 4.02$$

$$\frac{b_{MH}}{b_{LM}} = .71.$$

Taking square roots undercorrects more badly than logging overcorrects, since the slope ratio is poorer for square roots; let's log X and see how well that works. The logs of GNP per capita were found and entered in Table 12.6; the plot of logged X and raw Y is in Table 12.8.

Starting again with the plot, we see a great improvement. The points are nicely spread out, easy to see; and they look pretty straight overall. It seems that logging X has solved both our problems: displaying the data and fitting the curve. We check this further by arithmetic. The range rules are now satisfied and so are the other rules for thirds (we'll let you check this in detail yourselves). How about curvature? Let's find three summary points using trimeans now, since we can see that we are in the right ballpark and some added accuracy is worth the little extra time that trimeans take as compared to medians.

$$X_H = 2.87 \qquad X_M = 2.36 \qquad X_L = 1.89$$

$$Y_H = 95.0 \qquad Y_M = 54.6 \qquad Y_L = 23.3$$

$$\frac{b_{LM}}{b_{MH}} = \frac{66.6}{79.2} = .84$$

Table 12.8

Literacy and Logged Wealth

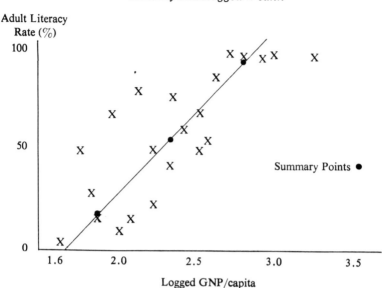

Logged GNP/capita

The slope ratio is in our discretionary range; we could try a logged X plus a Y transform to unbend the curve more exactly. It's best to take a look. The plot in Table 12.8 includes the three summary points (three circles) and a line drawn through them by eye. The summary points look fine as they are; there is perhaps a tiny bit of bend in them, but the bend is very slight indeed compared to the scatter of the data points. So the rules of thumb, like our visual impression, indicate that logging X has unbent the curve as well as displaying the data more effectively.

In interpreting the curve that we just fitted by logging X, we have to remember that logging is used differently from the use in the population example. For one thing, X was logged, not Y; so there is no use trying to think of steady rates of growth here. The percent adult literacy grows very rapidly as GNP per capita does, then less rapidly, and less rapidly still until the rate of growth seems to stop for the most highly developed countries. A ceiling effect comes to mind immediately: no matter how wealthy a country is, it cannot have more than 100% adult literacy. In fact, it cannot have more than 98% or 99% literacy, since a small fraction of any population is incapable of reading for one reason or another. This *ceiling effect* certainly helps to explain the Canadian point, which is well below its predicted value (well below the line in Table 12.8): to be on the line, Canada would need a literacy rate of about 125%! You may wonder about a *floor* effect here: after all, no matter how poor a country is it cannot have less than 0% literate. Such a floor effect might well have shown up if there were more countries near the floor: more countries like Nepal, with very low rates of literacy. Although this does not happen here, it is possible for a floor and ceiling effect to happen together, producing a sort of S-shaped curve, which requires a transformation slightly harder than those we use in this book ("logit" transforms often help with data bounded both above and below).

We don't feel happy with the ceiling effect as an explanation of the whole curve, since there is a curve even for countries well below the ceiling. Why? Perhaps it is easier to increase the literacy rate when the rate is low. Suppose the rate is 10% and goes to 20%; the additional 10% of the population is probably an elite in many ways, wealthier, more highly motivated and smarter (after all, literacy is a rare thing). On the other hand suppose that the rate is 80% and goes to 90%. Surely that 10% increase takes much more effort; the people involved are likely to be less advantaged educationally. That implies that raising the rate the same amount takes more effort (more expense) when the rate is higher to start with, so that it takes massive increases in GNP per capita to raise literacy 10% for wealthy nations where the rate is high but takes less of an increase in GNP per capita to raise the rate 10% for poorer nations where the rate is low.

Some Final Remarks

Coping with curviness via transformation has many advantages. First, it uses tools we already know how to work with: transforms and the basic straight line fit. Second, it is very flexible; we can transform *X* or *Y* or both, allowing us to cope with a great variety of simple curves. Third, we can work with it quite quickly by: (1) using the chart to see roughly what kind of transforms are in order and (2) checking out exactly which transforms work best by trying them on the three summary points. Fourth, it is often a great time-saver. Suppose we are getting curviness here and there in a data set because one or two of the variables straggle a lot: if we transform these variables early on, we often find that everything is nice and straight and easy. (This is not always the case, but things often work out as suggested.)

On the other hand, there are problems as well. Perhaps the most important problem is that transformation does not always work. First, our transformations can straighten out only the curves shown in the chart, curves which have only one bend and which either increase or decrease all the way. Transformations are not much help with curves which look like a U or a J; these have just one bend but *Y* increases with *X* in one part of the curve and decreases with *X* in the other part. For curves like these, one can use a more complex kind of equation:

$$Y = cX^2 + bX + a$$

There are both exploratory and confirmatory ways to make such fits, although we will not go into them here. Occasionally you see X by Y data with several bends; these more complicated curves take more complicated fits, either more complex transformations than we use here or more complex equations using X^3 or X^4 or even higher powers. Fortunately, such complex curves are quite rare in sociology. You will be able to cope quite nicely with nearly all of the data you are likely to see with the simple transformations used in this chapter. This chapter's approach should work as long as b_{LM} and b_{MH} both have the same sign and neither one is zero. (If they have different signs then the curve must be something like a J or a U.)

Second, it sometimes happens that the transformation needed to satisfy the range rule for X conflicts awkwardly with transformations suggested to unbend a curve. If this comes up, use your judgement. Is the curve strong enough to worry about? Can you cope by transforming X (for the range rule) and Y also (for the curve)? If things seem unmanageable, you may decide to satisfy the range rule and then fit a curved line with a cX^2 term. Things rarely are really unmanageable.

Finally, which variable should you transform, X or Y? Often this is up to you; do what you think is most convenient or makes most sense. Some possible grounds for decision are:

the simpler transformation is preferable; e.g. log X is usually better than the fifteenth power of Y;

if one of the variables is symmetric and the other has straggle, the straggling one should be transformed. Often the curve and the straggle have the same sources and both will respond to the same transformation (as is true in this chapter's population example).

Homework

Keep a copy of your homework results; you will need it for the next chapter. Choose *one* of the two following examples. Decide whether a curve fit is needed; if one is needed, choose a transformation; then make a line fit for the transformed data. Do not forget to discuss both the overall relationship (for example, if it was curved originally why was it curved?) and the more striking residuals.

1. *Weaning and toilet training revisited.* In chapter 9 we looked at twenty-five primitive societies for which stable estimates of age at weaning and at toilet training were available. Suppose you want to predict age at onset of toilet training from age at onset of weaning. Below are nineteen of the twenty-five societies; we've set aside six societies where the two ages appear overly disproportionate, that is, where one of the ages is more than twice the other.

Age at Weaning	Age at Toilet Training
2.3	1.8
2.7	3.0
1.5	1.2
2.5	2.0
2.0	1.5
2.0	1.5
2.5	3.0
2.8	2.2
2.2	2.0
1.3	2.2
0.5	1.0
2.0	2.2
2.3	1.9
1.5	1.7
2.3	2.8
2.0	1.7
2.0	2.2
2.7	2.2
2.8	2.0

2. Try using the adult literacy rates from Table 12.6 as X; for Y, get the corresponding rates of enrolment in higher education from the review example following chapter 6.

13

Linear Regression

The standard confirmatory approach to fitting a straight line for X by Y data is called linear regression. In many ways this approach is analogous to the exploratory techniques developed in the previous two chapters. The confirmatory line is useful in the same ways that the exploratory line is useful: the confirmatory line summarizes a relationship, can be used to make predictions, and so on. The line is fitted rather differently in a way that makes it less resistant than the exploratory line. However, confirmatory residuals are found in exactly the same way and can also be used in very similar ways to evaluate the fit and to go beyond it. Besides these parallel uses and procedures, the confirmatory techniques let us do one important thing we could not do before: we can ask whether a linear relationship is *significant*, whether there is likely to be a relationship in general and not just in our sample data.

Linear Fits: Two Sets of Goals

A confirmatory linear fit has goals somewhat different from those of an exploratory fit and is thus made somewhat differently. Both fits summarize an X by Y pattern, but the exploratory fit emphasizes speed and resistance whereas the confirmatory fit emphasizes mathematically useful procedures based on all the data. In exploratory work we have seen that a straight line can be fitted to a set of points simply and resistantly by breaking the points up into three parts and finding resistant summary points for each. The confirmatory approach, on the other hand, uses all the points (however unusual some of them may be); this alone loses resistance. Further, the confirmatory line is the one line that makes the sum of the squared residuals as small as possible. Squaring the residuals has handy properties from the mathematical point of view, but again it loses resistance. You may remember what happens when residuals are squared if you think back to the discussion of the variance in chapter 3: unusual values become even more unusual when squared, so that one outlying value can really have an impact on the results.

Consider the little plots in Table 13.1. Graph A shows a tidy direct relationship with some scatter (not a perfect relationship) but no really unusual values that stand out from the rest. Here, the exploratory and the

Table 13.1

A Simple Exploratory-Confirmatory Comparison

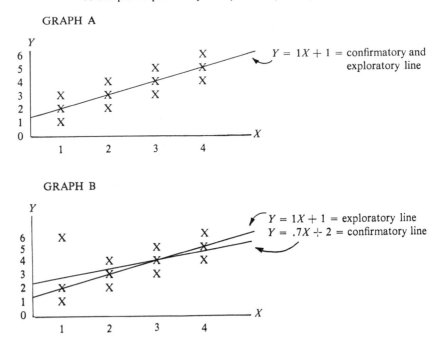

GRAPH A

$Y = 1X + 1 =$ confirmatory and exploratory line

GRAPH B

$Y = 1X + 1 =$ exploratory line
$Y = .7X + 2 =$ confirmatory line

confirmatory procedures give exactly the same line: $Y = X + 1$. (You can fit the exploratory line by eye, and you can fit the confirmatory one as a very easy warm-up for the confirmatory procedure described below if you wish.) Graph B is just like Graph A except that one point has been moved: $(1, 3)$ has become $(1, 6)$. The exploratory line is not affected, it is still $Y = X + 1$. But the confirmatory line is affected. For the confirmatory line all squared residuals are minimized, so an unusual point (like 1, 6) has quite a strong effect. The line moves clockwise to reduce that one very large residual. The residuals for most of the other points are increased in the process, but the average squared residual is made as small as possible. Thus the confirmatory line is based on all the data points, at the cost of decreased resistance to unusual points.

The two approaches to linear fitting have different strengths and weaknesses. The confirmatory fit is better if you want to go on to make a statistical test, or if you want the data summarized in a form suitable for publication (everyone should know linear regression: not everyone knows the corresponding exploratory technique yet). The exploratory way is best if you are working hastily and/or working with erratic data, looking for the main message of most of the data. Does this sound familiar? Of course: the differences here are very like those between the mean and the median, or between the standard deviation and the midspread.

Finding the Line

It can be shown that the following formulae for b and a produce a line which minimizes squared residuals:

$$b = \frac{N\sum X_i Y_i - (\sum Y_i)(\sum X_i)}{N\sum X_i^2 - (\sum X_i)^2}$$

$$a = \overline{Y} - b\overline{X}$$

The formula for a is very easy, but the one for b is a bit more complex so let's go over it:

(Top part) $N\sum X_i Y_i$ multiply each X value by the Y value it is paired with; next, add up these crossproducts; then multiply the total by N, the number of pairs (X, Y).

(∑X_i) (∑Y_i)   find the total of the X values, find the total of the Y values, and multiply the two totals.

(Bottom part) $N\sum X_i^2$ square all the X values; then add up these squares; then multiply by N.

(∑X_i)^2 add up all the X values and then square the total.

These are computing formulae, designed for speedy work rather than for intuitive appeal. Let's see the formulae in action by computing the confirmatory linear fit for the Angell data; then we can compare this fit to the exploratory one already made in chapter 11.

Table 13.2

Confirmatory X by Y Worksheet, Angell Data

X	Y	XY	X²	Y²	Y' Y + 1.831X − 45.98
19.0	15.0	285.00	361.00	225.00	3.809
16.4	13.6	223.04	268.96	184.96	−2.352
15.8	17.6	278.08	249.64	309.76	.550
15.2	14.7	223.44	231.04	216.09	−3.449
14.2	19.4	275.48	201.64	376.36	−.580
14.0	18.6	260.40	196.00	345.96	−1.746
13.8	35.1	484.38	190.44	1232.01	14.388
13.0	15.8	205.40	169.00	249.64	−6.377
12.7	21.6	274.32	161.29	466.56	−1.126
12.0	12.1	145.20	144.00	146.41	−11.908
11.3	22.1	249.73	127.69	488.41	−3.190
10.9	31.2	340.08	118.81	973.44	5.178
9.6	38.9	373.44	92.16	1513.21	10.498
8.8	23.1	203.28	77.44	533.61	−6.767
7.2	35.8	257.76	51.84	1281.64	3.003
$\sum X =$ 193.9	$\sum Y =$ 334.6	$\sum XY =$ 4079.03	$\sum X^2 =$ 2640.95	$\sum Y^2 =$ 8543.06	$\sum Y' = -.069$ $\sum (Y')^2 = 628.38$

A Worked Example: the Angell Data

Table 13.2 illustrates a useful kind of basic work sheet for getting the sums and sums of squares needed for confirmatory work. You have this sort of thing for analysis of variance; it can be tedious but is easy enough (especially with a calculator and a little help from your friends). The only rather new bit is the column of XY or "crossproduct" figures. Each crossproduct is the product of a paired X and Y; for example, for the first point the crossproduct is 19 times 15 for 285 (see the first line of the work sheet). Once the basic figures have been found in such a work sheet, they are just plugged into the formulae above:

$$N = 15$$

$$\sum X = 193.9$$

$$\sum Y = 334.6$$

$$\sum Y^2 = 8543.06$$

$$\sum X^2 = 2640.95$$

$$(\sum X)(\sum Y) = 64{,}878.94$$

$$(\sum X)^2 = 37{,}597.21$$

$$\sum XY = 4{,}079.03$$

$$b = \frac{N\sum XY - (\sum X)(\sum Y)}{N\sum X^2 - (\sum X)^2} = \frac{15(4{,}079.03) - (193.9)(334.6)}{15(2640.95) - 37{,}597.27}$$

$$= \frac{61{,}185.45 - 64{,}878.94}{39{,}615.25 - 37{,}597.21}$$

$$= \frac{-3693.49}{2017.04} = -1.831$$

$$a = \overline{Y} - b\overline{X}$$

$$= \frac{334.6}{15} - (-1.831)(193.9/15)$$

$$= 22.307 + 23.669$$

$$= 45.98$$

Note that we hang onto extra decimal places until the end, rounding only when we have the final figures for b and a. Confirmatory work involves so much arithmetic that small rounding errors can have a big cumulative effect, so we can't be quite as quick and approximate as we are in exploratory work. Note also that we have in fact used every data point in finding both b and a by linear regression. There are no summary points in this procedure, no way to cope with stray or flukey values.

Now let's compare the two fits for these data. The confirmatory fit is:

$$Y = -1.831 + 45.98$$

and the exploratory fit found in chapter 11 was:

$$Y = -2.4X + 53$$

The equations look roughly similar (both indicate that mobility is inversely related to integration) but it is hard to tell just how different they are. Let's make a visual comparison by turning to Table 13.3, which shows the scatterplot with the two fits drawn in. (To draw the confirmatory line, you must solve the equation for any two handy values of X, since there are no summary points to rely on.) Now we can easily see that the lines are pretty much the same; the slight differences between them do not look like much compared to the scatter of the data points. Even though these real-life data are much less regular than the artificial data of Table 13.1, Graph A, these data are still not eccentric enough to produce really substantial differences in the exploratory and confirmatory fits.

Evaluating the Fit

We can and should find residuals from the confirmatory fit as we found them earlier from the exploratory fit: we find $Y - (bX + a) = Y'$, though now, of course, the b and a are those found by linear regression. The residuals

Table 13.3

Two Fits for the Angell Data

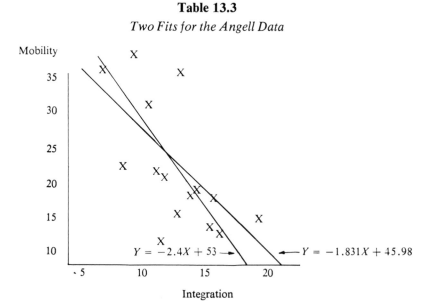

Table 13.4

Exploratory and Confirmatory Residuals for Integration and Mobility

Residuals from:

Confirmatory: $Y = -1.831X + 45.98$ Exploratory: $Y = -2.4X + 53$

	1	5.2
0.5, 4.4	1	
5.2	0	8.6, 8.9
3.0, 0.6, 3.8	0	0.0, 2.5, 0.5, 4.4, 0.1
3.2, 1.1, 1.7, 0.6, 3.5, 2.4	−0	1.8, 0.8, 0.9, 3.8
6.8, 6.4	−0	6.0, 8.8
1.9	−1	2.1
	−1	

stem: tens   *leaf*: units and tens

dq	7.3	8.2
range	26.3	27.3
Variance	44.88	47.94
$\dfrac{dq\,Y'}{dq\,Y}$	$\dfrac{7.3}{16.2} = .45$	$\dfrac{8.2}{16.2} = .51$
$\dfrac{\text{Var } Y'}{\text{Var } Y}$	$\dfrac{44.88}{77.09} = .58$	$\dfrac{47.94}{77.09} = .62$
$\sum (Y')^2$	628.38	672.86

from the confirmatory fit are shown in the last column of Table 13.2. These residuals ought to be examined closely, but once again we will omit this for lack of space.

We have contrasted the exploratory and confirmatory fits in Table 13.3; Table 13.4 contrasts the residuals in various ways. In the stems-and-leaves, we again see overall similarity. The residuals from the exploratory line are more likely to be either close to zero or to be quite extreme, because the exploratory line fits the middle mass of the data while the confirmatory line is very sensitive to cases with large residuals.

Once again the residuals from the fit serve to evaluate the strength of the fit. The more the spread of Y is reduced by the fit, the less there is of Y unexplained. So the spread of the Y residuals is compared to the spread of the original Y. Now, however, we make the comparison in confirmatory terms by using variances instead of dqs:

$$\text{proportion of } Y \text{ unexplained by regression} = \frac{\text{Variance } (Y')}{\text{Variance } Y}$$

In Table 13.4 we see that this works out to .58 for the confirmatory fit; so the linear regression leaves 58% of the variance in Y unexplained, that is to say that 58% of the variance in mobility is not explained by a linear fit to integration. On the other hand, it follows that 42% is explained, which is quite high as social science relationships go.

We have now broken the original variance of Y into two parts: the proportion explained by the regression and the proportion not explained. The proportion explained is symbolized

$$r^2 = \frac{\text{Amount explained by regression}}{\text{Variance of Original } Y}$$

The proportion not explained by the confirmatory line is

$$1 - r^2 = \frac{\text{Variance of Residuals}}{\text{Variance of Original } Y} = \frac{\text{Amount not explained}}{\text{Total } Y \text{ Variance}}$$

The second term $(1 - r^2)$ is the confirmatory parallel to the dq ratio we have used in exploration since both sum up the amount the line does not account for. The first term, r^2 is a bit more familiar in confirmatory write-ups, particularly the square root r, known as the product-moment correlation coefficient or, more simply, the *correlation* between X and Y. The correlation has the same sign as the slope b. So, for the Angell example the correlation is

$$-\sqrt{.42} = -.65 \quad \text{(negative because } b \text{ is)}$$

The sign of the correlation tells you the direction of the relationship: r is negative for an inverse relationship like that between integration and mobility, positive for a direct relationship. The correlation also indicates the strength of the relationship, although r^2 has a more natural interpretation: the proportion of the variance of Y explained by the fit. r^2 goes from a minimum of 0 (the fit explains none of Y) to 1.0 (the fit predicts Y perfectly). The correlation, r, goes from -1.0 (perfect inverse relationship) through 0 (no linear relationship at all) to $+1.0$ (perfect direct relationship).

Since the correlation is so useful, it is worthwhile to have a fast computing form for it:

$$r = \frac{N\Sigma XY - (\Sigma X)(\Sigma Y)}{\sqrt{[N\Sigma X^2 - (\Sigma X)^2][N\Sigma Y^2 - (\Sigma Y)^2]}}$$

All of the components can be found easily in a work sheet like Table 13.2, and most of them have already been found for the slope calculation anyway.

The correlation is a popular measure with a clear interpretation. However, it can be misleading if you do not watch out for a few common traps. First, the correlation tells you how much of Y is explained by a *linear* fit to X. Some other fit, like a curve, may work much better. It is even possible to have a correlation of 0 when X and Y are perfectly related, but related in a perfect curve rather than in a straight line form (see Table 13.5, Graph A). A second trap is lack of resistance. The correlation uses variances, and it sums up the strength of a confirmatory fit, so it is not very resistant and this can give various kinds of misleading results. One of the best known is the

Table 13.5

Examples of Misleading Correlations

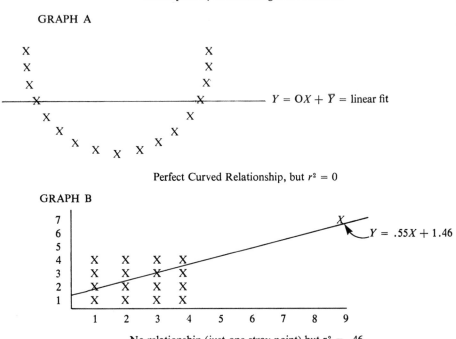

GRAPH A

$Y = 0X + \bar{Y} =$ linear fit

Perfect Curved Relationship, but $r^2 = 0$

GRAPH B

$Y = .55X + 1.46$

No relationship (just one stray point) but $r^2 = .46$

"one-point correlation." Graph B of Table 13.5 gives an extreme example: there are 16 points showing absolutely no relationship between *X* and *Y*, and one point off by itself. Common sense (and exploratory analysis) suggests that *X* and *Y* are unrelated and there is something odd about the discrepant point; it may well be an error of some kind. But linear regression produces a line with a fairly strong r^2 value of .46 — rather more than we got for the integration and mobility example where the points showed a more consistent and convincing pattern. The fit looks great if we only look at r^2.

The moral of this story is clear; always plot the data! A possible curve or misleading fits overly influenced by a few odd points can be seen immediately in plots, and not in the line equation or the r^2 value. A plot of *Y* by *X* is indispensable and a plot of *Y'* by *X* is also a good idea just as before, especially if the residuals are labelled.

Let us just stress once again that *r* depends on the strength of a *confirmatory, linear* fit; and that fit is the straight line which minimizes squared residuals over all points. For example, if we look at Table 13.4 again briefly we see that the sum of the squared residuals, $(Y')^2$, is smaller for the confirmatory fit than for the exploratory one (628.38 versus 672.86).

No other line will make the sum of the $(Y')^2$ smaller than the confirmatory line does. As a result, the proportion of Y left unexplained,

$$1 - r^2 = \frac{\text{Variance } Y'}{\text{Variance } Y},$$

will be smaller for the confirmatory line than for the exploratory line or for any other possible line. That's the job the linear regression is designed to do. In doing it, resistance is lost, so that the confirmatory line is often poorer than the exploratory line in exploratory terms, that is, residuals are more often moderate and less often extreme. We can see that happening in Table 13.4: big residuals are bigger, small ones are smaller. Curiously, the dq ratio is also a bit better for the confirmatory fit here, an effect of the many moderate values.

Another Version of the Confirmatory Slope

The formula we gave above for b is the best one for computation, but it does not say very much to most people. Here is another version with more familiar components:

$$b = r \frac{sd_Y}{sd_X}.$$

If you plug in the formulae for r, sd_X, and sd_Y and do lots of algebra you can get back to exactly the same computing formula we saw earlier. Now, what does this version suggest?

We see that r is part of b. That means that b and r should have the same sign, as we said earlier. Also the stronger the relationship the more different b is from zero (because the more different r is from zero). In fact, b is r if X and Y happen to have equal spreads ($sd_X = sd_Y$). However, this is not very likely unless we have standardized both X and Y (standardizing in confirmatory terms, of course, using sd and the mean). If we have, our regression equation becomes very simple indeed:

$$Y = rX$$

We have no great use for this fact now but it is handy in later chapters. In the meantime, be careful: b also includes sd_X and sd_Y, which are *not* usually the same and may not even be similar, so you can't tell how strong a linear fit is just by looking at the size of b (as beginners are often tempted to do).

Hypothesis Tests for Linear Regression

We have seen how to make a confirmatory linear fit which minimizes squared residuals from the line, and we have seen how to evaluate the strength of the fit by finding r^2, the proportion of the variance of Y explained by the fit. The confirmatory line tends to be similar to the exploratory one, unless there are some unusual points to which the less resistant confirmatory line is sensitive. We have also seen that the amount of Y not explained by the regression $(1 - r^2)$ is parallel to the dq ratio used in exploratory work: both are ratios of Y' spread to Y spread, or

$$1 - r^2 = \frac{Y' \text{ variance}}{Y \text{ variance}} \qquad dq \text{ ratio} = \frac{Y' \text{ midspread}}{Y \text{ midspread}}$$

Now we want to go beyond the confirmatory-exploratory parallels to what confirmatory alone can do: a test of significance for the fit. Is there a linear relationship in general in the universe?

This question could be stated in many ways; for example, we can ask whether b is significantly different from zero or we can ask whether r^2 is significantly different from zero. These are equivalent questions, so we might as well focus on the one with the easiest test procedure; thus we will look at r^2. Our null hypothesis becomes:

$$H_0: r^2 = 0 \text{ in the universe.}$$

If this is true then X does not explain any of Y, at least not in a linear way. Our alternative hypothesis is:

$$H_1: r^2 > 0 \text{ in the universe.}$$

If this is true then knowing X does help to predict Y to some extent (we don't specify just how big r^2 is). This may look like a one-tailed test, but it's really two-tailed; r^2 cannot be negative though its square root, the correlation, can be. In any example, we will probably find that r^2 is not exactly zero; even if H_0 is true, we will almost always get a little pattern in our sample data by chance alone. But as r^2 gets big, H_0 gets harder and harder to believe. It is also easier to reject H_0 if the sample size N is larger so that we feel more confidence in the sample estimate of r^2. This should sound rather like previous tests, in which more striking differences among means and larger N meant easier rejection of H_0. It is not too surprising to find that the test statistic looks like this:

$$F_{1,N-2} = \frac{r^2(N-2)}{1 - r^2}$$

Even the fact that the F-table comes into play again may not seem too surprising if we remind ourselves of what r^2 and $1 - r^2$ mean:

$$F_{1,N-2} = \frac{\text{Variance explained} \times (N-2)}{\text{Variance of Residuals}}$$

$$= \frac{(\text{Variance explained by regression})/1}{(\text{Error Variance})/(N-2)}.$$

This closely resembles $\dfrac{(\text{Between SS})/df}{(\text{Within SS})/df}$.

Regression and analysis of variance are very similar indeed, although a demonstration of that similarity takes more mathematics than we want to get into.

Computing the value of F for the sample is easy. As before, the critical value for F is found from the F-table and depends on the degrees of freedom and on the α-level chosen. We will show an example of an F-test for linear regression below, using the wealth and literacy example from the previous chapter, but we will not do so until the data have been checked to see whether they satisfy the assumptions which must be met for the test to be appropriate.

One assumption must be met very strictly: the sample should be a random sample of points independently observed. Proper data collection will meet this requirement. The data should also have an appropriate form. Odd as it may seem, this does not mean that X and Y must be normally distributed (which is probably what you're expecting): this assumption applies to the residuals! This assumption can be phrased very technically in ways that are difficult to understand or to check, but in practice it boils down to making sure that the X by Y plot looks reasonable. The points should form a fairly regular oval without badly straying values or large variations in the oval's thickness. (The oval as a whole may be thin or thick, depending on the strength of the relationship: the stronger the relationship the more nearly all the points come to falling on a straight line.) This assumption does not have to be met perfectly, since linear regression is robust (like analysis of variance) especially if N is large.

In concluding this section on testing for a linear regression in the universe, let us remind you that significance and strength of a regression are related but not the same. They are related because, as you've seen, it's easier to get significant results for stronger relationships: the bigger r^2 the bigger F. But F is also related to the sample size N. It is possible to get a nonsignificant result even when the correlation is large, where N is very small; and if N is large enough then almost any weed of a relationship will turn up as significant. r^2 tells you how strongly X and Y are linearly related in your sample; the F-test tells you whether there is likely to be a linear relationship of some degree of strength in the universe.

A Significance Test for Wealth and Literacy

For an example of the regression test procedure we turn to the data on Gross National Product per capita and adult literacy rates from the previous chapter. First, are the test assumptions met? The 22 cases in Table 12.6 were a very rough sample (every fifth case) but we can't think of any biases in that sampling procedure so we will go ahead. A trickier point is the form of the data: does the *X* by *Y* plot look like a rough oval? In raw data, as in Table 12.7, certainly not! This looks more like a hockey stick than an oval. But if GNP per capita is logged, as in Table 12.8, the plot does look roughly regular. Perhaps the oval's thickness varies a bit, with countries lower in wealth having more spread in literacy rates, but it's hard to say with only 22 points, and the variation does not look great. Remember, regression is robust so the plot does not have to be absolutely neat, just approximately oval like logged wealth and literacy or like integration and heterogeneity (but not like raw wealth and literacy, which is too far from oval).

We can proceed with a significance test. The first step is to make a confirmatory fit and find r^2:

$$Y = 56.4X - 77.4 \qquad r^2 = .65$$

We omit the details of the calculations (again, you might like to try the calculations to check your understanding of the formulae). The fit is plotted in Table 13.6; it looks reasonable, very similar to our earlier exploratory fit. Our null and alternate hypotheses are:

$$H_0: r^2 = 0$$

$$H_1: r^2 > 0$$

We might as well use the commonest significance level, $\alpha = .05$, and *N* is 22;

Table 13.6

Linear Regression for Literacy and Logged Wealth

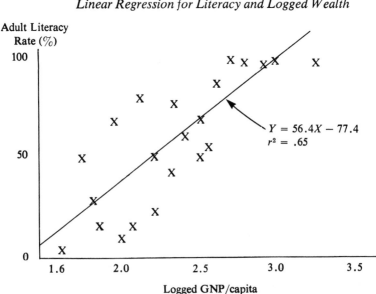

our F-table tells us that the 5% critical value for 1 and 20 degrees of freedom is 4.35. What F do we get for our sample?

$$F_{1,20} = \frac{r^2(N-2)}{1-r^2}$$

$$= \frac{.65(20)}{.35}$$

$$= 37.1$$

The null hypothesis looks quite unlikely. Our F is clearly significant, well beyond the .05 level. It seems very likely that literacy rates and logs of GNP per capita are linearly related in general, not just in our sample. (If you check the data for all available countries, given in the *World Handbook*, you find that these variables are indeed related.)

Unbending, Transformation, and Regression

We have just seen that transformations can be useful in satisfying the assumptions one must make before doing a test for linear regression. Transformations can also help avoid one-point correlation problems; if X or Y or both has a lot of straggle, the few highest or lowest points may have a disproportionate effect on the fit and on r^2. Transformation can help by pulling the unusual values into the main body of the data. Finally, transformation can be used just as we used it in chapter 12: to unbend curved data so that our simple linear fitting procedure will work better. The same general points apply in confirmatory work as in exploratory work, so we will not go over the procedure in much detail. First, the basic transformations used in this text will only unbend some curves: curves with just one bend which are either always increasing or always decreasing. More complex curves can also be handled, and easily, but they are beyond the scope of the book. Second, the chart in Table 12.5 tells what kind of transforms to try, although getting the best choice may involve some trial and error. This is a good place to mix in some exploratory technique because this will often give a transformation choice that works well for confirmatory regression too, although there is no guarantee. Once the data are transformed, the rest is routine: just do basic linear regression on the transformed data.

We have just seen that logging GNP per capita helps satisfy confirmatory assumptions. Take a look at the plot in Table 12.7 again to remind yourself of the problems posed by the raw data. The data are strongly curved, so a linear regression on the raw data will not be a good fit. Some of the points (those for the wealthiest countries) look out of pattern and may pull the confirmatory line off. Table 13.7 shows what happens if we go ahead and fit the linear regression line anyway (done only for illustration, and *not*

Table 13.7

Linear Regression for Raw Wealth and Literacy

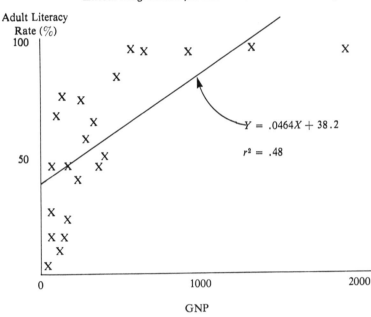

recommended). The r^2 of .48 is quite healthy, so if we only looked at the arithmetic we might conclude that we had a strong linear fit accounting for almost half of the variance in *Y*. But this is not the case, as the plot makes very clear: the pattern of points is not linear so the line summarizes it poorly. As we saw a moment ago, we get a much better fit if we remove the curve by logging *X*: r^2 goes from .48 to .65. For confirmatory as well as for exploratory fitting, the transformation has really helped. The plot in Table 13.6 also looks much better than that in 13.7: the fit seems to make visual sense, following the main pattern of the data. (It is also very similar to the exploratory fit in Table 12.8, although the rather unusual value for Canada has swung the confirmatory line clockwise just a shade.)

Conclusions

There are parallels between exploratory and confirmatory techniques in every part of this book; for *X* by *Y* techniques the parallels are especially strong. Both approaches are first and foremost designed to find a straight line that "well summarizes" a set of *X* by *Y* data; the line is useful in the same ways whether it is exploratory or confirmatory; residuals are found in the same way; and the line's success in summarizing the data is evaluated in the same general way, by a ratio of the spread of the residuals to the original Y spread. The lines are fitted somewhat differently because "summarizing well" can mean different things. In confirmatory work there is a unique best line, that one that minimizes squared residuals for all points. This line has useful mathematical properties and keeping residuals small makes sense; but squaring all the points leads to a lack of resistance. On the other hand, in exploratory work there may be several good lines, with different fits coming from different judgements by the analyst, as long as the line summarizes the bulk of the data. An exploratory line is resistant and easy, but cannot be quite as easily communicated as the more standard confirmatory fit.

Being so strongly parallel, the two approaches give very similar results, as long as the data are well-behaved. Some data irregularities, like curvature or straggling points, can be corrected through transformation. If irregularities cannot be fixed, as might for example happen if one or two points stray widely from the rest, then the more resistant exploratory fit will usually make much more sense. People sometimes try to adapt confirmatory procedures a bit to handle such situations better; for example, you may have seen reports in which a linear regression is given with and without an awkward point included. Dropping the awkward point is roughly similar to basing a fit on resistant summary points, which are not affected by one or two stray values. If regression is modified in this way the analyst should make the modification clear in his report and should not do a significance test; once he starts dropping out points he doesn't like, he no longer has a random sample.

The significance test for a linear regression has no exploratory parallel. With this test, and with suitable data that meet the test's requirements, we can decide whether X predicts Y by a linear rule in general, not only in our sample. The bigger r^2 and the bigger N, the more likely it is that we'll decide X and Y are really related. As always, making the decision involves risks: we may reject H_0 when X and Y are not linearly related but only happen to seem so in our sample, or we may accept H_0 because of poor sample results when X is in fact linearly related to Y in the universe.

We have encountered one new and very important measure in this chapter: the correlation, which indicates how strongly X and Y are related. If the correlation is squared (r^2) we get the proportion of Y's variance explained by a linear fit to X, a simple interpretation. The correlation can be seen as one particular example of a general group of statistics called *measures of association*, statistics which indicate how strongly two variables are related. In the next chapter we will look at several measures of association for two categorical variables. There are a great many such measures, designed for different data and different purposes.

As we have hinted in this chapter, exploratory and confirmatory X by Y techniques are especially powerful when used in combination. For example, exploration can help in finding transformations that unbend the data or make it more regular, thus making the data suitable for linear regression and significance tests. Exploratory thinking is useful in pursuing the residuals from a fit whether the fit is exploratory or confirmatory. On the other hand, confirmatory procedures allow tests of ideas generated in exploration. We have shown exploratory and confirmatory techniques on the same data so the techniques could be compared, but the best combination (if you have ample data) is to subdivide your data randomly, explore part, and test the exploration-generated ideas on the remaining part.

Homework

Return to the two homework problems in chapter 12.

1. Calculate confirmatory a, b, and r for both examples.

2. Do a significance test for both regressions and discuss the appropriateness of the test for each regression.

3. For the problem you did as homework in chapter 12, compare the two sets of results (exploratory and confirmatory) and discuss.

14

The Chi-Square Test

In this chapter we round out our collection of tools for analyzing the relationship between two variables. We have seen how to work with data where the independent variable is categorical and the dependent variable numeric: this calls for batch analysis in exploratory terms (chapters 2 through 6) and in confirmatory terms, comparisons of means of various batches (chapters 8 through 10). We have also seen how to work with a numeric independent variable and a numeric dependent variable: this calls for X by Y analysis and the fitting of exploratory and confirmatory lines (chapters 11 through 13). Here we consider chi-square, a simple and popular way to work with two variables both of which are categorical. We will begin with a very simple example of such data, go through the chi-square procedure in detail for this example, describe the assumptions that underly the use of chi-square in hypothesis testing, and then apply the procedures to a somewhat more complex example.

Female Response to Success by Men and Women

Levine and Crumrine (1975) examined the attitudes of males and females to the success of another person, male or female. Introductory sociology students were given a sentence and asked to make up stories about it. About half the students, both male and female, were asked to write in response to the sentence: "After first-term finals, Anne finds herself at the top of her medical school class." The other half of the students were asked to write about a sentence exactly the same except that the name "John" replaced the name "Anne." The stories were then analyzed in several ways. Parts of the results appear in Tables 14.1 and 14.12. For the moment, we will consider only the female students' stories. For those stories, we will investigate the possible relationship of two categorical variables. The first variable is the sex of the successful person the female students were asked to write about ("Anne" stories versus "John" stories). Obviously this is a variable with two categories, male and female. The other variable, extent of negative response to success, was a bit more complex. For each story, the percentage of negative sentences was found. For example, one sentence showing a negative response to success was: "Anne's roommate kills herself in a fit of

Table 14.1

A Simple Crosstabulation

Response to Success (Female Subjects)

Proportion Negative Sentences:	Person Written About		
	John	Anne	Total
Low	93	96	189
High	35	21	56
Total	128	117	245

Names of Parts of the Table

		Column Variable		
		John	Anne	
Row	Low	cell entry	cell entry	row marginal
Variable	High	cell entry	cell entry	marginal
		column marginal	marginal	Total N

jealous anger." Then the stories were categorized as either high or low in negative sentences ("high" meaning that 60% or more of the sentences in the story had negative connotations, "low" meaning 50% or less). This variable began as numeric but was collapsed into the two categories high and low negative. We have pointed out before that a variable can be categoric to start with (like sex of person written about, or John versus Anne) or it can be formed by breaking up a numerical variable into categories (percentage of negative sentences becomes high or low in negative sentences).

The results are shown in the top part of Table 14.1, a form of table which you have probably seen many times before. In general such tables are called crosstabulations, or crossclassifications, or contingency tables. The essential thing is that they are tables of counts; for example, the entry 93 on the upper left means that 93 female subjects wrote stories about John's success such that the percentage of negative sentences in the stories was low. To make it easier to talk about such tables, each part of the table has a name as indicated in the bottom part of Table 14.1. The number 93 just mentioned is a *cell entry*, or the number of people (or other units of analysis) that belong in the cell. Each cell is formed by combining a category from one variable with a category of the other (e.g. "John" combined with "low" percentage of negative sentences). Each *marginal* is the total number of people in one category of one of the variables, just the row or column total; for example, 128 is the total number of females who wrote "John" stories. The total N is the total number of female subjects reported on in this table; the total N is equal to the sum of the row marginals, or the sum of the column marginals, and also to the sum of all the cell entries, as you can easily check for the top part of Table 14.1.

We want to examine such tables for possible relationships between the row and column variables. For this particular example it is natural to ask: "Does the percentage of negative sentences depend on the sex of the person whose success is written about? Do the female subjects respond more negatively to the success of a male or to the success of a female or is there no difference?" This question assumes that the column variable (John or Anne) is the independent variable and the row variable is the dependent variable, which makes sense in this case. But sometimes it is not really clear which variable is the "X" and which the "Y"; it may be uncertain, or it may seem that the two variables influence each other. The chi-square technique introduced below does not make any assumptions about which variable is independent (an assumption which does have to be made in linear fits).

The relationship between negative response to success and sex of the successful person is not dramatically obvious in Table 14.1; if there is a relationship, there may be a slight tendency for women to be more negative about John's success, perhaps because they are more likely to empathize with and enjoy success by someone like themselves (i.e. of the same sex). But is this tendency marked enough to suggest a general pattern of responding more favourably to same-sex success? This sounds like the usual confirmatory question: is a sample result striking enough to suggest a pattern exists in the universe? But we are raising this old question for a rather new form of data, so let's examine the possible sample results a bit in Table 14.2A. The table on the left shows the strongest possible pattern of responding more favourably to one's own sex, with every story high in negative sentences being written about John and none about Anne. The table on the right shows no relationship between the two variables: there are a few more negative stories about John, but that's only because a few more of the female subjects (128 versus 117) were given John to write about. The proportion of negative stories is the same for stories about John, for those about Anne, or for all the stories together:

$$\frac{29}{128} = \frac{27}{117} = \frac{56}{245} = .23 .$$

Note that these hypothetical results have been set up so that the marginals are the same as for the actual results in Table 14.1; only the cell entries

Table 14.2A

Hypothetical Responses to Success

Strongest Possible Relationship, "John" Stories More Negative				No Relationship			
	John	Anne	Total		John	Anne	Total
Low	72	117	189	Low	99	90	189
High	56	0	56	High	29	27	56
	128	117	245		128	117	245

have been changed, and they have been changed so that they still add up to the marginals as they should. The marginals are taken as given: we assume that the results have to fit the marginals as we find them in the sample. This gives us a numerical basis for our calculations (like the hypothetical results in Table 14.2A) while leaving open the question of whether the row and column variables are related. The marginals alone have very little to do with the relationship between the variables. To see this, contrast the two tables in Table 14.2A: same marginals, very different relationship. Or look at the marginals by themselves in Table 14.2B.

Table 14.2B
Response to Success, Female Subjects

Negative Sentences	John	Anne	Row Totals
Low			189
High			56
Column Totals	128	117	245

What can we tell from this? We can see that the female subjects were fairly evenly divided between those writing about John and those writing about Anne (128 versus 117); and we can see that most of the stories were not very negative (189 out of 245 had a low percentage of negative sentences). But we cannot see how the two variables connect. We know how many females wrote about John, but not how negative those stories were; this information would be in the cell entries. We know how many females wrote stories with a high percentage of negative sentences, but not whether they were more likely to be negative about John or about Anne; again this information would be in the cell entries. To get at the relationship we must be able to look inside the table.

Table 14.2A shows us a couple of extreme possibilities for the inside of the table. Table 14.1 showed the actual results, which are somewhere in between. Should we conclude that there is really no relationship between the variables, and the tendency Table 14.1 may show is just a sampling accident? Or should we conclude that there is a relationship in the universe? This must depend on how far the actual cell entries get away from the "no relationship" entries in 14.2A: the more different they are from that flat pattern, the harder it is to believe that the two variables are unrelated.

This is the general strategy of the chi-square test, to which we now turn.

Analyzing Response to Success with Chi-Square

We want to see how far our results get from the "no relationship" pattern, so our first step is to make a more exact calculation of such a pattern. The version in Table 14.2A was rounded to whole numbers so it would look like a possible sample result, but for our test we want more accuracy. Now if the two variables are not related, knowing something about one of them tells us nothing new about the other one. For example, in the hypothetical "no relationship" table in Table 14.2A we saw that the percentage of negative sentences was the same whether we looked at all the stories (ignoring the John–Anne distinction) or whether we knew that the story had been written about a male or a female. But in the perfect relationship table, knowing the value of the column variable tells us a lot about the percentage of negative sentences: none of the Anne stories have a lot of negative sentences, while $56/128 = 44\%$ of the John stories do. To generalize this: if the row and column variables are not related, then the proportions inside the table will be the same as those in the marginals; but if the variables are related, then the proportions vary from row to row and column to column.

More formally, suppose H_0 is true:

H_0: the row and column variables are not related.

Then the number of cases in each cell just depends on how many cases there are in the row and column the cell belongs to. It is easy to calculate the number of cases we would expect:

$$\text{Expected values if } H_0 \text{ true} = \frac{(\text{Row Marginal})\,(\text{Column Marginal})}{\text{Table Total}}$$

The results are given to two decimal places in part A of Table 14.3; rounding these values gets back to the "no relationship" table in Table 14.2A. For example, the cell entry for women writing negative stories about Anne is

$$\frac{56 \times 117}{245} = 26.74, \text{ which rounds to } 27$$

Table 14.3

Finding Chi-Square for Female Response to Success

A. Expected Values

	John	Anne	Total
Low	98.74	90.26	189
High	29.26	26.74	56
	128	117	245

C. $(O-E)^2$

	John	Anne
Low	32.95	32.95
High	32.95	32.95

B. Observed—Expected

	John	Anne	Total
Low	−5.74	5.74	0
High	5.74	−5.74	0
Total	0	0	0

D. $(O-E)^2/E$

	John	Anne
Low	.334	.365
High	1.126	1.232

Of course, any real cell entries will be a little bit different from the expected values; for one thing, they'll be whole numbers! More importantly, the cell entries may be a bit higher or lower than expected just from sampling fluctuations even when the two variables are really unrelated in the universe. But if the actual cell entries get far enough from the H_0 expectations, we'll find H_0 too unlikely to be acceptable and we'll tentatively move to the alternative hypothesis

H_1: the row and column variables are related in the universe.

H_1 does not say how the variables are related; any extensive departure from the H_0 values is of interest, whatever the pattern of departure is. So our next step is to find out how different the observed cell values are from those expected if H_0 is true:

$$\text{Observed value} - \text{Expected value} = O - E.$$

These figures are reported in part B of Table 14.3. As an arithmetic check, note that the rows and columns must add up to zero. We see that there's some difference between the observed and expected values but it's hard to say whether the difference is important or something that could easily happen by chance. To help decide this familiar confirmatory question we will put all the differences in the $(O - E)$ table together to get an overall measure of how large they are. First we have to handle a couple of problems with the differences: some are positive and some negative, and they are not all equally impressive. First we dispose of the minus signs by squaring all the values to get

$$(O - E)^2$$

as in part C of Table 14.3. (You may have noticed that statisticians usually prefer squaring things to get rid of minus signs; once again squaring turns out to have useful mathematical properties.) Next we allow for the fact that the $(O - E)^2$ values are not all equally impressive even though they all happen to be the same number here. This may be easiest to think about if we turn back to the $(O - E)$ values in part B briefly, comparing them to the expected values in part A. Somehow the difference of 5.74 in the lower left hand corner, where we expect about 29 cases, looks more impressive than the difference of 5.74 in the upper right hand corner, where we expect about 90 cases. The lower left difference is a proportionally bigger departure from what we expect if H_0 is true. To get the departures in proportion to the expected values, we can just divide by the expected values. This brings us to

$$\frac{(O - E)^2}{E}$$

as in part D of Table 14.3. For example, the value in the John–Low cell is

$$\frac{(-5.74)^2}{98.74} = .334$$

Now chi-square, our overall measure of the difference between the observed data and the null expected, is just the total of the entries in part D:

$$\text{Chi-Square} = \chi_1^2 = \Sigma \frac{(O - E)^2}{E}$$

$$= .334 + .365 + 1.126 + 1.232$$

$$= 3.057$$

This value can be compared to a critical value from Table A.5 (p. 382). To use A.5 we need to know (1) what level of significance we want to use, and (2) how many degrees of freedom we have. As with anova we don't usually predict direction, so the test is ordinarily two-tailed. Let's use a 5% level of significance. The degrees of freedom for a chi-square test are found by multiplying the number of rows in the table less one $(R - 1)$ times the number of columns less one $(C - 1)$:

$$df = (R - 1)(C - 1)$$

In our example, $df = (2 - 1)(2 - 1) = 1$. Note that the degrees of freedom have nothing to do with the sample size, N, which has been crucial in all the other tests we've looked at. More on this later. Table A.5 tells us that the CV for one degree of freedom, 5% level, is 3.841. Our chi-square value is not that large, so we cannot reject H_0; the relationship between the sex of the person written about and the number of negative sentences is not significant at the .05 level. By this measure, at any rate, female response to success is not significantly affected by the gender of the successful person.

Finding a nonsignificant result was of considerable interest, since a previous study had suggested that women fear success and react more negatively to a woman's success than to a man's. Failures to replicate, and/or failures to find significant relationships where they are expected, are always interesting and can often be far more productive than getting the predicted result. It's the unexpected that makes you think the hardest. If there is any tendency in these data, it is one opposite to the "fear of success" prediction since the women were slightly more negative about John's success. The chi-square test, being nondirectional, tests for either possibility: for more negative response to John or for more negative response to Anne, or in general for any kind of difference from a flat "no relationship" pattern. So if the chi-square does turn out to be significant, we have some confidence that the two variables are related but we do not know how they are related; we must examine the data to see. Again this is similar to analysis of variance where we have to examine the means to see what a significant difference among them consists of. For a 2 × 2 table like the example just concluded, examination is easy, but for larger tables some visual display of the table pattern is useful. A table of $O - E$ values (like Table 14.3B) is not bad, but does not indicate which differences between observed and expected are proportionately larger. A more useful table for exploring a pattern is that for $\frac{(O - E)^2}{E}$ with minus signs in brackets to serve as quick reminders of which cells were lower than expected.

Degrees of Freedom for Chi-Square

In earlier tests the degrees of freedom were based on N, because a larger sample size meant more reliable estimates and thus less extreme critical values. Here, we find that the number of degrees of freedom does not depend on N at all but instead on the size of the table, or $(R - 1)(C - 1)$. Why? The chi-square compares observed to expected values cell by cell, so what really matters is the number of comparisons or the number of cells. So why not just R times C instead of $(R - 1)(C - 1)$? Consider the simplest possible table again, a two by two table like our response to success table. Suppose we know any one cell value: it doesn't matter which, let's say it's the Anne–Low cell. We also know the marginals, which are given throughout. So we have:

	John	Anne	Total
Low		96	189
High			56
Total	128	117	245

What do we know about the three blank cells? Everything! For example, the John–Low cell must be $189 - 96 = 93$; all the remaining cell values are fixed once we know the value of any one cell. So we really only have one independent comparison of observed and expected values. And the $(R - 1)(C - 1)$ formula tells us that we have one degree of freedom. Here is an illustration with a larger table:

			Total
5	10	?	20
10	5	?	25
10	10	?	25
?	?	?	15
Total 30	30	25	85

Once we fill in 6 cells, like the six filled in above for example, we know what the other cells must be. So we have six degrees of freedom; and $(R - 1)(C - 1) = 3 \times 2 = 6$.

Chi-Square Assumptions

As with any confirmatory test, chi-square can be used appropriately only if some assumptions about the data are met. First, the data must consist of randomly selected, independently measured cases. Second, the expected values must be large enough. "Large enough" depends on the size of the table primarily:

1. for 2 × 2 tables, the expected values in each cell should be 10 or more.
2. for tables larger than 2 × 2, the mean of the expected values should be six or more for tests at the 5% level; for tests at more demanding levels, like 1% or 0.1%, the minimum mean expected value should be somewhat higher.

These requirements for expected values are something new, so let's try to get a feel for them by looking at the simple 2 × 2 case again. In our example this assumption was met easily, since the smallest expected value was 26.74. Suppose it were not met; suppose we were doing a little trial run with fewer respondents and got this table of expected values from Table 14.4:

Hypothetical Table of Expected Values

	John	Anne	Total
Low	9.5	9.5	19
High	2.5	2.5	5
	12	12	24

Now, no matter what the observed values are, they must be at least a bit different from the expected values. Further, the last step in preparing cell values for chi-square is to divide through by the expected values; so if the expected values are small, such artifactual $O - E$ differences get even more exaggerated. The net effect is that the chi-square value can be increased a bit by arithmetic constraints that have nothing to do with the relationship between the two variables. The same sort of problem comes up in tables larger than 2 × 2, except that the effect is not quite as serious because it is spread over more cells, so the minimum mean expected value can be lower.

Suppose the expected values are not large enough? No problem, there are simple ways to cope. For a 2 × 2 table, find the $(O - E)$ values and then bring each cell one half unit closer to zero before proceeding with the rest of the test. This is called *correcting for continuity*. For example, suppose we had the hypothetical results in Table 14.4, part A. We find E values and $O - E$ values as usual (parts B and C) and then insert the correction for continuity (part D) before finding $\frac{(O - E)^2}{E}$ and chi-square (not shown).

For a table larger than 2 × 2 there is no way to correct for continuity. Instead, you can *collapse* the table; combine some of the categories with small marginals (and thus small expected values) to get bigger expected

Table 14.4

Hypothetical Example with Small Expected Values

A. Observed

	John	Anne	Total
Low	8	11	19
High	4	1	5
	12	12	24

C. O–E

	John	Anne	Total
	−1.5	1.5	0
	1.5	−1.5	0
Total	0	0	0

B. Expected

	John	Anne	Total
Low	9.5	9.5	19
High	2.5	2.5	5
	12	12	24

D. O–E, Corrected for Continuity

	John	Anne	Total
	−1.0	1.0	0
	1.0	−1.0	0
Total	0	0	0

values. Try to do so in some sensible, nonarbitrary way without peeking at the observed values.

Let's go through another, larger example. This will let us illustrate the details that are a bit different for larger tables, while reviewing the overall chi-square procedure.

A Larger Example: Response to Disaster

In January 1975 a downtown office building in North Bay blew up following a gas leak. The explosion, which happened at 3:30 p.m. on a workday, was very large and very loud and caused several deaths. News of the disaster spread through the community very rapidly, most often and most rapidly by word of mouth. The next day, a research team from Carleton University began doing interviews using a preset questionnaire devised to study disaster in general. This example looks at the data on how the news spread. The data were collected by tracing chains of communication about the disaster. The researchers began with a random sample of the community; each person sampled was asked how he heard about the explosion; if he named another person, that person was also interviewed to learn who he had heard from, and so on. Table 14.5 gives the "who tells whom" information by occupational category (students, housewives, and people in the work force in jobs of low, medium, or high status). For example, the 8 in the extreme upper left corner of the table means that 8 housewives were informed by other housewives. One interesting thing about this table is that the unit of observation is a communication tie (for example, a housewife–housewife communication of the news); the units are not people, as in the previous example.

Table 14.5

Communication Between Occupational Statuses

TO

FROM	Housewives	Students	Low Status	Medium Status	High Status	Total
Housewives	8	2	7	7	2	26
Students	3	4	3	1	0	11
Low Status	5	2	10	6	3	26
Medium Status	7	2	8	17	7	41
High Status	4	0	5	5	6	20
Total	27	10	33	36	18	124

Before proceeding we check out the chi-square assumptions. The data come from a random sample, and each communication link was separately traced, so the cases are probably a random sample of independent cases. Now, are the expected values large enough? To find the mean expected value we need only find the mean number of cases per cell or

$$\frac{N}{RC} = \frac{124}{5 \times 5} = 5$$

which is a bit small. We'll have to do some collapsing. The outstanding candidates for collapsing are the communications involving students, since there are so few of these. What should we collapse them with? Here judgement comes in. To us, it made sense to combine housewives and students as "nonworkers" on the grounds that communications among those in the formal work world (low, medium or high status) are perhaps rather different from other communications and should not be mixed up with them. This brings us to the simpler table in Table 14.6. Now the mean expected value is an acceptable 124/16 or about 8 so we can proceed with the chi-square test. Table 14.7 gives the expected values, which we note are all of a respectable size now. Table 14.8 gives $(O - E)$ values, and 14.9 gives $\frac{(O - E)^2}{E}$ with the signs noted in brackets to help exploration as we sug-

Table 14.6

Collapsed Communications

TO

FROM	Nonworkers	Low	Medium	High	Total
Nonworkers	17	10	8	2	37
Low	7	10	6	3	26
Medium	9	8	17	7	41
High	4	5	5	6	20
Total	37	33	36	18	124

Table 14.7
Expected Values for Table 14.6

TO

FROM	Nonworkers	Low	Medium	High	Total
Nonworkers	11.04	9.85	10.74	5.37	37.00
Low	7.76	6.92	7.55	3.77	26.00
Medium	12.23	10.91	11.90	5.95	40.99
High	5.97	5.32	5.80	2.90	19.99
Total	37.00	33.00	35.99	17.99	

Note: The marginals are the same as in Table 14.6 within rounding error.

Table 14.8
O–E for Table 14.6

TO

FROM	Nonworkers	Low	Medium	High	Total
Nonworkers	5.96	.15	−2.74	−3.37	.00
Low	−.76	3.08	−1.55	−.77	.00
Medium	−3.23	−2.91	5.10	1.05	.01
High	−1.97	−.32	−.80	3.10	.01
Total	.00	.00	.01	.01	.02

Note: The marginals are all zero within rounding error.

Table 14.9
$$\frac{(O-E)^2}{E} \text{ for Table 14.6}$$

TO

FROM	Nonworkers	Low	Medium	High
Nonworkers	3.218	.002	(−).699	(−)2.115
Low	(−).074	1.371	(−).318	(−).157
Medium	(−).853	(−).776	2.186	.185
High	(−).650	(−).019	(−).110	3.314

$$\chi_9^2 = 16.047$$

gested above. Finally, summing the entries in Table 14.9 gives us a chi-square value of 16.047. The degrees of freedom are $(R - 1)(C - 1)$ $= (3)(3) = 9$. Table A.5 gives 16.919 as the CV for nine *df*s; the chi-square for our table, 16.047, is close but lower, so we cannot reject the null hypothesis.

As usual, we do not let the absence of a significant relationship keep us from thinking about the data. These data are clearly worth exploring; since the relationship is close to significance, perhaps it would have been significant with a little more data. Table 14.9 shows a simple pattern that makes a lot of sense: people are more likely to pass the news to someone like themselves than to someone unlike themselves. This is clear from the positive, large values down the diagonal; for example, the entry for high status workers telling high status workers is 3.314, indicating that high status workers told more high status workers than one would expect by chance. Nonworkers talk to nonworkers, and workers talk to other workers of similar status.

Significance and Strength: Measures of Association

So far we've learned to use the chi-square test to answer one major question: is there a significant relationship between the row and column variables? Are the observed values different from the ones we would expect if there is no relationship, so different that we think there probably is a relationship? This is of course a very important question and one we must know how to answer, but there are other questions just as important; perhaps most important is the question, "How strong is this relationship?"

Let's look at a few examples to show how significance and strength differ and why. Earlier we looked at the proportion of negative sentences in stories written by females about John or Anne, getting this summary picture:

	John	Anne	Total
Low	93	96	189
High	35	21	56
Total	128	117	245

$$\chi_1^2 = 3.057$$

This value for χ_1^2 is not significant at the 5% level. Now let's suppose that someone with plenty of time on his hands decides to replicate this study with a sample size ten times larger; he does so, and happens to find a relationship that is identical except that everything is multiplied by ten:

Hypothetical Replication

	John	Anne	Total
Low	930	960	1890
High	350	210	560
Total	1280	1170	2450

$$\chi_1^2 = 30.57$$

Significant at .001 level.

Note that the chi-square gets multiplied by ten too! If we had doubled all the numbers in the table, the chi-square would have doubled; if we had tripled the numbers, the chi-square would have tripled, and so on. This hypothetical increase in sample size can affect the significance level even if the strength of the relationship stays the same. This is similar to what we found for the correlation coefficient in the previous chapter: if the N is large enough, even a very weak r^2 can be significant, so strength and significance are not exactly the same thing. For chi-square also, strength and significance are two separate though related questions.

Now we know how to ask if the relationship in our sample is significant, if it is likely to be present also in the universe from which the sample was taken: that is the question chi-square deals with. But what of strength? We can use chi-square for this if we can only remove chi-square's dependence on N. One very easy way to do this is to find

$$\phi^2 = \frac{\chi^2}{N}$$

(ϕ is the Greek letter pronounced "fee".)

In our little example, for the first (the real) table

$$\frac{\chi^2}{N} = \frac{3.057}{245} = .012 \; ;$$

while for the imaginary replication with increased N,

$$\frac{\chi^2}{N} = \frac{30.57}{2450} = .012 \; .$$

Whether we have 245 cases or 2450, this figure suggests that the relationship between negative sentences in stories and gender of person written about is a weak one, which fits with a common-sense look at the table. Thus ϕ^2 (pronounced fee square), is the kind of thing we want a measure of association between two variables to be: it suggests how strongly the variables are related whatever the sample size we happen to have.

For all tables which are either 2×2, $2 \times C$, or $R \times 2$, ϕ^2 has the very nice property that it goes from 0 to 1, 0 for no relationship and 1 for a perfect relationship. (r^2 does this too.) Unfortunately, ϕ^2 loses this nice property when both dimensions of the table are greater than 2. By modifying ϕ^2 a bit we get a measure which goes from 0 to 1.0 for any size of table, Cramer's V:

$$V = \sqrt{\frac{\chi^2}{N(S - 1)}}$$

where $S = $ either R or C, whichever is smaller.

If the row or column variable has just two categories then the smaller of $(R - 1)$ and $(C - 1)$ is $2 - 1 = 1$, so V is the same as $\sqrt{\phi^2}$. In bigger tables, there is a difference. Consider our table of communications among occupational groups in North Bay: $(R - 1) = 3$ and $(C - 1) = 3$ so

$$V = \sqrt{\frac{16.047}{124(3)}} = \sqrt{.0431} = .21$$

indicating a modest relationship.

There are many other measures of association. For 2 × 2 tables, one of the best and simplest measures is Yule's Q. If we simply label the counts in the cells of the 2 × 2 table as

$$\begin{array}{cc} a & b \\ c & d \end{array}$$

then:

$$Q = \frac{ad - bc}{ad + bc}.$$

This measure varies from -1 (if either a or d is zero) to $+1$ (if b or c is zero). It is much used in the social sciences. If you want to use Q and have a table that is larger than 2 × 2, Goodman and Kruskal (1954) have devised a measure that has the nice properties of Q but can be used more generally. They call this measure γ (pronounced gamma). The Goodman and Kruskal article is also an excellent overview of available measures of association and their properties.

Exploratory and Confirmatory

You may be wondering why we plunged into a confirmatory analysis of two categorical variables instead of doing an exploratory technique first, as we usually do. The reason is that chi-square is exploratory and confirmatory at the same time. To explore a table of counts, we would have to do something to show how the observed values differ from a "no relationship" pattern in order to make the actual pattern easily visible. Why not do that through chi-square, so the same arithmetic will serve for both exploration and testing? On the other hand, you can't do a chi-square properly without doing some exploration, since the chi-square test and a measure of association will tell you whether there is a relationship, and how strong it is, but not what it is.

Homework

Analyze Table 14.10 (communications between age groups in North Bay), or Table 14.11 (communications between educational groups), or Table 14.12, another aspect of the response to success. Table 14.12 gives data for both female and male respondents who wrote about John or Anne. In this table, a new aspect of their stories is considered: the presence or absence of a "denial of success." Denial of success refers to anything suggesting that John or Anne had not really been successful, accusations of cheating being typical. For example, "John's clever cocker spaniel reads and memorizes all the material and barks to John in code at the right moment" (Levine & Crumrine, 1975, p. 966).

Having chosen a table and checked the assumptions,

1. Find the expected values.
2. Discuss whether the assumptions of the chi-square test are met. If not, take appropriate action.
3. Find $O - E$ and $\dfrac{(O - E)^2}{E}$.
4. Find chi-square; is it significant at the 5% level? at the 1% level?
5. Discuss!

Table 14.10

Information Flow between Age Groups

TO

FROM	16–19	20–30	31–50	51+	Total
16–19	5	3	9	0	17
20–30	2	14	10	4	31
31–50	6	17	35	16	74
51+	2	5	8	15	30
	15	39	62	36	152

Table 14.11

Information Flow between Educational Groups

TO

FROM	Elementary	Some High School	High School	Some University	Total
Elementary	12	15	6	2	35
Some High School	4	19	17	5	45
High School	5	10	16	13	44
Some University	3	7	7	11	28
Total	24	51	46	31	152

Table 14.12

Denial of Success

Denial of Success	Female Respondent		Male Respondent	
	John	Anne	John	Anne
Present	52	28	56	84
Absent	122	129	121	101
	174	157	177	185

Third Review

Let us remind you of the importance of organic and sensibly limited analyses. Do not try a hectic mixture of attacks on the data, hoping it will somehow make sense at the last minute; pick a core topic and follow through on it in some orderly way, commenting as you go. For example, you might choose a dependent variable on which to focus X by Y analysis, explore a promising independent variable, examine residuals for suggestions about other possible independent variables, then do a corresponding confirmatory analysis, and finally compare the two approaches. This would follow the order of preceding chapters quite closely. Or you might start with confirmatory statistics and use exploratory methods to enrich this analysis. Don't just look at one combination of variables after another until one looks terrific; even a weak relationship can be interesting, and you are not going to be graded on the strength of relationships (that depends on reality, not on you!). We urge these points more strongly than ever because we are now giving you a lot of choice. In Example 1, you may choose from a wealth of possible variables; in Example 2, choose *one* of three tables to analyze. In both examples, give reasons for your choices.

Example 1. You met Vancouver municipal voting data in Table 11.9 and in the discussion of income, turnout, and East Side versus West Side in chapter 11. Table IIIR.1 gives more turnout data, together with the percentage of people casting ballots for a left wing candidate. During much of the period covered by these data, Vancouver had municipal parties which made it easy to classify candidates as left, right, or centre.

Example 2. You met the North Bay disaster study as part of chapter 14; here we give you some additional information about the respondents, their backgrounds, and how they heard the news about the downtown explosion which took several lives. There are three tables to choose from; for each, we used only the 168 respondents who were randomly sampled from residents of North Bay at the start of the study.

   In Table IIIR.2, the column variable is the respondent's own occupational status. For people other than housewives and students, we give a number which indicates the typical income and education of people in the respondent's occupation (3 means the income and education are rather low,

Table IIIR.1

Left Wing Vote and Turnout in Vancouver

Area	Mean Income 1961	Left Wing Vote (%)					Turnout (%)				
		1958	1960	1962	1964	1966	1958	1960	1962	1964	1966
1	2751	28	26	16	29	24	20	26	27	24	22
2	3315	37	30	18	34	27	22	25	29	26	25
3	3422	33	28	16	32	27	24	28	33	30	27
4	3864	35	29	15	36	28	32	35	44	42	39
5	3865	26	24	11	26	22	31	35	44	38	34
6	3865	36	31	13	32	27	33	37	43	38	32
7	3974	33	31	15	33	28	29	35	43	40	36
8	4003	36	29	15	35	28	33	35	42	39	37
9	4173	35	29	13	30	27	32	36	44	42	36
10	4186	36	31	14	32	29	29	33	41	38	34
11	4299	32	27	11	28	25	32	34	44	40	34
12	4383	28	23	11	26	22	34	36	48	43	40
13	4594	34	29	12	29	26	33	42	45	41	35
14	3589	20	18	10	20	19	26	28	32	27	26
15	3785	24	20	10	23	20	28	29	38	34	30
16	3786	22	19	10	22	19	25	27	33	30	27
17	4233	19	15	9	18	17	28	28	35	33	29
18	4558	21	17	9	22	18	33	37	47	41	39
19	4640	24	18	9	21	20	32	36	47	40	32
20	5701	16	13	7	16	14	44	54	66	58	50
21	5908	18	15	8	19	17	40	44	54	48	43
22	6267	15	9	8	15	12	41	46	60	55	47
23	7066	12	10	6	13	11	45	51	65	59	53
24	8477	9	8	5	12	10	40	40	58	52	48

Source: A. Ewing, *Socio-Economic Status and Voting Behaviour in Vancouver*, 1972.

8 that they are high). The row variable gives the same occupational scores as found for the respondent's father's occupation. Do you want to use all the data? Why or why not? Do you want to collapse the table? Note that the table includes 143 of the 168 people in the original random sample of

Table IIIR.2

Respondent's Status and Father's Status

Father's Status	Respondent's Occupational Status							
	Housewife	Student	3	4	5	6	7	8
3	2				2			
4	20	10	1	31	18	4	1	
5	7	4		10	10	3	1	
6		4		5	4	1	1	1
7	2					1		

Note: A total of 143 respondents gave information on both their own occupations and their father's.

North Bay residents. Some sampled people are excluded because they did not give information about their occupations and/or those of their fathers. This "missing data" problem crops up in virtually all social science research; how do you think it affects the analysis?

In Table IIIR.3, the column variable is the number of relatives which the respondent reported having in North Bay, and the row variable is how the respondent heard of the explosion. Here, in contrast to the first table, there is almost no missing data.

Table IIIR.4, the column variable is occupational status again, and the row variable is who the respondent first heard the news from. This table includes the fewest people, only 75; but (unlike Table IIIR.2) this is not primarily because of missing data. Instead, it is mostly because only 86 people in the entire sample heard the news from another person, so 86 is the maximum number to which the table could apply. The difference between 86 and 75 *is* due to missing data, mostly on the occupational variable. How would these two factors (not all people eligible, not all people giving full information) affect your conclusions?

Table IIIR.3
Number of Relatives and How the News was Heard

How Person Heard	Number of Relatives in North Bay									
	0	1	2	3	4	5	6	7	8	9 or More
Radio	8		3		1		3	1		9
TV or Paper	3	1	1	1						1
Person told	15	10	6	13	2	2	1	3	1	30
Overheard		3				1				2
Eyewitness	6	2	3	4	1	2	3	2	1	15

Note: A total of 160 respondents gave information on both variables.

Table IIIR.4
Occupation and Who Respondent Heard From

Who told you?	Occupation				
	HW	Student	Low	Medium	High
Family, Same House	11	4	6	4	2
Other Family		2	3	2	1
Fellow Worker			6	4	3
Friend	4	3	6	1	
Acquaintance	2		1	2	2
Known by Sight	1			1	1
Complete Stranger			2		1

Note: A total of 75 respondents heard the news from another person and gave information on both variables.

Section Four

Using Two Independent Variables

In the previous sections we learned how to work with one independent variable, X, and one dependent variable, Y. We have learned how to deal with the effect of X on Y under many different conditions. X and Y can each be numerical or categorical; our general style can be exploratory or confirmatory; the variables can have various levels, shapes and spreads. Let us remind you of what we have so far:

Variable Type		Statistical Techniques	
Independent (X)	Dependent (Y)	Exploratory	Confirmatory
categorical	numeric	batch analysis (ch. 2 to 6)	t-test, Z-test and one-way anova (ch. 8, 9, 10)
numeric	numeric	X by Y (ch. 11, 12)	linear regression (ch. 13)
categorical	categorical	chi-square interpretation (ch. 14)	chi-square test (ch. 14)

We even know how to use these methods for a numerical X or Y that is far from normal (we can almost always transform).

Suppose that we now want to examine the effects of two independent variables on Y? Suppose, for example, that we want to see the effects of heterogeneity and integration on mobility. This is a sensible goal, since mobility may well be a product of both integration and heterogeneity. Indeed, most social variables — if not all — are the product of many causes working together, not the result of just one.

This section is devoted to ways of predicting a numerical Y from two X variables in combination. First, we see how to combine two categorical X's. Chapter 15 shows how to summarize the effects of two categorical independent variables, with summarization either by means or by medians.

Chapter 16 shows one way to fit effects of the two variables in combination, or interaction effects. Then chapter 17 presents the basic confirmatory approach, two-way analysis of variance. In the second half of this section we work with two numeric X variables. Chapter 18 adds a second X to the exploratory X by Y techniques, while chapters 19 and 20 give the analogous confirmatory tools.

It is also possible to handle all the other combinations, although we will not try to cover the techniques here. A numeric X and a categorical X with a numeric Y? In our study of exploratory techniques we had a taste of this in chapter 11; you just combine X by Y and sub-batching, following your common sense. In confirmatory statistics one uses a kind of anova-regression hybrid called analysis of covariance. Two categorical X's and a categorical Y? Extensions of chi-square and related methods can be used here. In general, it is pretty hard to come up with a data set for which no standard technique exists, as there are lots of techniques available. The ones we give here are the ones most widely used. To read most journal articles, or handle most simple research problems, you may never need more.

Finally, the techniques presented here can be easily extended to handle three or more independent variables. They can also be seen as closely related techniques. Indeed, all of them are special applications of one approach, the "general linear model."

15
Elementary Analysis

We already know how to look at the effect of one categorical X on a numeric Y: divide up the Y values into batches, with each batch corresponding to a category of X, and find the batch levels. For example, we batched suicide rates (Y) by age groups (X) and found that the level of suicide increased with age. Now we extend this to the situation where two categorical independent variables together determine the level of Y.

First we make a table, like Table 15.1. The two categorical X variables are the row and column variables. The column variable in Table 15.1 is the proportion of white classmates that black students had in the previous years; the row variable is the students' grade. The Y variable appears in the cells of the table; here, Y is average reading comprehension on a standard reading achievement test normed by grade. The norming was done for all pupils (both black and white) so that the average score for all pupils in a grade was 50. For example, if we look at the lower right corner of the table we see the number 46.6. This means that black students in grade 6 more than half of whose grade five classmates were white scored 46.6 on reading comprehension on the average. This is a straightforward table of a kind you have probably seen often. Note that it is very different from a chi-square table although it may look similar at a quick glance. In chi-square there are two variables and the entries are counts for each cross classification. Here we have three variables, because the entries are scores on Y. This kind of table is often called a "two-way" table.

Table 15.1
A Simple Two-way Table:
Average Reading Comprehension*

Grade	Proportion of White Classmates Last Year			
	None	Less than Half	Half	More than Half
12	46.0	43.7	44.5	47.5
9	44.2	44.8	44.8	47.1
6	46.0	45.4	45.8	46.6

Source: Adapted from Table 3.3.1, page 332, James S. Coleman et al., *Equality In Education*; Washington, D.C., U.S. Department of Health, Education, and Welfare, Office of Education.

*Comprehension scores taken from results on two achievement tests given to Negro students in metropolitan areas of the northeast U.S.A.

In this chapter we will look at two methods of analyzing this kind of table; the two methods have the same goal, but one uses means and the other uses medians. Although the means analysis is not resistant, we will start with it because it is much simpler to compute. In this chapter and the next we think of both methods as exploratory approaches, although the use of means will turn up again in the confirmatory version.

Elementary Analysis Using Means

Let's put off thinking about the row variable "grade" for a moment. Each of the columns can be thought of as a batch of numbers; for example, in the column on the far left we see three reading comprehension scores for students who had no white classmates in their previous year. Well, this is a pretty familiar situation; we can just find the level of each of the four batches (columns) to see the effect of the column variable. Going from the category "no white classmates" to the category "over half white," the column means are: 45.4, 44.6, 45.0, 47.1. By looking closely at these four numbers we can see that there is an interesting curvilinear pattern here: the reading comprehension scores go first down and then up as the proportion of white classmates increases. We have to look rather closely because the numbers are all rather similar. We can make the effect of variation in the proportion of white classmates a lot clearer by setting aside the overall size of these numbers; this is just their mean, which is also the mean of the cell entries in the original table:

$$\overline{\overline{Y}} = \text{Grand Mean} = \text{mean of all the } Y \text{ cell entries}$$
$$= \text{mean of the column means}$$
$$= \text{mean of the row means}$$

$$\text{Here } \overline{\overline{Y}} = \frac{45.4 + 44.6 + 45.0 + 47.1}{4} = 45.5$$

Now we take away this "overall size of the numbers" component to get a clearer view of the column variable's effects: we simply subtract Y from each of the column means. The numbers we get in this way are known as the *column effects*. For example, the effect for the first column is

$$45.4 - 45.5 = \text{Column Mean} - \text{Grand Mean}$$
$$= -.1$$

Thus black students who had no white classmates in the previous year had reading comprehension very close to the average for all black students under consideration; their mean score is .1 under the overall average, but this is a small difference. We find much larger differences for the other columns, as we see in Table 15.2 where column means and column effects are given.

Table 15.2

Reading Comprehension: Column Means Removed

Grade	Portion of White Classmates Last Year			
	None	Less than Half	Half	Over Half
12	.6	−.9	−.5	.4
9	−1.2	.2	−.2	.0
6	.6	.8	.8	−.5
Column Mean	45.4	44.6	45.0	47.1
Column Effect	−.1	−.9	−.5	1.6
(= Column mean − Y)				$\bar{\bar{Y}} = 45.5$

Before going any further with the numerical work (which is pretty straightforward, as you can see) let's think about what this pattern of column effects might mean. Black students in black classrooms perform near the average (the effect, −.1, is near zero, so they are nearly average). Those with under half of their classmates white did poorly, and those with half their classmates white did almost as poorly (effects: −.9, −.5). On the other hand, having a majority of white classmates pulls the column effects way up to 1.5! Perhaps two trends account for this. First, it is probable that the higher the proportion white the better the school (better facilities, better teachers, and better home education for the students). Second, the all-black classrooms produce better results than one might expect from the first trend perhaps because racial distractions (e.g. tension, rivalry) are absent.

So far we have found and interpreted the effects of the column variable, using very simple arithmetic rather like that we used for batch analysis of levels. In batch analysis we did not stop there; we also removed levels in order to look harder at what remained, or the residuals. We do that here too:

Y residuals from column variable and grand mean
= Y − column mean
= Y − column effect − grand mean

These residuals have also been noted in Table 15.2. For example, consider the middle cell in the leftmost column, for grade nine students with no white classmates in the previous year. The original cell entry, from Table 15.1, was 44.2, so

Y residual from column variable
= 44.2 − 45.4
= −1.2

Now what might be going on with these residuals? The first thing to look for is the possible effect of the other variable: the row variable in this case. (We could have started with the rows and then gone to columns; the final result would be the same when using means.) Once again, to see the effects of the row variable we find the row means. We could do this just as we did for the columns: go back to Table 15.1, find row means, and subtract the grand mean. But we get exactly the same answer a little bit faster if we just find the row effects, or the means of the residuals in Table 15.2; then we don't have to bother removing the grand mean, which we took out in the previous step when we removed column means. So, for example, we find the row effect for grade twelve students by finding $\dfrac{.6 - .9 - .5 + .4}{4} = -.1,$

which tells us that the grade twelves were just a shade under average in reading comprehension. If we go the somewhat longer route of returning to Table 15.1, we find the row mean: $\dfrac{46.0 + 43.7 + 44.5 + 47.5}{4} = 45.4$, and then

we subtract the grand mean to get the row effect: $45.4 - 45.5 = -.1$, or the same result. That's one big reason why using means is so handy computationally: you can get the same result in several different ways. Table 15.3A gives the row means and effects, as well as the column means and effects we found earlier.

Table 15.3A

Reading Comprehension with Row Effects Removed;
Full Means Analysis

| Grade | Proportion of White Classmates | | | | | |
	None	Under Half	Half	Over Half	Mean	Effect
12	0.7	−0.8	−0.4	0.5	45.4	−0.1
9	−0.9	0.5	0.1	0.3	45.2	−0.3
6	0.2	0.4	0.4	−0.9	45.9	0.4
Mean	45.4	44.6	45.0	47.1	$45.5 = \overline{\overline{Y}}$	
Effect	−0.1	−0.9	−0.5	1.6		

What is the effect of the row variable? It is slight. The effects are much less extreme than those of the column variable: the row effects go from −.3 to .4, a range of .7, while the column effects go from −.9 to 1.6, a range of 2.5 or over three times as much; this gives us a rough feeling that the column variable makes a lot more difference to reading comprehension than grade does. The row effects also look rather small compared to the sizes of the residuals, many of which are farther from zero than the row effects are. All in all, the row variable has little impact; and it should have little impact, since the test of reading comprehension was supposed to be normed by grade. Actually, the small differences from grade to grade that turned up are rather interesting considering that we really don't expect any differences between grades. What could be going on? Since the norming was done for white students and black together, our row effects suggest that the black students in grade six are doing a little bit better compared to their white counterparts than the older students are doing compared to theirs. We will push this no further, since the row effects are so slight.

Naturally we go on to find the residuals. Again it saves time to go to Table 15.2, not 15.1:

Final residual
$$= Y - \text{column mean} - \text{row effect}$$
$$= Y - \overline{\overline{Y}} - \text{column effect} - \text{row effect}$$

The first formula is faster at this stage than the second and is of course the same thing. For example, consider grade six students more than half of whose classmates the previous year were white. From Table 15.2 we find that the residual from the grand mean and column effect is -0.5; the row effect for grade six is 0.4, so the final residual is $-0.5 - 0.4 = -0.9$, which is entered in Table 15.3A in the appropriate cell.

Please note that Table 15.3A, the full means analysis with $\overline{\overline{Y}}$ and column and row effects removed, is the same thing as the table we started with, Table 15.1. We have broken the original numbers down into their components or elements but we have not changed them. The elements are the pieces that make up our overall fit:

$\overline{\overline{Y}} = $ overall size of the cell entries

Column effect = the effect on Y of being in one column rather than another; the column mean minus the grand mean

Row effect = the effect on Y of being in one row rather than another; the row mean minus the grand mean

as well as residuals from the fit:

Residual = whatever is left over after fitting the above; the observed values in the cells minus grand mean, column effect and row effect.

In Table 15.3A, these various elements making up Y are separated and clearly displayed. $\overline{\overline{Y}}$ goes in the lower right corner; effects go in the margins of the table (means are put there too, largely for the benefit of those who like means better than effects); and the residuals go in the cells. At a glance we can see what the effects of the row and column variables are, and whether the row or the column variable appears to be stronger. If we put the elements together again, we get right back to our original table. For example, the upper right cell has a residual of .5, a row effect of $-.1$, a column effect of 1.6; and the grand mean is 45.5. Putting all these components together,

$$.5 - .1 + 1.6 + 45.5 = 47.5 = \text{original cell entry in Table 15.1.}$$

What We've Done So Far

We have outlined a very simple procedure which lets us look at the effects of two categorical X variables on a numeric Y variable. In doing an elementary analysis, you usually do all the arithmetic first and then discuss. The arithmetic is easy: start with one of the X's, find and remove its means; find the grand mean and then remove it from the first X's means to get effects; then find and remove the effects of the second X variable. This is just addition and subtraction and very fast to do. Sometimes people get a little mixed up at first in removing effects; they forget when to add and when to subtract. You may find it helpful to remind yourself that you want to fit some aspect of the data, say a row effect; when you have this fit, you move it *out of* the main body of the table and *into* the margins of the table where it can be clearly seen. So if a row effect is $-.1$, you put $-.1$ in the margin and subtract $-.1$ from the entries in that row (subtracting $-.1$ is the same as adding .1 to all the entries).

Because you are working with means, there are lots of arithmetic checks you can make. The grand mean should be the mean of the row means and the mean of the column means. The row and column effects should add up to zero. The residuals in any row or column of the final table should add up to zero. Of course, all these "shoulds" are true within rounding error. For example, in Table 15.3A, the residuals for the right hand column add to $-.1$, not zero, but $-.1$ is within rounding error.

The interpretation of row and column effects is pretty much the same as interpreting batch levels in the old days when we only had one X. So far, the only new wrinkle we have seen is that the strength of effects of the two X's can be roughly compared: the stronger X is the one with effects of wider range. We will see a real wrinkle in the next chapter, where we see how to work with combinations of the two X variables as well as looking at their effects separately as we do here.

Beyond the Basic Fit: Using the Residuals

We have a fit:

$$\overline{\overline{Y}} + \text{Column Effect} + \text{Row Effect}.$$

Naturally, we want to know how good a fit this is. As always with a numeric Y, we compare the midspread of the residuals from the fit to the midspread of the original Y. In an elementary analysis, the original Y values come from the cells of a table like 15.1 and the residuals from the cells of a table like 15.3. In our example,

$$\frac{dq\ Y'}{dq\ Y} = \frac{1.05}{1.65} = .64$$

Table 15.3B

Symbols from a Stem-and-Leaf

Upper Outliers	**X**	2		$N = 12$
		1		$X_U = .7$
Above q_U but not an outlier	x	1		$q_U = .45$
		0	755	Md $= .25$
q_U, q_L, or in between	.	0	44321	$q_L = -.6$
		-0	4	$X_L = -.9$
		-0	899	$dq = 1.05$
Below q_L but not an outlier	o	-1		Step $= 1.6$
		-1		
Lower outliers	●	-2		

stems: units   *leaves*: decimals

Outliers: none (upper outliers would be 2.0 or more; lower outliers would be -2.2 or less).

which suggests that our fit has helped explain Y but has left quite a lot unaccounted for. An intuitive look at Table 15.3, where the residuals look pretty large compared to the effects, leaves us with a similar impression.

Well, that's all the more reason to look hard at the residuals, a good idea in any case. In numerical form, as in Table 15.3A, the residuals can be rather hard to see because there is too much detail; the larger the table, the harder it can be to see patterns in the residuals. To make things more visual we make a "plot" of the residuals by replacing the numbers with symbols. Table 15.3B shows how we would define these symbols, using the reading comprehension example. Make the big **X**'s much bigger than the small ones; and use large solid dots (●) so you can easily see where the outliers are, if there are any. (In our example there do not happen to be any.) The plotted residuals are given in Table 15.4. We see that the curvilinear relation between proportion of whites and reading is strongest for grade twelve students; that the fit is best for younger students and for those with more white classmates; and that none of the residuals is really big (none is an outlier).

Table 15.4

Reading Comprehension: Residuals Plotted

Grade	Proportion of White Classmates				
	None	Under Half	Half	Over Half	Effect
12	x	o	.	x	$-.1$
9	o	x	.	.	$-.3$
6	.	.	.	o	.4
Effect	$-.1$	$-.9$	$-.5$	1.6	45.5

Getting a Resistant Analysis: Median Polish

So far so good; now we have an easy and sensible approach to pulling apart the two-way table. But what about this business of using means? Hardly the best thing for exploratory work! Our row and column effects will lack resistance if they are based on mean levels of row and column values after the grand mean $\overline{\overline{Y}}$ is gone. And our residuals will tend to be rather bland (remember, if there is an unusual case then it will affect the mean strongly and the oddball case will not look as odd as it would if a more resistant level were used). The reading comprehension residuals from grade and proportion of white classmates were large on the whole (many were as large as most of the row and column effects) but there were no really extreme ones (no outliers). Use of the mean has a flattening effect on residuals, which makes residuals less helpful for generating further insights.

Let's try using medians in place of means; we'll have the same basic idea, breaking Y up into components, but the components will be resistant levels instead of means. Now we could do this by just going back to the beginning again: go to the raw data in Table 15.1, find the grand median, then find column medians and so on. But that approach can be a lot of work, for reasons which will be explained below. It is a lot faster to carry on from the means analysis in Table 15.3, adjusting to make it a median analysis: this is called a *median polish*.

The steps in a median polish are illustrated in Table 15.5. In the first step, we look at our grand level $\overline{\overline{Y}}$ to see if it is a grand median for our data. To see, we look at the residuals from the previous step, recorded back in Table 15.3. Those residuals have a mean of zero, of course, but they have a median of 0.3, not zero. So we remove 0.3 from those residuals and add 0.3 to the overall level, getting new residuals recorded in the First Step part of Table 15.5. In this first step we did nothing to the row or column effects, so they are just carried over from the previous stage, Table 15.3.

We are done with the overall level now, but the row and column effects may need polishing too. Here we decided to look at the column effects first. We look at the residuals from the current stage, the First Step table, and see if their column medians are zero. Mostly they're not: from left to right the column medians are $-.1$, $.1$, $-.2$, and 0. Once again we subtract the medians from the residuals and add them to the fit, to the column effects in this step. Let's look at one column in more detail to see the procedure. The leftmost column has values $.4$, -1.2, and $-.1$ in the First Step; the median is $-.1$ and we want it to be zero. Otherwise, in median terms there is still some column effect left in the residuals. So we remove the remaining effect, $-.1$, by subtracting it from the residuals:

$$\text{residuals from current step} - \text{median} = \text{new residuals}$$
$$.4 - (-.1) = .5$$
$$-1.2 - (-.1) = -1.1$$
$$-.1 - (-.1) = .0$$

Table 15.5

Median Polish of Means Analysis in Table 15.3

First Step: Polish overall level; Subtract residual Md from residuals, add to $\overline{\overline{Y}}$

	New Residuals			Row Effects (Carried Over)
.4	−1.1	−.7	.2	−.1
−1.2	.2	−.2	.0	−.3
−.1	.1	.1	−1.2	.4

Column Effects −.1   −.9   −.5   1.6 $\overline{\overline{Y}} + .3 = 45.8 =$ New Overall Level
(Carried Over)

Second Step: Polish column effects; find column Md's from previous residuals, remove, add to column effects.

	New Residuals			Row Effects (Carried Over)
.5	−1.2	−.5	.2	−.1
−1.1	.1	.0	.0	−.3
.0	.0	.3	−1.2	.4

Md	−.1	.1	−.2	.0
Old Effect	−.1	−.9	−.5	1.6	Overall Level 45.8
New Effect	−.2	−.8	−.7	1.6

Third Step: Polish row effects; row Md's from Step Two are subtracted from residuals and added to row effects.

	New Residuals			Md + Old Effect = New Effect
.7	−1.0	−.3	.4	−.2 + (−.1) = −.3
−1.1	.1	.0	.0	.0 + (−.3) = −.3
.0	.0	.3	−1.2	.0 + (.4) = .4

Column   −.2   −.8   −.7   1.6
Effects   Overall Level = 45.8
(Carried Over)
Column Medians of new Residuals are all zero; no further steps required.

This fixes up the residuals, which now have a median of zero as we wish; we record them in the cells of the Second Step of Table 15.5. But what about that −.1 that we subtracted? We can't just ignore it, as it was part of the data. We add it to the column effect: −.1 + (−.1) = −.2. Now we have a new column effect in median terms, also recorded in the Second Step table. Note that nothing is lost as this polish goes on; we remove things from the residuals, but we add them to the fit at the same time. At any step in this procedure, the elements in a table add up to the original Y values.

The second step took care of column effects in median terms; how about row effects? To see what has to be done we look at the residuals in the Second Step table: are the row medians zero as we want them to be? For the grade six and grade nine rows they are, so we can leave those rows and row effects alone: but the grade twelve row has a median of −.2. Again, we subtract this effect from the residuals; this gives us new residuals in the grade 12 row in the Third Step table, where we also add this −.2 to the row effect, getting a new effect in median terms.

At the end of the third step we know that the row medians of the residuals must be zero; that's what the third step was for. But we do not know that the column residuals must be zero; for adjusting the row residuals may have thrown the column residuals off. This cannot happen when you find effects with means (one reason why the means analysis is so much simpler computationally) but it can happen with medians. In this case we are lucky: we look at the columns in the Third Step table and find they still have zero medians. Now both rows and columns have zero medians; both row and column effects have been fitted in median terms; and we are done.

In this last step (and in all the intermediate steps as well) the fit plus the residual must add up to the original Y. Let's just check the grade 12 row on this:

$$
\begin{array}{rcccl}
Grand\ Median + Row\ Eff + Col\ Eff + Residual & = & Original\ Y \\
45.8 \quad + (-.3) \quad + (-.2) + \quad .7 & = & 46.0 \\
45.8 \quad + (-.3) \quad + (-.8) + (-1.0) & = & 43.7 \\
45.8 \quad + (-.3) \quad + (-.7) + \ (-.3) & = & 44.5 \\
45.8 \quad + (-.3) \quad + (\ 1.6) + \quad .4 & = & 47.5 \\
\end{array}
$$

With median analysis as with means analysis, we have broken Y up into elements, which can be added up to give us the original Y again. The difference is that the components of the fit are resistant components after a median polish has been done. What kind of a difference is this?

Means Analysis versus Median Polish

Now we have two versions of the data in Table 15.1; we have a means analysis in Table 15.3 and a median analysis in Table 15.5, Third Step. How do they compare? We expected to see differences in the residuals especially, with the residuals from medians being more clear-cut. The two sets of residuals are compared in Table 15.6; clearly there is a difference of the kind expected. In the median analysis, there is a small number of residuals that look quite unusual; the three lowest certainly, and perhaps the largest. In the means analysis, the three lowest residuals look somewhat unusual but are not as sharply separated from the rest. In the median analysis most of the cells are fitted very closely: four of them have zero residuals (so they are perfectly fitted) and four more have small residuals. In the means analysis, no residuals are zero and the moderate residuals are more evenly spread out; the dq is 1.05 as opposed to .85 for the median analysis residuals. If we use our dq ratio to judge fit, the median analysis has a better one with a

Table 15.6

Residuals from Means vs. Medians

Y', Means Analysis (see 15.3)		Y', Median Polish (see 15.5, Third Step)
557	0	7
44123	0	0000134
4	−0	3
899	−0	
	−1	012

$$dq = 1.05 \qquad dq = .85$$

stem: units
leaf: decimals

ratio of $\dfrac{.85}{1.65} = .52$ where the means analysis has a ratio of .64. Once again, the means approach fits all the data while the resistant median approach just fits the bulk of the data but fits it more tightly (i.e. gives more tiny residuals) while showing up the unusual character of the data that aren't well-fitted (i.e. gives more relatively big residuals).

What about the patterns of effects and residuals in the two approaches? Do we get different versions of reading comprehension from the different tools? It is easiest to compare the two analyses in summary form: compare the two tables with plotted residuals, Tables 15.4 and 15.7.

In this case, the two approaches generally give similar pictures of the fit: (1) the overall levels are similar (45.5, 45.8); (2) both sets of row effects indicate that grade 6 scores were higher: (3) both sets of column effects indicate a curvilinear relationship between the proportion of white classmates in the previous year and reading scores. So we would use the same interpretation of the effects of grade and proportion white classmates on reading, whichever analysis we used. (Things are not always this simple; they are simple here because the data are based on very large samples and thus are better-behaved than most.) The patterns of residuals from the two fits are also rather similar. The main difference is that the three lowest residuals are more extreme residuals in the median version, although they

Table 15.7

Residuals from Median Polish Plotted

Grade	Proportion of White Classmates				
	None	Under Half	Half	Over Half	
12	x	o	•	x	−.3
9	o	•	•	•	−.3
6	•	•	x	o	.4
	−.2	−.8	−.7	1.6	45.8

do not become lower outliers. The residuals do not form a very clear-cut pattern in either analysis.

Some Complications

So far, elementary analysis looks — elementary. And indeed it is a pretty easy technique. There are one or two hitches that can come up; we'll introduce them now and then illustrate them using a more complex example than the reading comprehension example. But remember that the hitches are themselves minor things and elementary analysis stays simple even when the hitches do crop up. All these hitches occur for medians analysis, because medians do not add up as tidily as means do.

First, when finding the components of a median fit, round a figure off to zero if it is possible to do so. To make it clearer what we mean, look ahead a moment to the means analysis in Table 15.9 (p. 282). To polish this we will start with the rows; and the row residuals have medians −.010, −.005, .010, −.015. We usually round up in absolute value, which would make these medians −.01, −.01, .01, −.02. That is fine for every row except the second, which began as −.005; this could be rounded to zero and it should be. Why? To avoid going around in endless circles. If we round it to −.01 and remove that from the row then we will get a new row with median .005, which we round to .01 and remove, getting a row with median −.005 which we round to −.01 and . . . this we can do without!

Second, starting with columns or starting with rows makes no difference in a means analysis, but it does in a median analysis. If you start with rows and your buddy starts with columns, your fits and residuals may be slightly different, although they should not be very different. To illustrate this, we picked up the median polish in Table 15.5 at step two and polished rows, then columns (instead of columns then rows as before). This time the row effects came out as −.4, −.4, .4 instead of −.3, −.3, .4; and the column effects as −.2, −.8, −.6, 1.7 instead of −.2, −.8, −.7, 1.6. In all cases the differences are within rounding error.

Finally, our reading comprehension example was chosen in part because the median polish could be polished off very quickly: polish overall level, then row effects, then column effects, and you're done. Often a median polish is this fast, but sometimes it takes another round or two; one must polish the rows, then columns, then rows again, then columns again, until each row and column has a zero median. The basic steps do not change; they are simply reapplied until we get the desired result; this kind of circling in on a solution is called *iteration*. The example we turn to shortly illustrates iterative median polishing. In this example two rounds are enough and you will seldom if ever need more. But if you start from the raw data, instead of polishing a means analysis, you can easily find yourself doing several more rounds of polishing if the table is at all complex. That is why we urge you always to begin with a means analysis and then do a median polish. By and large, you can do both in less time than it would take to do a median analysis from scratch; so the median polish saves time. In addition, it gives you a double result, means version as well as median version, or two for less than the price of one.

Fertility in Ireland: a More Complex Table

Let's try going through a larger, more complex example in detail. The data are adapted from "Minority Status and Fertility" (Robert E. Kennedy, Jr., 1973; in particular see Table 6, page 95). The original sources are Irish Census reports.

Table 15.8

Average Number of Children

Occupational Status of Husband	Catholics NI	Catholics RI	Non-Catholics NI	Non-Catholics RI	Row Means
Upper	4.02	3.80	2.13	2.19	3.04
Middle	4.14	3.91	2.20	2.44	3.17
Lower	4.82	4.33	2.65	2.81	3.65
Agriculture	5.25	4.57	3.37	3.08	4.07
Column Means	4.56	4.15	2.59	2.63	$\bar{\bar{Y}} = 3.48$

Source: Robert E. Kennedy, Jr., "Minority Status and Fertility", *American Sociological Review*, vol. 38 (1973), pp. 85–96. Adapted from Table 6, page 95.

In this table Y is the average number of children born alive per woman aged 25–29 at marriage and married 20–24 years (thus the women have had roughly equal time in which to have children). The row variable is the status of the husband's occupation. The column variable is the most complex, being a combination of religion and part of Ireland: Catholics in Northern Ireland and in the Republic of Ireland, Non-Catholics in the North and in the Republic. At first, this might seem like jamming two variables together; but we will soon see that the combination of place and religion may well be thought of as a variable in its own right.

Table 15.9 reports the means analysis of this set of data. We will hold off on interpretation until we have the median polish as well. First we ask whether the overall level needs polish. The residuals in 15.9 have a median of .005, which is within rounding error of zero, so we leave the overall level alone (remember the rule stated above?). Next we polish rows in Table 15.10 and columns in 15.11; so far, this is just like the reading comprehension example. But in this case one polish for rows and one for columns

Table 15.9

Means Analysis of Table 15.8
Average Number of Children

Occupational Status of Husband	Catholics NI	Catholics RI	Non-Catholics NI	Non-Catholics RI	Row Means
Upper	− .10	.09	− .02	.00	− .44
Middle	− .11	.07	− .08	.12	− .31
Lower	.09	.01	− .11	.01	.17
Agriculture	.10	− .17	.19	− .13	.59
Column Effects	1.08	.67	− .89	− .85	$\overline{\overline{Y}} = 3.48$

Source: Kennedy (1973).

Note: We have taken means of cells of the original table, and then worked with means of these means; we do not have means over the individuals in these cells. As we pointed out in the suicide example earlier (chapter 3), means of aggregates are often not the same as means of individuals if the aggregates (whether cells or nations) have different numbers of individuals.

Table 15.10

First Row Polish

	C/NI	C/RI	NC/NI	NC/RI	Old Effect + Change = Row Effect
Upper	− .09	.10	− .01	.01	− .44 + (− .01) = − .45
Middle	− .11	.07	− .08	.12	− .31 + (.00) = − .31
Lower	.08	.00	− .12	.00	.17 + (.01) = .18
Agriculture	.12	− .15	.21	− .11	.59 + (− .02) = .57
Col. Effect	1.08	.67	− .89	− .85	Md$_Y$ = 3.48

Table 15.11

First Column Polish

	C/NI	C/RI	NC/NI	NC/RI	Row Effect
Upper	− .09	.06	.04	.01	− .45
Middle	− .11	.03	− .03	.12	− .31
Lower	.08	− .04	− .07	.00	.18
Agriculture	.12	− .19	.26	− .11	.57
Old Effect	1.08	.67	− .89	− .85	
+	+	+	+	+	Md$_Y$ = 3.48
Change	.0	.04	− .05	.0	
= Col. Effect	1.08	.71	− .94	− .85	

is not enough! For polishing the columns in 15.11 throws the rows a bit off again; the first row has a median of .03 and the third a median of −.02, whereas we want them to have zero medians. So we start iterating: we just polish the rows again, removing the offending .03 from the first row and adding it to the row effect and removing −.02 from the third row and adding it to the row effect; in short, more of the same. This gives us the second row polish in Table 15.12; then we still have some column action so we do the column polish in 15.13; and then, thank goodness, we are done: all the rows and all the columns have zero medians, so no row or column effects remain to be fitted.

Table 15.12

Second Row Polish

	C/NI	C/RI	NC/NI	NC/RI	Old Effect	+	Change	=	Row Effect
Upper	−.12	.03	.01	−.02	−.45	+	.03	=	−.42
Middle	−.11	.03	−.03	.12	−.31	+	.0	=	−.31
Lower	.10	−.02	−.05	.02	.18	+	(−.02)	=	.16
Agriculture	.12	−.19	.26	−.11	.57	+	.0	=	.57
Col. Effect	1.08	.71	−.94	−.85	Md$_Y$ = 3.48				

Table 15.13

Second Column Polish

	C/NI	C/RI	NC/NI	NC/RI	Row Effect
Upper	−.12	.03	.02	−.02	−.42
Middle	−.11	.03	−.02	.12	−.31
Lower	.10	−.02	−.04	.02	.16
Agriculture	.12	−.19	.25	−.11	.57
Old Effect	1.08	.71	−.94	−.85	Md$_Y$ = 3.48
Change	+.0	+.0	+(−.01)	+.0	
New Effect	1.08	.71	−.95	−.85	

Means versus Medians

In the previous example, using means or medians made little difference. Here, it makes a more marked difference. We will argue that the median version makes more sense, and that the nonresistant nature of the means version clouds the interpretation of the data.

First, we compare the residuals in another back-to-back stem-and-leaf in Table 15.14. The medians' residuals are far more clear-cut. The bulk of the residuals, the ones between the quartiles in this case, are very small, and the rest are quite big and clearly of a different kind. We see that about half the cells in the original table are well fitted and the rest are not. Two cases, with residuals .25 and −.19, are clearly the most poorly fitted. Both these cases come from the row for agricultural workers, which suggests that the country and the city may be very different in their childbearing patterns: not too surprising. These two cases also had the largest residuals in the means analysis but not as sharply marked because the column means were affected by these unusual values.

Table 15.14

Two Sets of Residuals

From Means		From Medians
	2	5
	2	
9	1	
02	1	022
997	0	
101	0	3322
2	−0	2242
8	−0	
0113	−1	211
7	−1	9

stem: tenths
leaf: hundredths

q_U =   .09 q_U =   .065
q_L = −.105 q_L = −.075
dq =   .195 dq =   .140
                                  step: .21
                    Outiers: none (upper, .275 or more
                                      lower, − .285 or less).

Now we move on to two versions of the fit and the two patterns of residuals; to make all this information easier to see, we use the plotted residuals form of the two analyses, which are reported in Table 15.15. We will discuss row effects, then column effects, and then residuals from the fit.

Effects of class (row effects): Both analyses give the same picture, a pleasantly simple one: the higher the class the fewer the children. Those higher in the class structure are generally more educated, and hence may be more exposed to modern values stressing the importance of birth control. Perhaps more important is access to birth control: successful birth control requires some knowledge, money, and medical supplies. These resources are more available to the wealthier (especially in Ireland, where birth control, despite recent modifications to the law, is not fully legal at the time of writing). Further, some people may actively desire and try to get large families. Perhaps this is why the agricultural row effects are so high; children can be very useful as cheap labour around a farm. Religious prohibitions on some birth control techniques may be most effective for farm people also, since people in rural areas tend to be more regular in performance of religious obligations.

Effects of place and religion (column effects): The two analyses produce similar column effects, though not as similar as the two sets of row effects. The order of column effects is *C/NI, C/RI, NC/RI, NC/NI* for both, but the median analysis indicates a larger difference between *NC/NI* and *NC/RI*. We will probably prefer the median version, since the *NC/NI* effect

Table 15.15

Two Approaches Plotted
(Original Data: Table 15.8)

	C/NI	C/RI	NC/NI	NC/RI	Row Effects
			Means Analysis		
Upper	•	•	•	•	− .44
Middle	o	•	•	x	− .31
Lower	•	•	o	•	.17
Agriculture	x	o	x	o	.57
Col. Effects	1.08	.67	− .89	− .85	$\bar{\bar{Y}}$ = 3.48

Note: See Table 15.9 for numeric residuals.

	C/NI	C/RI	NC/NI	NC/RI	Row Effects
			Median Analysis		
Upper	o	•	•	•	− .42
Middle	o	•	•	x	− .31
Lower	x	•	•	•	.16
Agriculture	x	o	x	o	.57
Col. Effects	1.08	.71	− .95	− .85	Md$_Y$ = 3.48

Note: See Table 15.13 for numeric residuals.

for means analysis has obviously been pulled up by just one case: the agricultural cell, which is nearly an upper outlier in the median plot but gets smoothed over in the means plot. So let's stress interpretation of the median analysis column effects. The columns are complex, really, being combinations of place and religion, so let's break interpretation up into easy stages.

1. *Religion alone:* Here we compare the first two columns (Catholics) to the second (non-Catholics) and find that the Catholics have more children. No surprise; we have already alluded to Catholic prohibitions on many forms of birth control. The sheer size of the difference between Catholics and non-Catholics is worth noting. Even the gap between the lower Catholic effect and the higher non-Catholic effect (.71 versus −.85, or a difference of 1.56) is far larger than the gap between the largest and smallest row effects (−.42 versus .57, or a difference of .99). Clearly religion makes much more difference to childbearing than class does in Ireland. This suggests that the Catholics, at least, may be quite religiously observant. Is it possible that ties based on religion are stronger and better organized than those based on class?

2. *Place alone:* Here we compare the first and third columns (Northern Ireland) to the second and fourth (Republic of Ireland). Well, it is not just a simple matter of level difference, of one place having a higher number of children than the other: *NI* effects are 1.08 and −.95, *RI* effects are .71 and −.84. There is no noticeable level difference there. But there is a *spread*

difference: the two *NI* values are more different from each other than the two *RI* values are. In other words, religion appears to make more of a difference in Northern Ireland. This brings us to the third step of column interpretation of these data.

3. *Place and Religion together:* Religion makes more difference in Northern Ireland; why? Well, as we all know, tension between Catholics and Protestants in Northern Ireland has been great for many years. Probably the Catholics and non-Catholics there live much more separated lives than those in the Republic, which could intensify within-group similarity and between-group differences. Hostility may even lead some Catholics in the North to prefer larger families as a way to capture the North by getting a majority of the votes (at least, this policy has been advocated by some people). There may also be a status effect here as well, since the Catholics of the North are poorer than the Protestants and less powerful and so on. Some of the effects of class were removed by the row effects, but the rows only deal with one aspect of class and there may be a bit left over.

Religion matters more in the North; does place matter more for one religion than for the other? Clearly so. Being in Northern Ireland rather than the Republic makes a big difference for Catholics (1.08 versus .71, or a difference of .37) but not such a big difference for non-Catholics (−.95 versus −.84, or a difference of −.11). This suggests that the social stituations of Catholics in the two places differ more. All of the factors in childbearing so far suggested could be relevant here. Further ideas could be developed. For example, the *NC/RI* and *C/NI* groups are both minorities, and both have relatively high numbers of children compared to majorities of the same religion. Could this be some sort of response to powerlessness?

4. *Residuals (plotted cell entries):* Here the two kinds of analysis diverge the most, and again the median version makes a lot more sense. Just look at the means residuals: they are flat, scattered, hard to get an angle on. Then look at the medians residuals: what a nice simple picture! We see that the basic additive model (observation = overall level + row effect + column effect) is fine except for one row and one column where it is very poor. The agricultural row is poorly fitted (even worse than it looks, perhaps, since one residual was nearly an outlier). The first column is poorly fitted as well, though not as poorly as the bottom row. What might be happening?

In general, it is not surprising that the agricultural row stands out; rural life is quite different from urban so we would expect rural people to differ in many ways from city dwellers. Getting down to specifics, we see that the number of children is relatively high in Northern Ireland and relatively low in the Republic (relative to the additive fit, that is). Perhaps farming is more modernized in the Republic so that children are less useful for labour; or perhaps those in agricultural work in the Republic are less well off so that children can't be supported as well.

For the Catholics of Northern Ireland column residuals we again have a nice simple pattern, with the wealthier Catholics having fewer children and the poorer having more than the additive model predicts. This is an accentuated version of the overall status effects summarized in the row effects. Why does status make more difference for Catholics in Northern Ireland than for other groups? Perhaps lower status C/NI people are doubly disadvantaged (they are poor as well as being underdogs in a very tense conflict) so they have especially poor access to birth control information and devices.

The fit overall: We seem to have done a pretty good job of squeezing the juice out of these numbers. The row and column effects were strong (very large compared to the residuals) and suggested several reasonable interpretations. We have very little unexplained material left.

We can evaluate the additive fit in the usual way:

$$\frac{dq\ Y'}{dq\ Y} = \frac{0.14}{2.13} = .07 \ (\text{medians})$$

$$\frac{dq\ Y'}{dq\ Y} = \frac{0.195}{2.13} = .09 \ (\text{means}) \ .$$

These numbers reinforce two things we have already seen: the fit works very well here, and it works even better in its median form. Class, place, and religion have strong effects on the number of children for Irish women. We can suggest some reasons for the few deviations from these effects, at least for residuals from the median analysis.

Exploratory and Confirmatory

The means version of elementary analysis is directly related to two-way analysis of variance, which is coming up soon. Means analysis is very useful indeed in figuring out what the two-way anova is telling you. On the other hand, we have just seen that the median polish of a means analysis may be essential for a clear, resistant interpretation. Both should be done and thought about.

The exploratory tools in this chapter and in chapter 16 are very important for interpreting the two-way anova results, much as exploratory thinking was essential for interpreting one-way anova's results. Most of the terms mean the same thing in either approach: "grand mean," "row effect," "residual," "additive fit," etc., are all terms used in confirmatory work.

Homework

Table 15.16 looks at life expectancy at birth by race and sex, and when born. Do both a means analysis and a median polish for the means analysis: What effect does the row variable have? Why? What effect does the column variable have? Why? Which variable seems to have the stronger effect? How well does the combined fit, overall level plus row effect plus column effect, account for *Y*? Do you see any striking patterns in the residuals? If so, what's going on?

What difference does median polish make: to the numerical residuals? to the effects? to the pattern of the residuals as plotted? How has your interpretation changed, if it has?

Table 15.16

Average Life Expectancy, Continental U.S.A.

Race and Sex	Time of Birth				
	1929–31	1939–41	1949–51	1959–61	1971
White Males	59.12	62.81	66.31	67.55	68.3
White Females	62.67	67.29	72.03	74.19	75.6
Other Males	47.55	52.26	58.91	61.48	61.2
Other Females	49.51	55.56	62.70	66.47	69.3

Source: For 1971 figures: Table 7, *Facts of Life and Death*; Rockville, Maryland, 1974. For other time periods: Table 12, *United States Life Tables 1959–61*, Volume 1 – No. 1; Washington, D.C. 1968. Both sources published by the U.S. National Center for Health Statistics, U.S. Department of Health, Education and Welfare.

These figures are taken from "current life tables," or tables based on current death rates. For example, a white male born in 1971 is given a life expectancy of 68.3 years; that is the average length of life if death rates at all ages stay at the 1971 values. No doubt these death rates will not stay the same, so the figure 68.3 summarizes the experience of people of all ages in 1971 rather than predicting what a child born in 1971 can expect over his lifetime.

16

Interaction Effects in Elementary Analyses

In the last chapter we learned a simple and effective way of analyzing two-way tables, elementary analysis, which breaks each observation up into the sum of the overall level, row effect, column effect and residual. This is a very useful fit when it works, because it is easy to work with numerically and easy to interpret. But sometimes the simple additive fit works poorly. When that happens we need a new concept and some new techniques. First, we'll return to the fertility example to illustrate the general difference between the simple additive fit of chapter 15 and the slightly more complex fit used here. Then we will turn again to the Vancouver voting data (Table IIIR.1, p. 265) to develop a technique for handling this complication.

Additive Fits and Interaction Effects

We now know how to make an additive fit; we isolate the effect of each of the independent variables on the dependent variable. Their sum is the fit, and the difference between an observation and this fit is, of course, the residual. Moreover, finding this effect is quite easy. Look again at Table 15.8 (p. 281); to find the non-Catholic/Northern Ireland effect we simply take the mean fertility of all four status groups and subtract the grand mean. Status effects don't enter into the value we find; they are "averaged out" of the column values, appearing separately as row effects. To see the effect of the two variables combined we just add their separate effects together: row effect + column effect. The column effect stays the same whatever row we are working on, and vice versa; for example, we add in −.95 for NC/NI whether we are finding the fit for high status husbands or agricultural husbands or whatever. Now this is fine as long as the effect of being non-Catholic in Northern Ireland is the same for all status groups. Is it? Pretty much so, as we can see from the residuals for this column, which are small on the whole. The additive fit works pretty well there.

However, it does not work as well in some other parts of the table. For example, we saw that the C/NI column had comparatively extreme residuals: negative residuals for higher status groups and positive residuals for lower status groups. There is something interesting going on that the additive fit is missing. It is not missing the overall effect of C/NI, which is accurately summed up in the column effect; nor is it missing the overall effects of the various statuses found in the row effects; the problem is that these overall effects don't quite describe the Catholics in Northern Ireland. If they are of higher status, they have somewhat fewer children than row effect + column effect predicts; if they are of low status, they have somewhat more children than the additive fit suggests. To predict these figures accurately we really need to make one fit for higher status C/NI and another for lower status C/NI; a different fit for different combinations of the two independent variables.

This is the kind of thing meant by interaction. There are lots of ways to define interaction, with all the versions meaning much the same thing. The no-nonsense, pure arithmetic version is: interaction is the extent to which the additive fit fails to work. Thus, we're talking about nothing more than a form of residual analysis. So, large residuals mean large interactions, and conversely. In the fertility example we looked at the C/NI column because it had unusually large residuals from the additive fit. This definition is clear-cut but, for most people, not all that informative. So here's another: interaction occurs to the extent that the effect of one variable depends on the value of another. In the fertility example, the effect of C/NI depended in part on what status level was involved. Or, to put the same thing another way, the effects of status weren't exactly the same for Catholics in Northern Ireland as they were for the other groups; status made a bit more difference for C/NI than for C/RI, NC/NI, or NC/RI. There was also a possibly interesting interaction effect in the "agricultural" row, where agricultural women had more children in the North, and fewer in the Republic, than the additive model indicated.

You can see that it's important to learn how to deal with interaction effects. It is somewhat more difficult than straightforward elementary analysis, but still easy enough. Since interactions occur frequently and may be vital theoretically, we will need to know how to look for, fit and interpret them.

Vancouver Left Wing Voting

The Vancouver voting data we look at here are patterns of left wing voting in five municipal elections (see Table 16.1, adapted from Table IIIR.1). The column variable is election year, from earlier to later; the row variable is area, from lower to higher income as reported from the 1961 Census. These "areas" were formed by averaging sets of districts together, since twenty-four districts are more than we could handle comfortably. For both

Table 16.1

Left Wing Vote by Income and Time

Area, Low to High Income	Election Year				
	1958	1960	1962	1964	1966
East Low	33	28	17	32	26
West Low	22	19	10	22	19
East Medium	34	29	14	32	27
West Medium	21	17	9	20	18
East High	31	26	11	28	24
West High	14	11	7	15	13

Incomes of Areas Above

Area	Mean Income	Range
East Low	$3163	$2751–3422
West Low	3713	3589–3785
East Medium	4017	3864–4186
West Medium	4377	4233–4640
East High	4425	4299–4594
West High	6684	5701–8477

Note: Incomes are averaged over districts included in each area.

the East and West side, districts were classified as high, medium, or low as regards income, trying to follow natural breaking points. Then the mean percentage left wing vote for districts in an area was found and entered in Table 16.1. (There are many other ways we could have constructed districts, and measures for them, of course.) To keep life simple and leave time for the main business of this chapter, we will just work with the elementary analysis by means (see Table 16.2). First we look at the additive fit: the row effects, or the overall impact of the row variable (area) and the column effects, or the overall impact of the column variable (year). From the row effects we see that the percentage left wing vote varied quite a bit from election to election, with 1962 being something of a disaster for the left (see

Table 16.2

Left Wing Vote, Means Analysis

	1958	1960	1962	1964	1966	Row Effect
East Low	1.0	.1	−.5	1.0	−1.4	6.2
West Low	−1.2	−.1	1.3	−.2	.4	−2.6
East Medium	2.0	1.1	−3.5	1.0	−.4	6.2
West Medium	−.8	−.7	1.7	−.8	.8	−4.0
East High	2.2	1.3	−3.3	.2	−.2	3.0
West High	−2.8	−1.7	4.7	−.8	.8	−9.0
Column Effect	4.8	.7	−9.7	3.8	.2	$\bar{\bar{Y}} = 21.0$

Ewing, 1972, for details). An analysis of the column effects will not be attempted since this would require too much specific information (on candidates and issues, for example). The row effects show an eyecatching pattern that we can discuss: every East district effect is positive and every West district effect is negative. That is, the East Side is more left wing, even for those districts with incomes close to those of some West districts. If we look closely we can also see that, for East districts alone or West districts alone, higher income goes with lower left wing vote. Thus two kinds of things are going on here. First, income is inversely related to left-wing voting as one would expect (left-wing policies being more oriented to the interests of those with lower incomes). Thus the less wealthy East Side is more left wing. Second, there is an East-West difference above and beyond wealth; perhaps campaign strategies or community structures are different in the two districts. Remember the turnout example from chapter 11? There also we found an income effect (higher income going with more turnout) and also an East-West difference (East areas having higher turnout than West areas with similar income). Overall, the additive fit makes a lot of sense: there are swings from election to election (column effects) and both low income and East Side placement go with higher left wing vote (row effects). How well does this additive fit do? The dq of the original Y values in Table 16.1 is 14, and the dq of $Y' = Y - (\overline{\overline{Y}} + \text{Row Effect} + \text{Column Effect})$ (see Table 16.2) is 1.8, giving an excellent dq ratio of .13.

But even when the additive fit is good, it's worthwhile to look for possible interaction patterns which may make the fit even better and add to the understanding of how the variables are related. To look for interaction, we look for meaningful patterns in the residuals, which are plotted in Table 16.3 to make looking easier. Hmm ... there are some striking individual residuals, one lower outlier and one upper, and some pretty substantial adjacents, but it's hard to see any simple patterns. Well, a lot depends on how the data are arranged. In Table 16.3 the rows and columns are arranged in a "natural" ordering: columns by time, areas by income. So if interaction effects were linked to time or income we would be able to see them; but if

Table 16.3
Residuals Plotted, "Natural Order"

	1958	1960	1962	1964	1966	Row Effect
East Low	•	•	•	•	o	6.2
West Low	o	•	X	•	•	−2.6
East Medium	X	X	●	•	•	6.2
West Medium	•	•	X	•	•	−4.0
East High	X	X	o	•	•	3.0
West High	o	o	X	•	•	−9.0
Column Effect	4.8	.7	−9.7	3.8	.2	$\overline{\overline{Y}} = 21.0$

they are linked to something else, this sort of ordering probably makes them harder to see. Obviously we need to try different row and column arrangements making some other kind of sense; another arrangement may reveal a simple pattern in the residuals which is hidden in 16.3.

Let's try reordering the rows. We know income per se does not fully explain area effects: being on the East or West Side matters a lot too. Instead of ordering rows by income, let's try ordering them by row effects, from the most left wing area to the least left wing area. A little quick recopying gives us Table 16.4. This new order of rows happens to make a lot of sense; now it is clearer than ever both that the East is more left wing and that rising income goes with declining left wing vote. And look what happens to the residuals! They are much simpler: the East and West residuals are almost exact opposites.

Table 16.4

Reordering 16.3 by Row Effect Size

	1958	1960	1962	1964	1966	Row Effect
East Low	.	.	.	.	o	6.2
East Medium	x	x	●	.	.	6.2
East High	x	x	o	.	.	3.0
West Low	o	.	x	.	.	−2.6
West Medium	.	.	x	.	.	−4.0
West High	o	o	X	.	.	−9.0
Column Effect	4.8	.7	−9.7	3.8	.2	$\overline{\overline{Y}} = 21.0$

Table 16.5

Effect Order Version of 16.3

(16.4 Reordered by Column Effect Size)

	1962	1966	1960	1964	1958	Effect
East Low	.	o	.	.	.	6.2
East Medium	●	.	x	.	x	6.2
East High	o	.	x	.	x	3.0
West Low	x	.	.	.	o	−2.6
West Medium	x	.	.	.	.	−4.0
West High	X	.	o	.	o	−9.0
Effect	−9.7	.2	.7	3.8	4.8	$\overline{\overline{Y}} = 21.0$

Reordering the rows by effect size seems to be helping, so let's try it on columns as well. We rearrange the columns of Table 16.4 and get Table 16.5, going from the election lowest in percentage left wing vote (1962) to the highest (1958). Now the pattern is very simple indeed: we tend to have negative residuals in the upper left and lower right and positive residuals in the other two quadrants. In a simplified form to help underline the pattern, the table blocked out schematically looks something like this:

High Left Area	0	X
Low Left Area	X	0

	Low Left Election	High Left Election

We seem to have found a pattern, all right. What does it mean? First we just want to get the pattern into words to help in thinking about it. In an election with high left wing vote, the highly left wing areas have positive residuals and the areas with a low left wing vote have negative residuals; that is, the left wing areas are more left wing and the low left wing areas are even less left wing than the additive model predicts. The differences between areas are heightened. On the other hand, when an election shows a relatively low vote for the left then the high left areas are voting left less and the low left areas are voting left more than the model predicts, which means they are more alike than the additive model would suggest. You might find it helpful to connect this verbalization with the raw data in Table 16.1. In the left's worst year, 1962, the difference between the most and least left wing area is 8% (17% − 9%); in the left's best year, 1958, the difference between the most and least left area is 20% (34% − 14%). The greater the support for the left, the more different the areas are in left wing vote. This is clearly an interactive effect, not an additive one, since it sums up the way one independent variable (area) has different effects given different values of another independent variable (election).

Why might this pattern happen? Perhaps it stems from the fact that percentage left wing vote is rather low in Vancouver in this time period, only about 21% overall ($\bar{\bar{Y}}$). So most of the time few people expect the left wing candidates to be very important. But when there is a swing leftward, as in 1958, the possibility of a left-wing victory is taken more seriously and both left and right voters respond more vigorously, the former voting left in the hopes of a victory, the latter voting right in order to prevent such a victory, and the centre losing ground. In elections where the left does poorly,

Table 16.6

Numerical Residuals in Effect Order

	1962	1966	1960	1964	1958	Effect
East Low	−.5	−1.4	.1	1.0	1.0	6.2
East Medium	−3.5	−.4	1.1	1.0	2.0	6.2
East High	−3.3	−.2	1.3	.2	2.2	3.0
West Low	1.3	.4	−.1	−.2	−1.2	−2.6
West Medium	1.7	.8	−.7	−.8	−.8	−4.0
West High	4.7	.8	−1.7	−.8	−2.8	−9.0
Effect	−9.7	.2	.7	3.8	4.8	$\bar{\bar{Y}} = 21.0$

on the other hand, people in left wing areas may stay home or vote for the least unappealing right wing or centrist candidate with a chance to win; while those in right wing areas may venture to vote for left wing candidates they like as individuals, knowing they will not be part of a left majority. Thus the differences between left and right get muted.

So we have found a pattern, put it into words, and generated a possible explanation for it. How about fitting it? Let's look at a simplified version of the residuals table again, but this time using "+" for a positive effect or residual and "−" for a negative one, to help see any arithmetic patterns:

	Effect	Low Left Election	High Left Election
		−	+
	Effect		
High Left Area	+	−	+
Low Left Area	−	+	−

There is a pattern here: positive residuals go with effects of like sign (row and column effects both high or both low) while negative residuals go with effects of different sign (row effects high and column effects low, or vice versa). We can predict the sign of a residual by multiplying the effects for the residuals cell. Why don't we try this for the whole table of actual residuals? Table 16.7 records

$$(\text{row effect}) \times (\text{column effect})$$

for each cell; let's call these products RC for short ($RC = $ Row times Column). For example, in the lower right corner you find $-43.2 = (4.8)(-9.0)$. The pattern of the RC values corresponds at least roughly to the pattern of the residuals in the preceding table, 16.6: the negative values are in opposite corners (upper left to lower right) and so are the positive values (lower left, upper right). It seems that RC values and residuals are directly related. To see the relationship more clearly we return to X by Y techniques and do a plot, with RC values on the X-axis and residuals from the additive fit on the

Table 16.7

Row Effect times Column Effect (RC)

	1962	1966	1960	1964	1958	Effect
East Low	−60.1	1.2	4.3	23.6	29.8	6.2
East Medium	−60.1	1.2	4.3	23.6	29.8	6.2
East High	−29.1	.6	2.1	11.4	14.4	3.0
West Low	25.2	−.5	−1.8	−9.9	−12.5	−2.6
West Medium	38.8	−.8	−2.8	−15.2	−19.2	−4.0
West High	87.3	−1.8	−6.3	−34.2	−43.2	−9.0
Effect	−9.7	.2	.7	3.8	4.8	$\overline{Y} = 21.0$

Table 16.8

Plot of Interaction Fit

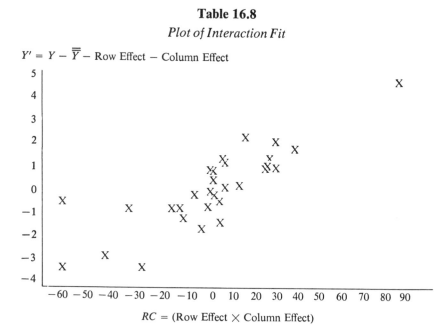

$Y' = Y - \overline{\overline{Y}} - \text{Row Effect} - \text{Column Effect}$

$RC = (\text{Row Effect} \times \text{Column Effect})$

Y-axis: see Table 16.8. The relationship is not perfect but it looks good and should help to account for a fair amount of Y'. We decide it is worthwhile to go on to make a numeric fit, again using familiar X by Y methods:

$$Y' = bX + a$$

Residuals from additive fit $= b(RC)$
$$= b(\text{Row effect})(\text{Column effect})$$

We set up a work sheet as in Table 16.9, where RC values are paired with corresponding Y' values (keeping the values matched, cell by cell, is the only tricky part of this technique). The ten cases lowest on RC give us our low third, and the nine cases highest on RC give the high third (we can't have ten in the top third because of a tied value). The range rule is not satisfied, but when fitting RC effects we may have to waive this requirement; it is rarely possible to meet this rule with RC as X, and the rule is not as important as usual because both the upper and lower thirds are ordinarily going to be very spread out. Finding trimean summary points,

$$X_H = 26.0 \qquad Y_H = 1.4$$
$$X_L = -26.0 \qquad Y_L = -1.4$$

and thus

$$b = \frac{1.4 + 1.4}{26.0 + 26.0} = \frac{2.8}{52} = .054$$

Table 16.9

Work Sheet for RC Interaction Fit

RC (see 16.7)	Y' (see 16.6)	b(RC) = .054(RC)	Y'' = Y' − b(RC)
87.3	4.7	4.7	.0
38.8	1.7	2.1	−.4
29.8	2.0	1.6	.4
29.8	1.0	1.6	−.6
25.2	1.3	1.4	−.1
23.6	1.0	1.3	−.3
23.6	1.0	1.3	−.3
14.4	2.2	.8	1.4
11.4	.2	.6	−.4
4.3	.1	.2	−.1
4.3	1.1	.2	.9
2.1	1.3	.1	1.2
1.2	−1.4	.1	−1.5
1.2	−.4	.1	−.5
.6	−.2	.0	−.2
−.5	.4	.0	.4
−.8	.8	.0	.8
−1.8	.8	−.1	.9
−1.8	−.1	−.1	.0
−2.8	−.7	−.2	−.5
−6.3	−1.7	−.3	−1.4
−9.9	−.2	−.5	.3
−12.5	−1.2	−.7	−.5
−15.2	−.8	−.8	.0
−19.2	−.8	−1.0	.2
−29.1	−3.3	−1.6	−1.7
−34.2	−.8	−1.8	1.0
−43.2	−2.8	−2.3	−.5
−60.1	−.5	−3.2	2.7
−60.1	−3.3	−3.2	−.1

What about a? If you bother to work it out, you'll find it's zero. Since RC and Y' both have levels of zero (why?), a must be zero as well. Thus our RC fit for interaction is

$$Y' = \text{residuals from additive model}$$
$$= .054 \, (RC)$$

To find out how good the fit is, we carry on with the rest of Table 16.9 to find a new set of residuals (Y'') from the RC interaction term as well as the additive fit:

$$Y'' = Y' - b(RC) = Y - (\overline{\overline{Y}} + \text{Row Effect} + \text{Column Effect} + b(RC)).$$

For these Y'' residuals, $dq = 0.9$; for the residuals from the additive model alone, or Y', the dq was 1.8; $\frac{0.9}{1.8} = 0.5$, so we have explained roughly half the spread of the residuals from the additive model by fitting an interaction effect. This is pretty good.

Combining Additive Fits and Interaction Fits

We have just seen that we can find, explain, and fit an interaction effect for the left wing voting example. This effect can be added to the original additive model to get a more complete fit for Y. Thus we go from the basic additive fit:

$$Y = \overline{\overline{Y}} + \text{Row Effect} + \text{Column Effect}$$

to the interaction fit:

$$Y = \overline{\overline{Y}} + \text{Row Effect} + \text{Column Effect} + b(RC).$$

To evaluate the interaction fit versus the simpler additive fit without interaction, we can look at two things:

1. the overall strength of each one or

$$\frac{dq\,(Y')}{dq\,Y}$$

for the basic additive fit, compared to

$$\frac{dq\,(Y'')}{dq\,Y}$$

for the basic additive fit with interaction included.

2. how much the interaction fit explains of the residuals not explained by the basic fit, or

$$\frac{dq\,(Y'')}{dq\,(Y')}.$$

Consider the first kind of comparison for our example: we get a dq ratio of .13 for the basic fit and a dq ratio of .06 for the basic fit plus interaction. The fit is very good with or without interaction and perhaps the interaction fit does not seem to make much difference. However, if we find

$$\frac{dq\,(Y'')}{dq\,(Y')} = .5$$

as above, we see that the interaction fit explains a lot of what the basic fit did not explain. The basic fit was very good, so the interaction fit was left little to work on; of that little we've explained half, which is pretty good.

We conclude that the strongest influences on percentage left wing vote in our table are year and area effects; there is a substantial interaction effect as well. The interaction takes the form of a heightened difference between left and non-left areas in years with higher leftward trends, and a reduced difference in years when the left is weak.

Other Interaction Fits

The interaction fit just illustrated is often useful, but it is not the only kind of interaction fit; there are other fits for other interaction patterns. First, consider one very mild variation. Suppose the block of residuals looks like this:

	Column Effect	
Row Effect	Low	High
High	X	0
Low	0	X

At first glance, this looks like the left wing voting example, but there's an important difference. In the earlier example, positive residuals came in cells where row and column effects were of similar sign. Here the same sign effects give negative residuals, while the opposite sign effects give positive residuals. Consider Table 16.10, which gives residential segregation indices for three southern U.S. cities for three census years. Since this is a small example, we can easily do a median analysis from scratch as in Table 16.11. The row effects show some city to city difference in residential segregation, and the column effects show that segregation increased from 1940 to 1950. (This did not happen in all cities.) The residuals show the sort of pattern sketched just above: the large positive residuals occur in cells with high row effect and low column effect or vice versa, while the one large negative residual occurs in a cell going with row and column effects that are both very low. The higher the rates are, the more alike they are. Probably we have a simple ceiling effect here, since the segregation index cannot be more than 100 and these values are very close to that. How can we fit this? Easily: use RC again, expecting to get a negative b instead of a positive one.

Table 16.10

Residential Segregation

	Census Year		
City	1940	1950	1960
Jacksonville	94.3	94.9	96.9
Atlanta	87.4	91.5	93.6
Dallas	80.2	88.4	94.6

Source: Karl E. Taeuber, "Residential Segregation." *Scientific American*, August, 1965.

Note: The segregation index ranges from 0 to 1, 0 if Negroes and whites are evenly distributed over residential areas and 1 if all Negroes live in Negro neighbourhoods and all whites in white neighbourhoods.

Table 16.11

Median Analysis of Table 16.10

Md = 93.6; *remove*

1940	1950	1960
.7	1.3	3.3
−6.2	−2.1	0
−13.4	−5.2	1.0

$Md_Y = 93.6$

Remove Row Effects

1940	1950	1960	Row Effects
−.6	0	2.0	1.3
−4.1	0	2.1	−2.1
−8.2	0	6.2	−5.2

$Md_Y = 93.6$

Remove Column Effects

	1940	1950	1960	Row Effects
	3.5	0	−.1	1.3
	0	0	0	−2.1
	−4.1	0	4.1	−5.2
Column Effects	−4.1	0	2.1	$Md_Y = 93.6$

Row Medians still zero – stop.

Sometimes interaction effects show up clearly with rows and columns in some order other than effect order. For example, our voting data could have shown some strong time patterns in the residuals, although as it happens they didn't. In such a case one might want to handle interaction by using Y' as a dependent variable and time as the independent variable, e.g. $Y' = b \times$ (Election Year). Often we forget the importance of geography; physical location, natural barriers (mountains, rivers, etc.), and having allies or enemies for neighbours all are often important in analyzing interaction effects, so plotting on a map may help. Sometimes a few rows or columns show a pattern of residuals related to time or income or some other variable; then you might fit the residuals for those rows or columns only, trying to explain why they depart from the additive fit and the rest of the table does not. (A strategy like this might help in the homework example in chapter 15.)

So far we have talked about interaction fits that use basic X by Y methods to add on another layer of explanation:

$$Y' = b(RC)$$
or $\;Y' = b(\text{Time})$
or $\quad = b(\text{income})$, etc.

Such strategies plus a little ingenuity will give useful results surprisingly often.

Another broadly useful strategy is — surprise — transformation. Earlier we described the percentage left wing vote interaction in this way: the areas are more different in their percentage left wing vote in election years with higher leftward swing. If you think about that for a moment, and/or look at the numbers, you'll see this is the same as saying: the columns with larger Y levels have larger Y spreads. It's also true that rows with higher Y levels have higher Y spreads. We'd like these spreads to be evened up, so that the column variable has the same sort of effect whatever the row and vice versa. And, as we have often seen, a covariation of level and spread can usually be removed with transformation.

This logic would suggest a transform like logs. The logging would be done on the original Y, not Y' (remember, we can't log negative numbers). If the transformation works well, the residuals for the basic additive fit for the transformed data will be very small and without pattern. This chapter is already quite complex so we won't complicate it further by going through an example using transformation. But this shouldn't be interpreted to mean that we regard transformation as a poor tool here. It is often even more effective than the RC fit. In the next chapter, we will describe how it can be used in confirmatory two-way analysis.

In this chapter, we've used insights gained from looking hard at interaction to make some interesting speculations about left wing voting patterns in Vancouver. These speculations could turn out to be correct or incorrect. The point is that interesting ideas were generated: by looking hard at interaction, we came up with ideas we might well have missed otherwise. Once we have them, we can decide whether they look worth testing.

We did do a little checking (if not formal hypothesis testing) for one of our interpretations with turnout data like those in chapter 11. If it is true that a leftward swing makes left wing voters hopeful and right wing or centrist voters worried, surely it should make them more likely to vote; so in this case a higher percentage of left wing votes in an election should go with higher turnout. Does it? Just the opposite! The percentage left wing vote is high when turnout is low. This suggests a second interpretation: the number of people voting left is fairly steady (perhaps, again, a committed minority?); it is the number voting for the right or centre which varies. So a larger turnout means a smaller percent left wing vote: the same numbers of left wing votes, roughly, but increased numbers of non-left wing voters. If this view is correct, the best the left can hope for is a deadly dull campaign, so most of the opposing voters will stay home. That's quite a provocative speculation. And how about . . . ? Well, enough's enough.

Recapitulation

In working with interaction effects, the first step is to see what they are. Begin with a means or median polish analysis to find a basic additive fit and residuals from it. Then look for patterns in the residuals. Patterns may emerge in a few special parts of the table, as in the Irish fertility data perhaps. Or there may be an overall pattern visible either with rows and columns in effect order.

Once you've seen a pattern, the next step is to put it into words and then try to explain it. This is the hardest step, at least when you first try it, but with some practice you'll be able to come up with interpretations. We've whipped up several possibilities for the left wing voting interaction to give you some idea of the kinds of things you can come up with.

The interaction pattern should also be fitted numerically. The procedures we illustrated are best for interaction patterns that show up in effect ordering (and most interaction is like that). The effect ordering pattern should look like either of the following simplified forms:

		Effect				Effect
0	**X**	High		**X**	**0**	High
X	**0**	Low		**0**	**X**	Low
Effect: Low	High			Effect: Low	High	

We can handle either of these by transforming the original data or making an interaction fit:

$$Y' = b(RC)$$

Suppose the data do not look so neat? Then you might try fitting Y' to some new variable, like time or income or geography. Finally, you might decide that the Y' values should not be further fitted in any way because these residuals are very small and unsystematic. Small unpatterned residuals may be nothing more than measurement error, so that fits based on them are meaningless (this is sometimes called "overfitting"). However, most people stop too soon rather than too late in explaining residuals. It is usually a good idea to keep trying to reduce the spread of the residuals for as long as your resources permit; this is especially useful in exploratory work.

Homework

For your homework, choose either Table 16.12 or Table 16.13. Table 16.12 is adapted from Molotch and Lester's (1975) study of newspaper coverage of a large oil spill in Santa Barbara. By examining the most detailed coverage, that in the local paper, Molotch and Lester made a list of occurrences connected with the spill during four time periods. Then nineteen other papers (of which we show only every third) were examined for the same four time periods; for each period, the percentage of occurrences reported in a given paper was found.

Table 16.12

Percentage of Occurrences Covered by Selected Newspapers

Newspaper and Region	Period Ending			
	2/21/69 (1)	6/30/69 (2)	12/1/69 (3)	12/31/70 (4)
San Francisco Chronicle (California)	63.6	18.2	31.0	16.7
New York Times (East)	50.0	10.9	8.6	0.0
Washington Post (East)	36.3	14.6	1.8	3.4
Atlanta Constitution (South)	18.2	5.5	6.9	0.0
Boston Globe (East)	22.7	3.7	3.5	0.0
New Orleans Times Picayune (South)	9.1	7.3	1.8	0.0

Source: Molotch and Lester (1975), *American Journal of Sociology*. Published by the University of Chicago. © 1975 University of Chicago.

Table 16.13

Percentage Turnout by Income and Time

Area, Low to High Income	Election Year				
	1958	1960	1962	1964	1966
East Low	22	26	30	27	25
West Low	26	28	34	30	28
East Medium	31	35	43	40	35
West Medium	31	34	43	38	33
East High	33	37	46	41	36
West High	42	47	61	54	48

Table 16.13 is similar to Table 16.1, except that we have the proportion of eligible voters actually voting (% turnout) as the dependent variable instead of left wing voting. In all other respects, the two tables are exactly alike.

Make a basic additive fit for the table you choose (you may only have time to do an analysis by means) and discuss briefly. Then make an interaction fit for the residuals and discuss more carefully. Would a transformation of the original data help here? If so and you are using a computer for this assignment, you might wish to try a few likely transforms. If you think a transformation would be helpful but you don't have the time to actually do it, indicate what sort of transform you think would help, and why.

17

Two-Way Analysis of Variance

By now we know how to look very hard at a two-way table. We can break an observation Y up into its components: observation = grand mean + row effect + column effect + interaction + residual. We can display these components clearly, whether separately or together, and we can interpret them in an orderly way. This is a very useful set of skills for exploratory work and will continue to be important for making sense of a confirmatory analysis. The confirmatory tools are all we lack and we will begin to learn them in this chapter.

Once again our basic problem is making inferences about a universe from a sample. If we already have data about the universe (as in the Irish fertility example from chapter 15) then we don't need statistical tests. We simply interpret the results with elementary analysis and report our conclusions about trends in the universe. But if our data are from a sample, we must use a test to tell us whether the apparent patterns are likely to be merely random sampling fluctuations or whether there is probably a similar pattern in the universe we want to make inferences about. We want to make decisions about three things: effects of the row variable, effects of the column variable, and interaction between row and column variables. It is possible that none of these is significant, that any one is, that any two are, or that all three are.

The confirmatory technique that we begin with here is two-way analysis of variance, which is a fairly straightforward extension of one-way analysis of variance but with a few extra wrinkles. The basic idea is the same. Remember that in one-way anova we used an F-test:

$$F = \frac{\text{MS between}}{\text{MS within}} = \frac{\text{How much the means vary about the grand mean}}{\text{How much they would be expected to vary by chance alone}}$$

We had just one independent variable, the various categories or groups, and all we had to do was compare the magnitude of the differences among these groups to the size of differences we could expect to get from random sampling fluctuations if the groups were not "really" different (i.e. not different in the universe). We estimated these chance differences by looking at the variability of observations within groups. When the observed differences are much larger than chance, the F-ratio is large, and we can reject the null hypothesis, which asserts that there is no difference among group means.

The problem we deal with here involves the same kind of logic but because Y is now seen as being made up of three components, row, column and interaction effects, three ratios will be needed. We find the observed variability of effects of each component, and compare these mean squares to estimates of how big they would be by chance. Thus, all three tests are based on the same principle we used in one-way anova and each is computed in an analogous way.

An Example: Experimenter Expectations

Table 17.1 reports some experimental data which we will use to illustrate the new procedure. This table is obviously just another two-way table. There is a row variable (O_1, O_2, O_3), a column variable (E_1, and E_2), and a Y variable reported in the cells. The only new feature is that each cell has eighteen Y observations, while the tables we have worked with in previous chapters had just one case (often a mean) per cell. Note that a "row" is a category of the row variable; so in Table 17.1 we have three rows, that is, O_1 and O_2 and O_3. We have two columns, E_1 and E_2. Finally, we have six cells: O_1E_1, O_1E_2, O_2E_1, O_2E_2, O_3E_1, O_3E_2. The numbers inside the cells (replications) do not count as rows or columns because their arrangement within cells is irrelevant and arbitrary. They are batches; they could be

Table 17.1

Experimenter Effects

Outcome Stressed	E_1 Expect High Ratings			E_2 Expect Low Ratings		
O_1 "good" data	25	0	-16	-25	-20	-2
	5	11	-6	-23	-24	12
	42	-2	-13	-28	-24	-8
	14	4	-22	-22	-22	-17
	19	6	9	-22	-23	-30
	13	-3	-6	-10	-19	-22
O_2 "scientific" data	-19	5	-13	6	-22	-5
	-24	-1	-1	-5	7	-5
	-4	-9	-3	14	14	-9
	-24	-5	-11	-11	15	3
	0	-6	-6	14	-6	-5
	-4	4	-4	-5	9	6
O_3 no stress	-26	-21	-10	-12	-4	20
	-1	-19	-37	-4	-10	9
	22	-12	0	13	-3	-8
	3	9	-10	-27	-11	8
	-26	-9	-6	-7	2	-6
	4	-27	-11	-20	-9	6

arranged in any convenient way in any order, as long as they are in the correct cell.

The data in Table 17.1 come from an experiment by Adler (1973) designed to find out about "experimenter effects," or biases stemming from the experimenter's expectations. There is a great deal of evidence showing that researchers are not completely objective, that they see what they expect to see. Moreover, in some as yet undetected way, researchers seem able to communicate their expectations to their subjects. This problem is of concern in many disciplines, medicine for one, and has been studied increasingly by social psychologists. In Adler's study, several research assistants acted as experimenters. They showed pictures of people's faces to respondents who were asked to estimate how successful or unsuccessful the people were. Thus the experiment seemed to be a study of physical appearance. In fact, it was not; the pictures used were all average-looking as far as successful appearance goes. The averageness was established by showing various pictures to judges beforehand and choosing only pictures that were judged to belong to moderately successful people.

What was really being studied was the experimenters and the different ratings they might get out of their respondents if they (the experimenters) had different expectations of what the respondents would do. The experimenters' expectations form the column variable: some were told that their respondents were likely to give high success ratings (E_1) and some were told that their subjects were likely to give low success ratings (E_2). In fact, there was no reason for the subjects to differ; they were randomly assigned to E_1 or to E_2 experimenters, and they were all rating pictures with approximately the same average appearance of success. So if E_1 ratings are different from E_2, they differ because of the experimenters' expectations.

Adler pushed this idea a bit further by also giving the experimenters different kinds of instructions: these instructions form the row variable. One third of the experimenters were instructed to try to get "good" data (O_1), one third were instructed to try to get "scientific" data (O_2), and one third were just told what to do without any stress on the kind of results they should try for (O_3). These may seem like small variations, but small changes in wording can often have big effects on how people behave in an experiment or interview. So the instructions given the experimenters could affect the way they conducted the experiment, which in turn could affect the ratings given by respondents.

Each cell is made up of the eighteen respondents (replications) who were interviewed by experimenters with the same instructions and the same expectations. The table entries, Y, are the ratings given by the respondents, but differences from row to row and column to column will tell us about the experimenter effects. If the experimenters' expectations and/or instructions had effects on subject ratings, then the ratings will differ from cell to cell; if not, all the cells will have roughly the same levels. The rating scale went from

+10 to −10, and the pictures used were rated at about zero in the pretest.

Before we test the effects of expectation, instruction, and their interaction, let us note just what kind of two-way anova we are dealing with. We will present the procedures for tests appropriate when:

1. there is more than one case per cell
2. the number of cases in each cell is the same (18 in our example)
3. the row and column categories are fixed, not random; we will say more about this later in this chapter.

In other cases (e.g. when there are unequal numbers of cell entries) the procedures need to be modified. We will tell you where to find such modifications if you need them, but for now we'll stick with the simplest case. We will begin by showing how this kind of analysis is done, discussing assumptions later.

Computing Two-Way Analysis of Variance

Basic Sums

As in one-way analysis of variance, it turns out to be very handy to calculate some basic sums of squares and then use them to construct the sums of squares and mean squares needed for our F-tests. Four of the basic sums (A, B, C_{col} and C_{row}) are essentially the same as the ones used in one-way anova. There is one new basic sum (D) which we need because two-way anova is slightly more complex. To keep the formulae for A through D straight, we need some subscripts:

Part of Table	Subscript	
rows	i	Note that "i" goes from one to "r" — that is, the number of rows is "r". In our case $r = 3$.
columns	j	"j" goes from one to "c" which is the number of columns; in our example, $c = 2$.
cells	k	"k" goes from one to "n," the number of replicates in each cell; in our example $n = 18$.

Thus Y_{ijk} is the kth entry in the cell in row i and column j.

Finally, N is the total number of entries in the table; this is the number of rows times the number of columns times the number of replications:

$N = rcn = 108$, in our case.

A pragmatic note: most of these sums involve adding up the table entries in various ways; so it is handy to have *cell totals*; these can be combined as needed, rather than having to add up the same numbers over and over again.

Here are cell totals, row totals, column totals, and grand total for our Table 17.1:

Cell Totals for Table 17.1

	E_1	E_2	Row Totals
O_1	80	−329	−249
O_2	−125	15	−110
O_3	−177	−63	−240
Column totals	−222	−377	Grand Total $= -599$

For example, the "80" for the O_1E_1 cell is the total of the 18 cases in that cell; the row total for O_1 is $(80 - 329) = -249$, which is the total of all the entries in that row; the column total for E_1 is $(80 - 125 - 177) = -222$, the total of all the entries in that column; and the grand total is $(-249 - 110 - 240) = (-222 - 377) = -599$, the total of all the entries in the table. Now we are ready to give the formulae and their verbal interpretations.

$$A = \sum_{i=1}^{r} \sum_{j=1}^{c} \sum_{k=1}^{n} Y_{ijk}{}^2$$

In words: square each entry separately and then add up the squares. In our example,

$$A = 25^2 + 0^2 + (-16)^2 + (-25)^2 + \ldots\ldots + (-9)^2 + 6^2$$

$$= 24,101$$

$$B = \frac{1}{N} \left(\sum_{i=1}^{r} \sum_{j=1}^{c} \sum_{k=1}^{n} Y_{ijk} \right)^2$$

In words: add up all the entries, square this total, and divide by the number of entries. So in our example,

$$B = \frac{1}{108}(25 + 0 - 16 - 25 \ldots \ldots - 9 + 6)^2$$

$$= \frac{(-599)^2}{108}$$

$$= 3,322.232$$

$$C_{\text{col}} = \frac{1}{nr} \sum_{j=1}^{c} \left(\sum_{i=1}^{r} \sum_{k=1}^{n} Y_{ijk} \right)^2$$

In words: go through the table column by column this time. For each column, add up all the entries in the column and then square the column total. Finally, add up the squared totals and divide by nr, the number of entries in each column. In our example,

$$C_{\text{col}} = \frac{1}{54}[(-222)^2 + (-377)^2]$$

$$= \frac{191413}{54}$$

$$= 3,544.685$$

$$C_{\text{row}} = \frac{1}{nc} \sum_{i=1}^{r} \left(\sum_{j=1}^{c} \sum_{k=1}^{n} Y_{ijk} \right)^2$$

In words: go through the table row by row, add up the entries in each row; square each row total; then add up the squared totals and divide by nc, the number of entries per row. In our example,

$$C_{\text{row}} = \frac{1}{36} [(-249)^2 + (-110)^2 + (-240)^2]$$

$$= \frac{131,701}{36}$$

$$= 3,658.361$$

Clearly C_{col} and C_{row} are much the same idea; C_{col} does for columns what C_{row} does for rows.

$$D = \frac{1}{n} \sum_{i=1}^{r} \sum_{j=1}^{c} \left(\sum_{k=1}^{n} Y_{ijk} \right)^2$$

In words: go through the table cell by cell. Add up the entries in each cell; square these cell totals; add up the squared totals and divide by n, the number of entries in each cell. In our example,

$$D = \frac{1}{18} [(80)^2 + (-329)^2 + (-125)^2 + (15)^2 + (-177)^2 + (-63)^2]$$

$$= \frac{165,789}{18}$$

$$= 9,210.5$$

Computing F-Ratios

Now that we have these basic sums, we can plug them into very simple formulae to get the sums of squares, mean squares, and F-ratios needed for our test. The formulae are summarized in Table 17.2. Let's go through the main features of this table to help clarify what's going on.

First of all, in every F-test we have MS Within as the denominator of the F-ratio. That is because the MS Within is our basic standard of comparison; it is the size of difference we could expect just by sampling fluctuations, even when there is nothing happening in the universe. Basically, MS Error is the "average" variance of cell batches. Like the error or "within" term in the simpler one-way case (chapter 10), within-cell variance has nothing to do with the effects of the independent variables, for row and column are constant for all replications within each cell. So differences inside cells should reflect differences just due to "error"; sampling fluctuations,

Table 17.2

Basic Two-Way Anova Table

(Fixed Categories)

Source of Variance	Sum of Squares	df	Mean Squares	F- ratio
Rows	$C_{row} - B$	$r - 1$	$\dfrac{C_{row} - B}{r - 1}$	$\dfrac{\text{MS Rows}}{\text{MS Within}}$
Columns	$C_{col} - B$	$c - 1$	$\dfrac{C_{col} - B}{c - 1}$	$\dfrac{\text{MS Cols}}{\text{MS Within}}$
Interaction	$B + D - C_{row} - C_{col}$	$(r - 1)(c - 1)$	$\dfrac{B + D - C_{row} - C_{col}}{(r - 1)(c - 1)}$	$\dfrac{\text{MS Interaction}}{\text{MS Within}}$
Within Cell	$A - D$	$rc(n - 1)$	$\dfrac{A - D}{rc(n - 1)}$	
Total	$A - B$	$N - 1$		

measurement error, the effects of other unmeasured independent variables, etc. Within-cell differences represent the magnitude of differences we can expect even if the row and column variables have no effect, so row effects or column effects or interaction effects must be greater than this before we can take them seriously.

So our basic strategy, once again, will be to compare observed variations in row, column, or interaction effects to the chance expectation: MS Within. We will use three ratios:

$$\frac{\text{MS Rows}}{\text{MS Within}} = \frac{\text{Differences between rows}}{\text{Differences we expect if } H_0 \text{ true}}$$

$$\frac{\text{MS Columns}}{\text{MS Within}} = \frac{\text{Differences between columns}}{\text{Differences expected if } H_0 \text{ true}}$$

$$\frac{\text{MS Interaction}}{\text{MS Within}} = \frac{\text{Differences between cells after row and column differences are gone}}{\text{Differences expected if } H_0 \text{ true}} .$$

In each case H_0 has the same general form:

For Rows, H_0 says: there are no differences in Y from row category to row category in the universe.

For Columns, H_0 says: there are no differences in Y from column category to column category in the universe.

For interaction, H_0 says: after row and column means are removed, there are no differences in Y from one combination of row and column categories to another combination, in the universe.

In short, H_0 asserts that there no real differences in the universe, and the apparent differences in our data could easily have arisen from mere chance fluctuations. MS Within gives us our estimate of what to expect if H_0 is true; we will reject H_0 only if our observed differences are significantly greater than MS Within.

We sum up observed differences between rows (MS Rows) by finding $C_{row} - B$ and dividing by the degrees of freedom, $r - 1$ (the number of rows less one). We saw earlier that C_{row} is a row-by-row computation. If you work through a lot of algebra, this short computing form of MS Rows turns out to be approximately a weighted form of the variance of the row means about the grand mean, just as MS Within turns out to be approximately the variance within cells.

We sum up the column differences (MS Columns) by finding $C_{col} - B$ divided by the degrees of freedom $c - 1$ (the number of columns less one). This is the same idea as MS Rows, of course: similarly MS Columns is approximately the weighted variance of column means around the grand mean.

Finally, we come to MS Interaction. This is approximately the variance of the cell-to-cell residuals after the grand mean, row effect, and column effect have been removed. This turns out to be $D - (C_{row} + C_{col} - B) = B + D - C_{row} - C_{col}$. If the basic additive fit predicts the cell means perfectly there will be no interaction: as the basic fit works more poorly the size of the interaction term will increase, just as we saw in the exploratory analysis.

F-Tests for the Adler Data

Let's work our example, and then look harder at the data to interpret what the numbers mean. We have the basic numbers A, B, C_{col}, C_{row} and D; we know r, c, n (see pp. 307-09). So we just need to plug these into the basic anova table, Table 17.2, which gives us Table 17.3. Next we consult an *F*-table to find out whether the *F*'s are large enough so that they are unlikely to have happened if H_0 were true. The size of the critical value for F depends on the degrees of freedom and the significance level chosen. For the sig-

Table 17.3

Anova Table for 17.1

Source	Sum of Squares	df	MS	F- ratio
Rows	336.129	2	168.065	1.151
Columns	222.453	1	222.453	1.524
Interaction	5329.686	2	2664.843	18.254
Within Cell	14890.5	102	145.985	
Total	20778.768	107		

nificance level we might as well use the familiar .05; the degrees of freedom can be read off from the basic table for our example, Table 17.3. For example, the F-ratio for rows is based on MS Rows divided by MS Within, so the numerator has two df and the denominator has 102 df, which is the case for all three ratios. For the F for columns, the df for the numerator is one; for the F for interaction the df for the numerator is 2. Looking at our table for critical F-values at the 5% level, we find:

Critical Values for F, 5%

Rows	$F_{2,102} = 3.07$
Columns	$F_{1,102} = 3.92$
Interaction	$F_{2,102} = 3.07$

If we compare these critical values to the computed F's for our data, we see that only the F for interaction exceeds the critical value. We cannot reject H_0 for rows and columns; that means that different instructions (rows) made no overall difference to the subjects' ratings (Y), and different expectations (columns) made no overall difference either. But we can reject the H_0 for interaction, which means that particular combinations of instruction and expectations probably did have an effect on the ratings.

But what combinations? What is happening here? The F-test can't tell us; we have to look at our data to figure it out. Table 17.1, the original data, is not helpful because there are too many numbers. We want to figure out interaction effects, which are differences between cells which row and column effects can't explain so we don't really need the eighteen replications. Let's go back to the table of cell totals from a few pages ago to find cell means and do a quick elementary analysis by means. Table 17.4 goes from the totals to the means analysis by stages.

The elementary analysis gives visual support for the F-test results. On column effects: the experimenters that expected high ratings did get somewhat higher ratings, as seems reasonable, but they didn't get much higher ratings (1.44 higher than average). On row effects: those instructed to get "scientific" data got somewhat higher ratings than others, but again not by much. What "much" means here is "by comparison with the magnitudes of the residuals from the basic additive fit." When the basic additive fit (without interaction) is working well, the row and/or column effects will be large relative to the residuals. Here it's the residuals that are large, which suggests that the interaction effect is what's important in this table.

Let's go through the residuals in Table 17.4 systematically to interpret interaction effects. The first row reports results for those experimenters told to get "good" data. We see that those expecting to get higher ratings got them (9.92 for those expecting high ratings versus −9.93 for those expecting low ratings). The stress on "good" data seems to produce a strong experimenter effect, with the experimenter getting what he expects to get. The second row reports results for those experimenters told to get "scientific"

Table 17.4

Elementary Means Analysis of 17.1

	Cell and Marginal Totals		
	E_1	E_2	Total
O_1	80	−329	−249
O_2	−125	15	−110
O_3	−177	−63	−240
Total	−222	−377	−599

	Cell and Marginal Means		
	E_1	E_2	Row Means
O_1	4.44	−18.28	−6.92*
O_2	−6.94	.83	−3.06
O_3	−9.83	−3.50	−6.67
Column Means	−4.11*	−6.98	$-5.55 = \overline{\overline{Y}}$

*e.g., $-6.92 = -249/36$, and $-4.11 = -222/54$.

	Elementary Analysis		
	E_1	E_2	Row Effects
O_1	9.92	−9.93	−1.37
O_2	−5.32	5.32	2.49
O_3	−4.60	4.60	−1.12
Column Effects	1.44	−1.43	$-5.55 = \overline{\overline{Y}}$

data. This is the opposite of the first row; those who expected high got low, and those who expected low got high. Perhaps this is a "bending over backwards" phenomenon: the experimenters know they expect certain ratings, consciously try to avoid bias, and end up overdoing it. Much the same thing in a slightly weaker form occurs in the third row, where the experimenters were given instructions without stress on any special kind of outcome. Only the instructions stressing "good" data produce the classic experimenter effect, perhaps because the instruction implies that there is a correct answer (high ratings or low ones) so an experimenter who doesn't get these correct results is not doing it right.

Are We Being Misled?

We have done the analysis of variance, come to the appropriate conclusions about H_0's, and interpreted the statistical results by means of an elementary analysis by means. So we have done the numerical work *and* seen what it means. But all this work was in confirmatory terms: means and variances have dominated this analysis. This could be misleading because the confirmatory methods lack resistance so let's go on to use a resistant procedure. Because the table is small but the number of replications is large, we will do a little more than just a median polish. If the resistant picture is the same as the elementary analysis by means, fine; if not, we will know where to interpret the confirmatory results with caution.

Table 17.5 presents a resistant analysis which is resistant in two ways:

1. the cell values were found from a resistant level, the trimean, for the eighteen cell values in Table 17.1;
2. the analysis of these trimeans was done in a resistant way, by a median elementary analysis.

Table 17.5

Resistant Analysis of 17.1

| | Cell Trimeans | |
	E_1	E_2
O_1	4.0	−21.3
O_2	−5.3	.5
O_3	−10.3	−3.5

| | Elementary Analysis by Medians | | |
	E_1	E_2	Row Effects
O_1	15.6	−15.5	−4.3
O_2	0	0	2.0
O_3	−.5	.5	−2.5
Column Effects	−2.9	2.9	−4.4 = Md_Y

We used trimeans for cell levels because there are a lot of cell entries, and medians for analyzing the cell levels because there are only a few cells. If we compare the cell trimeans of Table 17.5 to the cell means of Table 17.4, we see that they are very close: good. The row and column effects are slightly different (most amusingly, in median terms the experimenters who expected higher ratings got slightly lower ones) but the same overall impression remains: the row and column effects are small compared to the residuals — the interaction effect. Finally, when it comes to the interaction effects, the median analysis stresses the difference between O_1 ("good" data) and the other rows a bit more than the means analysis did. In median terms it looks like the "scientific" data and no stress instructions resulted in mild experimenter effects at most, while the "good" data stress led to strong experimenter expectation effects. Because O_1 is the "odd one out" here, the column medians are based on one of the other rows (O_2 for both columns as it happens); in those rows (O_2 and O_3) there is that "bending over backward" effect, which is why the column effects end up the reverse of the way they were for means. The means are much affected by the big numbers in row O_1 but the medians of course are not.

All in all, the resistant analysis is pleasantly similar to the analysis using means, suggesting no great distortion from extreme cases; but the resistant analysis emphasizes row O_1 somewhat more, instructing experimenters to get "good" data.

Assumptions in Two-Way Anova

Like all confirmatory statistics, two-way analysis of variance is based on a set of assumptions about the data. They should be checked before starting an analysis, though we report them afterwards here for clarity of presentation. We look at three assumptions.

First, in each cell the data should be normally distributed. This is surely no surprise. Most of the powerful and useful statistics assume normality. As in one-way anova, this assumption can be stretched if n (the number of cases per cell) is large. The larger the number of replications, the more non-normality you can put up with. If you have a close call to make, and you are unsure about whether your n is big enough to make up for patent straggling, consult an expert.

In our example, we have $n = 18$ which is quite large; we could accept a fair bit of straggle without seriously bending this assumption. In fact, we do not have much to accept; the stems-and-leaves of the six cell distributions (Table 17.6) show pretty balanced patterns. Some of the stems-and-leaves are not quite symmetric (O_1E_2 straggles up for example) but, on the whole, they are quite pretty.

What do you do if your data have pronounced departures from normality? If the cell stems-and-leaves show straggle in the same direction, it's easy: transform the data. If most cells straggle strongly in one direction, but a few straggle strongly in the other, you're probably safe after transforming, but it may be useful to talk to an expert. If the cells straggle seriously about half and half up and down, and cell sizes are fairly small, you probably need expert advice.

Second, in each cell the data should have equal variances. Again, this is familiar from one-way anova. And again, although the assumption is important it can be relaxed if the number of entries in each cell is equal.

In our example, the cell variances are:

	E_1	E_2
O_1	237.2	106.1
O_2	71.4	109.3
O_3	216.7	135.2

Table 17.6

Cell Stems-and-Leaves

O_1E_1
```
 4 | 2
 3 |
 2 | 5
 1 | 4931
 0 | 50469
-0 | 2366
-1 | 63
-2 | 2
```

O_1E_2
```
 1 | 2
 0 |
-0 | 28
-1 | 970
-2 | 32204423258
-3 | 0
```

O_2E_1
```
 0 | 045
-0 | 4411349566
-1 | 319
-2 | 44
```

O_2E_2
```
 1 | 4445
 0 | 67936
-0 | 5565595
-1 | 1
-2 | 2
```

O_3E_1
```
 2 | 2
 1 |
 0 | 3490
-0 | 196
-1 | 92001
-2 | 6617
-3 | 7
```

O_3E_2
```
 2 | 0
 1 | 3
 0 | 2986
-0 | 4743986
-1 | 201
-2 | 70
```

stems: tens
leaves: units

The largest variance (237.2) and the smallest (71.4) are in a ratio of about three to one. If the cell sizes were unequal, a ratio of three to one would be barely acceptable; a much larger disparity would be too great. In fact, our cell sizes are equal, so we could tolerate even more inequality among the variances. Since only very rough similarity of variances is required given equal cell sizes, we do not really need to go through the labour of computing all those variances; a rougher and faster comparison of spread is fine. For example, we could look at the midspreads and ranges:

	dq	range		dq	range
O_1E_1	19	64	O_1E_2	7	42
O_2E_1	10	29	O_2E_2	14	37
O_3E_1	21	59	O_3E_2	16	47

The midspreads vary a fair bit (O_3E_1 has a *dq* three times as large as that of O_1E_2 and the ranges somewhat less (the range of O_1E_1 being about twice that of O_2E_1). Thus the faster spread measures give an impression in the same ballpark as the variance (close enough when cell sizes are equal); but we probably should look at variances if cell sizes are unequal. With large, equal cell sizes, even a look at the stems-and-leaves needed to check normality can be enough. (Here we could look at Table 17.6.)

What can you do if your cell variances are very unequal and you do not have equal numbers in each cell? Transformation can help here too, if cell variances happen to be related to cell levels. Recall the log of spread versus log of level plot for finding the best transformation which we used in chapter 6. You could use this again, plotting each cell as a point to find the appropriate transformation. Log variance by log mean would be suitable. If this doesn't work, consult that expert. Moral: plan ahead and get equal cell sizes.

Third, errors (or the things not explained by the row, column, and interaction variables) should be independent. In practice, this means that each case should be gathered and measured independently so that the datum for one case is not a function of the datum for another. The best way to ensure this is to use randomization; randomly assign people (or factories or whatever you are studying) to cells; apply the row and column variables as called for; then measure the dependent variable to fill in the cells with Y values and do the analysis.

For example, when Adler did the study we have used as this chapter's example, she had a pool of subjects, who were randomly assigned to a combination of treatments. She also had a pool of experimenters who were randomly assigned to instruction and expectation conditions.

Randomization right at the start, followed by experimental manipulation of the independent variables, is a very powerful strategy which has many statistical (and other) advantages. Do it whenever you can; and if you can't do it, approximate it as much as you can. (A useful source on these matters is Campbell and Stanley, *Experimental and Quasi-Experimental Designs for Research*, 1966.)

Alas, this lovely strategy is very hard or impossible in most "natural" experiments where you take the category assignments as they come. For example, we don't decide (in chapter 15) what religion our Northern Irish are going to have. Still, we can make sure that data gathered for one cell are not tied to data gathered for another cell if we use our heads. For example, suppose one of our variables (row or column) was sex and we were looking at its effects on aggression. Suppose further we sampled some men for the male category, and then used their wives to fill in the female category. Obviously this will create problems. Spouses tend not to be independent of each other, so the male and female aggression rates in this imaginary table would be far from independent. To get a more accurate comparison of the sexes, we would have to sample men and women separately — independently Then the third assumption would be satisfied and it would make sense to use anova.

All in all, analysis of variance is a very robust technique: the assumptions do not have to be met perfectly, and can be met fairly imperfectly if a little advance planning has produced: (1) ample entries in each cell; (2) equal numbers of entries in each cell; (3) entries based on randomly sampled, independently measured cases.

Some Special Problems

What do you do if the data you have are suitable for analysis of variance (categorical X_1 and X_2 and numerical Y) but the practical details are messy? What if you do not have equal numbers in each cell? What if you have only one case per cell? And what happens when the categories are random instead of fixed? There are two essential points here. First of all, you can still do analysis of variance; it is a very flexible technique. Secondly, however, you can't do it exactly the way we have done it here. The formulae have to be modified. The modifications are not hard for the most part and you can find them in many standard books (e.g. Guilford, *Psychometric Methods*, 1954, or Snedecor, *Statistical Methods*, 1956).

We will say no more about having just one case per cell or having unequal numbers in the cells; if these happen, you will not have any trouble telling. But the next issue, the difference between fixed and random categories is less obvious so we will go over it a bit.

Fixed and Random Categories

As mentioned earlier, our discussion so far holds only for two-way analyses with row and column variables whose categories are fixed, not random. If the categories are fixed, inferences are made only about the categories directly studied in the anova table. If the categories are random, they are chosen to represent a whole range of possible categories and inferences are made for that whole range, including categories not in the anova table itself. This is a tricky distinction at first. In making it, you may find it helpful to ask yourself whether the variables were measured as categories from the start or whether they were based originally on numeric variables made into categories. So far, we have seen just categorical X's. In chapter 15, we looked at fertility by variables like religion/residence, or occupational status level. In this chapter we've looked at positive versus negative expectation by type of instructions. All these are fixed categories; when we finish our analysis, we would expect to make inferences just to these categories and no others.

But suppose that our independent variables were originally measured on interval scales, and that we had "sampled" on these scales to obtain the table's categories. For example, suppose that to induce expectation on the part of our experimenter/subjects we had prepared a tape that we played under their pillows while they were asleep. Suppose, further, that we could play this tape for any length of time from say four minutes to nine hours. We might end up comparing the effects of eight, four and two hours of exposure, but when we finish our analysis we would want to talk about exposure time as a continuous variable with eight, four and two hours as convenient representative levels. Now we are talking about random categories. In other words, if the various levels we actually study show strong effects as we hope, then we will conclude that our variable in general works the same way. If we have sampled our categories well, then they are likely to represent all possible categories and what is true in our study is likely true for the variable in general.

In one-way analysis of variance we did not stress fixed versus randomly-chosen categories because the distinction does not make much practical difference there. But it makes a lot of difference in two-way anova. Since random categories involve not one but two layers of random selection, with an ambitious attempt to generalize to universes of subjects *and* universes of categories, it is a somewhat more demanding affair than fixed categories. The tests are tougher. Tougher on the data, that is, not on you; you do no more arithmetic work for random categories than for fixed ones. In fact, you find the same basic quantities (A to D) and the same mean squares; the way these mean squares fit together in F-tests is a little different, however. Should one or both of your independent variables have random categories, look up the modified procedures in Guilford (1954), Snedecor (1956) or another such source. Watch out for the conventional terminology, which is far from intuitive. If both independent variables have fixed categories (the case we treat here), it is conventional to say that we have two variables with "fixed effects" and a "Model One" analysis of variance. If one or both variables have randomly selected categories, conventional usage refers to "random effects" and "Model Two" analysis of variance.

Exploratory and Confirmatory

By now you can see the full set of analogies between exploratory and confirmatory approaches to two-way tables. Both approaches break Y up into row, column, and interaction components; the exploratory components are resistant levels and the confirmatory components are means. Both offer ways in which the effects of the row and/or column variables can be evaluated. In exploratory statistics the strength of overall fit (row and column effects, or those plus interaction effects) is evaluated by comparing differences of quartiles. In confirmatory, each of the three possible parts of the fit (row, column, interaction) is tested. There are also confirmatory measures of the strength of each of these components (rather like r^2) although we have not gone into them here. Both approaches need eye-work: there is no way to interpret a means or a median analysis without looking hard at it.

Finally, the two approaches work very well together. One can do resistant analysis to develop ideas for later testing on fresh data, or one can do analysis of variance first and then interpret with exploratory approaches. The exploratory approaches supplement the confirmatory well in yet another way: they help us to tell if the confirmatory analysis has been pulled off by a few extreme cases. In this chapter's example, we saw that the median and means analyses were quite close, which made us much more confident that the confirmatory analysis was well founded.

Homework

Table 17.7 reports some of the results from a study of children's perceptions of status. Pupils in several schools were shown pictures of people and pictures of cars or houses and asked to match the pictures, for example to put the person with the house to which he belonged. All the pictures were chosen to reflect high or low status; for example, one of the houses was expensive and one inexpensive, one of the men was well dressed and one shabbily dressed, and one of the cars was a costly model while the other was a run-down Volkswagen (which belonged to the investigator, Bernd Baldus). The dependent variable is the number of correct matches of people with objects of corresponding status, which could range from 0 to 4. Several independent variables were examined; here we just give information on two, the pupil's grade (1, 3, or 6) and his family's status (white collar and blue collar). Both these variables could be related to status perception — why?

Table 17.7
Status Matchings by Grade and Family Status

	White Collar Family			Blue Collar Family		
Grade 1	4	3	2	4	3	2
	4	3	2	4	3	2
	4	3	2	3	2	1
	4	3	1	3	2	1
	4	2	1	3	2	1
	3	2	1	3	2	0
Grade 3	4	4	3	4	4	3
	4	4	3	4	4	3
	4	4	3	4	4	3
	4	4	3	4	4	2
	4	4	3	4	3	2
	4	4	3	4	3	1
Grade 6	4	4	3	4	4	4
	4	4	3	4	4	4
	4	4	3	4	4	3
	4	4	3	4	4	3
	4	4	3	4	4	2
	4	3	3	4	4	2

Do a two-way analysis of variance for these data. Do not forget to examine the assumptions first. Both independent variables have fixed categories here; the "grade" variable may look somewhat numeric, but the grades used were not chosen randomly and were meant to represent three distinct stages of development rather than three points sampled from an age or grade continuum. Consider the cell variances carefully (*hint:* try a power of Y). Do not forget to discuss the anova results and an elementary analysis by means (you probably won't have time for a resistant analysis).

Fourth Review

Here we have more data adapted from Janet Polivy's experiment on delay and insult (refer to the second review for a description of the experiment). There are two independent variables; gender of subject and a combination variable: whether the subject was insulted or apologized to after waiting and whether or not the subject could retaliate for the treatment by recommending a poor grade for the experimenter (a graduate student).

We present two new possible dependent variables: change in hostility scores (scores after treatment minus scores before treatment) and depression change scores (how depressed the subject reported himself after treatment minus depression before treatment). In fact, a third dependent variable is also possible; some combination of these that might be referred to as increase in emotionality.

A few remarks on the general theoretical framework of this study might be order here. First, not surprisingly, both frustrating delay and un-provoked attack are expected to generate anger and hostility which theo-retically can be reduced in several ways, including catharsis, here resulting from retaliation against the experimenter; or by empathy, here the result of getting an apology and explanation from the experimenter. Hence, where subjects were apologized to or could retaliate, change scores for hostility would be expected to be near zero (i.e. no change). Regarding depression, very generally, Freud and others argue that when a person is angry at a valued other, he might also feel some anger toward himself, thus, some depression.

The expected effect of gender of subject comes via research into sex-role socialization. Thus, while females are "allowed" to show sadness (e.g. by crying) this is more difficult for males. The reverse may well be true for anger; that is, males are "allowed" to show and act out anger, this being more difficult for females. For more discussion of the theory, look at the study by Atkinson and Polivy (1976).

Finally, a few suggestions about the data. If you decide that the data need transforming, you may find the presence of negative (and zero) values disconcerting, because many useful transformations can't be made with such data. There are several simple and useful things one can do here, the simplest being merely to add some number to all of the observations so that all become greater than zero, that is, if the greatest negative value were −50, then just add 51 to everything. Transforming the original scores would be best (if transformation is needed) but would make extra work for you.

Table RIV.1

Changes in Hostility and Depression*

Batch 1 Females; insult with no retaliation		Batch 2 Males; insult with no retaliation	
Hostility	Depression	Hostility	Depression
7	3	−4	0
11	1	9	10
25	−3	6	5
23	24	−3	7
25	26	4	3
5	−5	34	38
0	10	11	−7
3	3	20	11
−6	−1	14	−2
10	6	1	−14

Batch 3 Females; apology with no retaliation		Batch 4 Males; apology with no retaliation	
Hostility	Depression	Hostility	Depression
−17	−11	6	7
1	0	4	3
11	4	0	2
0	3	6	21
4	0	45	24
10	4	−1	−2
6	1	−3	5
9	−8	−3	−2
−21	−6	−16	−13
−1	5	3	8

Batch 5 Females; insult with retaliation		Batch 6 Males; insult with retaliation	
Hostility	Depression	Hostility	Depression
8	6	13	21
5	6	2	3
32	23	15	20
7	0	−23	−9
5	3	10	−9
57	16	24	7
−4	7	−1	−8
8	5	6	4
6	9	−6	−4
1	−1	−13	−11

Batch 7 Females; retaliation and apology		Batch 8 Males; retaliation and apology	
Hostility	Depression	Hostility	Depression
−6	−20	31	21
11	8	0	1
11	0	0	−3
0	−12	6	9
6	4	6	7
1	10	0	7
−3	0	−17	−9
−5	−2	−4	−10
−2	−7	−1	6
3	−11	−1	−25

Source: Atkinson and Polivy (1976), *Journal of Abnormal Psychology.* © 1976 by the American Psychological Association. Reprinted by permission.
* All scores were found by subtracting scores before treatment from scores after treatment.

18

Getting More From Residuals

Having rounded out our collection of tools for two categorical independent variables and a numeric Y, we now move on to tools for two numeric variables and a numeric Y. At this point you might want to look back to the introduction to Section Four to get your bearings.

One of the basic strategies of the good data analyst is the scrutiny of residuals. Many of the techniques of exploration were designed just to make it easier to spot suggestive residuals. This is the single best way of pushing research further, of getting just a bit more out of a body of data.

We have pointed out that one of the payoffs from making a numeric fit is precisely being able to get residuals so that further explanatory factors can be more easily sought. You have done enough poring over residuals by now to know that possible further factors can easily be suggested with some hard looking and a bit of thought. But when you've thought of them, what next? Thus far, we're rather short on methods for pursuing residuals from X by Y analysis.

We need ways to make fits involving more than one numeric explanatory variable at a time. Virtually every social phenomenon has many causes, so for any Y we should be able to work with several X's.

In this chapter we begin with the residuals from the simple X by Y analysis of integration and mobility in chapter 11. We get further insight about mobility by introducing a second independent variable, heterogeneity, to see whether it can account for part of the mobility variation not accounted for by integration alone. The second independent variable is investigated without anything really new by way of technique: we just use the basic linear fitting procedure again. First we make a linear fit for heterogeneity and integration and find the residuals, or the part of heterogeneity that integration does not explain. That step completes the full control of integration. Next we make a linear fit using the two sets of residuals; this gives us a picture of the relationship between heterogeneity and mobility with integration effects removed.

In essence this is a very simple application of old tools to new uses, so we will go through just one example which illustrates most of the complications that can arise. There aren't many and common sense will handle them easily.

Table 18.1

Integration, Mobility and Heterogeneity

City	X_1 = Integration	Y = Mobility	Y'	X_2 = Heterogeneity
Rochester	19.0	15.0	7.6	20.6
Worcester	16.4	13.6	0	22.1
Milwaukee	15.8	17.6	2.5	17.4
Buffalo	15.2	14.7	−1.8	22.3
Reading	14.2	19.4	.5	10.6
Cleveland	14.0	18.6	−.8	39.7
Peoria	13.8	35.1	15.2	10.7
Trenton	13.0	15.8	−6.0	23.5
Toledo	12.7	21.6	−.9	19.2
Baltimore	12.0	12.1	−12.1	45.8
Akron	11.3	22.1	−3.8	20.4
Tacoma	10.9	31.2	4.4	17.8
Spokane	9.6	38.9	8.9	12.3
Indianapolis	8.8	23.1	−8.8	29.2
Portland (Ore.)	7.2	35.8	.1	16.4

Source: R. C. Angell, *American Journal of Sociology* 57, 1951. Published by the University of Chicago. © 1951 University of Chicago.

Back to the Angell Data

Consider Table 18.1, which reproduces some material from chapter 11 for your convenience. Table 18.1 gives integration, heterogeneity, and mobility for fifteen U.S. cities, plus Y' or the residuals of mobility from the exploratory fit:

$$\text{Mobility} = -2.4 \, (\text{integration}) + 53$$

We are going on to several more fits using the Angell data, so let's introduce some simple notation that will help keep things straight. Mobility is Y as before; integration, the first variable we used to explain mobility, is X_1; and heterogeneity, the second independent variable we are going to use here, is X_2. The equations for the fits will have different b's and a's, since different relationships are involved, so we will underline that by subscripts. For example, let's put the integration and mobility fit into symbols:

$$Y = b_1 X_1 + a_1$$

Here $b_1 = -2.4$ and $a_1 = 53$. We'll see different b's and a's shortly. As long as you remember that these values differ from fit to fit, the subscripting does not matter; it's just a convenience.

The fit found in chapter 11 showed us that mobility into and out of a city declines as the city's integration increases, perhaps because higher integration (or lower crime rates with higher welfare effort) makes a city more pleasant to live in so that fewer people leave. This fit produced a *dq* ratio of .50, which is good but still leaves a lot of Y unexplained. Now we want to work on that unexplained part of Y, the residuals Y', by bringing in another independent variable.

Heterogeneity suggests itself partly because "it's there," hence convenient, and partly for conceptual reasons. Heterogeneity is an index of the numbers of non-whites and foreign-borns in a city, a variable which may well have some effect on mobility over and above the effects of integration. There could easily be a relationship in either direction. Perhaps high heterogeneity means a more diverse array of backgrounds and values in the city, leading to more social conflict, so people are more likely to move out whatever the level of integration; or perhaps that very variety makes it more likely that more people of more kinds are attracted to the city, so that more people move in. Furthermore, all foreign-borns had to move at least once just to get to the city. Such arguments suggest that heterogeneity will be positively related to mobility when integration is controlled. Alternatively, one could argue that the non-white and foreign-born are poorer than average and thus move neither in nor out as easily, so that heterogeneity would be negatively related to mobility when integration is controlled. Thus heterogeneity does seem like a reasonable variable to look at, although we do not know exactly what to expect of it. The best way to find out is to look, so on with our exploration.

Fully Controlling for X_1

Our first step will be to fit and remove the linear effects of X_1, integration on X_2, heterogeneity. You may wonder: why control for X_1 again?

We want to see what X_2 can tell us about Y, above and beyond what X_1 has told us already. The clearest way of seeing this is to remove as much of the "underbrush" as possible, to fully and consistently control for the effects of X_1. Then we can look at the relationship between X_2' and Y' as the relationship that X_2 and Y might have if X_1 were out of the picture entirely. This is easier to think about than a mixed picture in which X_1 effects have been controlled for one variable and not for the other. Besides clearer conceptualization, the relationship itself may be clearer with X_1 fully controlled. To clarify, imagine X_2 and Y' to be perfectly related. X_2 may well have some X_1 effects, if only slight ones, while Y' has been carefully created as residuals from X_1 or a variable with no linear X_1 effects. This means X_2 and Y' must be a bit different, just because of their different status with respect to X_1, and this would fog the relationship between X_2 and Y'. So we will remove the effects of X_1 from X_2 before going on, even though this means a bit more work.

This raises an important procedural point: we have to make at least three linear fits to use both X_1 and X_2 (a fit for X_1 and Y, for X_1 and X_2, and for Y' and X_2'), so it makes sense to cut all the corners we can to keep the work manageable. We'll plot and think first, since plots can often save time by warning of problems. We'll use just the two end summary points whenever possible, and do transformations only when we clearly must.

Table 18.2

Heterogeneity by Integration

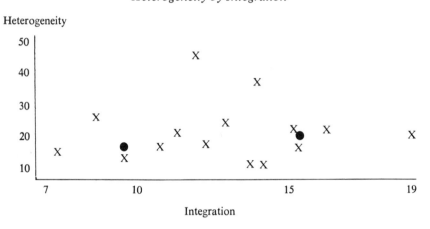

Heterogeneity

Integration

Table 18.2, gives a plot for $X_1 =$ integration and $X_2 =$ heterogeneity. Clearly this is a very weak relationship, but all the same we should fit and remove it. There may perhaps be a slight curve here, a curve like an inverted U, but we will ignore this possibility: we cannot fit such a surve simply via transformation, and we generally avoid fitting curves where the fit is poor, where the spread around the fit is so high. This also keeps the amount of work at a minimum. We'll reduce the arithmetic still further by fitting a straight line using only the two end summary points found with medians.

Since integration is the independent variable again, as in chapter 11, we know that the rules of thumb for thirds on X are satisfied by just splitting the data into three sets of five points each. The high and low summary points are:

	X_1 (independent)	X_2 (dependent)
High	15.8	20.6
Low	9.6	17.8

These points are also shown in Table 18.2, as filled circles. The line connecting those two points sums up a weak positive relationship which is an adequate fit for all but a few of the points. Higher integration goes with higher heterogeneity, though not very strongly. Perhaps immigrants and nonwhites are more likely to move to cities with good social services, but the connection is too faint to merit much attention.

We make a numerical summary of the integration-heterogeneity fit, or

$$X_2 = b_2 X_1 + a_2$$

by finding b_2 and a_2 in the usual way, except that we use only the two end summary points to find a_2 (saving a bit of time):

$$b_2 = \frac{20.6 - 17.8}{15.8 - 9.6}$$

$$= .45$$

$$\cong .5$$

a_2: (High) $20.6 - (.5)(15.8) = 12.7$
(Low) $17.8 - (.5)(\ 9.6) = 13.0$

$$a_2 = \frac{13 + 12.7}{2}$$

$$\cong 13$$

We use rounded values for b_2 and a_2, again saving time. We might use another significant digit if the relationship were stronger, but with such a weak relationship a little error in b_2 is not going to make much difference. This brings us to Table 18.3, a work sheet finding the residuals of heterogeneity from integration:

$$X_2' = X_2 - (b_2 X_1 + a_2)$$

giving us X_2' values with the linear effects of integration removed.

Table 18.4 plots Y' on the Y axis and X_2' on the X axis. This is a plot

Table 18.3

Work Sheet for Linear Fit Het = .5 (Int) + 13

Int (X_1)	Het (X_2)	$.5X_1$	$X'_2 = X_2 - (.5X_1 + 13)$
19.0	20.6	9.5	−1.9
16.4	22.1	8.2	.9
15.8	17.4	7.9	−3.5
15.2	22.3	7.6	1.7
14.2	10.6	7.1	−9.5
14.0	39.7	7.0	19.7
13.8	10.7	6.9	−9.2
13.0	23.5	6.5	4.0
12.7	19.2	6.4	−.2
12.0	45.8	6.0	26.8
11.3	20.4	5.7	1.7
10.9	17.8	5.5	−.7
9.6	12.3	4.8	−5.5
8.8	29.2	4.4	11.8
7.2	16.4	3.6	−.2

Table 18.4

Heterogeneity and Mobility, With Integration Controlled

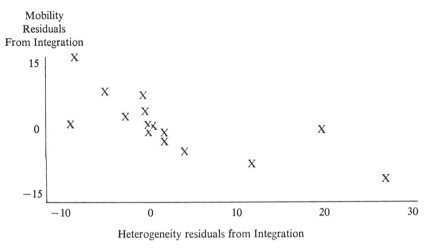

Heterogeneity residuals from Integration

of the relationship between mobility and heterogeneity with the linear effects of integration held constant. Our put another way, if all cities had the same level of integration, this is how mobility and heterogeneity would presumably be related. So we can now make a fit for this plot knowing that we are explaining a part of mobility not explained by integration; a part having no linear integration effect.

By this time you should be able to see how this way of introducing a new X variable works; the approach is generally familiar, as we said earlier. We also told you to expect a few complications even though the basic technique is straightforward. Now here's a complication: a long look at Table 18.4 makes it clear that an exploratory linear fit isn't going to be a success here, for two reasons. First, the range rule for the independent variable cannot be satisfied, since the high values of X_2' are too spread out; and second, this relationship is curved rather than straight. We might choose to ignore the curve if it were slight, but it isn't. It is clear-cut and too strong to mishandle with a linear fit. A transformation which will correct for upward straggle in X_2' should help here.

What Do We Transform?

When we first used transformation in chapter 11 as a way of satisfying the range rule for badly trailing data, we operated directly on either the independent or dependent variable. But in Table 18.4 both X_2' and Y' are residuals from another fit. We suggest that directly transforming the residuals is generally undesirable, for two reasons.

1. Residuals are often negative, and many of our favourite transforms don't work on negative numbers.
2. Even where all residuals are positive we will have to face the problem of putting what we did into words; it's not clear what transforming residuals means.

For these reasons we argue that it makes more sense to transform the original heterogeneity scores; looking at them, it's easy to see that X_2' trails up because X_2 trails up. Let's try logging heterogeneity; to avoid confusion, we will designate log(het) as X_3.

Table 18.5

Logged Heterogeneity and Integration

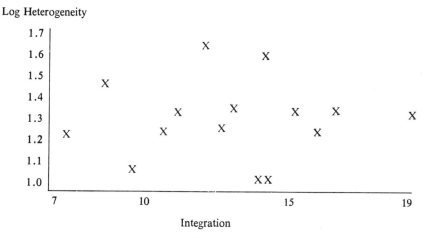

Log Heterogeneity

Integration

Starting Again with Logged Heterogeneity

Again there is no new technique involved; we ran up against a snag, we backtracked in order to use a familiar corrective tool, transformation, and now we just carry on as before. We start once again with a plot, now X_3 by X_1 or logged heterogeneity by integration, in Table 18.5. This looks much the same as the raw heterogeneity by integration plot, except that those points unusually high or low on heterogeneity now look a bit better balanced. So we repeat the earlier steps this time with logged heterogeneity scores. Table 18.6 gives the work sheet, from which we obtain the high and low summary points:

	X_1 (independent)	X_3 (dependent)
High	15.8	1.31
Low	9.6	1.25

Table 18.6

$log\,(Het) = .01\,(Int)$

X_1	X_3	$.01\,X_1$	$X'_3 = X_3 - .01\,X_1$
19.0	1.31	.19	1.12
16.4	1.34	.16	1.18
15.8	1.24	.16	1.08
15.2	1.36	.15	1.21
14.2	1.03	.14	.89
14.0	1.60	.14	1.46
13.8	1.03	.14	.89
13.0	1:37	.13	1.24
12.7	1.28	.13	1.15
12.0	1.66	.12	1.54
11.3	1.31	.11	1.20
10.9	1.25	.11	1.14
9.6	1.09	.10	.99
8.8	1.47	.09	1.38
7.2	1.21	.07	1.14

Now we could find another fit in the usual way:

$$X_3 = b_3 X_1 + a_3$$

Before doing that, let's think a moment about a_3. Do we really need it? We did fit and remove a_2, when dealing with raw heterogeneity and integration a moment ago; was that really essential? Look again at Table 18.4, the plot of X'_2 and Y'. If we had not fitted a_2, the plot would look exactly the same except that the level of the heterogeneity residuals would be higher by $a_2 = 13$, that is, the whole plot would be shifted thirteen units to the right. The relationship between X'_2 and Y' would not be affected: they would be related in the same pattern, with the same strength. The level in a numeric fit for their relationship would be affected, but the slope and the dq ratio and the residuals from the fit would not be. So why bother with a_2, or with a_3? We can save a little time harmlessly by making only a partial fit for slope but not level. Let's try that here. Returning to logged heterogeneity and raw integration, as plotted in Table 18.5, we find:

$$b_3 = \frac{1.31 - 1.25}{15.8 - 9.6}$$

$$= .01$$

and then remove this approximate partial fit in Table 18.6 to get X'_3, or logged heterogeneity with the linear effects of integration removed.

Has going back and starting again with logged heterogeneity done the job? Table 18.7 plots Y' against our new X'_3 showing how mobility is related to logged heterogeneity when integration is controlled. This plot looks much more promising than Table 18.4: the points are more evenly spread out

Table 18.7

*Logged Heterogeneity and Mobility With
Integration Controlled*

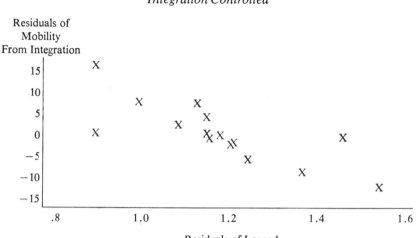

Residuals of Logged
Heterogeneity from Integration

Table 18.8

Y′ by X′₃ Work Sheet

X'_3	Y'	X'_3	Y'	$-35X'_3$	$Y'' = Y' + 35X'_3 - 42$
		Pairs Reordered on X'_3			
1.12	7.6	.89	.5	-31.2	-10.3
1.18	0	.89	15.2	-31.2	4.4
1.08	2.5	.99	8.9	-34.7	1.6
1.21	-1.8	1.08	2.5	-37.8	-1.7
.89	.5	1.12	7.6	-39.2	4.8
1.46	$-.8$	1.14	4.4	-39.9	2.3
.89	15.2	1.14	.1	-39.9	-2.0
1.24	-6.0	1.15	$-.9$	-40.3	-2.6
1.15	$-.9$	1.18	0	-41.3	$-.7$
1.54	-12.1	1.20	-3.8	-42.0	-3.8
1.20	-3.8	1.21	-1.8	-42.4	-1.4
1.14	4.4	1.24	-6.0	-43.4	-4.6
.99	8.9	1.38	-8.8	-48.3	-2.5
1.38	-8.8	1.46	$-.8$	-51.1	8.3
1.14	.1	1.54	-12.1	-53.9	$-.2$

$$b = \frac{-6.0 - 7.6}{1.38 - .99} = -35$$

a: $a_H = -6.0 - (-35)(1.38) = 42.3$
   $a_M = \quad 0 \; - (-35)(1.15) = 40.3$
   $a_L = \quad 7.6 - (-35)(\;.99) = 42.3$

$a = 41.6$
$\quad = 42$

from left to right and the relationship looks more nearly linear. Perhaps there is still some curviness; let's do some arithmetic to find out how bad it is.

Table 18.8 is a work sheet for Y' and X_3'. Until now, we've been using X_1 as an independent variable so the points have been ordered for us. Now, we must reorder on the new independent variable, being careful to keep Y' values matched with the corresponding X_3' values. We copied X_3' from Table 18.8 and Y' from Table 18.1 (the points are in the same order in both of these, ordered on integration) and then reordered the pairs. First we check the rules for thirds on X_3'. If we put five points in each third, as indicated by the two horizontal lines breaking up the third and fourth columns of the work sheet, all the rules of thumb are met. The range rule is just barely satisfied since half the X_3' range is $.65/2 \cong .33$, which is the range of the upper third. There is still a bit of upward straggle which a somewhat stronger transformation might have corrected but, remember, we're trying to keep the arithmetic as simple as possible here.

Next we check to see if a linear fit is appropriate. Since there was a distinct curve before transformation and may still be a bit of curve afterwards, we'll want to look at the middle summary point as well as the end ones:

	X_3' (independent)	Y' (dependent)
Low	.99	7.6
Medium	1.15	.0
High	1.38	−6.0

Then the check for curviness:

$$b_{\mathrm{MH}} = \frac{-6.0}{1.38 - 1.15} = -26.1$$

$$b_{\mathrm{LM}} = \frac{-7.6}{1.15 - .99} = -47.5$$

$$\frac{b_{\mathrm{MH}}}{b_{\mathrm{LM}}} = .60$$

The ratio, like the plot, suggests that there is some curve but that it's tolerable; we are in the discretionary range (see chapter 12). Again a slightly stronger transformation might have done better but we'd rather not spend the time looking for the "perfect" transformation when logging does an adequate job.

Completing the Second Layer of Fit

We are finally ready to make a fit for mobility and logged heterogeneity, with integration held constant. In Table 18.8 we find the linear fit in the usual way, getting

$$Y' = -35X'_3 + 42$$

Residuals are found in the last column of 18.8; next we find the dq ratio:

$$\frac{dq \ Y''}{dq \ Y'} = \frac{4.9}{8.2} = .60$$

The dq ratio tells us that heterogeneity has accounted for quite a lot of Y' or the part of mobility not explained by integration; we can indeed add to our understanding of mobility by fitting heterogeneity as well as integration.

Controlled Relationships

We have seen that the technique for finding the relationship between two variables with a third controlled is easy enough, just a common sense use of old techniques. Thinking about relationships with controls is a bit harder, because it is less familiar. Here we will underline the difference between a relationship without control of a third variable and the same relationship with such controls. We'll also discuss interpretation of controlled relationships a bit, and point out some of the problems that can arise.

First, it is vital to understand that the relationship between, say, X_3 and Y is not the same as the relationship between X'_3 and Y', or the same two variables with controls for a third. A relationship can change greatly when a third variable is held constant. As one illustration of this fact, contrast the heterogeneity-mobility relationship with integration controlled (Table 18.7) with the relationship without controls (Table 18.9). As it happens both are negative relationships, but the relationships differ in strength: the connection between logged heterogeneity and mobility becomes stronger after integration is controlled! The effects of integration were muddying the picture, concealing a rather close tie between the other two variables. As another illustration of the difference controls can make, recall the Vancouver turnout example from chapter 11. The East Side areas had lower turnout than the West Side areas. But then we controlled for area income by fitting turnout to income and finding the residuals. With income controlled, the East Side areas were higher in turnout residuals: the opposite of the pattern without controls. In general, the relationship between two variables can become stronger or weaker, and can keep the same direction or change it, when a third variable is held constant.

This difference should be reflected in the way we talk about controlled relationships. We speak of, for example, "heterogeneity and mobility with integration held constant" rather than of "heterogeneity and mobility." Besides our phrasing, our interpretation should recognize the difference be-

Table 18.9

*Logged Heterogeneity and Mobility
(No Integration Controls)*

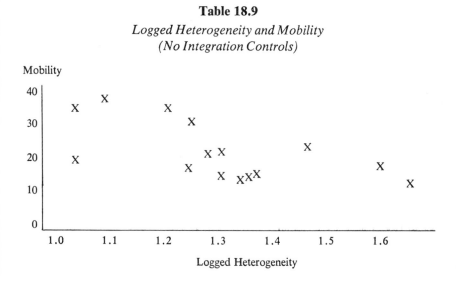

Logged Heterogeneity

tween analyses with and without controls. For example, we wonder why controlling integration makes the tie between mobility and heterogeneity stronger, or why the East Side areas have higher turnout than one would expect from their level of income. We cannot give any general rules for interpreting relationships with controls, since each case is a little different and must be thought through on its own, but we will give some suggestions about one use of controls in the next chapter when we discuss controls and causality briefly. Here we will just caution you not to control too freely. For example, suppose you are investigating the possible relationship of urban experience and modern attitudes. You find that urban dwellers are more modern in outlook than rural dwellers. You suspect that this is just because the urban dwellers have higher status so you control status and then look again. If urban dwellers are still more modern, it's not simply because they tend to be better off: it has something to do with urban life. But suppose you push this further and control for mobility, variety of interpersonal contacts, access to the mass media, and so on. Such variables may well be related to modern attitudes, and the urban-rural difference may well vanish when these variables are controlled. After all, in many ways these variables *are* the urban-rural difference! What is a city, if not a place where people move around a lot and meet lots of varied people and are bombarded by the media and so on? You may be controlling the urban-modern relationship for urbanism itself, which is not helpful. As Stouffer (1962, p. 267) notes, if we are not careful we are "likely to 'partial out' elements in such a way as to remove much of the commonly understood meaning from a particular index."

Conclusions and Comments

We have added to our understanding of a dependent variable by bringing in a second independent variable. We did so without anything really new by way of technique; instead, we used familiar X by Y methods plus common sense in trimming the arithmetic and in working our way around snags as they came up. You might ask if we could have avoided the main snag, the belatedly discovered need to log heterogeneity. After all, heterogeneity clearly straggles up, and if we had corrected for that at the start we would have saved a bit of trouble. The problem with attempted foresight of this kind is that it is very hard to foresee what will happen after a variable is controlled (as integration was here); heterogeneity could quite possibly have become well balanced after integration effects were removed. In general, it is more likely for variables to have linear relationships if they have the same shape and more likely for variables to have non-linear relationships if their shapes are very different; but this is not a hard and fast rule by any means. Keep plotting and thinking as you go, and you will be able to cope with most surprises the data have for you.

We added the second independent variable by linear fitting, because the second variable was a numeric one. But you already know that this is only one possibility of many. In chapter 11 we made a linear fit for turnout and income but a batch fit for the residuals with the categorical variable East Side–West Side. We saw still another possibility in chapter 16, where first layer of fit was two-way with categories as the row and column variables, while the residuals were analyzed by X by Y methods; we fitted the residuals to an interaction term (RC). It was noted that we could as easily have fitted the residuals to some new numeric variable such as time. Fits can be mixed. Use whatever combination of techniques, in whatever order, that seems promising to you.

We have seen how useful it can be to work in an additional layer of fit. But how far should this process be pushed? When should one stop adding new layers of fit? There are several criteria and you have to make your own choices in line with our own feelings about the data. One criterion is "stop when there is nothing left to explain." The difference of quartiles ratio is helpful here; if it is pretty close to zero then there is not much of Y left to worry about. You don't expect the ratio to get right down to zero, by the way; almost always there are some Y residuals left, either because of measurement error with no systematic explanation, or because of the effects of some variable not covered by your data. If you keep pushing on regardless, trying to get all of Y explained, you can get overfitting, which happens when you have milked so much out of the data that there is nothing left but measurement error. Fitting tiny measurement errors is not likely to do you much good. On the other hand, don't give up too soon. An additional layer can often produce interesting insights even when Y is substantially explained. Usually it's worthwhile to push as far as you can, stopping when you get silly-looking results (often a sign of over-fitting). Now, often you never get to use the "nothing left to explain" criterion because other issues enter in earlier. First, and most common, you may run out of time. Second, you may run out of potential X's. In the Angell data this happens pretty quickly since there are only three variables to play with; with effort one could dig up more, but this may not seem worthwhile. Finally, you may have looked at everything you feel is worth looking at.

How do you choose independent variables for further layer of fit? You may choose the variable that you think should be most closely related to Y (you may think this because you have a hunch, or because you know there are theories that predict X is important for Y). If you are short of ideas about causes of Y, you may plot a few interesting-looking possibilities and see which one has a relationship to Y that is strong, and makes sense (there is little point in using a fit that you cannot explain, since your understanding of Y is not increased much that way). This last approach can cause problems though. A very common one is the search for the perfect fit, where several imperfect but suggestive fits may be passed over in favour of continuing the search for the "best." Remember: if you're engaging in this kind of search, it's probably because you don't really understand the process you're investigating all that well. But a few suggestive exploratory fits can increase your understanding and make it easier for you to locate those better variables as a result. Of course, some of the ideas you try out will lead nowhere; but, as you should realize by now, this has advantages. Finding that a given X or X_1 or X_2 has nothing to add can actually be very useful. For one thing, you learn what to rule out; in addition, the very poorness of the fit may lead to very interesting questions (most commonly, "why didn't it work; and what can I learn from that?").

Exploratory and Confirmatory

The exploratory techniques in this chapter are directly parallel to the confirmatory technique *partial correlation*, the topic of the next chapter. The parallels will be discussed there. In both exploratory and confirmatory statistics, the strategy of controlling one variable while examining a relationship between two others is not confined to X by Y methods.

Homework

Naturally the homework for this chapter should consist of controlling some X_1 and looking at the relationship of X_2' and Y'. If possible, return to the homework example you did for chapter 11 and carry on with it; this will save you time since one of the necessary fits will be made already. If this does not appeal to you, try carrying on with the Vancouver voting data example from chapter 11. Let X_1 be the transformed income of an area, and Y be the 1964 turnout; Table 11.11 (p. 209) gives X_1, Y, and Y'. Let X_2 be the area turnout in the previous election in 1962 (see Table IIIR.1, p. 265). Does the 1962 turnout predict the 1964 turnout? (Discuss briefly.) Is the 1962 turnout related to the 1964 turnout when income is held constant? Discuss.

19

Partial Correlations and Causality

In chapter 11 we learned how to make an exploratory X by Y fit with one independent variable, and in the last chapter we learned how to go further by looking at the relationship between Y and a second independent variable with the first independent variable controlled. In this chapter we continue with the confirmatory parallels to the exploratory material used so far. We have already seen, in chapter 13, how to make a confirmatory X by Y fit with one independent variable: we use linear regression, which is strongly parallel to exploratory X by Y. Here we learn how to measure the strength of the relationship between Y and X_2 with X_1 controlled, or *partial correlation*. This is strongly parallel to the exploratory approach, except that we focus on the strength of the fit, rather than the fit itself.

To compute the partial correlation between two variables with a third controlled, one follows the same basic steps as in the previous chapter. The effects of the control variable, here X_1, are removed. That is, find $X_2' = X_2 - (b_2X_1 + a_2)$ and $Y' = Y - (b_1X_1 + a_1)$; but this time the b's and a's are found via linear regression, the confirmatory fitting method, rather than the exploratory X by Y. This having been done, all we need is the regression between X_2' and Y':

$$Y' = b_3X_2' + a_3.$$

The correlation that goes with this fit is the partial correlation of X_2 and Y with X_1 held constant.

We will also show a faster way to find a partial correlation by a computing formula. Finally, we will look at spurious correlation and causality, an important issue we have not yet touched on.

An Example of Partial Correlation

To underline the parallels between partial correlation and the approach used in the previous chapter, let's continue with the Angell data used there. Again, let us consider the relationship between heterogeneity and mobility

Table 19.1

*Necessary Numbers for Computing Partial Correlations
on Angell Data*

X_1 = Integration, X_2 = Logged Heterogeneity, Y = Mobility				
X_1	Y	$Y' = Y - bX_1 - a$	X_2	$X'_2 = X_2 - bX_1 - a$
19.0	15.0	3.809	1.31	− .0002
16.4	13.6	−2.352	1.34	.0328
15.8	17.6	.550	1.24	−.0665
15.2	14.7	−3.449	1.35	.0442
14.2	19.4	− .580	1.03	− .2746
14.0	18.6	−1.746	1.60	.2956
13.8	35.1	14.388	1.03	− .2741
13.0	15.8	−6.377	1.37	.0668
12.7	21.6	−1.126	1.28	−.0229
12.0	12.1	−11.908	1.66	.3580
11.3	22.1	−3.190	1.31	.0088
10.9	31.2	5.178	1.25	−.0508
9.6	38.9	10.498	1.09	− .2092
8.8	23.1	−6.767	1.47	.1717
7.2	35.8	3.003	1.21	−.0864

$$\sum Y' = -.069 \qquad \sum X'_2 = -.0068$$
$$\sum (Y')^2 = 628.3785 \qquad \sum (X'_2)^2 = .461886$$
$$\sum X'_2 Y' = -13.1394; \; r_{X_1 X_2} = .02; \; r_{X_1 Y} = -.64; \; r_{X_2 Y} = -.60.$$

with integration held constant. The first step is to remove the linear effects of integration on both mobility and heterogeneity. This has already been done for mobility back in chapter 13, where we found a linear regression fit:

$$Y = -1.831X_1 + 45.98$$
$$\text{Mobility} = -1.831 \, (\text{integration}) + 45.98$$

The residuals from this fit, or $Y' = Y - (1.831X_1 + 45.98)$, are recorded in Table 19.1. We also remove the linear effects of integration from logged heterogeneity. We used logged heterogeneity because we have seen from the exploratory work that it will be useful to transform heterogeneity; this will also keep the confirmatory and exploratory approaches as similar as possible. Further, recall the plots of integration with heterogeneity and with logged heterogeneity in the previous chapter. The plot with logged heterogeneity is more nearly a regular oval of points so it better satisfies regression assumptions. Partial correlation comes out of a sequence of regressions, so the usual assumptions for linear regressions are expected to hold (review chapter 13 if you have forgotten those assumptions). Using the standard linear regression formulae from chapter 13, we find

$$X_2 = .00117X_1 + 1.288$$
$$\text{Heterogeneity} = .00117 \, (\text{integration}) + 1.288$$

(a fit rather like the exploratory one, though this line is even flatter). The residuals, $X_2' = X_2 - .00117X_1 - 1.288$, are recorded in Table 19.1. Since we are doing a confirmatory technique involving a lot of arithmetic, rounding error may become important, so we have kept more significant digits for Y' and X_2' than we would in exploratory work.

Next we plot Y' and X_2' in Table 19.2, which shows the relationship between heterogeneity and mobility when integration is held constant. This plot looks very much like the parallel exploratory one, Table 18.7. Both plots were produced in the same way: linear effects of X_1 on both Y and X_2 were found and removed, then the residuals were plotted to show how Y and X_2 might be related in the absence of X_1. These data are well-behaved, with the linear fits to X_1 similar in the exploratory and confirmatory versions, so the residuals are very similar also; thus the two plots (19.2 and 18.7) look much alike.

Carrying on with the confirmatory analysis, let's measure the strength of the fit between heterogeneity and mobility with integration controlled. Using the standard formula, we simply find the correlation of X' and Y'_2:

$$r_{Y'X_2'} = \frac{N\sum X_2'Y' - (\sum X_2')(\sum Y')}{\sqrt{[N\sum(X_2')^2 - (\sum X_2')^2][N\sum(Y')^2 - (\sum Y')^2]}}$$

$$= \frac{15(-13.1394) - (-.0068)(-.069)}{\sqrt{[15(.461886) - .00004624][15(628.3785) - .004761]}}$$

$$= -.77$$

Table 19.2

Heterogeneity and Mobility, Integration Controlled

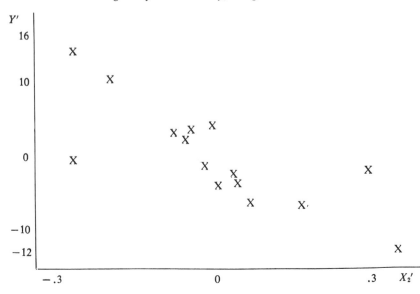

This is called the partial correlation of mobility and heterogeneity, holding integration constant. It is easier to express the strength of this partial relationship in terms of r^2, the squared correlation, here $(-.77)^2 = .59$; that is, heterogeneity accounts for 59% of the variation in mobility when integration is controlled. The amount not explained, or $1 - .59 = .41$ corresponds to the exploratory dq ratio, which we found in the last chapter to be $\dfrac{dq\ Y''}{dq\ Y'} = .60$. Both approaches suggest that after the effects of integration are removed, heterogeneity has much to add to our understanding of mobility.

We will not discuss these results here since the patterns are much the same as in the exploratory analysis. But we will note that in the confirmatory analysis, too, the relationship between heterogeneity and mobility is stronger after controlling integration. Without controls, the "zero-order" correlation of logged heterogeneity and mobility is $-.60$, so heterogeneity explains only about 36% of the variation in mobility. After controlling integration, as we just found, heterogeneity accounts for 59% of mobility, more than half again as much. Let us repeat that controlling one variable will not always strengthen the ties between other variables. Sometimes it will weaken or erase other ties, or have no effect on them, or reverse their direction: anything can happen. About the only way to find out what will happen is to try it and see, to control your X_1 and look at X_2' and Y'.

Finding Partial Correlations Directly

Controlling a variable is so useful that we would like to do it often, so it would be nice if we could do it quickly. The procedure we just used has some advantages (it uses nothing new, it is visual at every step, and one can clearly see what is happening) but it's not exactly speedy. Fortunately there is a simple formula for computing the partial correlation:

$$\text{partial correlation} = r_{X_2Y.X_1} = \frac{r_{X_2Y} - (r_{X_2X_1})(r_{YX_1})}{\sqrt{1 - r^2_{X_2X_1}}\ \sqrt{1 - r^2_{YX_1}}}$$

There is a bit of new notation here, so let's go through it part by part:

$r_{X_2Y.X_1} =$ partial correlation of X_2 and Y with X_1 controlled

$r_{X_2Y} - (r_{X_2X_1})(r_{Y\ X_1})$ This top part of the $r_{X_2Y.X_2}$ formula just puts simple correlations together, and does so in a reasonable way. You start with the r for X_2 and Y, the relationship before controlling for X_1; then you remove (subtract) the correlation of X_1 with Y and X_2 (i.e. $r_{X_1X_2}$). This makes sense since the idea is to remove the effects of X_1.

$$\sqrt{(1 - r^2_{X_2Y_1})}\sqrt{(1 - r^2_{YX_1})}$$ This bottom part of the $r_{X_2Y.X_1}$ formula is also based on simple correlations and also makes sense. We know that $1 - r^2$ tells us how much of a dependent variable is *not* explained: so here we have the amount of X_2 that X_1 does not explain and the amount of Y that X_1 does not explain. This product tells us how much action remains after X_1 is controlled; it is a kind of norming or standardizing factor which ensures that our partial correlation will go from -1 to $+1$ just like a correlation of raw data.

The partial correlation formula is another one of those things which are easier to do than explain: plugging in the numbers is no trouble. In our example,

$$r_{X_2Y.X_1} = \frac{-.60 - (.02)(-.64)}{\sqrt{1 - .0004}\sqrt{1 - .41}}$$

$$= \frac{-.59}{(1)(.77)}$$

$$= -.77$$

This is the same figure we got by the longer, but numerically identical, route of finding and correlating X'_2 and Y'.

Significance Testing for Partial Correlations

Since the partial correlation is a correlation, a correlation between residuals, we can treat is as such; most importantly, we can test the significance of a partial correlation in almost exactly the same way as we test a simple correlation. Find

$$F_{1,N-3} = \left[\frac{r^2_{X_2Y.X_1}}{1 - r^2_{X_2Y.X_1}}\right](N-3)$$

Once again we find the ratio of explained to unexplained variance (the partial r squared over one minus the partial r squared) and multiply it by the degrees of freedom, here $N - 3$. The only new wrinkle as compared to the simple correlation procedure in the previous chapter is this: the degrees of freedom become 1 and $N - 3$ instead of 1 and $N - 2$. We have "used up" one more degree of freedom because we have used one more variable (we controlled for X_1).

Let's try this for our example, assuming (perhaps not too accurately) that our data come from a random sample. The square of the partial correlation between heterogeneity and mobility with integration controlled is $r^2_{X_2 Y \cdot X_1} = .59$ so

$$F_{1,12} = \left(\frac{.59}{1 - .59}\right) \quad (12)$$

$$= 17.268$$

which is significant beyond the 1% level. So the apparent effect of heterogeneity on mobility, controlling integration, does not seem to be a mere fluke of random sampling. We should point out that we can't tell if mobility is having effects on heterogeneity, or heterogeneity is affecting mobility. Like the simple correlation, the partial correlation is symmetric: one can't tell whether heterogeneity is the independent variable and mobility is the dependent variable, or vice versa.

It is common to observe that a large correlation between X and Y doesn't necessarily mean that X is the cause of Y. But the matter need not rest here. Since this is an easy chapter, and since partial correlations can shed useful light on questions of causality, let's look now at the issue of spurious correlation and causation.

Related Variables and Causal Relationships

We can all probably think of numerous instances where variables appear to be related but causation is absent ("I only have to light a cigarette for the bus to come!"). It would be useful, though, if we had some techniques for dealing with spurious correlations. Let's look at a few examples.

Did you know that reading speed and length of thumb are positively correlated in the universe, and quite strongly too? Does that mean that they are causally related? If you are having trouble getting all your assigned reading done, should you get silicone injections in the tips of your thumbs or have them stretched on a rack? Hardly. Nor will reading more briskly make your thumbs grow. There is a relationship between these variables, but it's not causal. So why are they related? People with small thumbs tend to be small people, often children, and children generally read more slowly than adults. As age increases, so do both thumb length and reading speed. Therefore, if we control for age, the correlation between thumb length and reading speed will disappear. We can sum up the situation in a little diagram with arrows representing causal relationships, marking the arrows with a "+" if the relationship is positive and a "−" if the relationship is negative:

$$\text{AGE} \underset{+ \;\nearrow}{\overset{+ \;\nearrow}{<}} \begin{array}{l} \text{THUMB LENGTH} \\ \text{READING SPEED} \end{array}$$

Age is causally related to both thumb length and reading speed, both are by-products of maturation. Thumb length and reading speed are in no way causally related to each other (no arrow between them). However, thumb length and reading speed are positively correlated because each is related to age. Such a relationship is called a "spurious correlation": a correlation between two variables that do not have effects on each other, but are related because of the shared effect of some other variable or variables. Spurious relationships can be identified easily if you have information about the variable that is affecting the spurious pair; control for this variable and see if the relationship disappears.

Let's consider another example: the per capita expenditure on alcoholic beverages over time has a strong positive relationship with the average salary of clergymen. This sounds as though the only way we can keep people sober is to keep the clergy poor. This is probably false, so we'll assume that clerical income has no causal effect on expenditure on alcohol. It is barely possible that there is some causal link in the other direction, however: perhaps increased expenditure on alcohol leads to increased social problems and thus to increased demand for clerical services. But the most likely possibility is that this is a spurious correlation again. After all, both salaries and luxury expenditures tend to be related to overall wealth in the society. We could have something like this:

$$\text{Per capita GNP} \begin{cases} \xrightarrow{+} \text{per capita expenditure on alcohol} \\ \xrightarrow{+} \text{clerical salaries} \end{cases}$$

Then controlling per capita GNP should wipe out the correlation between clerical salaries and spending on alcohol.

Partial Correlations and Causality: An Example

Let's look at a small example including actual correlations so that we can see how partial correlations help in clarifying possible causal connections. Turning once again to the World Handbook, we find that death rates per 1000 population are inversely related to urbanization ($r = -.33$). Urbanization here is defined as the percentage of population residing in communities with a population in excess of 20 000. Now, there are many ways that this could be causally meaningful, for example, there are usually more doctors and hospitals, better sanitation, etc., in urban areas, but even these are actually aspects of another variable, general wealth. After all, hospitals and sewage systems are perquisites of the wealthy countries, and so is a large urban population. A high rate of urbanization implies, after all, that a sizeable proportion of the population has been freed from primary production. Let's examine how per capita GNP is correlated with the other variables.

	GNP per capita	Death rate per 1000	Urbanization
GNP per capita	1.0		
Death rate (per 1000)	−.41	1.0	
Urbanization	.71	−.33	1.0

This *correlation matrix* is a conventional, compact way to present correlations among variables and is especially handy if a lot of variables are involved. The main diagonal, upper left to lower right, gives correlations of variables with themselves; all these correlations are 1.0, of course, so they are often omitted. The area above the main diagonal is left blank because the entries there would just repeat the information given below the main diagonal (remember, correlations are symmetric).

The model we are suggesting is one where national wealth is the underlying cause of both an increase in urbanization and a decrease in the death rate; e.g.

If this is true, then the correlation between urbanization and death rate should vanish when GNP per capita is controlled. Let's try it. Plugging in the correlations we get:

$$r_{\text{UD.G}} = \frac{-.33 - (-.41)(.71)}{\sqrt{1 - (-.41)^2}\sqrt{1 - (.71)^2}} = -.06$$

It does virtually vanish. This is strong support for the model. However, it is also conceptually possible for an alternative causal structure to be at work here; wealth could be causing urbanization, as before, but city life might just be safer, for the reasons mentioned above as well as others. Then the model would look like this:

$$\text{GNP per capita} \xrightarrow{+} \text{Urbanization} \xrightarrow{-} \text{Death rate}$$

GNP per capita and death rate should have a zero partial because they are linked only through urbanization. Such a variable which acts as the causal link between two others is known as an intervening variable. If this model is correct, the $r_{\text{GD.U}}$ should vanish. Let's try it.

$$r_{\text{GD.U}} = \frac{-.41 - (.71)(-.33)}{\sqrt{1 - .71^2}\sqrt{1 - (-.33)^2}} = -.27$$

It is clear from this that the first model, in which wealth causes both urbanization and reduced death rate, is definitely preferable to this one.

In general, partial correlations can be very helpful in examining alternative causal possibilities, for those that do not conform to the observed partials can be eliminated. Perhaps there will be more than one plausible view that does match the observed partials; if so, turn to theory or consider the roles of some further variables. Simon (1954) describes some of the conclusions that can be drawn from partial correlations if a few simple assumptions are met. We will not go into this further here, but will just remind you not to jump to conclusions about causal relationships. It is possible for two variables to be correlated, but have no causal connection to each other. It is also true that two variables can seem unrelated, having a zero-order correlation of zero for example; yet when a third variable is controlled, their causal connection becomes manifest. Perhaps something like this was going on in the Angell data, where the connection between heterogeneity and mobility became much stronger after integration was controlled.

Exploratory and Confirmatory

We have seen that the exploratory and confirmatory techniques for making a second linear fit are directly analogous. In both cases, the dependent variable Y' (the residuals from Y controlling for X_1) is fitted to the new variable X_2' (X_2 with the linear effect of X_1 removed). This control of X_1 in both Y and X_2 clears away the underbrush, thus clarifying the $X_2 - Y$ relationship. The exploratory and confirmatory procedures are exactly the same, except for the kind of linear fit (exploratory or confirmatory) that is used.

When the controlled relationship between Y' and X_2' is examined, the amount of Y' unexplained by X_2' is

$$\frac{dq\ Y''}{dq\ Y'}$$

in the exploratory analysis, and is

$$1 - r^2_{X_2 Y \cdot X_1}$$

in the confirmatory analysis.

Homework

For the last chapter's homework you found a second layer of X by Y fit in exploratory terms. Now do the confirmatory equivalent, not forgetting a significance test and discussion of it. Consider one or two patterns of causal relationships that might exist among your variables.

20

Multiple Regression

In the previous two chapters we presented ways to examine situations involving two independent variables by looking at the effects of each in sequence; the process consisted of first making an ordinary linear fit for X_1 and Y, then looking at the relationship between X_2 and Y with X_1 controlled. Both exploratory and confirmatory approaches were given. These are useful techniques, but they do not tell us all we might like to know about two independent variables. In particular, they do not show us how the two can work together to make a combined fit for Y. *Multiple regression* is a confirmatory technique which combines X_1 and X_2 to predict Y using both variables at once. There are exploratory parallels to multiple regression (sometimes called "robust regression") but they go a bit beyond the fast and easy paper-and-pencil exploratory methods we've stuck to in this book. So rather than introduce more complex exploratory procedures, we'll point out ways that exploratory thinking can be combined with multiple regression procedures.

We will begin the chapter by describing the simplest kind of multiple regression, in which two independent variables are added together to make a combined fit. This is actually quite a familiar idea. Recall what we did in two-way elementary analysis. We predicted Y from a simple combination of the row variable and the column variable:

$$Y = \text{Row Effect} + \text{Column Effect} + \text{Overall Level}$$

For basic multiple regression, the effects of two independent variables are added together in a similar way:

$$Y = b_1 X_1 + b_2 X_2 + a$$

To make such a fit we have to find values for b_1, b_2 and a; the multiple regression computations are designed to find values which minimize the sum of the squared residuals from the fit (this is the "least squares criterion" again, the same one used in simple linear regression in chapter 13). We will describe the role and meaning of b_1, b_2 and a, but we will give only a few formulae for computing such values and these formulae will be left to an optional appendix at the end of the book. While the computations for most multiple regressions are simple in principle, they are very time-consuming in practice, so that the work is almost always done by computer. Every computer package (surely including one available to you through your instructors) has an inexpensive multiple regression program that is easy to use.

Once made, a multiple regression fit can be evaluated with a *multiple correlation coefficient*, which turns out to be just a special use of the correlation we met in chapter 13. The test for a multiple correlation is also very similar to the test for a simple correlation as done in chapter 13.

With basic multiple regression under your belt, it's easy to move on to a few simple and very useful variations. These extensions include making a curvy fit, making interaction fits, and working with additional independent variables.

Combining Two Variables

Let's start with two independent variables added together (a "linear combination" of two independent variables):

$$Y = b_1X_1 + b_2X_2 + a$$

We said above that the "effect" of X_1 is added to the "effect" of X_2, just as row and column variables are added in two-way analysis. Here the "effect" of each variable is worked in through the *regression weights* or the b_i values by which the X variables are multiplied. These weights are analogous to slopes in simple linear regression:

b_1 = the change in Y for a unit change in X_1, holding X_2 constant
b_2 = the change in Y for a unit change in X_2, holding X_1 constant

The new wrinkle here, compared to simple linear regression, is the part about holding the other independent variable constant. Why do we do that? Well, b_1X_1 should reflect the separate, distinct effect of X_1 on Y while b_2X_2 should reflect the separate, distinct effect of X_2; then we can add b_1X_1 and b_2X_2 together without duplication, without adding the same effect in twice.

Consider the Angell example again. We want to find

mobility = b_1 (integration) + b_2 (logged heterogeneity) + a

so that we can see how well integration and mobility together can predict Y, a question we have not been able to answer before. The multiple regression fit turns out to be:

$$Y = -1.78X_1 - 28.3X_2 + 82.2$$

where X_1 = integration and X_2 = logged heterogeneity as in the preceding chapter. (If you would like to see how the numbers were found, look in the appendix at the back of the book.) What does this fit tell us? Firstly, it says that when heterogeneity is held constant, integration has a negative effect on mobility. We can see this from the negative weight for integration, $b_1 = -1.78$. Secondly, it tells us that when integration is held constant, heterogeneity has a negative effect on mobility. We can see this from the negative weight for heterogeneity, $b_2 = -28.3$. If you would like to get a more vivid impression of what these regression weights mean, look back to chapter 19. Consider the relationship between logged heterogeneity and mobility, controlling integration (the plot is in Table 19.2). Suppose we do a simple linear regression of these two controlled variables (the numeric values are in Table 19.1). The slope for Y' and X'_2 is -28.4: the same, within rounding error, as the regression weight in the multiple regression above. Thus b_1 and b_2 are both slopes, but slopes with the other independent variable held constant.

The regression weights tell us the direction of each X's effect on Y with the other X controlled. Do they tell us any more? Unfortunately, no. It is especially important to note that they do not tell us the strength of each independent variable's separate effect on Y. This can be a problem because it is very tempting to think that the b's do reflect strength. For example, in the fit above it looks as though logged heterogeneity is substantially more important than integration because its weight is so much larger in absolute value (-28.3 versus -1.78, quite a difference). However, we just can't draw this conclusion: the problem is that the b's depend in part on how strongly each independent variable is related to Y, and also in part on the difference between the independent variable's scale and Y's scale. In our example, logged heterogeneity has a much smaller spread than mobility does, so logged heterogeneity must be multiplied by a large b_2 just to get $b_2 X_2$ into the same sort of units as Y.

You may recall that the same sort of problem cropped up in simple linear regression in chapter 13. At that time we pointed out that a linear fit could be made with standardized versions of X and Y to get a fit directly reflecting the real strength of relationship between X and Y: if Y^* and X^* are the standardized variables, the fit between them is just

$$Y^* = rX^*.$$

Standardizing eliminates the scale differences that can make interpretation of slopes misleading, leaving a nice simple picture involving nothing but the strength of the relationship. Why not try the same thing with multiple regression?

The Standardized Fit

We begin by standardizing all the variables used in the multiple regression:

$$Y* = \frac{Y - \overline{Y}}{\text{sd}_Y}$$

$$X*_1 = \frac{X_1 - \overline{X}_1}{\text{sd}_{X_1}}$$

$$X*_2 = \frac{X_2 - \overline{X}_2}{\text{sd}_{X_2}}$$

Then we do the same regression over again with the standardized variables to get a standardized multiple regression fit with standardized weights:

$$Y* = b_1^* X_1^* + b_2^* X_2^*$$

What should these new standardized regression weights be like? We still want to combine X_1 and X_2 to make a good combined fit predicting Y. How much weight should we give to each of the independent variables? Surely that should now depend only on how strongly they are related to Y. Take X_1, for instance. The more impact X_1 has on Y, aside from X_2's impact, the more weight X_1 should get. Similarly, the weight given to X_2 reflects the strength of X_2's effect on Y, with the effects of X_1 held constant. X_1 is held constant when considering X_2, and vice versa, so that the weights for each independent variable reflect the separate, distinct effect it has on Y. Then these distinct effects can be added up to get the overall fit above, in which

b_1^* = the effect of X_1^* on Y^*, holding X_2^* constant

b_2^* = the effect of X_2^* on Y^*, holding X_1^* constant

These $b*$ sound a lot like partial correlations, and indeed if you look at their formulae in the optional section you will see that they are very similar to partial correlations (though not identical). By looking at these $b*$ values one can immediately see both the relative importance of the X variables and the direction of their effects. Because $\overline{Y}^*$, $\overline{X}_1^*$ and $\overline{X}_2^*$ are all equal to zero, $a*$ is also zero, always.

Let's consider the Angell data again. If integration, mobility, and (logged) heterogeneity are standardized, the linear multiple regression fit for predicting mobility from the other two variables is

$$Y* = -.628X_1^* - .587X_2^*$$

mobility $= -.628$ (integration) $- .587$ (heterogeneity)

Now this means:

1. When integration is held constant, heterogeneity has a negative effect on mobility; we see this from the negative b_2^*, $-.587$, for heterogeneity. This is the same thing we learned from the raw weight b_2, and also from the partial correlation of heterogeneity and mobility with integration held constant, found in chapter 19.

2. When heterogeneity is held constant, integration has a negative effect on mobility; we see this from the negative weight $-.628$ for integration.

3. Integration and heterogeneity have about the same strength of effect, with integration being perhaps a bit stronger; we see this from the nearly equal b^* values, with integration's weight a little larger. Again, this is the same message given by the partials: $r_{X_1 Y.X_2} = -.79$ is slightly larger than $r_{X_2 Y.X_1} = -.77$. We could not see anything like this from the unstandardized regression.

Regression equations with standardized variables and standardized weights are easy to interpret because the weights mean what they appear to mean. Whenever possible, then, we will prefer to work with standardized variables and regression weights.

We should emphasize that the unstandardized and standardized versions of a regression are the same fit; it's easier to make sense of the standardized version, though, and we prefer it for that reason. On the other hand, the raw weights can sometimes be very useful. For example, Inkeles and Smith (1974) report a study of individual modernity in six developing nations. They wanted to know, among other things, the extent to which people are modernized through formal education and the extent to which they are modernized through modern work experience, that is, through working in a factory. They can and do report results using standardized weights, but they also report results using raw weights, in part because the raw weights have a clear interpretation: one can compare the modernity gained from a year of education to the modernity gained by a year of factory work. (See Table 19-3, Inkeles and Smith, 1974.)

Evaluating the Fit as a Whole

The fit described above combines two independent variables in the way that best predicts Y. The criterion for a good fit is the same as it was for simple linear regression: the squared residuals are minimized. The residuals are just

$$Y' = Y - (b_1 X_1 + b_2 X_2 + a)$$
$$= \text{observation} - \text{fit}.$$

Since multiple regression is designed to minimize squared residuals for all the data points, it will not be very resistant. Even though residuals from non-resistant fits are not entirely satisfactory, they are better than nothing. And since most computer programs are equipped to print out residuals, you should request and scrutinize them as a standard practice.

As always, we want some measure of how well the fit is working, of how close the predicted Y values are to the actual Y values. Well, we have two sets of numbers and we want to see how well they are related; why not just correlate them? The correlation of observed Y values and the Y values predicted from two or more X variables is called a *multiple correlation* and is symbolized as a capital R (to distinguish it from simple correlations using just one X_1). R goes from 0 to 1.0: if R is 0 there is no linear relationship between X_1 or X_2 or their additive combination and Y, while if R is 1.0 then X_1 and X_2 predict Y perfectly. A multiple correlation, unlike the r for just one independent variable, cannot be negative. Again the easiest thing to interpret is the squared multiple correlation, R^2, rather than R: R^2 is the proportion of the variance of Y that is accounted for by the multiple regression fit. For example, the R^2 for the Angell example is .76, which means that a linear combination of heterogeneity and integration explains 76% of the variation in mobility. Integration alone explained 41% and heterogeneity alone explained 36%, so we obviously do a lot better using the two variables together than we could do using them separately. This is partly because integration and heterogeneity are both strongly related to mobility but virtually unrelated to each other (their correlation is .02, remember) so they do not duplicate each other's efforts.

A Significance Test for R^2

There is a very simple test for R^2 that is very much like the F-tests for simple linear regression and for partial correlation.

The null and alternate hypotheses are:

H_0: $R^2 = 0$. In the universe, X_1 and X_2 have no linear effects on Y.
H_1: $R^2 \neq 0$. In the universe, X_1 and X_2 have a combined linear effect on Y.

To actually do the test find

$$F_{2,N-3} = \frac{R^2}{(1 - R^2)} \frac{(N - 3)}{2}$$

if you have two independent variables. Later in the chapter, we will see how this formula can be generalized. For the Angell example,

$$Y = .628X_1 - .587X_2$$
$$R^2 = .76$$

so the observed F value is

$$F_{2,12} = \frac{.76}{.24} \left(\frac{12}{2}\right) = 19$$

The critical value for $F_{2,12}$ at the 1% level is 6.93, so our F is much too high for H_0 to be retained. As always, the test is based on some assumptions about the data which should be tested ahead of time. Technically, the assumptions apply to the sub-batches of Y defined by combinations of values of X_1 and of X_2: given any (X_1, X_2) combination, Y should be normal, and the spread

Table 20.1

Y Within Levels of X_1 and X_2

X_2 Logged Heterogeneity	X_1 (Integration)	
	Under 13	13 and Over
Under 1.28	3 | 196 2 | 1 |	3 | 5 2 | 1 | 89
1.28 or Over	3 | 2 | 223 1 | 2	3 | 2 | 1 | 54596

of Y should be the same for every (X_1, X_2) combination. Now this is a hard set of assumptions! It is hard to visualize, and also hard to check. One could try something like Table 20.1, where we have broken X_1 and X_2 into high-low categories and found stems-and-leaves for Y. Clearly we need a larger number of cases before we can decide whether the four Y sub-batches are normal, or whether their variances are roughly equal. If we used a finer breakdown for X_1 and X_2 we would need still more cases and would have to go to still more trouble.

Fortunately multiple regression, like the other confirmatory techniques in this book, is very robust. The assumptions need only be met roughly; so they only have to be checked roughly. One reasonable approach is to plot Y by each of the independent variables and check to see whether the plots are roughly oval; this is easy to do and is worthwhile for other reasons as well, like checking for curvilinear relationships. We have already seen, in chapters 13 and 19, that the plots of mobility by integration and mobility by logged heterogeneity look fine. You can refine this approach a bit by plotting Y against one independent variable with the other held constant, for example as in Table 20.2 where we plot mobility by heterogeneity twice: once for integration high, once for integration low. Both the plots look very roughly oval. The plots are also useful for other reasons, as we will see shortly.

Table 20.2

Integration High (Over 13)   *Integration Low (13 and Under)*

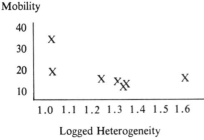
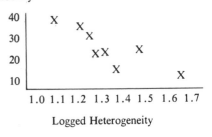

The data should also be based on a random sample, as always. This assumption may not be met for the Angell data, but we assumed it was for the sake of illustrating the test procedure.

Interpreting Multiple Regressions: More Examples

Since multiple regressions are usually done by computer, people working with multiple regressions spend most of their time interpreting regression fits provided for them by the computer or by a research article. To help you get used to reading multiple regression equations, we'll give a few more of them along with interpretations in words. The Angell example had two negative weights, so we'll present examples where both weights are positive as well as where one is positive and one negative.

First consider some regressions predicting occupational prestige in the United States and in Canada. In both countries, the prestige ratings of a large set of occupations have been found by asking a sample of people to rate occupations. Duncan (1961) argued that prestige in the U.S.A. should be related to the income and education of people in an occupation. He developed measures of X_1 (occupational income) and X_2 (occupational education) and used these to predict Y (the occupation's prestige rating). He found this equation (using raw weights):

$$Y = .59X_1 + .55X_2 - 6.0 \qquad R^2 = .83$$

Recently, Blishen and McRoberts (1976) found a similar multiple regression for Canada, using Canadian ratings of occupations and income and education measures based on the 1971 Canadian census. Rounding their equation to two significant digits to keep it parallel to Duncan's, it is:

$$Y = .30X_1 + .37X_2 + 12.0 \qquad R^2 = .84$$

What are these two equations saying? First, in both of them the weights for income and education are positive: the prestige of an occupation is higher if the people in it are better paid and better educated. Second, the pattern of weights looks roughly similar in both equations, suggesting that the underpinnings of prestige may be similar in both countries; this would be plausible given that the two nations are culturally and economically related. Third, both fits are very good, with over 80% of prestige explained by income and education combined. We cannot be sure of the relative importance of education versus income in determining prestige, since these are raw regression weights (it turns out that education and income are roughly equal in their effects). Why did we give raw weights? Only raw weights were reported by Blishen and McRoberts, because these weights were used for prediction. The multiple regression was done using only 85 occupations (there is a limit to the number whose prestige can be rated in practice) while there are hundreds reported in the census. The prestige of the remaining occupations can be estimated from the regression equation and the income and education information in the census.

A variable can be an independent variable in one analysis and a dependent variable in another. We have just seen income used to predict prestige; Stolzenberg (1975) tries to predict income. His Y is the median earnings of people in an occupation. To predict this, he uses $X_1 =$ median years of schooling and $X_2 =$ years of specific vocational preparation needed to perform the occupation's work at an average level (X_2 was based on ratings by experts; all the data came from the U.S. census). He found:

$$Y = 391.5X_1 + 412.1X_2 - 49.1 \qquad R^2 = .22$$

It is no surprise to find that occupations with more highly educated people and with more training requirements are better paid. It is more interesting to see that years of general schooling (X_1) have a positive effect on income even when specific job training is held constant and vice versa; both general and specific education go with increased earnings. However, together they explain only 22% of the variation in occupational income, so other independent variables should be considered.

Chase-Dunn (1975) uses multiple regression in a very different way from the previous authors. He is interested in the effects of "investment dependence," the "profits made by foreign direct investment in the 'host' country," on the rate of economic development. The effects could be positive (because investment stimulates economic growth by providing new capital) or it could be negative (because foreign investment is a form of foreign control and exploitation which will hinder development rather than fostering it). In any case, looking at the simple relationship between investment dependence and development clearly won't do; for example, if we find they are positively correlated, does that mean investment leads to development or does it mean more developed countries attract more investment? To clarify the causal position, Chase-Dunn used data from two points in time. Using logged GNP per capita to measure development, he looked at

1970 Development $= b_1$ (1950 Development) $+$
$\qquad\qquad\qquad\qquad b_2$ (1950–55 Investment Dependence) $+ a$

The 1950 development is included because countries more developed in the past are usually more developed in the present, aside from other factors like investment; by including past development in the regression we control for it. Then we can see what effect past investment has on current development controlled, or whether past investment dependence led to changes in development. The regression fit was:

$$Y = 1.32X_1 - .097X_2 - .17$$

(The R^2 is not given but is described as "high.") The weight for 1950 development is both positive and over 1.0, which suggests that development tends to increase over time; the countries with high GNP per capita in 1950 have even higher ones now. No surprise there. On the other hand the weight for 1950–55 investment dependence is negative, suggesting that countries with heavier foreign investment in the past have lost ground in development compared to others. The author uses other measures of development and finds the same result: investment dependence tends to hamper development.

Some Extensions of the Simple Case

Now that we know how to use two independent variables in a multiple linear regression, we can push the idea just a bit further to get ways of making curvilinear fits, working with additional X variables, and working with interaction. All of these are very useful capabilities: often the data are not linear, or Y is related to more than two other variables, or the independent variables have nonadditive effects. We have already seen some examples of curvy relationships in chapter 12 and of interaction effects in chapter 16.

Fitting a Curved Relationship

Back in chapter 12 we showed how to use transformations to straighten out one kind of curve: a curve with just one bend that is always increasing or always decreasing. Once the curve is straightened, either confirmatory or exploratory fits can be made. Fine; but what if the curve is a U or J shape, so it is not always increasing or always decreasing? Then we have to make this kind of fit:

$$Y = b_1X_1 + b_2X_1^2 + a$$

which will fit any one-bend curve well enough, even a U or J. In the exploratory chapter we left things there, since working with transformations was enough for one chapter: we did not show you how to make an exporatory fit of the form above, although this can be done fairly easily.

With multiple linear regression, making a fit like this is extremely easy. What difference is there between this fit and the one we just made earlier in the chapter? That is, what difference is there between

$$Y = b_1X_1 + b_2X_1^2 + a \quad \text{(curve fit)}$$

and

$$Y = b_1X_1 + b_2X_2 + a \text{ (regression with two independent variables)}$$

where X_2 is just X_1^2? It should be clear that there's no difference. So let's do that. We make a curvilinear fit by doing a multiple regression of a special kind; everything we said about multiple linear regression earlier still goes.

Let's consider our example again. Suppose we want to predict mobility with integration, and we want to know whether the fit should be linear or curvilinear. We must choose between these two equations:

$$Y = bX_1 + a \qquad \text{Linear fit}$$

$$Y = b_1X_1 + b_2X_1{}^2 + a \qquad \text{curvilinear fit}$$

Working out the equations for standardized data, we find

$$Y = -.64X_1 \qquad\qquad r^2 = .410$$

$$Y = -1.34X_1 + .706X_1{}^2 \qquad R^2 = .460$$

Should we make the curvilinear fit instead of the linear one? Probably not. The curved fit is more complex; it involves one more independent variable, $X_1{}^2$. Because of this we do not want to use it unless it has something substantial to add to the simpler linear fit. The amount of Y explained by the curved fit (46%) is only 5% greater than that explained by the linear fit (41%) which is not a great increase, especially since we are working with such a small number of points. You may wonder how to decide when a curvilinear fit "has something substantial to add": how much is substantial? One criterion is statistical significance: use the curvilinear fit if the R^2 for the curvilinear fit is significantly greater than the r^2 for the linear fit. Most computer packages for multiple regression provide this or equivalent information for you.

In this example, the confirmatory results agree with our earlier exploratory look at the relationship between mobility and integration; it did not look very curved, and the confirmatory work agrees that there isn't much of a curve. Once again, there is no substitute for looking at the plot. You may be able to see a curvilinear pattern right away, or you may see something even more complex.

Using More than Two Independent Variables

Multiple linear regression with three or more X variables is very much like regression with two X variables. Suppose we are using three X's: X_1, X_2 and X_3. The fit is

$$Y = b_1X_1 + b_2X_2 + b_3X_3 + a$$

The formulae for the b's get more complicated because more variables are involved, but the basic idea remains the same. Each slope gives the change in Y with a change in one independent variable, with all the other independent variables held constant. For example, b_1 is the change in Y given a unit change in X_1, holding X_2 and X_3 constant. If the unstandardized variables are used, the b's are not good guides to the relative importance of the variables, because they also include a scale correction. If the standardized versions of Y, X_1, X_2, and X_3 are used, then the b^*'s do reflect the relative strength of each X's contribution to the combined prediction for Y. The fit as a whole, or $Y = b_1X_1 + b_2X_2 + b_3X_3 + a$, is the "best" possible, where "best" means that the squared residuals are minimized. Finally, the multiple correlation R is the correlation between the predicted values Y (or $(b_1X_1 + b_2X_2 + b_3X_3 + a)$) and the observed values of Y, as before. The test for R is modified a bit to allow for the fact that more variables are involved. Let k be the number of independent variables involved in a regression. Then the null hypothesis $R^2 = 0$ can be tested with

$$F_{k,N-k-1} = \frac{R^2}{1 - R^2} \left(\frac{N - k - 1}{k} \right)$$

If $k = 1$, we get the familiar formula for r^2 in a simple regression with just one X. If $k = 2$, we get the formula for the R^2 for two independent variables given earlier in this chapter.

Let us return to the six-nation study of individual modernity (Inkeles and Smith, 1974) for an example. What makes people more modern in their attitudes: more open to new experience and ready for change, more ready to hold opinions and respect those of others, more oriented to the future, more comfortable with time scheduling, more confident in their ability to control their own lives, more ambitious, more favourable toward technical skill, more informed about modern industry, and so on? An overall measure of modernity was used as the major dependent variable which was compared to many combinations of independent variables. One of the more important was education, mass media exposure, and factory experience; each of these should increase modernity by increasing a man's exposure to modern ideas and modern experiences. Separately, each is positively related to modernity. But how do they work in combination? Consider the standardized regression for factory workers in Argentina, for example:

Modernity = .48 (education) + .24 (mass media exposure)
+ .20 (factory experience)

We can easily see that each of the three variables makes a contribution to modernity, even with the other two variables controlled. Education is clearly the most important single influence on modernity but mass media and factory work are also important.

This six-nation study is an excellent example of how useful numeric fits can be in summarizing information. The same regression as shown for Argentina was run for Chile, East Pakistan, India, Israel, and Nigeria. It would be rather hard to get an overall feeling for all this just using plots; but it is easy with a summary table of the regression weights for all six regressions (Inkeles and Smith, 1974, Table 19-2). The results for all six nations can be quickly seen to be similar; this is a rather surprising and interesting result, suggesting that the processes of individual modernization are similar even in nations with very dissimilar social structures.

Using Interaction Terms

Suppose we suspect that a simple linear combination of X_1 and X_2 may not do justice to the situation because X_1 and X_2 have interactive effects, where interaction means the same thing here as it did in two-way analysis of variance or elementary analysis; the effects of X_1 are different for different values of X_2 or vice versa. In Table 20.2, which we asserted would come in handy for more than checking regression assumptions, we see clear indication of an interaction effect. The effect of logged heterogeneity is quite different for different levels of integration. When integration is high, the heterogeneity-mobility plot except for one point is essentially flat: there is little or no relationship. But when integration is low, the relationship between heterogeneity and integration is strongly negative. Clearly the combination of the two independent variables is important.

How could we work this into our regression fit procedures? Once again we can draw on what we learned in elementary analysis. There we found that interaction could often be easily fitted through an interaction term $RC = $ (Row Effect) $\times$ (Column Effect). Why not do the same for regression? Why not fit interaction with an interaction term X_1X_2? Table 20.3 gives some of the arithmetic such a fit requires. $X_1 = $ integration, $X_2 = $ logged

Table 20.3

A Fit for Interaction

X_1	X_2	X_1X_2	Y
19.0	1.31	24.89	15.0
16.4	1.34	21.98	13.6
15.8	1.24	19.59	17.6
15.2	1.35	20.52	14.7
14.2	1.03	14.63	19.4
14.0	1.60	22.40	18.6
13.8	1.03	14.21	35.1
13.0	1.37	17.81	15.8
12.7	1.28	16.26	21.6
12.0	1.66	19.92	12.1
11.3	1.31	14.80	22.1
10.9	1.25	13.63	31.2
9.6	1.09	10.46	38.9
8.8	1.47	12.94	23.1
7.2	1.21	8.71	35.8

$$Y = -1.576 \, X_1X_2 + 48.9$$

$$r = b\frac{sd_X}{sd_Y} = -1.576 \, \frac{4.647}{8.780}$$

$$= -.834$$

heterogeneity, and the third column is X_1X_2, their product; for example, the first entry in the X_1X_2 column is $24.89 = (19.0)(1.31)$. We create a new variable by multiplying the two independent variables together one case at a time. Then we can treat the new variable X_1X_2 just like any other variable. For example, we found the basic linear regression using just one independent variable, X_1X_2:

$$Y = -1.58X_1X_2 + 48.9 \qquad r^2 = .70$$

Compare this to the linear combination of X_1 and X_2 that we used earlier:

$$Y = -1.78X_1 - 28.3X_2 + 82.2 \qquad R^2 = .76$$

The single variable for interaction explains nearly as much of Y as the two independent variables used separately! This is a surprise. Until we looked at Table 20.2, we had no way to know that interaction between X_1 and X_2 might be this important. And it is important: it accounts for much more of Y than either variable used separately (the r^2 for integration and Y is .41, and the r^2 for heterogeneity and Y is .36), it explains nearly as much as their linear combination, $b_1X_1 + b_2X_2$, and it means that we only must fit one independent variable.

It must be worthwhile to take a hard look at the interaction pattern. Rather than make a lot of X by Y plots, which could be very hard to see as a whole, let's get the interaction into one table like those we used for ele-

Table 20.4

Mobility by Integration and Heterogeneity

	Mobility		
Integration	Log (Het) low (1.03–1.24)	Log (Het) medium (1.25–1.34)	Log (Het) high (1.35–1.66)
High (14.2–19.0)	17.6 19.4	15.0 13.6	14.7
Medium (12.0–14.0)	35.1	21.6	18.6 12.1 15.8
Low (7.2–11.3)	38.9 35.8	22.1 31.2	23.1

Means of Cell Entries Above

	Mobility		
Integration	Log (Het) low	Log (Het) medium	Log (Het) high
H	18.5	14.3	14.7
M	35.1	21.6	15.5
L	37.4	26.7	23.1

mentary analysis. In Table 20.4, the row variable is integration (high, medium, or low) and the column variable is logged heterogeneity (high, medium or low) while mobility values are entered in the cells. Except for the fact that heterogeneity has been logged, this is just a rearrangement of the original data in Table 11.1. There is a clear diagonal pattern: the mobility values decline pretty steadily as you go from the lower left to the upper right of this table. That is, mobility into and out of a city is very high when both integration and heterogeneity are very low, perhaps because low integration (or low welfare effort combined with high crime rate) makes a city an undesirable place to live while low heterogeneity (or a low proportion of nonwhites and foreign born) implies high enough SES so that people who want to leave can afford to do so; thus low integration and low heterogeneity imply both reasons for leaving and ability to leave, or high rates of outward mobility. On the other hand, mobility is at its lowest when integration and heterogeneity are both high, perhaps because there is little reason to leave and the nonwhite or foreign born could not easily afford to leave anyway. Fairly low levels of both integration and heterogeneity together seem needed before mobility gets very high. For example, moderate integration with high heterogeneity (or moderate heterogeneity with high integration) produces no more mobility than when both variables are high (14.3 or 15.5 versus 14.7). Finally, note that the amount of difference one variable makes depends on the value of the other. If integration is high then the difference between low and high heterogeneity is $18.5 - 14.7 = 3.8$, but if integration is low then the difference for low heterogeneity versus high is $37.4 - 23.1 = 14.3$, quite a bit more. In short, this is the same kind of interaction that we encountered in elementary analysis and it can be both fitted and discussed in similar ways.

Exploratory and Confirmatory

Obviously the confirmatory and exploratory materials tie in with each other in many ways in multiple regression problems. A multiple regression may be run as a test of ideas developed in an exploratory analysis. If so, remember that the data used for the test must be a new set of data. Often, if you have lots of cases, it's a good idea to explore a modest subset of the cases and then do the confirmatory work on the rest. When doing exploratory work, there is no limit to the number of fits you can try with a modest subset of data (or rather, the only limits are those set by your judgement, interest, and available time). But in confirmatory work it is best to make just a few simple fits if you have a small number of cases. Overly complex fits can look very impressive quite artificially. To give an extreme example, suppose you have just two cases and you make an X by Y fit: naturally the fit is perfect, since the two points can be connected with a straight line. Similarly, three cases can be perfectly fitted with two X variables, four cases with three X variables, and so on. In less extreme cases there are no hard and fast rules governing how complex a fit is justifiable for how many cases. You must use your judgement, much as we suggested in chapter 12 when we said that choosing a curved or straight fit depended on a number of things including the sample size and the strength of the fit. In the Angell example, we used only fifteen cases in order to keep the arithmetic simple; then we made a large number of fits, some with two independent variables. We have probably done more with those data than is entirely safe from a confirmatory point of view. It would be a good idea to take the fit or fits we like the best (probably the interaction fit) and test them anew on the cases we left out.

Before a multiple regression is run, the confirmatory assumptions should be tested, which involves exploratory thinking in checking for normality of the variables. After a regression is run, exploratory thinking comes in again when you try to interpret the results. For example, interpreting an interaction term may be a lot easier if you use a little of the data to make a table like that of Table 20.4. You should always get all the plots that your computer program can be persuaded to give so you can see the relationships; often one quick look will alert you to the distorting influence of a few extreme cases, or will make it clear that a curve fit was needed at some point. We will not go into plots in more detail here because the kind you can get depends on the program that has been made available to you. Whatever statistical package you are using, it is always possible to get the residuals from the regression and these should be carefully examined. First, you can plot the residuals against the independent variables; this will often suggest modifications in the fit if they are needed. Second, you can look over the extreme residuals for ideas about new variables that may be worth examining.

These uses of exploratory thinking are the same ones we became used to for simple linear regression; but they are even more important for multiple regression because it is easy to be seduced by the computer, to take its printout at face value instead of looking hard at the data to check the analysis.

Finally, there is a way to use multiple regression itself in a somewhat exploratory way. This procedure is called *stepwise regression*: most statistical packages have this option. Stepwise regression proceeds by steps in a way very similar to the exploratory layer of fit approach. In the first step, the machine runs a regression with just one independent variable: the one that does the best job in one-variable regression, which means the one with the biggest simple correlation (the biggest r). At the second step, the machine runs another regression with two variables: the one from the first step plus the one that adds the most to that (this means the one with the biggest partial correlation with the first step independent variable controlled). At the third step, the machine examines the independent variables not yet used and again adds in the one that improves the R^2 the most. This process may be continued; at each step, the independent variable with the most to add is added to the fit. The process stops when there are no more independent variables or whenever there are no more that raise the R^2 enough to bother with, whichever happens first. The program also does a significance test on the increase in R^2 from each new variable. This is a useful procedure if you have a lot of possible independent variables and are not sure which combination will do the best job in predicting Y. Stepwise regression can meaningfully be used in an exploratory spirit, as a way to get into the data quickly and get started thinking about it. But it is no substitute for thinking up meaningful explanations! Because the criteria for adding variables are completely statistical, stepwise regression sometimes can give rather peculiar results. Thus, after you have digested the stepwise results, you may well decide that the regression you want is a slightly different one, one with a more theoretically compelling mix of variables — even if the theoretically interesting version has a somewhat smaller R^2.

Multiple regression is a flexible and widely used technique. We have dealt with a few of the more familiar uses of the approach. There are many other useful extensions of multiple regression which you will meet in later courses and more advanced texts.

Fifth Review

The following data were collected by Norman Shulman as part of his research for his doctorate. We consider only respondents living in East York, at that time a Toronto residential area with many long-time residents of British origin. Shulman asked his respondents to describe both themselves and their intimates, or the up to six people they felt closest to; his overall goal was an understanding of networks of close ties. For some background reading on networks, you might want to look at Elizabeth Bott, *Family and Social Network* (1971); Michael Young and Peter Willmott, *Family and Kinship in East London* (1957); Barry Wellman, Norman Shulman, and Jack Wayne, *Personal Communities* (forthcoming); or Shulman (1976).

We subsampled twenty-six of the married respondents in order to keep the data set of an easily manageable size. Below, we have left a space between data for different respondents. The first line of information for a respondent begins with his identification number and goes on with data on him and his first intimate. The next lines give data on the respondent's other intimates, with data on the respondent left out to make easier reading. If you keypunch the data, you will probably want to repeat the respondent's data on all of the cards for him and his intimates.

From a variety of variables we selected the following:

Proportion intimate kin: This is just the proportion of the respondent's intimates who are related to him by birth or marriage. The first person listed, number 96, has four intimates who are all relatives so his score here is 1.0.

Intimate density: The respondent was asked which of his intimates knew each other; then the ratio of actual relationships to all possible relationships was found. The second person listed, 89, had 6 intimates so there could have been $6 \times 5 = 30$ relationships among them. Only 6 such ties were reported, though, so the score on density is $\frac{6}{30} = .2$.

Closeness: The intimates were listed in order, from most to least intimate; this variable gives the intimacy rank. Note that higher values on this variable mean *less* closeness. Many of the respondents did not give six intimates.

Interactions last 30 days: The respondent reported how often he had seen each intimate in the last 30 days, and how often he had telephoned each one in the last 30 days. These figures were added to get an overall measure of interactions in the last 30 days. The figures here are approximate, especially for higher values. For example, the first person listed reported seeing his closest intimate 3–5 times and phoning him 3–5 times; we assumed he saw and phoned 4 times each, for a total of 8 interactions. But the real value could be from 6 to 10.

Ego gives help; Ego gets help: The fifth and sixth variables record respectively how often the respondent gave help to an intimate with the intimate's problems, and how often the respondent got help from an intimate with the respondent's problems. The scores mean: 1, often; 2, occasionally; 3, rarely; 4, once; 5, never. Note that higher values on these variables mean that *less* help was given or received.

Length of residence: This tells us how long the respondent had lived in his present home at the time of the interview. The codes mean: 1, under a year; 2, 1–2 years; 3, 3–5 years; 4, 5–10 years; 5, 10–20 years; 6, over twenty years.

Length of marriage: Here the codes mean: 1, under a year; 2, 1–5 years; 3, 6–10 years; 4, 10–20 years; 5, 20–30 years; 6, 31–40 years; 7, over 40 years.

Number of neighbours known; Number of neighbours visited: The ninth and tenth variables have the same coding: 1, none; 2, 1; 3, 2–3; 4, 4–5; 5, 6–10; 6, 10–20; 7, over twenty.

Kin: This variable just tells us which of the intimates are related to the respondent; if an intimate is a relative, he is scored 1, and if not he is scored zero.

Table VR.1

Data on Networks of Close Ties

Resp #	Proportion Int Kin	Int Density	Closeness	Interactions last 30 days	Ego gives help	Ego gets help	Length residence	Length marriage	# Neighbours known	# Neighbours visited	KIN = 1
96	1.0	1.0	1	8	1	2	5	4	6	4	1
			2	3	2	2					1
			3	6	2	5					1
			4	4	1	5					1
89	.5	.2	1	0	3	3	5	5	4	1	1
			2	0	5	3					1
			3	12	2	1					1
			4	24	1	1					0
			5	6	4	5					0
			6	10	5	1					0

Table VR.1 (cont.)

Data on Networks of Close Ties

Resp #	Proportion Int Kin	Int Density	Closeness	Interactions last 30 days	Ego gives help	Ego gets help	Length residence	Length marriage	# Neighbours known	# Neighbours visited	KIN = 1
84	.4	.8	1	4	5	5	5	6	3	3	1
			2	2	5	5					1
			3	0	5	5					0
			4	15	5	5					0
			5	15	5	5					0
76	.4	.9	1	8	2	5	4	6	4	1	1
			2	8	5	5					0
			3	8	5	5					0
			4	1	5	4					1
			5	8	5	5					0
72	.67	1.0	1	4	5	5	4	4	6	4	1
			2	10	5	2					1
			3	10	5	5					0
65	.5	.67	1	19	3	5	4	4	5	1	0
			2	6	5	5					0
			3	8	5	5					1
			4	12	5	5					1
54	.75	1.0	1	5	2	1	3	6	3	2	1
			2	8	2	1					1
			3	1	5	2					1
			4	12	1	2					0
48	.4	.7	1	0	2	5	5	4	6	5	0
			2	8	2	2					1
			3	4	2	5					0
			4	0	3	5					0
			5	5	2	3					1
42	.67	.8	1	2	5	2	3	4	1	1	0
			2	15	2	2					0
			3	12	2	4					1
			4	4	5	5					1
			5	34	2	2					1
			6	5	1	5					1
194	.25	.33	1	5	2	2	5	4	5	1	1
			2	3	2	2					0
			3	0	5	5					0
			4	0	5	5					0

Table VR.1 (cont.)

Data on Networks of Close Ties

Resp #	Proportion Int Kin	Int Density	Closeness	Interactions last 30 days	Ego gives help	Ego gets help	Length residence	Length marriage	# Neighbours known	# Neighbours visited	KIN = 1
189	.6	1.0	1	45	3	3	6	6	5	5	1
			2	16	2	5					1
			3	12	5	5					1
			4	4	5	5					0
			5	6	5	5					0
173	.75	1.0	1	45	5	5	3	4	1	1	1
			2	6	5	5					0
			3	19	5	5					1
			4	19	5	5					1
165	.5	.53	1	38	2	2	6	5	5	2	1
			2	10	5	5					0
			3	2	2	2					0
			4	19	2	2					0
			5	30	3	3					1
			6	2	3	3					1
159	.6	.75	1	2	4	5	2	2	1	1	0
			2	0	5	5					0
			3	2	2	3					1
			4	2	5	5					1
			5	2	5	5					1
131	1.0	1.0	1	12	5	5	5	6	6	1	1
			2	23	5	5					1
			3	8	5	5					1
			4	0	5	5					1
			5	0	5	5					1
			6	0	5	5					1
112	.4	1.0	1	8	3	1	5	6	7	3	0
			2	8	3	3					0
			3	8	5	2					1
			4	6	5	2					0
			5	34	2	3					1
179	.4	.4	1	50	2	2	2	2	3	1	0
			2	12	5	5					0
			3	4	5	5					0
			4	1	5	3					1
			5	1	5	3					1
129	.33	1.0	1	5	2	5	5	5	5	1	1
			2	8	5	5					0
			3	1	5	5					0
			4	1	4	5					0

Table VR.1 (cont.)

Data on Networks of Close Ties

Resp #	Proportion Int Kin	Int Density	Closeness	Interactions last 30 days	Ego gives help	Ego gets help	Length residence	Length marriage	# Neighbours known	# Neighbours visited	KIN = 1
			5	0	5	5					0
			6	1	5	5					1
71	.33	1.0	1	16	3	3	5	5	5	5	1
			2	4	5	5					0
			3	30	5	5					0
152	1.0	1.0	1	6	5	5	5	5	7	4	1
			2	2	5	5					1
			3	1	5	5					1
185	.0	1.0	1	16	5	5	4	4	7	4	0
			2	16	5	5					0
			3	8	3	3					0
			4	8	5	5					0
			5	6	5	5					0
			6	16	5	5					0
83	.67	1.0	1	28	5	5	5	4	6	1	1
			2	6	4	5					1
			3	23	5	5					0
110	.25	1.0	1	34	4	5	6	6	6	5	1
			2	5	5	5					0
			3	5	5	5					0
			4	4	5	5					0
23	.67	1.0	1	23	3	5	6	5	7	2	1
			2	19	2	5					1
			3	8	5	5					0
			4	4	5	5					0
			5	8	5	5					1
			6	4	5	5					1
22	.8	1.0	1	34	1	5	3	2	5	1	1
			2	8	1	5					1
			3	6	3	3					1
			4	8	2	5					1
			5	10	2	2					0
85	.5	.27	1	0	5	5	2	2	4	2	1
			2	0	5	5					1
			3	1	3	5					1
			4	4	5	5					0
			5	8	4	4					0
			6	3	5	5					0

Some Comments

Units of analysis
For some purposes, you will want to treat each of the lines of data as a case; for example, if your interest is in helping relationships then you have 124 relationships to examine. For other purposes, you would treat each respondent as a case. For example, if you want to see if longer marriage goes with longer residence then you have just twenty-six cases. You might like to keypunch all the data, then use all 124 cards for relational questions but pull out just one card per respondent for questions that relate just to the respondent himself. Otherwise, you'll "weight" respondents who name more intimates more heavily than those who name fewer.

Dummy variables
One of the variables (the last) is a dummy variable or one with only two values: the intimate is kin or not kin to the respondent. Such a variable is categorical, not numeric, and should be used somewhat cautiously in a regression analysis. If kinship seems interesting, you might consider doing two analyses: one for kin alone, one for just non-kin.

Ordinal variables
Ordinal variables are not as well suited to regression or X by Y analysis as numeric variables are, but they can be used and often have to be. For example, we really cannot expect our respondents to remember exactly how often they helped or interacted with each of six people; an answer like "Oh, three or four times" is as much as we can expect and probably none too accurate anyway. The ordinal nature of most of the data means that the plots *cannot* look much like regular ovals, as we would like them to; the plots instead will tend to look like rectangles. You can still keep an eye out for unusual cases.

There are a lot of things you could do with this data set. Restrain yourself! Consider picking an especially interesting dependent variable and try to explain it using a few small subsets of the other variables. Write down your reasons for choosing these variables. Then analyze, discussing after each step. Don't pile up masses of printout and then try to make sense of them.

Appendices

Appendix A: Background Math

Negative Numbers

You may have gotten a little rusty at working with negative numbers. You'll need to work with them easily because we use them a great deal; for example, we often remove fits by subtraction, as in Table 4.5. The all-purpose guideline is: an even number of negative signs preceding a number makes it positive, an odd number makes it negative. So if you are subtracting a positive number (often a level) from a larger positive number, it's simple subtraction; e.g.

$$10 - 6 = 4.$$

However, if you subtract a number from a smaller number you get a negative answer, like this:

$$4 - 6 = -(6 - 4)$$
$$= -(2)$$
$$= -2.$$

That is, you find what the answer would be if the order of subtraction were reversed; then put a minus sign in front of it. Sometimes you will subtract negative numbers from positive numbers, such as

$$6 - (-4).$$

Now there are two minus signs in a row, and an even number of minus signs makes the number positive. So

$$6 - (-4) = 6 + 4$$
$$= 10.$$

Finally, you may subtract a negative number from a negative number, as in

$$-10 - (-4) \quad \text{or} \quad -2 - (-4).$$

Just take it in stages, first simplifying:

$$\begin{array}{ll} -10 + 4 & -2 + 4 \\ = -6 & = 2 \end{array}$$

In a string of signs the plus signs don't count, e.g.

$$-10 + (-6) = -10 - 6 = -16.$$

For practice, check some of our subtractions in Tables 4.5 and 4.8 (ch. 4). For example, the dq of the standardized summary values for the youngest batch is

$$dq = q_U - q_L = 0.3 - (-0.7) = 0.3 + 0.7 = 1.0.$$

Similar rules apply for multiplications involving minus signs. An odd number of negative values multiplied together gives a negative result, for example

$$(-6)(-8)(-2) = -96 \quad \text{and} -(6)(8)(2) = -96.$$

An even number of negative values multiplied together gives a positive result, for example

$$(6)(-8)(-2) = +96$$

Finally, the same idea goes for division:

$$\frac{6}{12} = .5 \quad \frac{-6}{12} = -.5 \quad \frac{-6}{-12} = .5 .$$

Significant Digits

The basic idea of significant digits is familiar to all of us. If someone says, "I make $10 649.00 a year," then we know that he is giving us a very exact report of his income (perhaps because he has just filled out his income tax form, or just moved to a new salary level; otherwise he would not be likely to know his salary so exactly). But if he says, "I make ten thousand a year," he can mean anything between nine thousand and eleven thousand. In the first case he has given us his income to five significant digits (10 649) or five digits that give us information beyond mere magnitude; he implies that he really has measured his income to the dollar. In the second case he gives us his income with only two significant digits (the 10 in ten thousand) plus an indication of magnitude (the thousand in ten thousand); the implication is that he only knows his income to the nearest thousand.

We can usually recognize degrees of accuracy in words, but they are not always so clear in numbers unless we use the appropriate way of recording the numbers. For example, how many significant digits are there in this income figure: $15 000? There is no way to be sure. Perhaps there are only two (1 and 5) because income is known only to the nearest thousand. Perhaps there are three (1, 5, and the first 0) because income is known to the nearest hundred; or perhaps there are four or even five. To avoid such ambiguity, the number of significant digits should be clearly indicated in some way. You owe this to your readers; they have the right to know how accurately your data have been measured, or how many significant figures are justified.

You can indicate the accuracy of measurement in words, for example by putting "to the nearest thousand" or "to the nearest hundred" at the bottom of a table of income figures. Do not report more significant figures than are justified. For example, if you know your income data is accurate to the nearest hundred then a figure like $54 943.00 is quite wrong because it gives the misleading impression that it is accurate to the penny. The figure should be reported as $54 900 with detailed information only to the hundreds.

The accuracy of measurement can also be indicated by reporting the numbers in a form often used by scientific workers. In this form a number is broken into two parts: a set of significant digits plus a power of ten which gives the magnitude of the number. The significant digit part is generally written with one digit to the left of the decimal place. For example, consider again an income of $54 943 where income is measured only to the hundreds with any accuracy. This number would be written

$$5.49 \times 10^4.$$

The first part, 5.49, gives all the significant digits justified by our accuracy of measurement: three of them. The second part gives the order of magnitude so that we can tell 54 900 from 5490 (which is 5.49×10^3) or from 549 (which is 5.49×10^2) and so on. The ambiguity mentioned above is easy to handle now. If we have an income figure of $15 000, the number of significant digits can be easily recorded. Say there are three; then we write 1.50×10^4. Say there are five; we write 1.5000×10^4.

Finding the right power of ten is easy: move the decimal place as many places over as necessary, and the number of places moved is the power of ten needed. If you move to the left, the power is positive. For example, above we found

$$1\underset{4\ \ 3\ \ 2\ \ 1}{5\ 0\ 0\ 0,} = 1.50 \times 10^4$$

If we have to move to the right, the power of ten is negative. For example, suppose we are recording the number .0015, with two significant digits:

$$\underset{1\ 2\ 3}{.0\ 0\ 1,}5 = 1.5 \times 10^{-3}$$

(Remember, 10^{-3} is $\frac{1}{10^3}$ or $\frac{1}{1000}$ or .001.)

Finally, note that we have been talking mostly about rules for presenting the original data. Values computed from the data may be reported to one or two more significant digits than the data itself. In the process of computing these values (like the means and variances introduced in chapter 3) lots of detail should be kept until the final figure is found; this avoids rounding error. Avoiding rounding error is usually less important in exploratory work than in confirmatory.

Appendix B: Some Proofs

Proof that total sum of squares is the sum of the "within" and the "between" sums of squares

The sum of squares from which the variance is computed is

$$\sum_i\sum_j(x_{ij} - \overline{\overline{x}})^2 = (N - 1)\,\text{VAR}$$
$$= \sum_i\sum_j[(x_{ij} - \overline{x}_i) + (\overline{x}_i - \overline{\overline{x}})]^2$$

That is, we've just added and subtracted the means of each group. This equals, by expanding the squared expression,

(1) $\sum_i\sum_j(x_{ij} - \overline{x}_i)^2 + \sum_i\sum_j(\overline{x}_i - \overline{\overline{x}})^2 + 2\sum\sum(x_{ij} - \overline{x}_i)(\overline{x}_i - \overline{\overline{x}})$.

Now the first term is just the sum of squares within groups; the second term is the sum of deviations of the group means from the grand mean, the between groups sum of squares. What about the third term,

$$2\sum_i\sum_j(x_{ij} - \overline{x}_i)(\overline{x}_i - \overline{\overline{x}})\,?$$

Now $(\overline{x}_i - \overline{\overline{x}})$ is the sum of each group mean minus the grand mean and when summing over j it is a constant. So the formula above becomes

$$2\sum_i[(\overline{x}_i - \overline{\overline{x}})\sum_j(x_{ij} - \overline{x}_i)]$$

The last term here, $\sum_j(x_{ij} - \overline{x}_i)$ is just the sum of the deviations of a batch of observations about the batch's mean, and that sum *must* equal zero (you might want to refresh your memory by looking at chapter 3). In fact, the other term, too, must equal zero, but it doesn't really matter; as long as one of them equals zero the whole product equals zero. Consequently, (1) becomes

$$\sum_i\sum_j(x_{ij} - \overline{\overline{x}})^2 = \sum_i\sum_j(x_{ij} - \overline{x})^2 + \sum_i\sum_j(\overline{x}_i - \overline{\overline{x}})^2$$

or the total SS = within groups SS + between groups SS.

Formulae for Two Independent Variables

Earlier we said that we would have an optional appendix showing how b's and R are computed when two independent variables are used. We include these formulae because some people like to know what the computer is up to, or like to read formulae to get a mathematical sense of what multiple regression does. Other people find formulae no help at all or find them deeply counter-productive. Read this section or not, accordingly. We will give no formulae for more complex multiple regressions (with three X variables, for example), not because the formulae are difficult but because they get very cumbersome.

Standardized Regression Weights

The computations for $b_i{}^*$ are quite straightforward and require nothing but the set of zero-order correlations:

$$b_1{}^* = \frac{r_{YX_1} - r_{YX_2}r_{X_1X_2}}{1 - r^2_{X_1X_2}}$$

In the text, the formulae for the standardized regression weights were described as being quite similar to those for the partial correlations. Compare $b_1{}^*$ to the formula for $r_{YX_1 \cdot X_2}$:

$$r_{YX_1 \cdot X_2} = \frac{r_{YX_1} - r_{YX_2}r_{X_1X_2}}{\sqrt{1 - r^2_{X_1X_2}} \, \sqrt{1 - r^2_{YX_2}}}$$

As you can see, the formulae are identical in the numerators though rather different in the denominators. $b_2{}^*$ is computed in an exactly analogous way.

Unstandardized Regression Weights

Let's look at the formula for b_1, the unstandardized coefficient for X_1:

$$b_1 = \frac{\text{sd}_Y}{\text{sd}_{X_1}} \, b_1{}^*$$

This equation is built up of sensible and familiar pieces. One part of b_1 is scale correction.

$$\frac{\text{sd}_Y}{\text{sd}_{X_1}}$$

gets from X_1's spread to Y's. First X_1's spread is removed (divided by) and then Y's spread replaces it (multiplied by).

If Y and X are standardized then $\text{sd}_Y{}^* = \text{sd}_{X_1}{}^* = 1$, so we get back to $b_1{}^*$ as the regression weight.

Scale includes level as well as spread; level differences are fixed up through a, which is (as usual) simple to find:

$$a = \overline{Y} - b_1\overline{X}_1 - b_2\overline{X}_2$$

If we are using standardized variables they all have zero means, so a is zero too.

Let's work out the values for the Angell example. We need to know these figures:

$$
\begin{array}{ll}
r_{X_1X_2} = \quad .02 & \text{sd}_Y = 8.780 \\[4pt]
r_{X_1Y} = -.64 & \text{sd}_{X_1} = 3.099 \\[4pt]
r_{X_2Y} = -.60 & \text{sd}_{X_2} = \quad .182
\end{array}
$$

Then we can find raw and/or standardized weights:

$$b_1 = \frac{sd_Y}{sd_{X_1}} \quad b_1^* = \frac{sd_Y}{sd_{X_1}} \frac{r_{X_1Y} - r_{X_1X_2}r_{X_2Y}}{1 - r^2{}_{X_1X_2}}$$

$$= \frac{8.780}{3.099} \cdot \frac{-.64 - (.02)(-.60)}{1 - .0004}$$

$$= \frac{8.780}{3.099} \cdot (-.628) .$$

So $b_1^* = -.628$ and $b_1 = -1.78$. We can do the same for heterogeneity, X_2:

$$b_2 = \frac{sd_Y}{sd_{X_2}} \cdot \frac{r_{X_2Y} - r_{X_1X_2}r_{X_1Y}}{1 - r^2{}_{X_1X_2}}$$

$$= \frac{8.780}{.182} \cdot \frac{-.60 - (.02)(-.64)}{1 - .0004}$$

$$= \frac{8.780}{.182} \cdot (-.587)$$

$$b_2 = -28.3 \qquad\qquad b_2^* = -.587$$

Finally we get a for the unstandardized regression:

$$a = \overline{Y} - b_1\overline{X}_1 - b_2\overline{X}_2$$

$$= 22.307 + 1.78\,(12.927) + 28.3\,(1.303)$$

$$= 82.2.$$

There are several alternative formulae for R^2. For example,

$$R^2 = r^2{}_{X_1Y} + (1 - r^2{}_{X_1Y})r^2{}_{X_2Y \cdot X_1}$$

$$= .4096 + (.5904)(.5929)$$

$$= .76 .$$

Appendix C: Statistical Tables

Table A.1

Random Sampling Numbers

15 77 01 64 69	69 58 40 81 16	60 20 00 84 22	28 26 46 66 36	86 66 17 34 40
85 40 51 40 10	15 33 94 11 65	57 62 94 04 99	05 57 22 71 77	99 68 12 11 14
47 69 35 90 95	16 17 45 86 29	16 70 48 02 00	59 33 93 28 58	34 32 24 34 07
13 26 87 40 20	40 81 46 08 09	74 99 16 92 99	85 19 01 23 11	74 00 79 41 63
10 55 33 20 47	54 16 86 11 16	59 34 71 55 84	03 48 17 60 13	38 71 23 91 83
05 06 67 26 77	14 85 40 52 68	60 41 94 98 18	62 20 94 03 71	60 26 45 17 92
65 50 89 18 74	42 07 50 15 69	86 97 40 25 88	14 17 73 92 07	93 11 93 15 15
59 68 53 31 55	73 47 16 49 79	69 80 76 16 60	58 53 07 04 53	66 94 94 18 18
31 31 05 36 48	75 16 00 21 11	42 44 84 46 84	83 20 49 17 12	21 93 34 61 16
91 59 46 44 45	49 25 36 12 07	25 90 89 55 25	83 47 17 23 93	99 56 14 60 16
63 59 73 21 67	80 00 25 58 25	72 06 12 86 74	54 79 70 85 88	71 58 21 98 48
89 72 47 46 94	78 56 10 65 97	84 79 42 31 49	94 15 41 13 09	45 43 03 82 81
70 51 21 03 18	50 21 99 49 73	06 99 19 24 96	39 43 10 14 12	94 08 55 54 70
14 15 99 60 44	62 72 38 18 36	63 92 61 55 93	77 66 82 10 91	81 51 67 01 47
92 46 90 39 99	64 08 00 97 27	54 96 63 40 54	34 70 27 48 18	68 59 91 83 32
81 23 17 13 01	37 57 92 16 34	15 80 90 25 64	67 77 29 95 84	80 84 84 87 22
87 54 42 46 56	28 89 02 06 98	59 90 74 13 38	98 66 23 20 23	90 55 31 83 48
74 73 84 98 13	11 48 25 33 39	27 36 08 99 57	60 42 88 68 25	22 89 67 83 16
94 55 14 00 97	32 51 92 47 03	92 33 73 20 21	29 77 37 06 98	64 63 34 31 43
69 21 94 26 20	73 90 70 92 76	49 14 60 34 43	90 51 72 11 07	75 94 19 49 40
82 36 36 89 29	87 70 08 71 98	49 00 89 89 99	29 08 02 72 32	68 16 29 82 19
25 06 22 30 87	87 44 48 90 91	38 53 10 60 29	40 07 58 97 84	09 04 33 56 72
82 37 97 60 92	76 39 17 84 34	67 65 52 89 90	62 97 04 33 81	91 27 56 46 35
83 71 07 22 15	17 55 56 82 62	88 83 86 38 14	63 89 39 81 90	25 62 58 68 87
73 13 79 15 12	18 34 22 24 75	56 47 45 22 81	30 82 38 34 52	57 48 30 34 17
91 28 00 57 30	92 12 38 95 21	15 70 78 50 88	01 07 90 72 77	99 53 04 34 73
33 47 55 62 57	08 21 77 31 05	64 74 04 93 42	20 19 09 71 46	37 32 69 69 89
56 66 25 32 38	64 70 26 27 67	77 40 04 34 63	98 99 89 31 16	12 90 50 28 96
88 40 52 02 29	82 69 34 50 21	74 00 91 27 52	98 72 03 45 65	30 89 71 45 91
87 63 88 23 62	51 07 69 59 02	89 49 14 98 53	41 92 36 07 76	85 37 84 37 47
32 25 21 15 08	82 34 57 57 35	22 03 33 48 84	37 37 29 38 37	89 76 25 09 69
44 61 88 23 13	01 59 47 64 04	99 59 96 20 30	87 31 33 69 45	58 48 00 88 48
94 44 08 67 79	41 61 41 15 60	11 88 83 24 82	24 07 78 61 89	42 58 88 22 16
13 24 40 09 00	65 46 38 61 12	90 62 41 11 59	85 18 42 61 29	88 76 04 21 80
78 27 84 05 99	85 75 67 80 05	57 05 71 70 21	31 99 99 06 96	53 99 25 13 63
42 39 30 02 34	99 46 68 45 15	19 74 15 50 17	44 80 13 86 38	40 45 82 13 44
04 52 43 96 38	13 83 80 72 34	20 84 56 19 49	59 14 85 42 99	71 16 34 33 79
82 85 77 30 16	69 32 46 46 30	84 20 68 72 98	94 62 63 59 44	00 89 06 15 87
38 48 84 88 24	55 46 48 60 06	90 08 83 83 98	40 90 88 25 26	85 74 55 80 85
91 19 05 68 22	58 04 63 21 16	23 38 25 43 32	98 94 65 35 35	16 91 07 12 43
54 81 87 21 31	40 46 17 62 63	99 71 14 12 64	51 68 50 60 78	22 69 51 08 37
65 43 75 12 91	20 36 25 57 92	33 65 95 48 75	00 06 65 25 90	16 29 34 14 43
49 98 71 31 80	59 57 32 43 07	85 06 64 75 27	29 17 06 11 30	68 70 97 87 21
03 98 68 89 39	71 87 32 14 99	42 10 25 37 30	08 27 75 43 97	54 20 69 93 50
56 04 21 34 92	89 81 52 15 12	84 11 12 66 87	47 21 06 86 08	35 39 52 28 99
48 09 36 95 36	20 82 53 32 89	92 68 50 88 17	37 92 02 23 43	63 24 69 69 91
23 97 10 96 57	74 07 95 26 44	93 08 43 30 41	86 45 74 33 78	84 33 38 79 78
43 97 55 45 98	35 69 45 96 80	46 26 39 96 33	60 20 73 30 79	17 19 08 47 28
40 05 08 50 79	89 58 19 86 48	27 98 99 24 08	94 19 15 81 29	82 14 35 88 93
66 97 10 69 02	25 36 43 71 76	00 67 56 12 69	07 89 55 63 31	50 72 20 33 36

Source: A. Hald, Statistical Tables and Formulas, © 1952 by John Wiley & Sons, Inc. Reprinted by permission of John Wiley and Sons, Inc.

Table A.2
The Standardized Normal Distribution

Z	.00	.01	.02	.03	.04	.05	.06	.07	.08	.09
.0	.5000	.4960	.4920	.4880	.4840	.4801	.4761	.4721	.4681	.4641
.1	.4602	.4562	.4522	.4483	.4443	.4404	.4364	.4325	.4286	.4247
.2	.4207	.4168	.4129	.4090	.4052	.4013	.3974	.3936	.3897	.3859
.3	.3821	.3783	.3745	.3707	.3669	.3632	.3594	.3557	.3520	.3483
.4	.3446	.3409	.3372	.3336	.3300	.3264	.3228	.3192	.3156	.3121
.5	.3085	.3050	.3015	.2981	.2945	.2912	.2877	.2843	.2810	.2776
.6	.2743	.2709	.2676	.2643	.2611	.2578	.2546	.2514	.2483	.2451
.7	.2420	.2389	.2358	.2327	.2297	.2266	.2236	.2206	.2177	.2148
.8	.2119	.2090	.2061	.2033	.2005	.1977	.1949	.1922	.1894	.1867
.9	.1841	.1814	.1788	.1762	.1736	.1711	.1685	.1660	.1635	.1611
1.0	.1587	.1562	.1539	.1515	.1492	.1469	.1446	.1423	.1401	.1379
1.1	.1357	.1335	.1314	.1292	.1271	.1251	.1230	.1210	.1190	.1170
1.2	.1151	.1131	.1112	.1093	.1075	.1056	.1038	.1020	.1003	.09853
1.3	.09680	.09510	.09342	.09176	.09012	.08851	.08691	.08534	.08379	.08226
1.4	.08076	.07927	.07780	.07636	.07493	.07353	.07215	.07078	.06944	.06811
1.5	.06681	.06552	.06426	.06301	.06178	.06057	.05938	.05821	.05705	.05592
1.6	.05480	.05370	.05262	.05155	.05050	.04947	.04846	.04746	.04648	.04551
1.7	.04457	.04363	.04272	.04182	.04093	.04006	.03920	.03836	.03754	.03673
1.8	.03593	.03515	.03438	.03362	.03288	.03216	.03144	.03074	.03005	.02938
1.9	.02872	.02807	.02743	.02680	.02619	.02559	.02500	.02442	.02385	.02330
2.0	.02275	.02222	.02169	.02118	.02068	.02018	.01970	.01923	.01876	.01831
2.1	.01786	.01743	.01700	.01659	.01618	.01578	.01539	.01500	.01463	.01426
2.2	.01390	.01355	.01321	.01287	.01255	.01222	.01191	.01160	.01130	.01101
2.3	.01072	.01044	.01017	$.0^2 9903$	$.0^2 9642$	$.0^2 9387$	$.0^2 9137$	$.0^2 8894$	$.0^2 8656$	$.0^2 8424$
2.4	$.0^2 8198$	$.0^2 7976$	$.0^2 7760$	$.0^2 7549$	$.0^2 7344$	$.0^2 7143$	$.0^2 6947$	$.0^2 6756$	$.0^2 6569$	$.0^2 6387$

Source: **A Hald, Statistical Tables and Formulas,** © 1952 by John Wiley and Sons, Inc. Reprinted by permission of John Wiley & Sons, Inc.

Table A.2 (cont.)

Z	.00	.01	.02	.03	.04	.05	.06	.07	.08	.09
2.5	$.0^{2}6210$	$.0^{2}6037$	$.0^{2}5868$	$.0^{2}5703$	$.0^{2}5543$	$.0^{2}5386$	$.0^{2}5234$	$.0^{2}5085$	$.0^{2}4940$	$.0^{2}4799$
2.6	$.0^{2}4661$	$.0^{2}4527$	$.0^{2}4396$	$.0^{2}4269$	$.0^{2}4145$	$.0^{2}4025$	$.0^{2}3907$	$.0^{2}3793$	$.0^{2}3681$	$.0^{2}3573$
2.7	$.0^{2}3467$	$.0^{2}3364$	$.0^{2}3264$	$.0^{2}3167$	$.0^{2}3072$	$.0^{2}2980$	$.0^{2}2890$	$.0^{2}2803$	$.0^{2}2718$	$.0^{2}2635$
2.8	$.0^{2}2555$	$.0^{2}2477$	$.0^{2}2401$	$.0^{2}2327$	$.0^{2}2256$	$.0^{2}2186$	$.0^{2}2118$	$.0^{2}2052$	$.0^{2}1988$	$.0^{2}1926$
2.9	$.0^{2}1866$	$.0^{2}1807$	$.0^{2}1750$	$.0^{2}1695$	$.0^{2}1641$	$.0^{2}1589$	$.0^{2}1538$	$.0^{2}1489$	$.0^{2}1441$	$.0^{2}1395$
3.0	$.0^{2}1350$	$.0^{2}1306$	$.0^{2}1264$	$.0^{2}1223$	$.0^{2}1183$	$.0^{2}1144$	$.0^{2}1107$	$.0^{2}1070$	$.0^{2}1035$	$.0^{2}1001$
3.1	$.0^{3}9676$	$.0^{3}9354$	$.0^{3}9043$	$.0^{3}8740$	$.0^{3}8447$	$.0^{3}8164$	$.0^{3}7888$	$.0^{3}7622$	$.0^{3}7364$	$.0^{3}7114$
3.2	$.0^{3}6871$	$.0^{3}6637$	$.0^{3}6410$	$.0^{3}6190$	$.0^{3}5976$	$.0^{3}5770$	$.0^{3}5571$	$.0^{3}5377$	$.0^{3}5190$	$.0^{3}5009$
3.3	$.0^{3}4834$	$.0^{3}4665$	$.0^{3}4501$	$.0^{3}4342$	$.0^{3}4189$	$.0^{3}4041$	$.0^{3}3897$	$.0^{3}3758$	$.0^{3}3624$	$.0^{3}3495$
3.4	$.0^{3}3369$	$.0^{3}3248$	$.0^{3}3131$	$.0^{3}3018$	$.0^{3}2909$	$.0^{3}2803$	$.0^{3}2701$	$.0^{3}2602$	$.0^{3}2507$	$.0^{3}2415$
3.5	$.0^{3}2326$	$.0^{3}2241$	$.0^{3}2158$	$.0^{3}2078$	$.0^{3}2001$	$.0^{3}1926$	$.0^{3}1854$	$.0^{3}1785$	$.0^{3}1718$	$.0^{3}1653$
3.6	$.0^{3}1591$	$.0^{3}1531$	$.0^{3}1473$	$.0^{3}1417$	$.0^{3}1363$	$.0^{3}1311$	$.0^{3}1261$	$.0^{3}1213$	$.0^{3}1166$	$.0^{3}1121$
3.7	$.0^{3}1078$	$.0^{3}1036$	$.0^{4}9961$	$.0^{4}9574$	$.0^{4}9201$	$.0^{4}8842$	$.0^{4}8496$	$.0^{4}8162$	$.0^{4}7841$	$.0^{4}7532$
3.8	$.0^{4}7235$	$.0^{4}6948$	$.0^{4}6673$	$.0^{4}6407$	$.0^{4}6152$	$.0^{4}5906$	$.0^{4}5669$	$.0^{4}5442$	$.0^{4}5223$	$.0^{4}5012$
3.9	$.0^{4}4810$	$.0^{4}4615$	$.0^{4}4427$	$.0^{4}4247$	$.0^{4}4074$	$.0^{4}3908$	$.0^{4}3747$	$.0^{4}3594$	$.0^{4}3446$	$.0^{4}3304$
4.0	$.0^{4}3167$	$.0^{4}3036$	$.0^{4}2910$	$.0^{4}2789$	$.0^{4}2673$	$.0^{4}2561$	$.0^{4}2454$	$.0^{4}2351$	$.0^{4}2252$	$.0^{4}2157$
4.1	$.0^{4}2066$	$.0^{4}1978$	$.0^{4}1894$	$.0^{4}1814$	$.0^{4}1737$	$.0^{4}1662$	$.0^{4}1591$	$.0^{4}1523$	$.0^{4}1458$	$.0^{4}1395$
4.2	$.0^{4}1335$	$.0^{4}1277$	$.0^{4}1222$	$.0^{4}1168$	$.0^{4}1118$	$.0^{4}1069$	$.0^{4}1022$	$.0^{5}9774$	$.0^{5}9345$	$.0^{5}8934$
4.3	$.0^{5}8540$	$.0^{5}8163$	$.0^{5}7801$	$.0^{5}7455$	$.0^{5}7124$	$.0^{5}6807$	$.0^{5}6503$	$.0^{5}6212$	$.0^{5}5934$	$.0^{5}5668$
4.4	$.0^{5}5413$	$.0^{5}5169$	$.0^{5}4935$	$.0^{5}4712$	$.0^{5}4498$	$.0^{5}4294$	$.0^{5}4098$	$.0^{5}3911$	$.0^{5}3732$	$.0^{5}3561$
4.5	$.0^{5}3398$	$.0^{5}3241$	$.0^{5}3092$	$.0^{5}2949$	$.0^{5}2813$	$.0^{5}2682$	$.0^{5}2558$	$.0^{5}2439$	$.0^{5}2325$	$.0^{5}2216$
4.6	$.0^{5}2112$	$.0^{5}2013$	$.0^{5}1919$	$.0^{5}1828$	$.0^{5}1742$	$.0^{5}1660$	$.0^{5}1581$	$.0^{5}1506$	$.0^{5}1434$	$.0^{5}1366$
4.7	$.0^{5}1301$	$.0^{5}1239$	$.0^{5}1179$	$.0^{5}1123$	$.0^{5}1069$	$.0^{5}1017$	$.0^{6}9680$	$.0^{6}9211$	$.0^{6}8765$	$.0^{6}8339$
4.8	$.0^{6}7933$	$.0^{6}7547$	$.0^{6}7178$	$.0^{6}6827$	$.0^{6}6492$	$.0^{6}6173$	$.0^{6}5869$	$.0^{6}5580$	$.0^{6}5304$	$.0^{6}5042$
4.9	$.0^{6}4792$	$.0^{6}4554$	$.0^{6}4327$	$.0^{6}4111$	$.0^{6}3906$	$.0^{6}3711$	$.0^{6}3525$	$.0^{6}3348$	$.0^{6}3179$	$.0^{6}3019$

Source: Hald, Statistical Tables and Formulas, 1952, p. 34.

Table A.3

*Critical Values for t
Significance Test*

df $(N-1)$	0.4 0.8	0.25 0.5	0.1 0.2	0.05 0.1	0.025 0.05	0.01 0.02	0.005 0.01	0.001 One tail 0.002 Two tails
1	0.325	1.000	3.078	6.314	12.706	31.821	63.657	318.31
2	.289	0.816	1.886	2.920	4.303	6.965	9.925	22.326
3	.277	.765	1.638	2.353	3.182	4.541	5.841	10.213
4	.271	.741	1.533	2.132	2.776	3.747	4.604	7.173
5	0.267	0.727	1.476	2.015	2.571	3.365	4.032	5.893
6	.265	.718	1.440	1.943	2.447	3.143	3.707	5.208
7	.263	.711	1.415	1.895	2.365	2.998	3.499	4.785
8	.262	.706	1.397	1.860	2.306	2.896	3.355	4.501
9	.261	.703	1.383	1.833	2.262	2.821	3.250	4.297
10	0.260	0.700	1.372	1.812	2.228	2.764	3.169	4.144
11	.260	.697	1.363	1.796	2.201	2.718	3.106	4.025
12	.259	.695	1.356	1.782	2.179	2.681	3.055	3.930
13	.259	.694	1.350	1.771	2.160	2.650	3.012	3.852
14	.258	.692	1.345	1.761	2.145	2.624	2.977	3.787
15	0.258	0.691	1.341	1.753	2.131	2.602	2.947	3.733
16	.258	.690	1.337	1.746	2.120	2.583	2.921	3.686
17	.257	.689	1.333	1.740	2.110	2.567	2.898	3.646
18	.257	.688	1.330	1.734	2.101	2.552	2.878	3.610
19	.257	.688	1.328	1.729	2.093	2.539	2.861	3.579
20	0.257	0.687	1.325	1.725	2.086	2.528	2.845	3.552
21	.257	.686	1.323	1.721	2.080	2.518	2.831	3.527
22	.256	.686	1.321	1.717	2.074	2.508	2.819	3.505
23	.256	.685	1.319	1.714	2.069	2.500	2.807	3.485
24	.256	.685	1.318	1.711	2.064	2.492	2.797	3.467
25	0.256	0.684	1.316	1.708	2.060	2.485	2.787	3.450
26	.256	.684	1.315	1.706	2.056	2.479	2.779	3.435
27	.256	.684	1.314	1.703	2.052	2.473	2.771	3.421
28	.256	.683	1.313	1.701	2.048	2.467	2.763	3.408
29	.256	.683	1.311	1.699	2.045	2.462	2.756	3.396
30	0.256	0.683	1.310	1.697	2.042	2.457	2.750	3.385
40	.255	.681	1.303	1.684	2.021	2.423	2.704	3.307
60	.254	.679	1.296	1.671	2.000	2.390	2.660	3.232
120	.254	.677	1.289	1.658	1.980	2.358	2.617	3.160
∞	.253	.674	1.282	1.645	1.960	2.326	2.576	3.090

Source: Table A.3 is taken from Table III of Fisher and Yates: *Statistical Tables for Biological, Agricultural and Medical Research*, published by Longman Group Ltd., London (previously published by Oliver and Boyd, Edinburgh), and by permission of the authors and publishers.

Table A.4
Critical Values for F, α = .05

df for Within	\multicolumn{19}{c}{df for Between}
	1	2	3	4	5	6	7	8	9	10	12	15	20	24	30	40	60	120	∞
1	161.4	199.5	215.7	224.6	230.2	234.0	236.8	238.9	240.5	241.9	243.9	245.9	248.0	249.1	250.1	251.1	252.2	253.3	254.3
2	18.51	19.00	19.16	19.25	19.30	19.33	19.35	19.37	19.38	19.40	19.41	19.43	19.45	19.45	19.46	19.47	19.48	19.49	19.50
3	10.13	9.55	9.28	9.12	9.01	8.94	8.89	8.85	8.81	8.79	8.74	8.70	8.66	8.64	8.62	8.59	8.57	8.55	8.53
4	7.71	6.94	6.59	6.39	6.26	6.16	6.09	6.04	6.00	5.96	5.91	5.86	5.80	5.77	5.75	5.72	5.69	5.66	5.63
5	6.61	5.79	5.41	5.19	5.05	4.95	4.88	4.82	4.77	4.74	4.68	4.62	4.56	4.53	4.50	4.46	4.43	4.40	4.36
6	5.99	5.14	4.76	4.53	4.39	4.28	4.21	4.15	4.10	4.06	4.00	3.94	3.87	3.84	3.81	3.77	3.74	3.70	3.67
7	5.59	4.74	4.35	4.12	3.97	3.87	3.79	3.73	3.68	3.64	3.57	3.51	3.44	3.41	3.38	3.34	3.30	3.27	3.23
8	5.32	4.46	4.07	3.84	3.69	3.58	3.50	3.44	3.39	3.35	3.28	3.22	3.15	3.12	3.08	3.04	3.01	2.97	2.93
9	5.12	4.26	3.86	3.63	3.48	3.37	3.29	3.23	3.18	3.14	3.07	3.01	2.94	2.90	2.86	2.83	2.79	2.75	2.71
10	4.96	4.10	3.71	3.48	3.33	3.22	3.14	3.07	3.02	2.98	2.91	2.85	2.77	2.74	2.70	2.66	2.62	2.58	2.54
11	4.84	3.98	3.59	3.36	3.20	3.09	3.01	2.95	2.90	2.85	2.79	2.72	2.65	2.61	2.57	2.53	2.49	2.45	2.40
12	4.75	3.89	3.49	3.26	3.11	3.00	2.91	2.85	2.80	2.75	2.69	2.62	2.54	2.51	2.47	2.43	2.38	2.34	2.30
13	4.67	3.81	3.41	3.18	3.03	2.92	2.83	2.77	2.71	2.67	2.60	2.53	2.46	2.42	2.38	2.34	2.30	2.25	2.21
14	4.60	3.74	3.34	3.11	2.96	2.85	2.76	2.70	2.65	2.60	2.53	2.46	2.39	2.35	2.31	2.27	2.22	2.18	2.13
15	4.54	3.68	3.29	3.06	2.90	2.79	2.71	2.64	2.59	2.54	2.48	2.40	2.33	2.29	2.25	2.20	2.16	2.11	2.07
16	4.49	3.63	3.24	3.01	2.85	2.74	2.66	2.59	2.54	2.49	2.42	2.35	2.28	2.24	2.19	2.15	2.11	2.06	2.01
17	4.45	3.59	3.20	2.96	2.81	2.70	2.61	2.55	2.49	2.45	2.38	2.31	2.23	2.19	2.15	2.10	2.06	2.01	1.96
18	4.41	3.55	3.16	2.93	2.77	2.66	2.58	2.51	2.46	2.41	2.34	2.27	2.19	2.15	2.11	2.06	2.02	1.97	1.92
19	4.38	3.52	3.13	2.90	2.74	2.63	2.54	2.48	2.42	2.38	2.31	2.23	2.16	2.11	2.07	2.03	1.98	1.93	1.88
20	4.35	3.49	3.10	2.87	2.71	2.60	2.51	2.45	2.39	2.35	2.28	2.20	2.12	2.08	2.04	1.99	1.95	1.90	1.84
21	4.32	3.47	3.07	2.84	2.68	2.57	2.49	2.42	2.37	2.32	2.25	2.18	2.10	2.05	2.01	1.96	1.92	1.87	1.81
22	4.30	3.44	3.05	2.82	2.66	2.55	2.46	2.40	2.34	2.30	2.23	2.15	2.07	2.03	1.98	1.94	1.89	1.84	1.78
23	4.28	3.42	3.03	2.80	2.64	2.53	2.44	2.37	2.32	2.27	2.20	2.13	2.05	2.01	1.96	1.91	1.86	1.81	1.76
24	4.26	3.40	3.01	2.78	2.62	2.51	2.42	2.36	2.30	2.25	2.18	2.11	2.03	1.98	1.94	1.89	1.84	1.79	1.73
25	4.24	3.39	2.99	2.76	2.60	2.49	2.40	2.34	2.28	2.24	2.16	2.09	2.01	1.96	1.92	1.87	1.82	1.77	1.71
26	4.23	3.37	2.98	2.74	2.59	2.47	2.39	2.32	2.27	2.22	2.15	2.07	1.99	1.95	1.90	1.85	1.80	1.75	1.69
27	4.21	3.35	2.96	2.73	2.57	2.46	2.37	2.31	2.25	2.20	2.13	2.06	1.97	1.93	1.88	1.84	1.79	1.73	1.67
28	4.20	3.34	2.95	2.71	2.56	2.45	2.36	2.29	2.24	2.19	2.12	2.04	1.96	1.91	1.87	1.82	1.77	1.71	1.65
29	4.18	3.33	2.93	2.70	2.55	2.43	2.35	2.28	2.22	2.18	2.10	2.03	1.94	1.90	1.85	1.81	1.75	1.70	1.64
30	4.17	3.32	2.92	2.69	2.53	2.42	2.33	2.27	2.21	2.16	2.09	2.01	1.93	1.89	1.84	1.79	1.74	1.68	1.62
40	4.08	3.23	2.84	2.61	2.45	2.34	2.25	2.18	2.12	2.08	2.00	1.92	1.84	1.79	1.74	1.69	1.64	1.58	1.51
60	4.00	3.15	2.76	2.53	2.37	2.25	2.17	2.10	2.04	1.99	1.92	1.84	1.75	1.70	1.65	1.59	1.53	1.47	1.39
120	3.92	3.07	2.68	2.45	2.29	2.17	2.09	2.02	1.96	1.91	1.83	1.75	1.66	1.61	1.55	1.50	1.43	1.35	1.25
∞	3.84	3.00	2.60	2.37	2.21	2.10	2.01	1.94	1.88	1.83	1.75	1.67	1.57	1.52	1.46	1.39	1.32	1.22	1.00

Source: Table A.4 is taken from Table V of Fisher and Yates: *Statistical Tables for Biological, Agricultural and Medical Research*, published by Longman Group Ltd., London (previously published by Oliver and Boyd, Edinburgh), and by permission of the authors and publishers.

Table A.5
Critical Values for Chi-Square

							Probability							
df	.99	.98	.95	.90	.80	.70	.50	.30	.20	.10	.05	.02	.01	.001
1	.0¹57	.0⁶28	.00393	.0158	.0642	.148	.455	1.074	1.642	2.706	3.841	5.412	6.635	10.827
2	.0201	.0404	.103	.211	.446	.713	1.386	2.408	3.219	4.605	5.991	7.824	9.210	13.815
3	.115	.185	.352	.584	1.005	1.424	2.366	3.665	4.642	6.251	7.815	9.837	11.341	16.268
4	.297	.429	.711	1.064	1.649	2.195	3.357	4.878	5.989	7.779	9.488	11.668	13.277	18.465
5	.554	.752	1.145	1.610	2.343	3.000	4.351	6.064	7.289	9.236	11.070	13.388	15.086	20.517
6	.872	1.134	1.635	2.204	3.070	3.828	5.348	7.231	8.558	10.645	12.592	15.033	16.812	22.457
7	1.239	1.564	2.167	2.833	3.822	4.671	6.346	8.383	9.803	12.017	14.067	16.622	18.475	24.322
8	1.646	2.032	2.733	3.490	4.594	5.527	7.344	9.524	11.030	13.362	15.507	18.168	20.090	26.125
9	2.088	2.532	3.325	4.168	5.380	6.393	8.343	10.656	12.242	14.684	16.919	19.679	21.666	27.877
10	2.558	3.059	3.940	4.865	6.179	7.267	9.342	11.781	13.442	15.987	18.307	21.161	23.209	29.588
11	3.053	3.609	4.575	5.578	6.989	8.148	10.341	12.899	14.631	17.275	19.675	22.618	24.725	31.264
12	3.571	4.178	5.226	6.304	7.807	9.034	11.340	14.011	15.812	18.549	21.026	24.054	26.217	32.909
13	4.107	4.765	5.892	7.042	8.634	9.926	12.340	15.119	16.985	19.812	22.362	25.472	27.688	34.528
14	4.660	5.368	6.571	7.790	9.467	10.821	13.339	16.222	18.151	21.064	23.685	26.873	29.141	36.123
15	5.229	5.985	7.261	8.547	10.307	11.721	14.339	17.322	19.311	22.307	24.996	28.259	30.578	37.697
16	5.812	6.614	7.962	9.312	11.152	12.624	15.338	18.418	20.465	23.542	26.296	29.633	32.000	39.252
17	6.408	7.255	8.672	10.085	12.002	13.531	16.338	19.511	21.615	24.769	27.587	30.995	33.409	40.790
18	7.015	7.906	9.390	10.865	12.857	14.440	17.338	20.601	22.760	25.989	28.869	32.346	34.805	42.312
19	7.633	8.567	10.117	11.651	13.716	15.352	18.338	21.689	23.900	27.204	30.144	33.687	36.191	43.820
20	8.260	9.237	10.851	12.443	14.578	16.266	19.337	22.775	25.038	28.412	31.410	35.020	37.566	45.315
21	8.897	9.915	11.591	13.240	15.445	17.182	20.337	23.858	26.171	29.615	32.671	36.343	38.932	46.797
22	9.542	10.600	12.338	14.041	16.314	18.101	21.337	24.939	27.301	30.813	33.924	37.659	40.289	48.268
23	10.196	11.293	13.091	14.848	17.187	19.021	22.337	26.018	28.429	32.007	35.172	38.968	41.638	49.728
24	10.856	11.992	13.848	15.659	18.062	19.943	23.337	27.096	29.553	33.196	36.415	40.270	42.980	51.179
25	11.524	12.697	14.611	16.473	18.940	20.867	24.337	28.172	30.675	34.382	37.652	41.566	44.314	52.620
26	12.198	13.409	15.379	17.292	19.820	21.792	25.336	29.246	31.795	35.563	38.885	42.856	45.642	54.052
27	12.879	14.125	16.151	18.114	20.703	22.719	26.336	30.319	32.912	36.741	40.113	44.140	46.963	55.476
28	13.565	14.847	16.928	18.939	21.588	23.647	27.336	31.391	34.027	37.916	41.337	45.419	48.278	56.893
29	14.256	15.574	17.708	19.768	22.475	24.577	28.336	32.461	35.139	39.087	42.557	46.693	49.588	58.302
30	14.953	16.306	18.493	20.599	23.364	25.508	29.336	33.530	36.250	40.256	43.773	47.962	50.892	59.703

For larger values of df, the expression $\sqrt{2x^2} - \sqrt{2df} - 1$ has the Z-distribution; see Table A.2

Source: Table A.5 is taken from Table IV of Fisher and Yates: *Statistical Tables for Biological, Agricultural and Medical Research*, published by Longman Group Ltd., London (previously published by Oliver and Boyd, Edinburgh), and by permission of the authors and publishers.

REFERENCES

Adler, Nancy E. 1973. "Impact of Prior Sets Given Experimenters and Subjects on the Experimenter Expectancy Effect." *Sociometry* 36: 113–126.

Angell, R. C. 1951. "The Moral Integration of American Cities." *American Journal of Sociology* 57, No 1, Part 2.

Baldus, Bernd and Tribe, Verna. 1976. "The Development of Perception and Evaluations of Social Inequality Among Public School Children." Mimeographed. Toronto: Dept. of Sociology, University of Toronto.

Blishen, Bernard R. and McRobert, H. A. 1976. "A Revised Socioeconomic Index for Occupations in Canada." *Canadian Review of Sociology and Anthropology* 13: 71–79.

Blood, Robert O. Jr. and Wolfe, D. M. 1960. *Husbands and Wives*, Glencoe: Free Press.

Bott, Elizabeth 1971. *Family and Social Network* (2nd ed.). London: Tavistock.

Brownlee, K. A. 1965. *Statistical Theory and Methodology in Science and Engineering*, 2nd ed. New York: John Wiley & Sons.

Campbell, Donald T. and Stanley, Julian C. 1966. *Experimental and Quasi-Experimental Designs for Research*. Chicago: Rand McNally.

Chase-Dunn, Christopher. 1975. "The Effects of International Economic Dependence on Development and Inequality: A Cross National Study." *American Sociological Review* 40: 720–738.

Coleman, James S.; Campbell, E. Q.; Hobson, G. J.; McPartland, J.; Mood, A. M.; Weinfeld, F. D.; and York, R. L. 1966. *Equality of Educational Opportunity*; Washington, D.C.: U.S. Department of Health, Education and Welfare, Office of Education.

Davis, A. and Havighurst, R. J. 1946. "Social Class and Color Differences in Child Rearing." *American Sociological Review* 11: 698–710.

Dominion Bureau of Statistics. 1950. *1941 Census of Canada*, vol. 1. Ottawa.

———— 1969. *1961 Census of Canada*. Cat. 92-539 (Bull 1.1-10) and Cat. 98-529 (Bull SX-15). Ottawa.

Doyle, Sir Arthur Conan. 1930. *The Complete Sherlock Holmes*. Garden City, New York: Doubleday.

Duncan, Otis D. 1961. "A Socio-economic Index for all Occupations." In *Occupations and Social Status*, edited by A. J. Reiss. New York: Free Press.

Ewing, Anthony. 1972. *Socioeconomic Status and Voting Behaviour in Vancouver*. M.A. Thesis, Dept. of Sociology, Carleton University; Ottawa.

Fisher, R. A. and Yates, F. 1948. *Statistical Tables for Biological, Agricultural and Medical Research*. Edinburgh: Oliver and Boyd.

Geekie, H. 1974. "A Review of CMA Policies and Positions on Abortion." *Canadian Medical Association Journal* 111: 475–477.

Goodman, L. A. and Kruskal, W. H. 1954. "Measures of Association for Cross Classifications." "*Journal of the American Statistical Association* 49: 732–764.

Gove, W. R. and Tudor, J. F. 1973. "Adult Sex Roles and Mental Illness." *American Journal of Sociology* 78: 812–835.

Guilford, J. P., 1954. *Psychometric Methods*. 2nd ed. New York: McGraw-Hill.

Hald, A. 1952. *Statistical Tables and Formulas*. New York: John Wiley & Sons.

Hays, W. L. 1973. *Statistics for the Social Sciences*. 2nd ed. New York: Holt, Rinehart & Winston.

Huff, D. 1954. *How to Lie With Statistics*. New York: Norton.

Inkeles, Alex and Smith, D. H. 1974. *Becoming Modern*. Cambridge: Mass. Harvard University Press.

Kennedy, Robert E. Jr. 1973. "Minority Status and Fertility." *American Sociological Review* 38: 85–96.

Kish, Leslie. 1965. *Survey Sampling*. New York: John Wiley & Sons.

Kuhn, T. S. 1970. *The Structure of Scientific Revolutions.* 2nd ed. Chicago: University of Chicago Press.

Levine, A. and Crumrine, J. 1975. "Women and the Fear of Success: A Problem in Replication." *American Journal of Sociology* 80: 964–975.

Luce, Sally R. 1974. *Classroom Behaviours as Predictors of Achievement.* Unpublished M.A. Thesis, Carleton University.

Molotch, H. and Lester, M. 1975. "Accidental News: The Great Oil Spill as Local Occurrence and National Event." *American Journal of Sociology* 81: 235–260.

Pearson, E. S. and Hartley, H. O., eds. 1954. *Biometrika Tables for Statisticians.* vol 1. Cambridge: Cambridge University Press.

Russett, B. M.; Alker, H. R. Jr.; Deutsch, K. W.; and Lasswell, H. D. 1964. *World Handbook of Political and Social Indicators.* New Haven: Yale University Press.

Shulman, Norman. 1976. "Network Analysis: A New Addition to an Old Bag of Tricks." *Acta Sociologica* 19: 7–13.

Simon, H. A. 1954. "Spurious Correlation: A Causal Interpretation." *Journal of the American Statistical Association* 49: 467–479.

Snedecor, G. W. 1956. *Statistical Methods.* 5th ed. Ames, Iowa: Iowa State College Press.

Statistics Canada. 1973. *1971 Census of Canada.* Cat. 92-708, vol. 10, Part 1 (Bull. 1.1-8). Ottawa.

—— 1973. *Therapeutic Abortions 1972.* Cat. 82-211. Ottawa: Information Canada.

—— 1974. *Therapeutic Abortions 1973.* Cat. 82-211. Ottawa: Information Canada.

Stolzenberg, R. M. 1975. "Occupations, Labor Markets and the Process of Wage Attainment." *American Sociological Review* 40: 645–665.

Stouffer, S. 1972. *Social Research to Test Ideas.* New York: Free Press.

Taeuber, Karl E. 1973. "Residential Segregation." In *Cities, Readings From Scientific America.* San Francisco; Freeman, 1973.

Tanur, J. M., ed with Mosteller, F.; Kruskal, W. H.; Link, R. F.; Pieters, R. S.; and Rising, G. R. 1972. *Statistics: A Guide to the Unknown.* San Francisco; Holden-Day 1972.

Taylor, C. L. and Hudson, M. C. 1972. *World Handbook of Political and Social Indicators.* 2nd ed. New Haven: Yale University Press.

Tukey, John W. 1977. *Exploratory Data Analysis.* Reading, Massachusetts: Addison-Wesley, forthcoming.

United Nations. 1975. *Yearbook of National Accounts Statistics 1973.* vol. 3: International Tables. New York.

—— 1976. *United Nations Statistical Yearbook 1975.* New York; United Nations Statistical Office.

U.S. Department of Commerce, Bureau of the Census. 1971. *Statistical Abstract of the United States 1971.* Washington, D.C.

U.S. Department of Health, Education and Welfare. 1968. *United States Life Tables 1959–61.* Washington, D.C.: National Center for Health Statistics.

—— 1974. *Facts of Life and Death.* Rockville, Maryland: National Center for Health Statistics.

Wellman, Barry S.; Shulman, N.; and Wayne, J. *Personal Communities.* New York; Oxford University Press, forthcoming.

Whiting, J. M. and Child, I. L. 1962. *Child Training and Personality.* New Haven: Yale University Press.

World Health Organization. 1974. *World Health Statistics Annual 1971.* Geneva.

Young, M. and Willmott, P. 1957. *Family and Kinship in East London.* London: Routledge and Kegan Paul.

Zajonc, R. B. 1968. "The Attitudinal Effects of Mere Exposure." *Journal of Personality and Social Psychology* 9, monograph supplement: 1–27.

INDEX